ZAMBEZI

Journey of a river

Michael Main

SOUTHERN
BOOK PUBLISHERS

To Gypsey, a small tan and white Jack Russell terrier — thanks for the company.

ISBN 1 86812 257 3

First edition, first impression 1990
First edition, second impression 1992
First edition, third impression 1998

Published by
Southern Book Publishers (Pty) Ltd
P O Box 3103, Halfway House, 1685

Cover design by Insight Graphics
Maps by Ingrid Booysen
Set in 10 on 12 pt Hanover
by Unifoto, Cape Town
Printed and bound by CTP Book Printers (Pty) Ltd.
Caxton Street, Parow, 7500, Cape Town
MIC1207-2

Contents

Preface

THE Zambezi challenged me, physically as well as mentally. Like arriving at the summit of a mountain, finishing this work evokes feelings not of victor and vanquished, but respect and therefore sadness at the parting. For the river has dominated my life for three years and after all the travel, the reading and the studying, I experience no sense of conquest, but instead, a feeling of awe. Awe at how little I have learnt compared to how much more there is to learn. I leave the experience of the Zambezi humble, but elated, for it has also been a time of great excitement and achievement.

I have a passion for learning about things that are of interest to me, I thrive on excitement and adventure and meeting interesting people. The Zambezi has given me all this in great abundance. Above all, I like sharing the knowledge and experiences with others and that, I hope, this book will do.

Looking back over the events of the last few years, I realise that I have been fortunate and privileged to enjoy experiences that are beyond price and that, because they are now memories, can never be taken away.

For example, how could I forget walking across the lip of Victoria Falls? Others have done it also. At the right time of year it is not particularly dangerous — but for me it was elemental, exciting and unforgettable. For obscure reasons, Livingstone is one of my own names and, although we are not related by blood, I cannot help an identification with the man. For this reason the visit to Livingstone island was doubly momentous for me.

So too was reaching the source. It had became a symbol of the whole project and for months afterwards, I did silly things like carrying round a few litres of water from the source. Small amounts were imposed upon chosen (and tolerant) friends!

Feeling the electric atmosphere when the Litunga of the Lozi people struck the first beat of the royal drums; watching, heart in mouth, as my Jack Russell Gypsey raised her hackles at a huge bull elephant which, gentleman that it was, majestically gave ground to her diminutive form; kyaking through the wild white water of the upper river and riding rubber rafts through the maelstrom of the rapids below Victoria Falls — these are some of the Zambezi experiences that have led to the making of this book.

The book is not, however, the diary of an incautious or reckless adventurer. To me it has been a way of communicating, of sharing with others, a small portion of what is exciting and fascinating about the river and its people.

In the course of my research, I learnt much about the Mwene Mutapa empire, about strange two-toed people, trees that kill animals and send messages to one another, concubines in Sofala and cannibals in Mozambique. How could I possibly resist telling you of a tennis court with flowers painted upon it in the heart of a malaria-ridden mangrove swamp? Or fail to point out Livingstone's transformation from a missionary to an explorer and then follow the highlights of his journey across Africa? Nor could I ignore the tragedy for Livingstone of Cahora Bassa or resist the authenticated facts of silver mines of fabulous wealth.

It would be criminal to know of, and not share with you, the story of the man who crossed Africa in a boat and talked his way out of difficulties with a bagful of glass eyes! Surely I would also be wrong to omit the facts about a frog-eating bat or turtles whose sex is determined by temperature?

The Zambezi overflows with anecdotes and amusing, interesting stories. I hope you enjoy reading them as much as I've enjoyed finding them.

It is impossible to travel nearly the whole length of the Zambezi and to spend as much time in libraries and research institutions as I have done without the assistance of a host of people — I would like to thank them all.

There is the support system that I could not have managed without; so, for your endless help and encouragement, thank you — John and Sandy Fowkes, Maurice Boaler who still faithfully tends home fires, Judy and Alec Campbell, John and Sylvia Cooke, Ian and Shona Lockhart, Gerrie and Helen Jooste. A special thank you to Phillip Welch who, as he has done for years now, generously kept me supplied with vehicles that have run as perfectly and reliably as only he can make them do.

There are those who, as friends, made contributions to this book far and above what could have been fairly asked of them.

Included among these, not always willing, martyrs are, with my special thanks: Caroline and Andy Anderson, Alec Campbell, Prof. Tom Huffman, Joan Hoyte and David Foster, Des Jackson and Jackie and John Minshull from the Bulawayo Museum, Prof. John Orpen, Alan and Ann Wardle.

A special note of appreciation is due to the Director, the staff and the photocopier at the National Archives in Harare. It would not be fair to acknowledge this debt without also paying tribute to the photocopier and the staff who run it in the Bulawayo Museum. Without those two machines this stage would never have been reached!

And speaking of machines, Ralph Wheeler of Data Processing, Gaborone, is gratefully thanked for the miracles of mini-mechanics he performed on the innards of my computer.

Photographic support came unfailingly, as it always does, from Jane at Cas Camera, from the team at Procolor and from Gaele Mogwe who generously helped with film.

For reading the manuscript and offering ideas and discussion that have helped shape the final product: Vonna Hermans, Prof. John Cooke, Janet Barnes, Marie Kinsella, Di Lock, Andy Moore and my wife Janis.

Many other people helped with their time, ideas and knowledge. To the following, my sincere thanks: Dr Reg Allsopp, Geoff Anderson, Abel Baptista, Dr 'Basher' Attwell, Senhor Bega, Daniel (Daan) Bester, Gavin Blair, Dr D. Broadley, Jeremy Brooke, Ken Budd, Dick Callow, Heather Carr-Hartley, Dr M. Chella, Dr Graham Child, Chief Chundu, Godfrey Chundu, Dr Victor d. V. Clarke, Victor Clarke, Peter Clemence, Wally and Collette Coetzee, Paul and Marie Connolly, Dr Cran Cooke, Dave Cumming, Kim St J. Damstra, Clive and Barbara de Milita, Jill and Maurice Diamond, Ian Dixon, Bob Drummond, Glen Dunlop, Raul du Toit, Lionel Dyke, Ian and Maggie Erasmus, Peter Fisher, Ruth and Per Forch-hammer, Mrs Mary 'Fred' Forrest, Alan Fox, John Fox, Rob Gee, Leo and Virginia Goodfellow, Don Granger, Bonani Hadebe, Graham Hall, Dr John Hargroves, Willie Harrington, Bomber Harris, Dr John Hatton, Kathleen and Piet Herbst, Prof. Tom Huffman, Dr John Hutton, Dr James Jijide, Nicholas Katanekwa, James Katoka, Sally Kemp, Lady Ruth Khama, Harold Kierstead, Albert Kumirai, John Langerman, Les Lessing, Dr L. Lister, Jean and Gerry Lousada, Jillian Lovell, Dr John Loveridge, Richard Lowe, Ruby and Eddie MacGregor, Miss C. MacNaughton, Peter Malesu, Antonio Manna, Dr Brian Marshall, Ian McKillop, Gert Meintjes, Dr Andy Moore, Stanley Msendo, George Muanda, Richard Mubita, George Muenge, Francis Musonda, Misheke Muyongo, Stella Nduku, Enock Ndumba, Andy Norval, Chris Nugent, Karuma Nykutepa, Fabian Nypossa, Ian Nyschens, Prof. R.J. Phelps, John Pile, Chris Pollard, Dr Neil Ransford, Willie Reed, Fernando Rosas, John Santa Clara, Charles and Linda Saunders, Bernard Siakalau, Mike Slowgrove, Bodo and Tieselotte Sollich, Nadia and Ray Stocker, Alison and Joe Susman, Estinath and Rainos Tawonameso, Charlotte Tagart, Glen Tatham, Maggie Taylor, Russell Taylor, Glenda, Dave and Eric 'Pops' Thompson, Rolly Thompson, Esther Townsend, John Urie, Xavier van den Berg, Angus van Jaarsveldt, Tony Venn, John, Dennis and Tommy Vlahakis, Dave Willis, Janet Wilson, Viv and Paddy Wilson, Farlie Winson, Brian Worsley.

For much fun, laughter and companionship along the road, my sons Jeremy and Andrew and, of course, Gypsey.

Finally, I would like to thank my wife for her patience and understanding, her tolerance and her help through what for her were three long and lonely years.

In compiling this work, I have drawn extensively on published scientific and popular material. While I have not wanted to clutter the text excessively, I do believe it is important that the work of others should be acknowledged and I have done this wherever possible. To these people I owe a special gratitude for I have relied heavily upon their work. The interpretations and conclusions that I have reached are, however, my own responsibility.

1 The Great African Divide

HIGH in the heart of Central Africa's savannas is the place where the Zambezi is born. It is not a place of mountains, grey dripping mists or hanging moss, nor is it home to dramatic scenery or wild white foam-filled rivers tearing at the earth. It is a region of pervasive, gentle beauty, as if such a nurturing base is a necessary counterpart to the violence, tumult and tempestuous passage the river will encounter as it carries, bit by bit, its own life-giving continent to the sea.

There is an intangible feeling in the air of the Zambezi's home that is at once distinctive yet hard to convey. Perhaps it springs from within me and I alone am aware of it. Partly, no doubt, it has to do with treading at the very start of a river that has occupied so much of my time, energy and thought. It is a reverential sensation, tinged with excitement and adventure.

At the source, there is no impression of height, for one stands upon an ancient and much eroded upland area. What mountains may once have been, are rendered into gently rounded shoulders of rock and earth, clothed in a patterned shawl of tree and grass.

The road in northern Zambia follows the watershed through an endless succession of beautiful meadows interspersed with stands of tall forest. The meadows are natural and swathes of towering grass reflect not only the fertility of the region but the high and frequent rainfall.

For me the watershed itself is the basic ingredient of the region's special magic for, inconspicuously, it divides the very continent. It is possible to stand on the moist, grass-covered earth under the trees at any one of an infinity of places where, on either side, the ground slopes imperceptibly away from you. Here is the invisible line that irrevocably separates coast from coast. A drop of rain that falls to my left will travel by way of the Congo to the great western sea: one on my right will follow the Zambezi to the coral-clad shores of the Indian Ocean.

Just off a shoulder of rising ground, in an area of open woodland, a trail of dark green riverine forest leads up-slope to a tiny valley. Shaped like the hollow of a cupped palm, its brown bracken sides slip beneath the canopy of green to become the permanently wet forest floor. Here, the roots travel overground, fearing suffocation below, supporting the bodies

1

of last year's leaves and linking one to another in a tangled network, anchored by the buttressed bulk of a forest giant.

Beneath the roots and between the ochre, red and yellowing leaves, the gurgle of running water sounds, leading the listener to the heart of the amphitheatre and the silence of small stilled pools which reflect the sky, the trees, reeds, ferns and the listener's face. This is the beginning.

It is my intention, during the course of the chapters that follow, to acquaint you with fact and anecdote about, or associated in some way with, the Zambezi River. It may well be in order now, therefore, to describe in broad outline the Zambezi's course so that you might more easily follow the journey and anticipate our direction. ·

From its source, at the very north-western tip of Zambia, the Zambezi first travels north before turning west, past the foot of Kalene Hill, and crossing into Angola, heading towards the Atlantic. Shortly, however, it turns south and, by now a substantial river, re-enters Zambia at Chalose about 400 km from its origins.

In western Zambia the river passes through an area once known as Barotseland but that is now simply part of Western Province. This region of the country is relatively flat and is distinguished by its covering of Kalahari sands which, in places, may be as deep as 50 m.[1] The sands of the Kalahari are aeolian in origin and, for this reason, the grains are rounded. Wind-blown for millennia, they are a remnant of a once vast desert and although the area is by no means a desert today, they remain extensive in their distribution, stretching without a break from the Orange River in the south to the most northerly reaches of the Congo.

It is in the shallow valleys and floodplains of Barotseland that the Zambezi annually inundates huge tracts of land. On these floodplains and on the islands within them, the Lozi people established their kingdom and live to this day, maintaining their tribal integrity and their colourful tribal ceremonies.

Ngonye Falls in the south of Barotseland mark the point at which the river encounters dykes of basalt which have slowed the downward cutting of its channel, creating the waterfall and, beyond it, a series of rapids that extends for 120 km to Katima Mulilo. At that point the river, tracing a great 'S' shape, turns to the east, approaching Victoria Falls.

Apart from the basalt dykes that have barred its way, the Zambezi thus far has flowed through an immensity of sand. At Kazungula, about 70 km from Ngonye Falls, it passes over a table-like formation of basalt that extends in total for nearly 200 km. Through the last 130 km of this basalt the Zambezi has cut deeply down in a wild but beautiful gorge. At Victoria Falls the process is still under way.

Beyond the Batoka Gorge, marked by the entry of the Deka River and a transition from basalt to sandstone, begins a section of the river known as the Gwembe Trough. This, as we shall see, is an area of great geological interest, although, of course, today it lies beneath Lake Kariba. In the Gwembe severe faulting created a valley that offers, with its steep and blue-hazed distant walls, outstanding scenery.

The downstream end of the trough is marked by the distinctive narrowing of Kariba Gorge. Here it was, in 1958, that the famous dam wall was thrown across the river's path to create the lake of the same name. The gorge is interesting in that there are three more like it along the river's length and all four have in common a most unusual feature: they each cut directly through an area of elevated and ancient geology far older than the river and demand, therefore, an explanation of how such an unlikely thing could come about. More will be said about this phenomenon later.

Downstream from Kariba Gorge the Zambezi continues northwards for a short distance before curving to the east and the final run down through Mozambique to the coast. Here it enters its most spectacular valley. Known as the Zambezi Valley, it is the most easily recognised of the so-called rift valley features, for on both north and south sides of the river, the flat alluvial valley floor ends abruptly in steep mountain slopes that rise spectacularly to cooler summits above. Within this valley is the second of the unusual gorges — Mupata.

Flowing east now, the Zambezi passes the junction with the Luangwa coming in from Zambia and the north. Today the pace of the Zambezi slackens at this point because the impoundment at Cahora Bassa affects the river as far upstream as Zumbo. Underneath the waters of this dam lies the gorge that defeated David Livingstone and caused him and others much heartache.

Past this point and downstream to the Mozambique town of Tete, the river has lost much of its power and magnificence. Tamed by two major dams, it flows but sluggishly on. It is dwarfed as it passes through the final gorge of Lupata, beneath towering cliffs of basalt. Escaping, it continues to the south-east before being joined on the north bank by the Shire River which draws water from Lake Malawi. Together the combined rivers flow into the sea at a great delta, set about with shifting sands and shallow entrances, ignored now by all but the smallest boats.

As I have already mentioned, there are four places along its course where the Zambezi has cut a channel through mountainous areas. This requires an explanation; after all, a river can hardly be expected to flow up one side of a mountain range and down the other, cutting a gorge through the middle. So how did the gorges come about?

An explanation that comes easily to mind is that the mountains rose beneath the existing river course at a rate equal to the river's down-cutting speed. This is perfectly feasible and is known to have happened elsewhere. However, there is a problem associated with this explanation where the exposed rocks are particularly ancient; precisely the situation in three of the four Zambezi gorges.

If one looks at Kariba Gorge, for example, the entrance cuts through Precambrian gneisses and paragneisses that are 2 500 million years of age or more.[2] This incredible span of time represents half of the earth's entire existence and, as will become clear later in the chapter, it is unthinkable that the present Zambezi has been flowing in the same course for all of that time.

Exactly the same applies to the gorge at Mupata, nearer the lower end of the Zambezi Valley. Here the river flows through very rugged hill country, over gneisses of various ages, none of which are likely to be younger than the Kariba rocks.[3] Parts of the gorge at Cahora Bassa are of exceedingly ancient basement rocks and these too have been cut through by the Zambezi.[4]

At Lupata Gorge below Tete, the situation is a little different. Here, the river winds between striking cliffs of basalt that tower nearly 300 m above it. The rocks, however, are younger and, at about 160 million years of age, are part of the relatively recent Stormberg succession of the Karoo Supergroup.[5] One geologist suggests that this lava was lifted beneath the river as the river cut down through it[6] but it seems to me more likely that the explanation which so neatly fits the other gorges applies equally here.

A widely accepted interpretation relies upon the concept of superimposition. To understand this, try to imagine a valley in an era of desertlike conditions when rivers ceased to flow. Within it, include a high ridge of extremely hard rock that runs from the crest of the valley wall to the river's edge. Over time under such desert conditions, the valley would be completely filled with sand and sediments. The ridge would disappear from view, covered by hundreds of metres of deposits. Imagine that, eventually, conditions change, rivers flow once more and begin again to excavate the softer material below. In this way a new channel is cut but it would not necessarily follow the line of the original, now deeply buried.

If it should happen that, in the downward erosion of its new course, the river comes across harder material, it cannot change the direction in which it flows and so is compelled to continue cutting downwards. In this manner a river is superimposed on an older landscape. Eventually as it erodes a passage through the harder material, a gorge may result. As more time passes, the softer deposits which overlaid the harder rock are removed and we are left with exactly the situation that occurs frequently along the river today.[7] There seems to be no doubt that all four of the Zambezi's famous gorges are examples of superimposition.

What is interesting about this explanation is that it requires us to accept dramatically different conditions to those that prevail today. Are such changes possible? The short answer is yes. The history of the river's development is remarkable for the extraordinary variation in its geomorphology and geology.

One cannot talk about these issues with precision for, of necessity, the speculations of scientists about the Zambezi's palaeo-geomorphology can only be at the most general level and are based on circumstantial evidence. It is also true that the further one goes back in time, the less remaining evidence is available and the more speculative the exercise becomes. Despite these limitations, intelligent analysis provides us with a fascinating palaeo-history.

It is widely accepted today that within, say, the last five million years, the present Zambezi began its existence in two separate portions which, for the sake of convenience, we shall call the Upper and the Lower, with the division between the two being the region of present-day Victoria Falls. The story of the Zambezi below the falls is far more ancient and is better told as part of the geological history. The Upper section, perhaps because it is younger, has been subject to far more changes.

It is a curious fact that one scientist who has spent a great deal of time on the palaeo-drainage of the Upper Zambezi is an ichthyologist, not a geomorphologist. Graham Bell-Cross, driven to answer his own questions on the origins and distribution of southern Africa's fish, was compelled, with others, to study the evolution of the Zambezi's drainage.[8]

Somewhere between two and five million years ago, at about the end of the Tertiary period, the Upper Zambezi was very different from today (Figure 1.1 overleaf). In the north-west it was considerably lengthened by the addition of the Kasai, subsequently lost by river capture to a northward-flowing stream, which now carries the modern Kasai as a major tributary of the Zaïre River and not the Zambezi.

In the north-east, the Kafue River was extended by the addition of the Chambeshi, which today flows almost from the southern border of Tanzania. This combined body of water continued in a south-westerly direction until it eventually reached the Upper Zambezi, almost certainly in the vicinity of what was to become the Caprivi Strip, well upstream of Victoria Falls.

Since that time, of course, the Chambeshi has been captured and, after flowing into Lake Bangwelu in northern Zambia, becomes part of the Luapula and Zaïre system (Figure 1.2 overleaf). The Kafue also has undergone dramatic realignment, the most obvious evidence of which appears in the abrupt left turn it takes to the east at Itezhi-Tezhi in central Zambia. Almost certainly due to river capture, the change in course joins the Kafue and Zambezi some distance below Kariba Gorge. The evidence of the Kafue's previous course remains clear, however.

In the present low watershed which separates the Kafue and the Upper Zambezi there is a gap, about 2 km wide, just a little south of where the Kafue now makes its sharp turn. It was through this gap that it originally flowed before being captured by an eastward-flowing stream.[9] This now takes it across the Kafue floodplains, down through its awesome gorge, to rejoin the Zambezi some 600 km downstream of its original entry point!

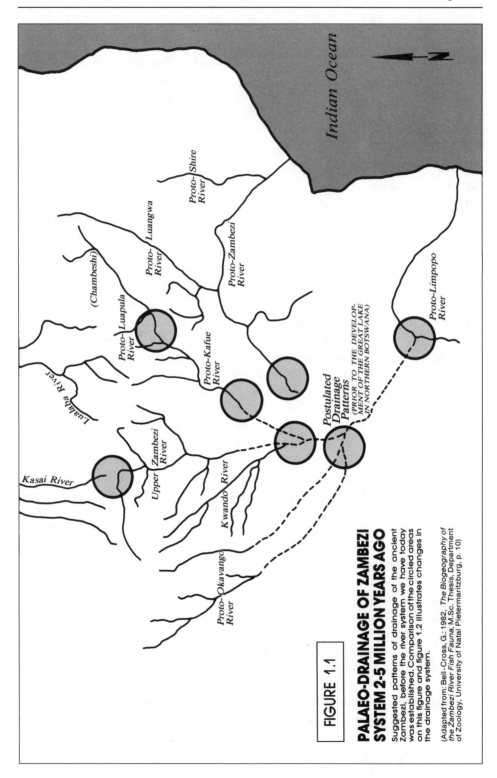

FIGURE 1.1

PALAEO-DRAINAGE OF ZAMBEZI SYSTEM 2-5 MILLION YEARS AGO

Suggested patterns of drainage of the ancient Zambezi, before the river system we have today was established. Comparison of the circled areas on this figure and figure 1.2 illustrates changes in the drainage system.

(Adapted from: Bell-Cross, G.: 1982, *The Biogeography of the Zambezi River Fish Fauna,* M.Sc. Thesis, Department of Zoology, University of Natal Pietermaritzburg, p. 10)

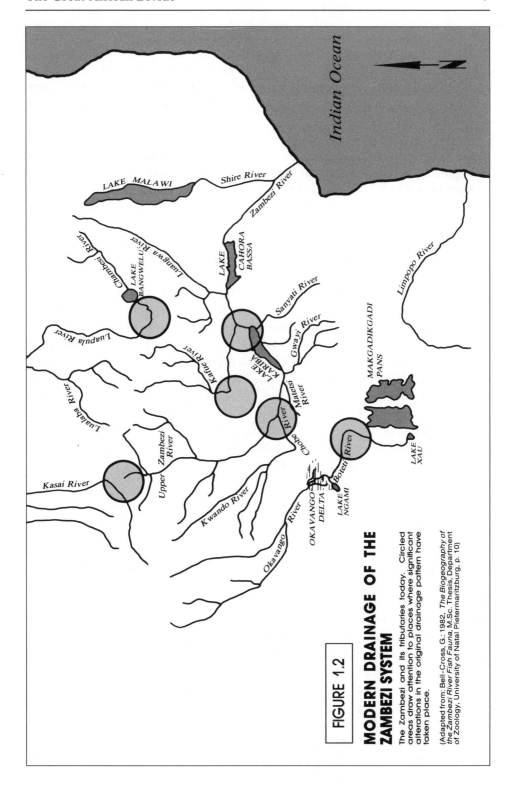

FIGURE 1.2

MODERN DRAINAGE OF THE ZAMBEZI SYSTEM

The Zambezi and its tributaries today. Circled areas draw attention to places where significant alterations in the original drainage pattern have taken place.

(Adapted from: Bell-Cross, G.: 1982, *The Biogeography of the Zambezi River Fish Fauna*, M.Sc. Thesis, Department of Zoology, University of Natal Pietermaritzburg, p. 10)

Considerations of climatic change aside, the additional volume of the palaeo-Upper Zambezi, including the Kasai, the Chambeshi and the Kafue, must have been substantial indeed. Between about seven and four million years ago, this huge quantity of water made its way to the sea, not by way of the present Lower Zambezi but, almost certainly, by way of the Limpopo.

As the Upper Zambezi crossed the vicinity of Caprivi Strip, it was joined by two other major rivers — the Kwando, Linyanti or Chobe, as it is called in various places, and the Okavango. These three combined somewhere in the heart of northern Botswana to flow east-southeast across the Kalahari, probably down the course of the modern Motloutse, joining the Limpopo near Botswana's eastern tip.[10]

The end of the Miocene and the beginning of the Pliocene, about five million years ago, saw a series of major tilting movements affecting the southern half of Africa. Concurrent with them, an axis of relatively slight uplift was created which extended from the centre of northern Zimbabwe, south-west through Bulawayo and down the eastern side of Botswana. The effect of this low ridge of slightly raised land, passing at right angles across the course of the proto-Limpopo, was to sever it, causing the great river, trapped behind it, to 'pond' and to spread out in an enormous lake.[11]

Professor John Cooke of the University of Botswana pioneered, in a series of absorbing papers, the work of establishing more detail about this fascinating lake.[12] The lake now no longer exists but traces of it are obvious in the 13 000 km^2 of Makgadikgadi Pans. As the investigation has progressed, so the extent of the lake has proved to be greater than first thought. Initial estimates ranged from 37 000 km^2 to 43 000 km^2 but after perusal of Landsat imagery these limits were moved to 80 000 km^2.[13] As a result of his recent research in north-west Botswana and the Caprivi Strip, Dr Paul Shaw believes the lake may have been as large as 100 000 km^2.[14]

The fate of Lake palaeo-Makgadikgadi is critical to an understanding of how and when the Upper and Lower Zambezi came to be linked. In principle, the how is simple, although the detail still eludes researchers. Unable to overcome the barrier placed across its path at the Motloutse, the superlake overflowed at the next lowest point. Current thinking has it that this was towards the north and took the escaping waters across a huge tableland of basalt to eventually begin, as we shall shortly see, the cutting of the Batoka Gorge and the creation of Victoria Falls.

According to Dr Lister at the University of Zimbabwe, it was only after this event took place, at the earliest Pliocene and therefore between about three and five million years ago, that the present course of the Zambezi River was fully established.[15]

An interesting aspect of the Zambezi's evolution to a single unit is illustrated by the Matetsi River for, according to some authorities, this was the original headwaters of the Lower Zambezi, as we have defined it, before the Pliocene conjunction took place. If this were so, we would expect to find evidence that the Matetsi is very much older than the Zambezi. Such evidence exists and its revelation to me was a useful reminder of the value of simple but intelligent observation.

The Matetsi flows north-east for a distance of about 120 km, from Botswana's border, on a converging course with the Zambezi which it joins at the end of the Batoka Gorge. An important point is that it flows across exactly the same basalt formation as the larger river. Of course, such a short river will carry nothing like the same volume of water nor will it remotely approach the erosive power of the Zambezi. The Zambezi is so powerful in this latter regard that, especially where they are young, the edges of the gorge are sharply defined and sheer. Indeed, as an observer noted, often one is not aware of the gorge until the very lip is approached. In other words, the Zambezi has cut no real valley to speak of, it has simply incised a deep and narrow gorge.

The basin of the Matetsi, on the other hand, is enormous by comparison, measuring 10 km to 20 km across in places. It is the most conspicuous physiographic feature of the basalt country.[16] How can such a small river achieve this result where a much larger and more powerful neighbour has failed? Is not the answer that the Matetsi had been working at a slower rate for a very much longer period of time, strongly suggesting that it substantially pre-dates the Zambezi?

I walked part of the Matetsi, for there is an object of great curiosity along its course. In exactly the same way as the Zambezi, but on a smaller scale, it is steadily cutting back through the basalt and, like the Zambezi, has carved a gorge and created a minor waterfall. It was this that I went to see, for I was looking at the Zambezi in microcosm. Considering the tiny volume of water that flows along this river, the gorge is dramatic and the waterfall, although disappointingly small (not more than 6 m or 7 m, I would estimate), striking. More striking still is the impressive size of the valley cut by this small river, leaving me with an even stronger impression of its greater antiquity.

Reluctantly, I must leave the fascination of the Zambezi's geomorphology and turn now to an equally absorbing subject — the geology of selected parts of the river: Victoria Falls, the Gwembe Trough and the Zambezi Valley. As we switch from geomorphology to geology, the time scale changes and where, up to this point, we have spoken in millions of years, we now talk in hundreds of millions of years.

We will take a detailed look at the geology of Victoria Falls in Chapter 5. Here I want to put it in perspective and, to do this, it is necessary to go back to Triassic times, some 200 million years ago, when the supercontinent of Gondwanaland was still united and the entire area, including almost all of southern Africa, was covered with an enormous sand desert. Over a period of about 100 million years, there began issuing forth from great rents in the earth's surface a flowing mass of lava. Not violently volcanic, in the sense of an explosive eruption, but a steady oozing of molten lava, fluid enough to flow into and fill hollows, troughs and valleys, smoothing out the landscape, leaving an almost horizontal aspect and trapping many hundreds of metres of sandstones beneath it. It is this lava over which the Zambezi flows today and in which the Batoka Gorge and Victoria Falls have been so deeply incised.

The lava appeared in widely separate parts of the supercontinent, and at different times, but the individual sheets often flowed together, eventually covering an estimated area of 2 000 000 km[2] and leaving traces still found today in India, Australia, Antarctica and South America.[17] The age of the basalt, as the lava is called, varies but in the area of Victoria Falls, it is estimated to be approximately 180 million years old.[18]

Immediately, erosion began to shape the new land surface. At the same time, between 160 and 120 million years ago, Gondwanaland began to break up, giving rise to the continental outlines of the southern hemisphere with which we are familiar today.[19]

Although the original distribution of Stormberg lavas might once have been universal within the supercontinent, that pattern has now been changed dramatically by subsequent erosion, so that in southern Africa, for example, there remains some 140 000 km[2]. The thickness varies considerably. Where the lava originally filled deep valleys, or at localities of particularly copious outpourings, great depths of it still remain and in southern Zimbabwe, for example, these reach down to between 7 km and 8 km. Elsewhere, depths of 9 km are known.[20]

Understandably, the basalt is preferentially removed from exposed locations and remains almost untouched in sheltered areas such as river valleys or grabens. The Drakensberg mountains in South Africa, for example, a highly exposed area of basalt, have been eroded 200 km westwards since they were laid down 160 million years ago.[21]

If the basalt is contained in a downfaulted zone and thus protected from erosion, it will persist indefinitely. This explains why, at Victoria Falls, so old a deposit has remained intact until quite recently, when nearly all of the great quantity of Stormberg lava, deposited elsewhere in the area now drained by the Zambezi, has long since been removed.

A common assertion is that the valley bounding west and north Zimbabwe is an extension of the Great East African Rift Valley (GEARV) (Figure 1.3). The truth of this depends largely upon what one means by that system, for there are subtle differences between it and both the Gwembe Trough and Zambezi Valley, although there are also similarities.

The GEARV is sometimes called an 'aborted ocean', implying that it is a fracture in the African continent which, had it continued, would have resulted in a portion breaking off and a separate land mass being formed.

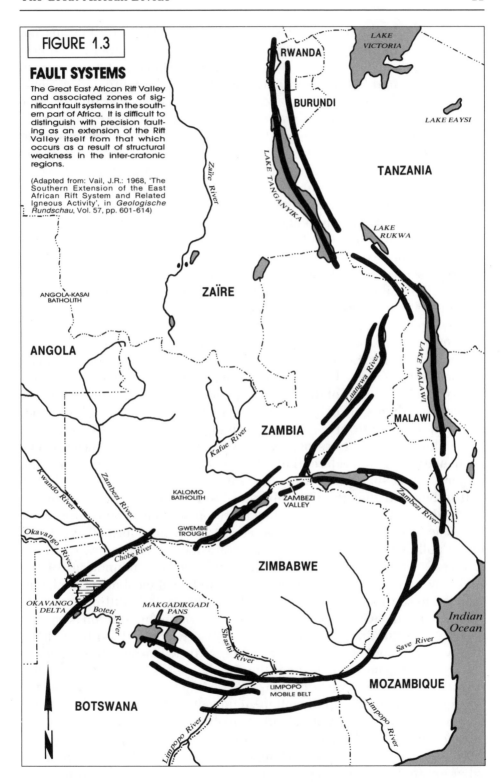

FIGURE 1.3

FAULT SYSTEMS

The Great East African Rift Valley and associated zones of significant fault systems in the southern part of Africa. It is difficult to distinguish with precision faulting as an extension of the Rift Valley itself from that which occurs as a result of structural weakness in the inter-cratonic regions.

(Adapted from: Vail, J.R.: 1968, 'The Southern Extension of the East African Rift System and Related Igneous Activity', in *Geologische Rundschau*, Vol. 57, pp. 601-614)

It has been active in three phases, during the Triassic, the Cretaceous and in the last 20 million years. Of course, it may be only temporarily quiescent. It extends for roughly 6 500 km from Lebanon in the north to Mozambique and Botswana's Okavango Delta in the south and, as some claim, includes the Luangwa and Zambezi valleys as well as the Gwembe Trough. One theory is that it was originally caused by the collapse of the continental surface following vast outpourings of lava from beneath it.[22]

The situation in southern Africa is not quite the same. Despite the apparent underlying geological unity of Africa as a continent it seems that, in the southern parts at least, rather than being a continuous whole, it is made up of smaller, discrete units. These consist of 'islands' of basement rocks, Precambrian in age, referred to as cratons. A handy way to view them (which is bound to make geologists turn in their graves) is rather like a large dish with a few half peaches set in custard. The cratons are represented by the peaches while the custard is the 'continental cement' that holds the whole thing together. Cratons are, if you like, the core pieces in the continental matrix.

In every continent in the world there are tracts of country made up of granite and older rocks which form these cratons.[23] Examples include the Kaapvaal craton in South Africa, the Zimbabwe craton, the Angola-Kasai craton and the Kalomo batholith. The point is that, if the continental mass is subject to pressures of distortion, whether due to rising convections in the deep-earth magma below or unequal distribution of mass above, and, as result, is going to 'give', then that 'giving' is much more likely to take place along existing lines of weakness. The faulting that accompanies such activity will preferentially follow the spaces between existing cratons, rather than penetrating the cratons themselves.

It is believed that the Gwembe and Zambezi Valley are part of the GEARV, only in the sense that they represent a superficial continuation of it. The Rift Valley in East Africa seems to have been formed as a result of the 'pulling apart' of the land mass or subsidence from below while the Zambezi's valley follows the western and northern boundaries of the Zimbabwe craton and, as such, is an inherent line of weakness which will respond to continental movement with fracturing and faulting.

Given that the west and north margin of the Zimbabwe craton is an area of weakness, drainage of some kind will always preferentially have followed it, but not necessarily the Zambezi River. The possibility of great changes in the enormous span of time available is so great that one distinguished writer has no hesitation in asserting that, if one goes back far enough, the Luangwa could well have flowed to the vicinity of the Okavango via the Zambezi Valley and Gwembe Trough. In other words, reverse drainage UP the course of the present river![24]

To understand the scale of changes possible, it is of interest to learn what events took place over the course of 250 million years in just one

well-studied part of the modern valley. This is a convenient period to take
for it includes the whole of what is known as the Karoo System which
contains the Zambezi's prolific coal deposits and, for that reason, is very
well known.[25, 26]

At the beginning of that time, where the Gwembe Trough is now, it was
exceedingly cold — near polar conditions prevailed. Glaciers had just
departed, leaving distinct traces in deposits of glacial tillite, the melt-
water collecting in small lakes. Gradually the climate warmed a little and
plant life became established. Tavener-Smith describes the area of the
mid-Zambezi basin as then being an extensive region of flat swampy
country thickly covered with vegetation, interspersed with shallow pools
and lakes.

Throughout those times, there was a constant balancing act between
the basin floor level and arriving sediments, with the valley subsiding,
perhaps in response to the mass that was being put upon it. In time, a lake
was formed but then subsidence stopped and slowly the lake filled with
transported silt and sands. Extraordinary as it may seem, ripple marks
from the muds of those times, perhaps 220 million years ago, are still
preserved as fossilised patterns in the rocks!

Eventually, subsidence began again, allowing more sediments to
collect, forming the mudstones of today. The climate, however, was
slowly drying and a foretaste of the desert conditions to come appears in
accumulations of wind-blown dust. An interesting aspect of the geological succession from Dwyka ice to Stormberg lava is how it shows a
steady increase in temperature, possibly reflecting a northward migration
of the entire continent from polar to subtropical latitudes.[27]

It must not be imagined that this long period of time was one only of
sediment collection. Far from it. Professor Bond identified at least four
cycles of erosion. Each was initiated by a period of continental uplift
which often dramatically altered the shape of the land. What took place
at the beginning of Stormberg times was probably typical. The elevated
areas surrounding the Zambezi basin were raised still higher so that,
following the consequent rejuvenation of rivers, erosion and deposit of
sediments into the basin proceeded at an ever faster rate.

Interestingly, during this period the manner of transportation changed
from water-borne to wind-blown, which reflected the ever-increasing
aridity of the time. For so long did desert-like conditions persist that not
only was the depositional basin filled, but it overflowed so that deposits
of aeolian sand lay on the much older rocks that surrounded it. As we have
already seen, it was onto this huge expanse of sand that the Stormberg
lavas were poured.

Towards the end of Stormberg times, after the lava flows had ceased
to appear, perhaps 140 million years ago, there was a period of extensive
faulting and tilting, possibly associated with the stresses of the break-up

of Gondwanaland. The present fault pattern largely dates from this time
and, particularly, the major fault line that created the modern north-
facing escarpment of the Zambezi Valley appeared in place during this
era.

Dr Lister's Ph.D. work focuses in fascinating detail on events that
followed the demise of Gondwanaland. They include six separate erosion
cycles, one of which lasted for 75 million years and saw the continent
nearly levelled. It was during this, the African Cycle, that the principal
drainage lines that affect the Zambezi were established — although they
were still very different from those of today.

It is probable, says Dr Lister, that it was during this period, say between
20 and 40 million years ago, that the Upper Zambezi and Kafue rivers
were established more or less in their present courses and formed, with
the Kwando and Okavango, the Proto-Limpopo, discussed earlier. The
Lower Zambezi may have been starting on its age-long task of cutting
back into the sediment-filled valleys over which it now flowed, somewhere on the northern side of the Zimbabwe craton, perhaps approaching
modern Kariba Gorge.[28] But, as we have seen, it was not until just a few
million years ago that the modern Zambezi River appeared for the first
time by the joining of the upper and the lower sections at Victoria Falls.

An interesting aspect of the Zambezi's geology over this incredible span
of 250 million years is that right from the beginning, life has been much
in evidence. Indeed, the oldest fossil insect in the southern hemisphere
was found in the Gwembe Trough where it had died beside an open-water
lake.[29]

The geology of the Zambezi yields a remarkable variety of fossils,
ranging from plants and plentiful, well-preserved spores, through fish,
amphibians and reptiles to molluscs. A curious fact is the inverse
relationship between the occurrence of plant and animal fossils. For
reasons that cannot yet be explained, the two are never simultaneously
abundant and appear, almost, to be mutually exclusive in the fossil
record.[30]

Dinosaur remains are the most exciting of the fossils and, from the
Zambezi River, have been reported almost exclusively along the Zimbabwe section. A steadily increasing number of dinosaur fossils have
been found in recent decades. Most are located in the sandstones beneath
the Stormberg lava. Their presence indicates that, despite the all-per-
vasiveness of the great Triassic desert of 220 million years ago, water and
food must have been locally available.

Both *Syntarsus*, with its bird-like feet and broadly splayed toes, and the
comparatively small and agile *Massospondylus* were, however, well
adapted to desert conditions. Several dinosaur fossil sites have now been
located in the Zambezi Valley itself and, undoubtedly, many more remain
to be found.

A most unusual and remarkable dinosaur fossil comes from an island in modern Lake Kariba. Here, precisely at the junction in time and geology between the sandstone and the succeeding lava, *Vulcanodon karibaensis* died and was encapsulated in a lava tomb. What makes the find unusual is that it lies in a sandstone lens, sandwiched between two lava flows, which prompts speculation as to the manner of its passing.[31] How did these and other creatures survive the lava flows that apparently turned their world to stone? One must assume that animal life was driven to other parts of the continent from whence recolonisation subsequently took place.

So far in this chapter I have moved quickly through a fraction of the Zambezi's geomorphology and geology, being able to accomplish in this space little more than the most superficial of introductions. Now, however, I would like to shift the focus from the general to something more specific and to return to the area of the river's beginning. There, we can begin a journey down the river and I can introduce some of the people and events that make up part of the Zambezi story.

The Zambezi's source is located in the Mwinilunga district of northwestern Zambia, an area renowned among botanists and entomologists alike. By a combination of altitude, soil and climate it has a great diversity of plant and insect species, added to by the close proximity of flora and fauna specific to the Congo and the Kalahari biospheres and the miombo woodlands of Zambia. The number of different woody plant species alone is estimated to be over 1 000.[32]

Game animals in the district and near the source are regrettably rare today; but it has not always been so. Owen Letcher, writing in 1913, was able to talk of great numbers of buffalo that roamed the watershed.[33] Sakeji school, to which we will return later, still has plenty of stories about game. Once, a lion ate the leather seat of a teacher's bicycle! For many years the school relied on the shooting of locally available antelope for meat.[34]

History does not appear to have discovered yet who was the first European at the source of the Zambezi. The chances are, however, that it would have been one of the 19th century missionaries, for they travelled extensively in this part of Africa and they came, not from the south, but from the west.

One of these missionaries, Fred Arnot, had been inspired as a young man by the vision and explorations of Dr David Livingstone. He had first been to Africa in 1871 and had spent seven years here. In 1888 he returned to England to gather recruits and within six months was back in Angola with a wife and a brother-in-law. The latter, Dr Walter Fisher, was a remarkable man who remained a lifelong friend. Together Arnot and Fisher experienced the challenge, the tragedy and the humour of an Africa still new to European eyes. Initially, these men worked together in central

Angola but constantly moved to new stations, eventually reaching the Zambezi.

Transport was a never-ending problem. One innovative missionary brought from England wheelbarrows specifically designed for the carriage of the mission's ladies, but when the local porters placed the barrows on their heads and complained of how unwieldy they were, the missionary realised he was beaten!

Later, Fisher himself sensibly took a bicycle to central Africa and pedalled many thousands of kilometres along the bush paths of eastern Angola to the decided consternation of the natives. It was 1893 and nothing like so sophisticated a machine had been seen so far inland.[35]

A combination of pioneering spirit and events beyond his control took Fisher progressively eastwards across Angola towards the Zambezi. His stations of Kavungu and Kazombo, now in the Angolan war-zone, were both on the banks of the Zambezi. Kalunda, which he established in 1904, was even further east. It was from the Zambezi, during a period of leave he took in 1903, that Walter Fisher walked east, not west, for home, and on his way to England joined a small group of hardy people to complete a crossing of Africa on foot.[36]

Living among the tribesmen of the Upper Zambezi was not an occupation for the squeamish, for their ways were very different from those to which the missionaries were used. Fisher described graphically the events that followed the death of a local chief.

Within minutes of the chief's passing, all his houses were destroyed except the one in which ten of his wives were expected to sit through the night with his body on their laps. An even less pleasant tradition sometimes demanded that the wives hold their dead chief in that position for months after death until only the bones remained.

Normally, at least five of the wives would have been killed and buried with the chief. Possibly another two would have had their arms and legs dislocated and been placed, alive, at the head and the foot of the grave, there to remain and die of starvation or be taken by hyenas. That this did not happen was due to Fisher's successful appeal for intervention by the Portuguese whose administrative authority reached into this remote part of eastern Angola.[37]

Eventually, continued eastward migration brought Fisher at last to Kalene Hill in 1906, just 30 km from the Zambezi's source. The hill is a low ridge of rock around which the river circles at a distance as it swings from north to west on its journey to the sea. Here Walter Fisher built his hospital which still serves the people of the region.

A perpetual problem for missionaries in Africa was the education of their children. In the absence of local schooling the parents had two choices. Either they separated and one stayed overseas with the children — to the detriment of the marriage and the remaining partner, or the children remained alone overseas to the detriment of the family as a unit. Fisher's solution was to motivate the building of a school on the Sakeji River, the first significant tributary of the Zambezi, and a short distance from Kalene Hill.

Opened in 1925, the school's particular attraction was its central location in that part of Africa. The intention of its creators was that it would be available for the children of missionaries in any nearby part of the continent. It was highly successful and by the end of 1975 more than 830 pupils had attended. The school continues today, alive, vibrant and fondly remembered by all who attended it. One of those, whom I recently met, has some unusual tales to tell.

Fred Barnett took his wife and children north to a mission site at Chavuma on the Zambezi in about 1931. Both parents were missionaries and set to with a will in their new home. Tragically, Fred was drowned in the river in 1933 but his wife, Dorothy, decided to stay and continue the work, despite what many might have considered to be the disadvantage of four young children.

Inevitably, the schooling question arose but for Dorothy, Sakeji was the answer — except that it was more than 400 km away, in an era before cars or roads. Gavin Barnett, now a successful business consultant in Johannesburg, told me that there was only one thing to do — like their kind all over the world, he and his sisters walked to school!

Four times a year, it became a favourite family outing. Twenty porters carried all that was required and the safari covered the distance to the school in ten to 14 days. The youngest children, who were not yet of school-going age, could not be left alone at home and so they went along, being carried in hammocks most of the way.

Game was everywhere extraordinarily plentiful and Gavin, to this day, recalls the herds of elephant and buffalo through which they walked, and the rivers, teeming with hippo and crocodile, which had to be crossed.

Gavin's mother made every trip and turned the outing into an opportunity for her evangelical work. Each night was spent in a village and in return for some salt and a piece of cotton material the chief or headman would offer them a chicken to eat. After the meal Dorothy would take out her guitar and sing hymns to those who gathered round.

By the middle of the Second World War the motor vehicle had reached even this remote corner of Empire and Gavin has a vivid recollection of his first meeting with one, when he was about seven. He, his mother and sisters set off on the usual safari through the wilds to Sakeji, but on this occasion they were to rendezvous with a man who had recently acquired a motor truck and who was to carry them the remainder of the journey. They reached the end of the track cut through the bush and Gavin remembers the frightening, noisy monster that emerged like some fearsome beast from the trees and took him away from his mother! Happily, he was quickly reconciled with the truck and on future journeys it was to cut the trip to school to a mere five days.[38]

The school and Kalene Hill have seen great changes in nearly 65 years. When Dr Fisher went there, slavery and slave capture were a very real part of daily life. The people about were so secretive that the doctor had to watch for the smoke from their fires in the evening and march on a compass bearing the following day to find them.

The school, remote as it remains today, has many of the amenities of modern life; one of the first to arrive was a piano. It was purchased in the Congo in 1928 and required transport through more than 100 km of wilderness. This problem was overcome with the assistance of 18 porters who, in carrying it, must have set one of Africa's records for the most unlikely load ever!

Another of the school's amenities is electricity. As a system, the electricity supply at Sakeji school is a monument to man's ingenuity and to God's miraculous powers — for it surely must be He and not David Foster, the Headmaster, who really keeps it all together! Apparently made of assorted discards from various motor cars, tractors and bicycles, powered by a water wheel and held together with large quantities of faith and insulating tape, it is a truly amazing achievement. Its central component appears to be an old station clock which in some way, mysterious to behold but associated with archaic mercury cup switches, renders the entire arrangement automatic!

2   A River Kingdom

NOWHERE in its sinuous course across the face of Africa, neither at the source nor at the subdued merging with the sea, is there to be found, along the entire length of the Zambezi River, a region quite as beautiful as Barotseland in western Zambia. Nor is it surprising that here, among the Lozi people, one encounters some of the warmest and most friendly of riverside people. I am sure this is partly to do with their beautiful home and partly with their history, but it owes more, I think, to their sense of pride in belonging to the 'superfamily', which is their tribe. In response to the tangible sense of ceremony and history in Barotseland, it is perhaps fitting that it should be on these remarkable floodplains that there survives, among the Lozi, one of Africa's most colourful indigenous tribal ceremonies — the Kuomboka.

We have seen the Zambezi leave its birthplace in Zambia's north-west and head westward through Angola towards the Atlantic. Soon, however, it turns to the south and re-enters Zambia. It then flows over vast areas of once wind-blown sand that are part of the immense Kalahari system. These are the floodplains of Barotseland.

The floodplains do not have, in all places, a clearly defined margin and so one cannot be precise about their extent. Generally, however, flooding takes place within a region some 250 km in length and 80 km or 100 km in width. That flooding occurs at all is due entirely to the unusual geography of the region.

Western Zambia is covered with Kalahari sand, a remnant of an ancient desert. In some places the sand is more than 50 m deep. Little is known about what lies beneath it, since all is smothered by the aeolian blanket. The shape of the ancient landscape is concealed from view below a featureless and nearly level sandy plain. It is across this plain that the Zambezi flows and would, long since, have incised a deep valley, were it not for the chance placement of numerous basalt dykes across its path.[1]

These dykes serve as barriers through which the river can but slowly cut and so they prevent the formation of a deep valley. Each, of course, forms a rapid or waterfall. Some of these are beautiful, particularly the largest, known as Ngonye or Sioma Falls. The falls are the first of the breached dykes and they mark the southern end of the floodplains. As such, they are the key to the entire floodplain ecosystem. As this point is lowered by the headward erosion of the river, so, in time, the floodplains

will become less extensive.[2] From here onwards, although navigable, the
river is much more broken and there are 24 sets of rapids between Ngonye
and Katima Mulilo.

Ngonye varies with the time of year at which it is viewed. In the wet,
apart from the noise and the spray, it is more awesome than striking, for
it is totally engulfed in the deluge of water that passes over it. In the dry
season, it is different. Then the cataracts above and below can be seen,
and particularly the beautiful half-moon shaped cascade of water that
drops 23 m into a short but ferocious gorge.

The Zambezi has not yet cut far enough into Ngonye's basalt to create
a deep upstream valley. In the absence of such a valley, vigorous annual
floodwaters quickly overflow the river's banks and vast areas of Barotseland are swiftly inundated.

My first glimpse of the floodplains was memorable. I had come to their
edge at night, to a place where they end abruptly. Here a fault line throws
up a low crest of higher land some 30 m above the plain. Unknowingly
I camped on this very crest. At dawn I was startled by the beauty I saw.
Beneath the tall and dark forest trees that clothed the steep slope, the
ground dropped to the plain below. The plain extended to the western
horizon and at first sight appeared to be a flawless expanse of green, endless and reaching in every direction. In time I noticed the streaks of blue
that told the real truth, for the plain was flooded and under more than a
metre of water.

Each year, when the Zambezi rises above its low banks and its waters
begin their annual soaking of the plains, the grass, stimulated by this
abundance of moisture, puts on a sustained spurt of growth, which allows
it to grow faster than the rising flood. In this way, over the entire plain,
a carpet of green shades the water, sometimes standing a metre or more
above it. These are the flooded plains of Barotseland and this is the home
of the Lozi people.

The Lozi have their origins in the great Lunda-Luba empire of the Congo
basin and probably came to the floodplains in the latter half of the 17th
century. Like other Zambian tribes of Zaïrese origin, the early Lozi had
a female leader called Mwambwa, and were matrilineal, although they are
not so now.[3] As are many tribal groupings in Africa, the Lozi are a mixed
people and the so-called Barotse nation is made up of some 25 smaller
tribes.[4] They have a complex mythology, a sophisticated tribal structure
and a system of government in which authority is highly centralised in
the figure of the king or Litunga.

Some of the characters and events in Lozi traditions and legends are
fascinating for their reiteration of familiar themes. The central figures are
Nyambe, the Creator, and his wife Nasilele. Nyambe made the world and
everything in it, including the first man, Kamunu and Kamunu's wife. As
in many African traditions, at the beginning of time, men and animals

could speak to each other and only because of mishap was this skill lost. Eventually, Nyambe distanced himself from his creations and took up an abode 'in the sky'. Kamunu then assembled all the people and with their help attempted to build a platform tall enough to reach the sky and Nyambe. Reminiscent of the story of the Tower of Babel, the Lozi construction collapsed when it grew too heavy to support.[5]

The Lozi trace with pride their history from Mwambwa and her daughter who became the second ruler in the new lands. She was succeeded by or abdicated in favour of her son, who began a period of Lozi expansion. By the beginning of the 19th century the state was well established and had developed the instruments of centralised administration that, in the long term, gave it stability and continuity. This level of organisation has allowed the Lozi nation to exist as a discernible political entity for nearly 200 years and to have survived 40 years of domination by a migrant Sotho group in the 19th century.

Mulambwa, the heroic ninth Litunga who ruled from 1780 to 1830, and his successor had to face the nation's greatest threat in the shape of a horde of battle-hardened warriors who were familiar with new weapons and new tactics and whose appetite for conquest was still unsatisfied.[6] To understand the nature and origins of this threat, which itself becomes an integral part of the Zambezi's story, we must move to a distant part of the continent and to events that were taking place there.

In the first decades of the 19th century, there occurred in south-eastern Africa, in what is today Zululand, the most extraordinary phenomenon. This event and the consequences are known by two names. Among the Ngoni people (Nguni is the language), in whose land it originated, it is called the Mfecane, meaning 'to crush', as in a total war. Those who lived in the hinterland, mainly Sotho-speaking groups, called it the Difaqane, which means 'forced migration' or 'hammering'.[7]

Such emotive and telling names nevertheless do not convey the terror of those times, nor do they suggest the remarkable chain of events that was set in motion. The origins of the Mfecane had to do with social, cultural and military changes among the Ngoni tribes who lived in what is now Zululand. Small things contributed to the momentous change: Dingiswayo's abolition of the traditional circumcision groups, the introduction of age regiments which created a standing army, drought, population pressure, food shortages and Shaka's military genius which produced the stabbing spear, a better shield and improved battle tactics. These and many other factors brought about deep-seated changes in Zululand.

Formerly, the land had been peopled by small tribal groups and disputes tended to take the form of feuds rather than standing battles. Disagreements were often settled by one group moving away. Increasingly in the crowded southern part of Africa, this was no longer possible. Confrontation became more common and the victors were those who were better armed and organised. Shaka, who enjoyed Dingiswayo's patronage and eventually succeeded him, was eminently suited for the role of victor.

By 1819, Shaka had dealt with all serious rivals and his own position was secure. Having created it, he then extended the Zulu kingdom by systematically absorbing numerous smaller independent chiefdoms. Unlike his predecessor who ruled through conquered royalty, it was Shaka's habit to eliminate completely the enemy élite and massacres of women and children sometimes followed. This was done to prevent any possibility of resistance.[8]

In this way, an era of mayhem and terror was unleashed. A deadly domino sequence was set in motion as tribal integrity and social organisation disintegrated. Fleeing fear and famine, refugees in their thousands scoured the land, for no fields had been tilled or crops harvested. Those who were without, conquered and took from those who had, but the victors soon became the defeated as food was quickly consumed. The only escape was to move further from the centre and conquer anew. Thus was set in motion the Difaqane.

This remarkable and explosive chain of events irrevocably affected much of Africa south of the equator. Groups of Ngoni people travelled vast distances, bringing war and leaving famine and death in their wake. Inevitably, Ngoni conquests displaced others whose wanderings, in their turn, had no less catastrophic an effect. Like an exploding fireball the Difaqane sent searing arcs of destruction curving across the continent.

Four of these groups form part of the Zambezi story and we shall return to them in future chapters. They were the Ngoni who destroyed the great states of Zimbabwe and who settled in Zambia, Tanzania and Malawi, those who fought through Mozambique and then stayed to become a part of it, the Matabele who speared their way across the highveld of South Africa through Botswana and into Zimbabwe where they established the Matabeleland of today, and finally, the Kololo. They were not Ngoni at all but had been displaced by the consequences of Zulu emergence and were also victims of the Difaqane.

It was in response to the chaos of the Mfecane that Chief Sebitoane addressed his people in 1823 and persuaded them to forsake peace to march in search of a new land in which to live. His people were the Patsa, a section of the Bafokeng who were recognised as the senior of many tribes known as the Basotho. In 1822, Sebitoane had succeeded to the chieftainship of the Bafokeng and he was soon to lead them into an extraordinary chapter of history.[9] Glorious and tragic, it lasted for 60 years, after which his people were no more.

From the area of the Transvaal, in which they had been living, Sebitoane, fearing that there was no choice if they were to survive, led his people on the path of conquest. Initially, he was not always successful but with experience he improved and soon acquired a sizeable army. He now called his followers 'Makololo' in honour of his favourite wife who belonged to the Kololo clan.[10] The Kololo fought their way up the eastern side of Botswana and across the Kalahari via the great Makgadikgadi Pans to Lake Ngami and the Okavango. From there, after a brief foray into the vicinity of Ghanzi, Sebitoane led them north again, through the Caprivi Strip to the banks of the Zambezi. Here, in the vicinity of Victoria Falls, they encountered and defeated a Batonga force. This led to the occupation by Sebitoane and his army of the cool, healthy and fertile highlands that extend north-eastwards from the falls through modern Kalomo and Monze. Here they might have remained but for a singular irony of history.[11]

At about this time, Mzilikazi had established himself in the town of Bulawayo in Matabeleland. Mzilikazi was a Ngoni who had not been able to accommodate himself to the regime in Zululand. He too was a victim of the Mfecane and, like Sebitoane, had fled. After a bloody journey of many years, he had arrived to the south of the Zambezi with a strong desire to increase even further his distance from the white man, with whom he had had several violent clashes in the Transvaal, and to conquer the Kololo.

By an unlikely coincidence, two large, powerful and well-organised military groups, with different origins but fleeing from the same violence, had settled in adjacent regions, almost 2 000 km from where they had started. Mzilikazi, aware of the good cattle country occupied by the Kololo, launched raids against them. The raids were not successful and were seriously hampered by the river crossing, but they were a sign of the times. Sebitoane could see an uncomfortable future with his Matabele neighbours and decided to move. It was then, in 1843, that his eyes rested covetously on the kingdom of the Lozi, comfortably ensconced in its wide and fertile valley, like a ripe fruit waiting to be picked.

Mulambwa, the powerful and revered Litunga, king of the Lozi, had died and the kingdom had divided in support of the two contenders for the vacant throne. Selunalumi, the former king's brother, and Sepopa, his son, could find no common ground and battle may have followed had it not been for the providential appearance of Sebitoane. The king's brother immediately asked that his kingdom be annexed by the stranger as a way of resolving the problem. Sebitoane obliged — and began immediately to exterminate every possible source of future resistance. Sepopa and his supporters fled to the far north where they remained in exile for 40 years.[12]

In the meantime Sebitoane, who was an extremely competent and intelligent individual, set about consolidating Kololo rule over the Lozi people. So successful was he in this endeavour that the language of his people became that of the Lozi and remains so to this day. His aim was to consolidate the disunited groups, to restore the integrity of the Lozi nation and to use it as a buffer against the continually aggressive Matabele. He ruled first from the village of Sesheke, the former Lozi southern capital, and then, for the greater security that the additional river and swamps provided, moved to Linyanti near the bend of the Chobe in the Caprivi Strip.

Here he unwittingly placed himself and his people within the grasp of an unknown and unseen enemy. Some authorities state that, by this time, most of his original Sotho followers were dead, victims of malaria, which was rife in Barotseland and especially bad at Linyanti. They had been replaced by assimilated prisoners but the drive and ambition that had taken the Kololo so far and achieved so much now seemed, with Sebitoane's passing, to take its leave.[13] David Livingstone and William Cotton Oswell were both present at the time and record the moving circumstances of Sebitoane's death in 1851.

Sekelutu, his son, was only 18 when he became the new leader. He was not the accomplished man his father had been and soon rebellion erupted in many parts of the kingdom. By 1864, Sekelutu was dead and it was now the turn of the Kololo to be riven by succession rivalries. For a few short months Mbolowa, Sebitoane's brother, held the reins of power but time for the Kololo had run out. Aware of the dissension within the ruling ranks and of the increasing unpopularity of the Kololo, Lozi plotters decided to act. Under the leadership of Sepopa, who had fled to the north, every Kololo was struck down — man, woman and child — in one night. A handful escaped but they were killed by those among whom they sought refuge.[14] The Lozi kingdom had been restored and the Kololo were no more.

In blood the restoration took place and in blood it continued for some years. Power turned the head of Sepopa who was increasingly seen as a cruel tyrant. He was ousted by his people in a conflict and died from his injuries — there are at least three different accounts of his death. Mwanamwina succeeded him but within two years, in 1878, he too was replaced. The next claimant was known as Lubosi and, with him, some semblance of stability returned. Lubosi held the throne for six years until he was driven into exile for a year.[15] He returned in 1885 with a changed name; Lubosi had stood for 'the escaped one', Lewanika meant 'the conqueror'.[16]

Much had changed in the Barotse Valley by the time Lewanika was firmly established on the throne. David Livingstone had passed through the country on four occasions and the world now knew of his exploits and discoveries. Traders, explorers, missionaries, fortune hunters and imperialists were to follow. Among those Europeans who came into contact with the Lozi and their kings, two stand out above all others; the trader George Westbeech and the missionary François Coillard. Probably, no two foreigners did as much to shape the development of the kingdom or to influence the choices that were made. Coillard's achievements and his relationship with Westbeech are examined in Chapter 3, but let us turn now to George Westbeech and the role he played.

Westbeech emigrated to Natal from England in 1862 and within two years had made a trading journey to Matabeleland. Early in his career he already exhibited the qualities that contributed much to his success. His strengths were his honesty, his integrity, his diplomacy and his intelligence. He and his partner, George Arthur 'Elephant' Phillips, gained the respect and confidence both of Mzilikazi and the future king, Lobengula. They once accompanied Lobengula and a Matabele regiment to the far north of Zimbabwe and both men were present at the installation of Lobengula as king of the Matabele in 1870.[17]

At about that time, the elephant hunting business, which was the backbone of every trader's enterprise, was in trouble. Two essential elements had underpinned its commercial success: ivory could be carried out on horseback and ox-wagons could be used to haul it. By 1870, however, this was no longer possible. Elephant populations in areas free of tsetse fly had been eradicated. Now elephants could be found only in fly-infested areas where neither ox nor horse could travel. This meant that they had to be hunted on foot and the ivory removed by porters. Hunting was now much more dangerous and the method slower and more time-consuming. It was Westbeech's innovative approach that overcame this problem. His technique was to employ armies of African hunters who did the hunting and killing for him.[18]

His first contact with the Lozi came in 1870 when he and his partner arrived at the junction of the Chobe and the Zambezi with three wagons of goods. Sepopa was king and he welcomed the visitors, striking up a deep friendship with Westbeech, whom he detained at his village for a year and a half. When at last he allowed Westbeech to leave, the wagons were filled with ivory — from the sale of which Westbeech profited £12 000, an enormous sum. Not surprisingly, Westbeech decided to continue as a trader in Barotseland. He travelled constantly between his supply points in the south and his new home on the Zambezi, spending periods of a year, sometimes two, in Barotseland. In 1875, he took his bride there.[19]

Westbeech almost became an institution. At Pandamatanga he established a trading post and store. This was the point furthest north to which one could travel before reaching the edge of the tsetse fly area. Here, with increasing regularity, came the visitors to Victoria Falls. They left their horses and oxen and moved to the falls on foot.

According to one authority, Westbeech was well educated, well mannered, generous and helpful to all who came to him. During the remainder of Sepopa's reign, Westbeech and his associate Blockley were the only whites permitted into Barotseland and the only ones allowed to hunt elephant. It is said that, during those years, Westbeech was able to move between 10 and 15 tonnes of ivory a year!

To the kings of Barotseland he was a trusted confidant and was elected a member of the Barotse council of state. This was remarkable when one considers his background and the turmoil in Lozi politics at the time, when no one could be trusted. Yet Westbeech survived and continued to assist five kings, a great tribute to the regard in which he was held and his ability to be a friend to all. It is not too much of an exaggeration to claim that Westbeech's presence may have neutralised the Portuguese influence in Barotseland, encouraging in its stead an inclination to favour closer links with Britain.[20] It is also true that his power and influence must have had some bearing on the success enjoyed by the Paris Evangelical Mission which was soon to be established at the Lozi capital. This question is looked at more closely in Chapter 4.

Living close to the Lozi capital during those tumultuous years, Westbeech saw at first hand both the vices and virtues that accompany the traditional exercise of untrammelled tribal authority. Violence and witchcraft were entrenched in the way of life. Sepopa's first act on being appointed king was to have two of his three brothers killed.[21] In 1884, when Lubosi was driven off the throne and out of the valley, Akufuna Tatila, who took his place, massacred all Lubosi's supporters he could find.

The following year, in 1885, Lubosi was back. Calling himself Lewanika, he had returned to stay; to make that more certain, dreadful purges were ordered. Westbeech described it: 'All those who were caught or came to surrender themselves to his former clemency were immediately killed; even the women, wives of rebels, were ripped open by the assegai and thus left to die'. Others were taken out onto the plains where their arms and legs were broken and they were left to die of hunger or thirst. Young children were thrown to the crocodiles.[22]

The well-known missionary F.S. Arnot stayed at Lealui, the Lozi king's capital, for two years, from 1882 to 1884, and witnessed with horror these and other examples of how cheaply human life was held. Events or possessions that were important were often sanctified with human blood. First the fingers and toes of victims were cut off and the blood sprinkled over the hut or boat in question. Bound still, the victim, usually a child, would then be ripped open and thrown into the river. Another form of sacrifice was to tie the victim hand and foot, staked to the ground, near an ants' nest. Within a few days, it was said, only the bones would be left, picked clean.[23]

Witchcraft was widespread and its perpetrators, the witchdoctors, held enormously powerful positions. Even trivial misfortunes were attributed by the tribespeople to some form of sorcery. The excesses of witchcraft probably reflected the unsettled nature of the times; witchcraft took a huge toll in human life and maimed many. When the 'bones' had been cast and a victim stood accused, he was usually tried by one of two ordeals.

Either he plunged his hand into boiling water or he drank some 'mwati' poison. There was no formal hearing of his case and the outcome by ordeal was left to rather predictable fate.[24]

If the exploits of Livingstone and reports of missionaries like Arnot and Coillard created one form of awareness about Africa, the discovery of diamonds and gold in the South African Republics created another. Everywhere, prospectors fanned out across the African veld, inspired by Kimberley and the gold of the northern and eastern Transvaal. In 1886, the great gold reef of the Witwatersrand was discovered and there could no longer be any doubt that Africa held the potential for fabulous mineral wealth.

It was the possibility of this wealth that provided much of the motivation for the great northward expansion of British interests, initially under the guise of the British South Africa Company. In Ngamiland, in Matabeleland and now in Barotseland, agreements were sought with kings and principal chiefs who were asked to grant exclusive mineral rights in questionable exchanges related more to what the seller would take than to what the goods sold were worth. This intrinsic unfairness was not, however, solely confined to one side, as we shall see.

Harry Ware of Kimberley was one of those who had been, in the late 1880s, fortunate enough to gain access to Lewanika's capital at Lealui. Here, he had badgered the king until a mineral concession had been granted to him. In return for the payment of £200 a year, plus a 4% royalty on all mineral wealth, Ware was assigned for a period of 20 years the sole rights for the mining of gold, diamonds and other minerals in the Batonga country. As well as paying the rent and the royalty, Ware pledged to respect the fields and the villages of the Barotse (not the Batonga!), not to kill elephants and to keep out all intoxicating liquors. The country of the Batonga was not specified in detail but it would have been the land occupied by the people to the east of Barotseland, between it and the Zambezi.[25]

Ware, seemingly, was an opportunist. He quickly sold the concession to a group of Kimberley speculators led by H.J. King and C.E. Nind. History has not recorded what reward Ware received for his enterprise. The concession had been granted to him in June 1889, the time when Cecil Rhodes's BSA Company was at its most acquisitive and formidable. Rhodes had already heard that Lewanika was contemplating British protection, and so he had decided that Barotseland was worthy of his company's attention. With this in mind, and so that failure to possess it would not hinder the plans he was developing, he acquired from King and Nind the Ware concession. For this they were paid £9 000 and received 10 000 shares in the British South Africa Company.[26]

The concession soon became part of and was swamped by more grandiose agreements. The agreement clearly shows that Lewanika had plenty of common sense as well as cunning. Strictly speaking, he had no authority whatsoever to dispose of mineral rights in Batonga lands. They were not a subordinate people, they were not conquered, nor did their land fall within the Lozi kingdom![27]

The Ware concession itself was not particularly significant, but it was a portent of what was rapidly to come. To see this in perspective, we have to shift the focus of events from politics at the level of a tribal kingdom to the more complex backdrop of international events.

The late 1880s saw the 'scramble for Africa', as it has come to be called, at its peak. By 1890, most of the easy gains had been accounted for and the European powers were now turning covetous eyes to the less accessible parts of the continent. It had already been agreed by France and Germany that the territory to the north of the Zambezi was part of the Portuguese sphere of influence. Britain had not been party to this agreement but its existence was enough to make her tread more carefully. Such an agreement was also likely to hinder Rhodes from achieving his cherished 'red route' through Africa, apart from enjoying the commercial and mining opportunities that Barotseland might offer. He realised that it would be difficult to persuade Britain to declare a protectorate over that region merely on the strength of a mining concession from Barotseland. Something more was required and with characteristic directness, Rhodes set about ensuring that it appeared.

A constant threat to Lewanika himself and the continuity of his kingdom since his return to the throne in 1885 was the fear of Matabele incursions. Prior to his dethronement, Lewanika had received a delegation from Lobengula, king of the Matabele. With presents of spears and shields, Lobengula had asked him to join forces against the white man. Already in contact with Khama, Chief of the Bamangwato in Bechuanaland, and persuaded, too, by F.S. Arnot, Lewanika chose to seek Khama's friendship and alliance, rather than that of the Matabele.[28] It was a brave choice between might and right but it was to give Lewanika many sleepless nights.

Spurning Lobengula's offer of friendship had increased the Matabele threat. So when, in 1887, Lewanika received definite warning that the Matabele were considering a raid against him, he wrote again to Khama enquiring about protection and what it meant. The raid did not materialise but the threat remained. In 1889, as a result of his continuous exchanges with Khama, Lewanika wrote to Sir Sidney Shippard, the Administrator of Bechuanaland, and formally requested British protection for Barotseland. It took eight months for that letter to reach the Foreign Office and, when it did, it received a friendly but lukewarm reply. There matters might have remained but for the machinations of Mr Rhodes.[29]

Knowing of Lewanika's leaning towards, and later request for, protection, Rhodes could see at once how he could take advantage of the si-

tuation. To put his plans into effect he chose a former officer of the Bechuanaland Police, Frank Elliot Lochner, whose task it was to visit Lewanika
and obtain a mineral concession from him. Lochner was chosen for a number of reasons: he knew the African people well, he was used to travelling long distances through the bush and, above all, he was well known
and respected by Chief Khama.

With three companions, Lochner set out in October 1889. Heavy rains
delayed them and it was not until March 1890 that they arrived at Lealui,
exhausted, ill with malaria and without provisions of any kind. Coillard,
the French Protestant missionary, took them in and cared for them.

Ware's concession, which had already been signed, had generated considerable opposition among the Lozi councillors who, in the subsequent
absence of Ware or any of his representatives, were beginning to feel they
had been duped. Lewanika appears to have assumed that Lochner and his
British South Africa Company were, in some way, representatives of the
Crown. He made it plain that, as far as he was concerned, British protection and mineral concessions were the same thing. His only interest
was to be satisfied that Lochner and his companions were, indeed, the
representatives of the Queen.

This presented some problems for Lochner since he was not the Queen's
representative but rather a servant of the BSA Company. He at once saw
that to explain the true commercial nature of the company to the king
would be the end of any concession. He therefore resolved to mislead
Lewanika and assured him that a treaty with the company was the same
thing as a treaty with the Queen. This was an act for which both Rhodes
and Lochner were severely criticised by the press in later years.[30]

Many of Lewanika's councillors whose presence was required for the
discussions were absent on a raiding party. Lochner's plans were delayed
by this and his own ill-health but eventually, at the end of May,
negotiations began. At this point Lochner employed some marketing
techniques to very good effect. He hosted a 'games day' in which there
were sports of all kinds and in honour of which he purchased and had
killed four oxen for a feast. The day ended with a display of fireworks
which were certainly the first ever seen by most of the people, if not all.
It is easy to imagine the kind of impression that this show of 'technology'
would have created.

Boosted to high popularity by this social success, Lochner was invited
to present his full proposals for discussion before the king and his 'pitso',
the tribal council. The raiding party with its absent councillors had returned triumphant and all seemed propitious for the meeting. But it did
not go smoothly. There were several white traders at Lealui whose interests would not be served by the fulfilment of Rhodes's plan, and they
spoke against it, denouncing Lochner and his claims. Both Coillard and
his assistant Jalla refuted these allegations but the suspicions of the coun-

cillors had been aroused. The issue hung in the balance and Lochner needed to do something dramatic to win the day. With the most accomplished stage management, not to mention flair and last-minute organisation, he did exactly that.

Into the open area of the 'kothla' — the king's meeting place where the 'pitso' was in session — came an elderly and dignified man who had clearly travelled far. After making his obeisance to the king, he obtained permission to deliver, to the assembly, the message he claimed he had brought from Khama the Great. The message was to the effect that Khama, who compared British protection to a savoury dish, had tasted the dish and wished to share it with his friends. He went on to vouch for Lochner and ended with the assertion that Lochner and the company he represented were, indeed, the Queen's men. In the face of such testimony, the day was inevitably won. Lochner and Cecil Rhodes gained the concession they sought.[31]

It is difficult to credit chance with the arrival of such an emissary bearing the fortuitous message that he carried. If anyone suspected manipulation, they were right, but it was not until much later that the truth was discovered. The messenger, whose name was Makoatse, had been paid by Lochner and instructed what to say![32]

The concession was signed on 27 June 1890, at a time when Rhodes and the BSA Company were stretched to their limit. Rhodesia was being colonised and there were no resources for further expansion. In many ways, the Lochner concession was a farce: as one historian has noted, in the years that followed it, the company reneged on almost every article. It was seven years before the first administrator appeared. No payments were made to the king or his councillors during that period. No schools or industries were developed and, in time, the power of the king and his councils was severely impaired.[33] It is perhaps possible that the only serious short-term objective of Lochner's work was to ensure, by means of the treaty, that other competitors were excluded. If this is so then it was, indeed, successful. It brought Barotseland and ultimately the whole of Northern Rhodesia under British rule.

An unexpected complication arose in 1893. Possessing mineral rights to a kingdom really requires that one know the extent of that kingdom. In this regard, it was necessary for Portugal and Britain to agree on the western limits of Barotseland. Lewanika claimed that they extended far west of the Zambezi but the Portuguese would not accept this. A provisional boundary was agreed, one that followed the Zambezi, while the matter was referred to the king of Italy for arbitration. He gave his judgement in 1905, largely supporting Lozi claims and thereby adding (or returning) more than ten million hectares to the kingdom![34]

The British government was not satisfied with the administration by the British South Africa Company after the 1890s and, on the advice of

Lord Milner, decided to undertake a more active role. In 1900 the Coryndon Treaty was signed at Victoria Falls. Britain accepted responsibility for the administration of Barotseland. This was to be carried out by the BSA Company's officials but under the authority of the High Commissioner at the Cape.[35]

It was necessary, of course, swiftly to establish an administrative infrastructure and a small but steady flow of officials moved north across the Zambezi. These young men often found themselves solely responsible for many thousands of square kilometres and had to perform unexpected and unlikely tasks. Such was the lot of Major Colin Harding.

The Barotseland Native Police had been established and Harding was their commander. It was one of his early duties to carry out a tour of the north-western extremes of Barotseland, taking with him speeches from the Administrator as well as Lewanika. These advised the people of their new status under British protection. There was nothing particularly unusual in this — except that the speeches were recorded on a gramophone![36] If the intention was to impress the local tribespeople, this was a most effective way of doing so. One can imagine the reaction at the sound of their king's voice emanating from a wooden box. More startling still was the reaction when chiefs were invited to record their own messages of loyalty and support to Lewanika. I have never been completely sure 'how the West was won' but there is no doubt in my mind that the west of Barotseland was 'won' with the gramophone!

Much has changed since those early days. Northern Rhodesia is no more and the independent nation of Zambia proudly stands in its place. Lewanika has long since passed away. He saw his nation pass successfully into the modern world and died in 1916. The name of Barotseland is used no more; it has become an undesignated part of Western Province. But the Lozi people and the land they love live on. Today the king is Yetta IV, but he is no longer called king. His title now is Litunga and he carries awesome responsibilities. He remains the traditional leader of the Lozi people but is also the senior government representative for Western Province and has a seat on the highest council in the land.

His task is difficult for, as their leader, he must meet the traditional needs of his people while at the same time maintaining the status and dignity of his government position. I did not meet the Litunga when I visited his island home but I did watch him combine the ancient and the modern with effortless ease, bridging the cultural and social differences of centuries with impressive and humbling dignity. This was done in the ceremony beloved by the Lozi and known to them as Kuomboka.

It has a special value because it is unspoilt, uncommercialised and still untainted by modern tourism. Although as many as 15 000 people are said to attend, they are not tourists but those for whom Kuomboka is a meaningful part of their lives. They come to witness it and participate out of

loyalty, joy and pride. At close quarters, there is a tangible air of excitement and a sense of sharing. To be present is to share a closeness with
an Africa sadly departing, an Africa rarely experienced today.

Simply put, Kuomboka is the annual ceremonial departure of the Lozi
king and his people from the flooded plains to the dry mainland. It
symbolises the king's leadership and the loyalty of his people and re-
cognises the dominating role of the annual flood in the lives of the Lozi.
The move is by boat, with royalty travelling in splendid barges and with
the inhabitants, forbidden to leave before the king, following in numerous
smaller vessels. The forthcoming departure is announced to the people by
the call of royal drums — an event I had the good fortune to witness and
one I shall never forget.

The island of Lealui is set about with towering trees between which
there is an open sandy space. Here the public business of the tribe is conducted, in the sight of the people and outside the place of the Litunga.

At night, the people gather in this space, waiting for the drums to start.
Adults sitting, kneeling or standing, chatting in small groups; children
racing, falling, screaming, jumping helter-skelter through the sand. The
usual kind of fire is absent for despite the surrounding trees wood is
scarce on the floodplains. Instead, a bundle of thatching grass is lit and
allowed to burn to ash before another takes its place. The red glow flares
and fades in a strange and ghostly silent rhythm that seems to pulse the
night with energy and underlines the unspoken excitement and expectation.

This was one of those velvet nights that only the tropics can provide.
The sky was profoundly black, pierced by a thousand points of sparkling
light that seemed brighter and more compelling because of the blackness
from which they shone. The scene was timeless, ancient beyond the recall
of memory, and somehow unchanged. Only in retrospect did I see that in
some way I had slipped back through time. I was in the real Africa.

Unannounced, unaccompanied, the Litunga appeared from the
shadows. Children instantly stopped their play, the people knelt in total
silence. I could hear the Litunga's approaching footsteps in the sand. Tall,
erect, dignified, he wore a simple robe around his shoulders. This talented
and sophisticated graduate in every way epitomised the proud and noble
chief and in him the two images became one. He stood beside the largest
drum and picked up the drumsticks. Two of his senior indunas took up
similar positions at the other drums and I was close enough to see them
looking intently, not at the Litunga's hands, but at his eyes.

I watched and waited. It seemed that the whole world and all of us did
the same. The atmosphere was electric, the tension tangible. The Litunga
pushed his drumsticks across the tightly stretched hide. I heard clearly
the faint scraping sound. He pulled them back again, paused and then in
a sudden and powerful movement raised them and brought them crashing

down. The silence of the night shattered and the world seemed to erupt into a wild and savage, pounding tumult that dominated all.

With that uncanny sense of musical precision that Africans seem to have, the two indunas struck their own drums precisely in time with the Litunga's lead. Each playing a different rhythm, the three combined in a barrage of synchronised sound that penetrated the night and reverberated across the whole island, shaking it with the power of the beat. It was gripping, exciting and, in every sense, an elemental African experience. Kuomboka had begun.

The royal drums are called Maoma and are sounded only at the direction of the Litunga. There are three of them (with one spare). Each drum is a metre or more across and as much in depth. An examination shows that each is a solid piece of wood carved from a single tree. The oldest drum is said to have been cut in 1816. Each is named and in order of size they are called Kanaono (the largest), Munanga and Mundili.[37]

For Kuomboka, Maoma are sounded a day or two before the event. Drumming begins at about 21h00 and continues until midnight. It starts again at 04h00 the following morning, when the drums are played until dawn. They can be heard for at least 15 km. Only the Litunga may begin but once he has departed, it is the custom that all who wish to do so may take turns to play. The young men and remaining indunas crowd the players for a turn and when there is a change, not a single beat is missed. No woman is ever allowed to beat the drums.

Only men may paddle the barges and those in the principal vessels wear distinctive regalia. The Litunga's barge, the giant Nalikwanda painted with broad black and white stripes, is propelled by 120 paddlers of whom only those who are indunas may stand in the front half, in front of the royal passenger. All paddlers are bare-chested. All must wear a wraparound cloth that covers them from waist to knees, called a 'sitenge'. There is no objection to trousers being worn underneath it.

Those who can afford it wear, in place of the sitenge, a curious garment known as a 'sisiba'. Not unlike a kilt or short skirt that reaches to the knees, it consists of two pieces of pleated material, ideally each about 10 m in length. With some excitement I had hoped to show that David Livingstone might have introduced this garment. However, the museum in Blantyre believes it unlikely that the explorer ever travelled with a kilt.[38] The origin of the garment remains a mystery.

When all is ready, the paddlers wait on the beached barges at Lealui for their royal passengers to board and commence the journey to the distant mainland. The Litunga, surrounded by local and provincial dignitaries, leads the way to Nayuma, Nalikwanda's special harbour, and is soon aboard. Rapidly, the barge is poled to an open lagoon and begins to circle while a procession is formed.

Nalikwanda, with its crew of 120, dominates the scene by its size and striking colour. A royal orchestra of drums and Lozi xylophones loudly elaborates on the basic rhythm provided by Maoma, whose now monotonous but still compelling and tingling beat will set the pace for the rest of the day. The Litunga's personal flag, large, vividly red and with the silhouette of an elephant in white upon it, streams out over the barge, proclaiming to all the majesty within.

The barge Notila, carrying the queen, joins in the ritualistic circling, adjusting its position in relation to Nalikwanda as deemed proper. The standing paddlers in both vessels, already reflecting the heat in their beading perspiration, dip and heave their paddles in response to the beat which echoes out across the water. Their craft, monumentally regal, sweep on, ignoring all in their path. It is here that the impact of Kuomboka is at its most vivid.

Smaller craft crowd the water in their hundreds, creating great difficulty for the two small 'spy' boats charged with clearing a path for the king. Eventually, Nalikwanda sets off at a tangent towards the distant hills, leading a flotilla of white and black and brilliant red across the bright green fields of flooded meadow.

As the barges begin to penetrate the taller grass and the distance distorts the detail, a stranger might think the Barotse floodplain an endless meadow of bowing green stems peopled by men with long sticks. For, as the smaller vessels disappear from view in the grass, all that remains to be seen is their standing occupants apparently moving without effort, following on foot some invisible path.

Kuomboka ends when Nalikwanda touches the shore at Limulunga, a short distance north of Mongu. The ceremony is a wonderful and exciting reminder of an Africa past and Barotseland as it always has been. Despite being engulfed in a modern nation Barotseland, for me, will always retain a special distinctiveness that makes it uniquely attractive and unforgettable.

3   In the Name of the Father

IN this chapter, I want to show something of the great efforts made by missionaries to bring Christianity to the Zambezi and, more especially, of the incredible price in human lives that was paid. The chapter starts with the most famous African missionary of them all, David Livingstone, and I try to show that, although he may have started out on his journeys of exploration as a missionary, his personal aspirations changed. I believe that by the end of his association with the Zambezi, he no longer saw himself as a missionary. He was an explorer — even though his work, like that of so many others, might have been undertaken in the name of the Father.

David Livingstone's transformation from missionary to explorer was effected in subtle stages that echoed his physical progress into and across the continent of Africa. The changes in him were not immediate. Despite the indisputable metamorphosis there were facets of Livingstone that remained unchanged: his lively mind, his analytical approach, his brilliant reporting, his strength and stamina and, above all, his faith in his God.

As testament to his qualities of mind and body, we have the records he left, our knowledge of the huge distances he walked and the fact that his level of achievement was sustained over a period of 23 years. As to his faith, nothing testifies more eloquently to it than the manner of his death. Immobile and in immense pain, his last night was spent alone, in a grass hut. A guard was set to watch him but fell asleep. In the morning, when his friends came to check, they found that somehow, impossibly, he had dragged himself into a kneeling position and there, in contact still with his Maker after 60 incredible years, he had died.[1]

William Cotton Oswell was the Livingstone catalyst. It was he who ignited Livingstone's desire for exploration by indicating what could be done and how it could be achieved. Not that Livingstone was new to travel in Africa. He had arrived as a missionary at Kuruman in 1841 at the age of 28 and the first thing he did was to complete a trek of some 1 100 km.

Just over two years later his restlessness drove him on again. He established three new stations in four years. He must have driven his seniors mad! In a sense, each of these moves was a form of exploration and each helped add to his self-confidence and a sound knowledge of conditions in the bush; but it was not discovery for the sake of discovery. It took Oswell to introduce this new, challenging and intellectually satisfying element. In return Oswell received small thanks for his efforts — at least in so far as sharing the honours of discovery was concerned.

It was Oswell's idea to search for Lake Ngami in the north-west of modern Botswana. He provided the wagons and the supplies. Livingstone was his guest. Livingstone wrote of and published the discovery first and captured the limelight. His account acknowledges Oswell's financial contribution but claims the discovery as his own. It was Livingstone who accepted an award from Queen Victoria and Livingstone who received a prize of 25 guineas from the Royal Geographical Society. Pleased with the publicity that Livingstone's journey reflected on them, the London Missionary Society gladly accepted the additional funds his success brought.[2]

While there was a feeling in the Oswell family that Livingstone had had more than his due, Cotton Oswell himself was apparently less concerned. Whatever he felt did not prevent him from arranging another journey with Livingstone and, indeed, it was he who bore most of the cost for the expeditions of 1849, 1850 and 1851.[3]

The second expedition was not a success, because Livingstone and Oswell did not join forces until its end. Livingstone had been aiming for the north-west and whatever rivers lay there, but the thirst and the heat had driven his party back. Undoubtedly, his wife and two children suffered terribly, Mary especially, as she was carrying her third child and was in her ninth month as they neared home.

At Kolobeng, near modern Gaborone, capital of Botswana, their third child Elisabeth was born, just as they reached home with Oswell's help. Six weeks later, Elisabeth was dead of 'an inflammation of the lungs' that she may have caught from the two elder children who had returned from the expedition so ill they were unable to stand unassisted.[4] Already, it seems to me, the forces that impell a person through hardship and difficulty into discovery, were moulding the change in Livingstone from caring missionary to hard-driving explorer.

The seed of discovery, planted at Lake Ngami, had yet to burst into life. Swelling in anticipation of imminent birth, however, it awaited only the final expedition with William Cotton Oswell for its nativity and a new life to begin. Incredibly, Mary and the two children, Thomas and Agnes, accompanied Livingstone on the journey with Cotton Oswell to Linyanti near the junction of the Chobe and Zambezi.

Whatever difficulties had dogged their previous expedition were, on this one, multiplied fivefold. They were multiplied further by Livingstone's haste. On the way, his party met a group of three traders who were also anxious to meet Sebitoane, the Kololo chief. Livingstone could not tolerate the thought that others might reach Linyanti ahead of him and so he took a short-cut. He had been warned that this proposed route was difficult due to unreliable water — regardless, however, he took the chance. He won his race but at astonishing risk. They did run out of water and, once again, his family suffered. At one stage, the parents recognised that their children might die of thirst before their very eyes.[5]

Eventually, the Chobe was reached and contact made with Chief Sebitoane (Chapter 2). The contact was both brief and poignant for Sebitoane died within two weeks. But not before winning the sincere respect of the two explorers and meeting Mary Livingstone. Being in fear of raiding Matabele, Sebitoane was well aware that the famous missionary, Dr Moffat, now stationed among the Matabele, was Mary Livingstone's father. Through her and Livingstone Sebitoane may have hoped to influence Mzilikazi, the Matabele leader.

The pair of explorers were delayed by the chief's death and it was five weeks before they obtained permission to go to the great river that lay further north and of which the chief had spoken. The time was usefully employed, as both were able to make copious notes and maps of the district. Mary, at last, had a life of some ease, and was able to relax. When permission finally came for her husband and his friend to move north, she remained in the comfort of the Chobe's shaded banks.

It was evident that Livingstone had been doing more than making notes and drawing maps while he kicked his heels in the Kololo village. Quite suddenly, he announced to Oswell that he had determined to walk to the west coast and, with his typical taciturnity, said no more.[6]

At the end of July they received the permission they sought and rode out of camp. Four days and some 160 km later, they both stood gazing, amazed, at the sight of the great Zambezi rolling majestically past. A boat took them to Sesheke on the other side of the river and slowly the doors to central Africa were opened before Livingstone's astonished eyes and ears.

The most important discovery he made concerned the slave trade. At Linyanti he had reached the southern limit of the trade and the personal encounter was to have far-reaching effects on him. Livingstone was quick to notice that the Kololo in Linyanti were not naked as he expected, but were all wearing cheap clothes of European manufacture. At Sesheke he learnt that Mambari traders (half-caste Portuguese) from the west had, for half a year according to those who lived there, been trading guns and cloth for young boys. Two hundred youngsters, recently captured in raids, had been sold at a rate that was usually one gun to one boy. The Kololo hastened to add that their need for firearms was prompted only by the incessant raiding of the Matabele.[7]

Livingstone must have seen the mists of his future suddenly clear. The seed of discovery, planted at Ngami, now burst forth into flower and found itself in a rich and fertile environment. Towards the north, Africa was not a great desert as people thought; there were rivers and lushness unheard of in the south and a new world lay there, waiting to be discovered. A motive was conveniently at hand, for the hated slave trade stood poised to soil this unexpected Eden. Help to combat it had hastily to be sought.

However much into the ascendancy the explorer now wished to rise, two factors restrained the missionary. Perhaps an innate caution and a need for material support and backing made him hesitate to throw off too hastily the blanket of Missionary Society support. When he returned to Kuruman, his proposals still spoke of establishing missions, not exploring continents.

The other factor that restrained him was his wife's pregnancy. It is difficult to understand what Livingstone expected of Mary. They left Kolobeng on 26 April 1851 to go to Linyanti. Mary's son was born during the return journey on the banks of the Boteti River on 15 September. It is inconceivable that the child was four months premature and so Mary must have been pregnant before they left. She, obviously, knew. Surely Livingstone did also? On what grounds could he have exposed her and his unborn child to such risks? In the event, his second son, Oswell, nicknamed Zouga after the river by which he was born, survived. That Mary also survived is a miracle.[8]

Had Livingstone felt compelled to make a choice at the start of the Linyanti expedition? Had he thought that, if he failed to go with Cotton Oswell because of Mary's pregnancy, he might never go at all and an opportunity would be irrevocably lost? Was his choice between going and risking his wife's and child's life but perhaps winning fame, and staying, in every sense, behind? If that were so, then the answer was plain. Livingstone's mind was practically made up. He had chosen exploration and not the drudgery of mission work as his future. He was waiting only for the stage to be properly set before declaring himself. In the meantime, his wife and family would not be allowed to stand in the way.

Their having survived the ordeal of his unspoken choice, the long-term problem of his family had to be solved. Livingstone had discussed it with Oswell during the waiting days at Linyanti. It was agreed to send them back to England to await him there: they left from Cape Town in April 1852. Livingstone was now free to pursue his plans. The ever generous Oswell paid the Livingstone family's passage and bought them suitable clothes for the journey.

After eight months Livingstone departed from Kolobeng for the last time and in May 1853 was back at Linyanti. There he met Sekeletu, a young man of 18, Sebitoane's eventual successor. Livingstone was greeted with every possible sign of respect and received a gift of 12 elephant tusks. In return he gave the chief an improved breed of goats, chickens and a pair of cats.[9] That such animals were acquired in Cape Town and successfully conveyed the whole distance to Linyanti without mishap must surely be a story in its own right!

FIRST PAGE
Among fallen leaves and ferns the Zambezi flows from the very heart of Africa.

PRECEDING PAGE
The ceaseless search for protein in Africa begins in the Zambezi less than 30 km from its source.

PRECEDING PAGE, INSET
And the catch barely rewards the effort.

RIGHT
Fallen flowers, like tears, lie on the newly cut stump of an ancient tree in the protected riverine forest at the source of the Zambezi.

BELOW
Mekoro traffic near Mongu on the flooded plains of Barotseland.

Sekeletu suggested a trip to Sesheke, an idea Livingstone managed to turn into a plan for a much longer journey up the Zambezi River. Several events delayed them and it was during this time that Livingstone met a number of interesting and unexpected people.

Before we see who these were and of what importance they were to Livingstone, let us not forget that Livingstone had already resolved to walk to Luanda. Almost two years to the day had passed since he had made the remark to Oswell when last at Linyanti. He had said nothing about his purpose to anyone (I wonder if his wife knew?) and, ostensibly, was back at Linyanti to choose a suitable mission site in Barotseland. Meanwhile, having tasted the fruits of discovery, his mind was firmly fixed on the possibilities his present journey offered to explore a route to the coast.

Livingstone's proposed journey was not unique. As we shall see in a moment, a number of people had already crossed the continent; others continued to do so. The first to appear in historical records are two Portuguese-speaking Africans. Inspired by the potential if not the results of Lacerda's famous expedition of 1795 (see Chapter 17), traders in Angola in 1802 despatched Pedro Joao Baptista and Amaro Jose, with instructions to walk to Mozambique.

On 30 October 1806, these two unfortunates arrived at the court of Kazembe, a powerful mid-African kingdom reached by Lacerda and at which he had died. There they were detained for four years, finally reaching Tete in February 1811. After this incredible journey that had taken nine years, they turned round and walked safely back again — although in a much shorter time![10]

Livingstone's journeys are noteworthy not because of the rather meaningless 'firsts' that once seemed important, but because of the extraordinary wealth of detailed knowledge he conveyed to the outside world. Never before had a man with his training, scientific background and ability to observe, reason and record ever travelled the routes upon which he was about to embark. This is why Livingstone is justly famous. If only he had been a little more generous in acknowledging the help he received from others.

A man who has cast himself in the role of discoverer will not be pleased if reality rules out the hoped-for uniqueness of his journeys. During his enforced stay in Linyanti, Livingstone met or heard of a number of people whose presence compelled him to recognise the extent to which others knew of and travelled this Africa, new to him and his world perhaps, but clearly familiar to them. It was a difficult fact to face and he dealt with it in an interesting way. He denied it. Reports of those he met were either omitted from his journals or the individuals were falsely denigrated and held to be of no account.

The first of those he met, on 23 June, was Caetano Jose Ferreira and his companion Norberto Pedro de Sena Machado. These two spoke vaguely of crossing to Mozambique but seemed more intent on local exploration. Livingstone described them as slave traders and half-castes, a statement to which Silva Porto, whose close friends they were, took strong exception as they were neither. They were respectable farmers from Porto's own home district.[11] Slave traders or not, Livingstone questioned them about the route west to the coast, drew diagrams in his journal and made notes. To this extent he was much assisted by the meeting.[12]

Just a few days later, on 12 July 1853, Livingstone met Antonio Francisco da Silva Porto. In Angola, Silva Porto was well known as an explorer and had reached the Upper Zambezi near Sesheke five years earlier, in 1848. On the present journey he was attempting to cross Africa but had been delayed by illness. Several of his men, however, completed the traverse. His meeting with Livingstone was as cordial and as helpful as had been Livingstone's with Ferreira and, once again, notes on distances and routes were recorded by Livingstone. Talks with both Ferreira and Silva Porto must have reinforced in Livingstone's mind just how comparatively accessible the west coast was. Only the hinterland stood between him and the developed areas of Portuguese occupation. It is also possible that he was aware of an increasing level of interest in the trans-Africa route and perhaps felt the need to move with greater speed.

On 22 July 1853, finally, Livingstone and Sekeletu departed on their journey to Barotseland. By right of conquest Sekeletu and the Kololo were rulers of the Lozi and their beautiful floodplains (Chapter 2). The procession northwards by ox and horse and later in fleets of canoes was that of an African ruler and his retinue receiving obeisance from his subjects. It must have been a rare and exciting experience for Livingstone to witness.

The procession continued north and, in time, reached the village of Naliele, the northern capital of Barotseland, from where Sekeletu's mother ruled on her son's behalf. Near here, Silva Porto had established his camp, Katongo (close to modern Mongu). From there he had travelled down to Linyanti to make contact with Livingstone in July.

Hearing of Livingstone's arrival, Porto again visited, bringing a present of bread, preserved pears, locally grown vegetables and two Dutch cheeses![13] There were difficulties in communicating since neither spoke the other's language well and they had no third language in common. Nevertheless, from the exchanges, Livingstone gathered that the Portuguese were exploring a route over the continent as an alternative to the 80-day sea journey around the Cape of Good Hope.[14]

On 31 August Livingstone paid a return call to Katongo which he saw was a substantial establishment indeed. There was a stockade with two dwellings and a pole from which flew the Portuguese flag. There were more than 200 people at the camp whom Livingstone described as 'Mambari' — a term in common usage denoting half-caste slave trading people from Angola.

On this occasion Silva Porto was not present but still Livingstone was greeted with kind hospitality — even being given the use of Porto's bed. It was here that, within the space of ten weeks, he met another three individuals linked to west coast travel. They were Arabs from Zanzibar and were about to complete a double crossing of the continent!

They had arrived in Benguela from Zanzibar on 23 April 1853, having been escorted there from the vicinity of Katanga. Their accomplishment created marked interest in Angola, to the extent that the governor was prevailed upon to make some arrangements for their safe return on foot. A reward was offered as an inducement, not only to help the Arabs return but in the interests of promoting exploration and communication between the two Portuguese states on opposite sides of Africa.

The reward was small and Silva Porto, who was the one who had accepted the challenge, was granted permission to trade during the journey so that there might be some commercial advantage to him also. So it was that he had left his farm in distant Bihe in Angola and by February 1853 had established himself at Katongo beside the Zambezi in Barotseland.

From there, two groups of his staff went east. One set off for Quelimane but had difficulties with local chiefs on the way and were robbed. They returned as they had gone, without seeing the Indian Ocean. The other group accompanied the Zanzibaris back to their island home, which they reached in November 1853 and, from there, the guides returned by sea to Benguela.[15]

If this account of the apparently frequent traffic across the continent is in danger of becoming a little bewildering, how much more so must it have been for Livingstone. He, who would like to have believed that he was entering an area totally unknown to the outside world, left his meeting with the Arabs and returned to his own village, there to meet yet another of these trans-continental trippers!

This time, it was Ben Habib, another Arab whom he was to meet again more than once. On this occasion Habib and his small party were making at least their second journey from east to west. In Livingstone's words 'they seem to pass and repass across the country'. Livingstone entertained his Arab friends with courtesy and hospitality, a factor that was to stand much in his favour in the future. His immediate gain was considerably more information about conditions and the route to the west.[16] We can be sure that, had he any doubts as to in which direction to travel, whether to the Indian Ocean or the Atlantic, it was his experiences in Barotseland and the information he gained there that persuaded Livingstone to go first to the west and Luanda.

After exploring some distance further north and verifying to his satisfaction the inaccuracy of the Portuguese map he carried with him, Livingstone went back to the waiting Sekeletu and with him returned directly to Linyanti. He arrived there in early September 1853, planning with some excitement, no doubt, his journey to the coast which he set for November when the rains should have begun.

Before his departure he had one more, unexpected, caller. This one he refused to meet.

The caller was Laszlo Magyar, a Hungarian. Born Ladislaus Amerigo Magyar, he was a capable and well-educated man. He had trained as a naval officer but emigrated to Africa in 1847, undertaking extensive journeys in the central and western part of the continent. Eventually, marrying the daughter of a chief, he settled in Angola where his skills and knowledge of the country and its peoples were recognised and highly valued by the government.[17]

Magyar's part in the Livingstone story is told in fascinating detail by Judith Listowel in her book *The Other Livingstone*. Let me say here only that his explorations in the western half of Africa equalled, at least in extent, those of Livingstone. He too kept diaries and journals and, as an educated man, spoke German, Italian, Portuguese and Spanish in addition to his native tongue and many local dialects. Fame eluded him for he was an unlucky victim of unreliable mail and a lack of financial means; he was also too slow to publish.

Nevertheless, it is highly probable that Livingstone knew all about him and his reasons for avoiding this man are therefore curious. Magyar had spent time with Sekeletu in October 1852 and they had formed a good friendship. Magyar explained his purpose in having come from Benguela as solely to meet Livingstone. He was invited to remain but lacked funds and had to return to Angola. However, Magyar was well known among the Kololo whose language he spoke and who were familiar with his exploits and his reputation. The route they followed when they guided Livingstone to the coast was based on information received from Magyar.

It has been suggested that Livingstone chose not to see his visitor because he knew that Magyar was 'white', not Portuguese. He therefore avoided dealing with a European and someone he could not brush aside as easily as he could a mulatto (half-caste) or a slaver. Magyar might well represent a threat to the exclusivity of discovery that Livingstone so earnestly sought — and so he refused to meet him.[18]

Throughout his time with Sekeletu, Livingstone had been delivering sermons and spreading the word of God — still fulfilling his role as a missionary. Thirty years later another Scottish missionary passed through Barotseland and claimed that Livingstone had left so strong an impact that his ways and words were still clearly remembered, and some of the older men could still recite his sermons.[19] Livingstone was fulfilling what he saw as his duties as a missionary, but this was to be his swan-song: the continent of Africa was calling him. He was to be its discoverer and its ambassador.

His response to Africa's call was remarkable. He left Linyanti for the west coast on 11 November 1853, arriving on 31 May the following year.

He left for the return journey on 20 September and took a year to cover what had taken him six months on the way west, reaching Linyanti on 10 September 1855. Here he rested but a few weeks before leaving on 3 November, reaching Victoria Falls on the 16th.

From the falls he followed a course parallel to the Zambezi, but on the highland to its north-west, and eventually reached the Kafue River which he followed until it rejoined the Zambezi. From this point he walked along the north bank to the junction with the great Luangwa River that flows in from the north. Here he passed a critical watershed, in the view of Oliver Neil Ransford.[20]

Ransford is himself a remarkable man: medical doctor, anaesthetist and author. His research into Livingstone's life led to his third Ph.D. The thesis on which this degree is based proposes that Livingstone's career was, to a large extent, determined by what is known as a cyclothymic temperament. We recognise this kind of temperament in its extreme form as a manic-depressive psychosis.

Such a state is neither 'bad' nor 'wrong' and the swings from 'down' to 'up' often lead to great achievements. Indeed, as Ransford claims, many of the great achievers of our world have suffered from this affective disorder, including Oliver Cromwell, Charles Lamb and John Ruskin.

As part of his study, Ransford marked, on a roll of paper 3,83 m long, a space for each day of Livingstone's life from 1841 to his death. On this, established from all available evidence, including letters, journals and other writings, he plotted his objective assessment of Livingstone's mood. Neil took great pleasure in showing me this one evening, making me stand in his lounge, holding one end of the roll while he backed slowly across the room, out of the french windows, across the verandah, onto the lawn by the pool . . .

But what an amazing record! There, swinging from side to side across the roll, regular as clockwork, moving from high to low and back again, a sinuous red line marked the alterations between euphoria and angst in Livingstone's psyche. Every major decision of Livingstone's that led to yet another achievement was made during a period of 'upness'.

Compared to the journey across Angola, the walk over the highlands downstream of the falls was a jaunt. For the first time, Livingstone was able to relax, to let up on the driving sternness and discipline that had taken him through disease, danger, mud, jungle, constant rain and hardship of every kind. On the highlands, the climate was cool and comfortable and his recurrent attacks of malaria became a thing of the past. He had time to stop, to think, to relax and to ponder events.

During this period his changing perceptions of himself became clearer. It was as if he had awoken in the eye of a storm and understood that what he had been through was a baptism, a testing, which he had survived. No longer the missionary, he was an explorer; not an ordinary explorer, but the advocate of Africa. Steadily, his faith in a special form of divine protection began to grow.

The first evidences of this change emerge in his journal, which shows him obviously relaxed; he prepares a memorandum to the king of Portugal even before reaching the coast. In it he makes suggestions on how the king should develop the states of Angola and Mozambique, sketches guidelines for the use of mineral and agricultural resources, talks about labourers to replace slaves and laments the shortage of both women and books.[21] This memorandum is a clear indication of his growing confidence in the new role he saw for himself. The key to that confidence turned on the Luangwa River.

He had walked in comfort and without difficulty down the beautiful north bank of the river and reached the point at which to cross. There was only one boat and his party numbered 120 people. Warriors of Chief Mouruma plainly intended to obstruct him and Livingstone was in a quandary as to whether to turn back or risk the crossing.

That night he took his Bible and found comfort, courage and what he took to be a special message of inspiration on the page at which it opened. Certain now of divine guidance and protection, he resolved not to cross in darkness, as he had planned, but to do so brazenly the next day. After dawn, closely surrounded by murmuring warriors clutching their spears, he ferried his men and cattle in small groups across to an island, leaving himself and a few others until last. Eventually, they all crossed safely despite increasing threats from the warriors.

For Livingstone, the crossing was a moment of visionary insight that finally convinced him he was an instrument, designated by God to fulfil a part of his divine purpose. From this point onwards, the sense that he was being led through life by an all-powerful force strengthened.[22] This is a very different Livingstone from the one who had accompanied William Cotton Oswell to Lake Ngami. The humble missionary was gone and God's ambassador had taken his place.

As Livingstone and others like him opened wide the continent to reveal the Christian voids that lay within, so those inspired by missionary ideals followed closely behind. Their task was no less daunting than that which faced their predecessors and often they had to cope with the same long distances, difficult journeys, pain, hardship and death. Perhaps the most extraordinary aspect of this early activity was the high level of ignorance, poor planning and poor organisation that characterised some ventures — nowhere better illustrated than in the Helmore-Price tragedy.

On Livingstone's recommendation, the London Missionary Society agreed to establish a station at Linyanti and, to this end, it selected personnel for the task. The intention was that they should proceed by wagon from Kuruman in the northern Cape, across the Kalahari, following the route taken by Livingstone. The latter, who was leading the Zambezi expedition at the time, was expected to join the mission and help them to become established and settle down when he returned with his Kololo porters from Tete.[23]

The small party set out in four wagons on 8 July 1859. There were two missionary families: Henry Helmore, his wife and four young children, and Roger Price with his pregnant wife. Price was new to Africa and knew little about it or its people. Helmore was much more experienced and spoke the local language. They had with them one of the guides who had travelled with Livingstone.[24] On the journey, Mrs Price became another of those women, brave and unfortunate enough to give birth on an ox-wagon somewhere in the middle of the Kalahari.

The journey was no less harrowing than the one Livingstone had experienced and it was perhaps made more so by the fact that, while he and Oswell had managed it in 115 days, Price and Helmore took 165, almost half as long again, arriving on 14 February 1860.[25]

Sixteen days later Malatsi, Price's ox-wagon driver, died. Five days after him the Helmores' youngest child was dead, followed two days later by the baby, Eliza Price. In quick succession fell Thabe, another Helmore child, then a deacon of the church and then Mrs Helmore herself. Setlhoke, who was responsible for Price's cattle, was the next to go and he was followed by Mr Helmore. In 35 days, the party had been decimated. Eight people had died.

Sensibly, Price and his wife decided urgently to leave Linyanti and return to Kuruman, taking the two surviving Helmore children with them. The circumstances of their departure and their relationship with Sekeletu and the Kololo are too lengthy to describe here. It is enough to say that the treatment they received in their last weeks and days amounted to a special kind of horror. Mentally tortured, they left their camp in Sekeletu's village with practically nothing, having been deprived by Sekeletu of everything they owned. In this incident is shown a side of the young chief that Livingstone apparently did not see.

Price set out with his wife and the two children, across the deep sands of Chobe. He was heading east and south, over the forbidding and featureless Mababe Depression. Here, on 5 July 1860, in the final tragedy, his wife died and Price buried her under a lonely tree in that great flat plain. The maliciousness of Sekeletu was not at an end, however.

The guides that Sekeletu had provided handed the small party into the care of San (Bushmen) who were asked to lead Price into the tsetse fly area and abandon him and his cattle there. This they did. Price survived only by walking to the banks of the Thamalakane River at the south-eastern end of the Okavango Delta and following that to the village of the Tawana chief, Letsholathebe. On the way back to Linyanti, as Price later learned, the returning Kololo had disinterred Mrs Price and mutilated her body to make 'medicine'.[26]

Many aspects of this affair deeply shocked people at the time and have occupied volumes since. Sekeletu may have had some reason for being hostile; Price may not have been a paragon of virtue. Here, however, I am more concerned with what the incident shows about the failures of missionary activity.

The major question that must be answered first is, 'What caused so many deaths?' A sensationalist public outcry naturally clung to the idea of poison and murder but those who knew enough thought not. Possible causes, in addition to poison, included enteric fever, sleeping sickness and malignant malaria. On balance, there seems little doubt that malaria was responsible.[27]

What an extraordinary capacity we, as human beings, have for reinventing the wheel. We seem to do it with such incredible consistency. In country after country, individual after individual makes the same mistakes as those before have done. Missionaries, it seems, are no different.

There was no malaria at Kuruman but the disease was very well known in southern Africa. Livingstone himself experienced his first attack of it at Linyanti[28] and then suffered badly, despite his self-made cure, on his walk through Angola.

What sense was there in sending people who had never been exposed to it at all into the heart of a bad malaria area, so distant and remote as to be beyond all immediate help? Why send children and pregnant women along without any means or knowledge of treating the disease if they should be stricken?[29]

There were other mistakes as well. The group had no horses with them, making hunting on the journey very difficult, so food supplies were erratic. This extended the journey and helps to account for the exhausted state in which they arrived. Their wagons were not well chosen and were overloaded. In addition, some important items were omitted while unimportant ones were included.

Missionaries, including the London Missionary Society, had not been living in a vacuum. The 19th century in southern Africa must have been *the* century of missionary endeavour, the most challenging and exciting years of missionary existence. How then could a mission like that to Linyanti be so badly organised? And yet, 20 years later, it all happened again.

We shall take a general look at Jesuit missions in southern Africa in a moment but, to make a point, I'd like to focus first on one of the Jesuits' early attempts to establish a mission on the middle Zambezi, in the Gwembe Valley.

In July 1880, Fathers Depelchin, Terorde and Vervenue set out from Pandamatenga for Chief Moemba's village on the Zambezi, about four days' walk downstream from Chief Hwange's kraal. They arrived at Moemba's on 9 August, having been guided there by George Westbeech's man, Blockley. He was the interpreter who explained to Chief Moemba what the Jesuits wanted, and seeing the priests as a possible buffer against marauding Matabele, the chief gladly consented for them to stay. Overnight, as it were, a mission had been established.

A nearby site was selected the next day for the Holy Cross Residence and shortly after this highly satisfactory piece of work, Depelchin departed, leaving Terorde and Vervenue the task of actually establishing the mission.[30] Depelchin barely crossed the river before he was struck down by the most frightful malaria. He was so ill he could not walk and Blockley arranged a machila (a chair or bed carried by four bearers) for him. Slowly they made their way out of the malaria-ridden valley towards hoped-for help. Blockley had sent a messenger ahead.

On 14 September, as they continued their slow progress back to Pandamatenga, they were met by the rescue party; Depelchin now so ill as to be hardly recognisable. The next day a runner from the new mission on the river arrived with news of Terorde's death and Vervenue's serious illness. Help reached the mission on 21 September and confirmed Terorde's death. Vervenue was delirious and was carried back to Pandamatenga. The mission had claimed one life, very nearly two others, and had lasted 42 days.[31] Surely, in 1880, they must have known about malaria?

Southern Africa had been, by default and since earliest times, the preserve of Protestant denominations. Mozambique and Angola were, without question, under the aegis of the Catholic Church. What lay between the three was there to be claimed by whomever felt it worthy of the effort. In the 19th century, that effort was made largely by the London Missionary Society which tended to follow quickly in the footsteps of traders and explorers.

Great names led the church then: one was Robert Moffat who founded Kuruman and extended Protestant influence into Bechuanaland. He also established a friendship with the Matabele in the Transvaal and maintained it when they moved to Bulawayo. On the strength of this the Inyati Mission started in 1859 and, in 1870, Hope Fountain. At these mission stations worked Moffat's son John, Thomas Morgan Thomas and William Sykes, all brilliant leaders and missionaries in their own right.[32]

Until 1879, there was little or no missionary effort from the Catholic Church in southern Africa and there were only a handful of priests in the Cape and Natal. In that year, however, Father Henry Depelchin led a group of Jesuit brethren from Grahamstown on a great expedition to the land north of the Limpopo. They faced a number of obstacles.

Not only were they trying to penetrate an established Protestant preserve with its entrenched Protestant values, but they were often opposed by powerful trader resistance, as we shall see. Finally, their late start and lack of experience left them naive about Africa. They were poorly briefed regarding the risks of malaria, other diseases and medical matters in general. It seems possible that many Europeans of this era, missionaries included, did not realise that the indigenous people were able to build up a level of natural protection against malaria. Without this protection, malaria was lethal.

We have seen how tragically Jesuit plans foundered on the Zambezi in Gwembe. On the upper river, in Barotseland, they were within a hair's breadth of success but, in the end, lost that opportunity also. How did all this come about?

François Coillard of the French Protestant Missionaries of Basutoland, with the support of his mission, attempted in 1877 to establish a church in Mashonaland but having neglected the small detail of asking Lobengula first, found himself out of the country and seeking the help of Khama in Bechuanaland.

With Khama's assistance, they travelled north to the Zambezi, hoping to make contact with Lewanika and obtain his authority to establish a mission. Arriving on the southern borders of Barotseland in mid-1878, they were treated with hospitality and the usual delays with which Africa is so generous. During this time Mrs Coillard became the first white woman to see Victoria Falls on 6 August 1878. In the meantime the couple waited for a reply to their request. The reply took five months to arrive and indicated that Lewanika was building a new capital. They were asked to return the following year! In the event, it was four years before they were able to follow up this favourable lead.

George Westbeech, introduced in Chapter 2, was established as a trader and confidant of kings in Barotseland from 1871. In the rejection of the Jesuit mission and the eventual selection of Coillard, Westbeech played an extremely important role, although his motives are still unclear.

Father Depelchin based his expedition at Pandamatenga, a store and stopping-off point on the road to the Zambezi, established and run by Westbeech. It was from here that Terorde and Vervenue had left on their tragic attempt to start a mission in the Gwembe Valley, and it was from here that Depelchin, seeking another opportunity, wrote to Lewanika.

The Litunga replied favourably and in June 1881 Depelchin's party set off up the river. They were received with great hospitality and an encouraging response from Lewanika. So enthusiastic was he that the Jesuits were asked to start their mission there and then. Incredibly, although he had two Brothers with him and could easily have left them there, Depelchin departed, promising to return when the necessary preparations had been completed.[33] This move was to cost him the mission.

In the two years that were to pass before the second Jesuit mission to Barotseland in March 1883, Lewanika changed his mind and the reason he did this has exercised the minds of academics ever since.

There are a number of possible explanations: the presents the returning Jesuits gave Lewanika were regarded by him as being somewhat niggardly.[34]

Coillard thought the Jesuits' aloofness and ignorance of the language, which were taken for dislike and contempt, was the reason. Others suggested the attempt to establish the mission station at Moemba's kraal may have offended Lewanika since he considered that chief to fall within his sphere of influence. Still others believe that Westbeech might have been the cause, for the Jesuits seemed not to know or care that he was the most powerful trader in the region and was, therefore, a man of great influence whom they should not have overlooked.[35]

Westbeech's diaries and reports from others seem to bear this out. Aside from allegations and denials concerning a £500 'inducement' Westbeech claims the Jesuits offered him, there are recollections of public statements he made in support of Coillard. Some visitors did not forget the petty feuds between Westbeech and the Jesuits at Pandamatenga when, sometimes, they did not speak to one another for months!

There was not a great deal of affection wasted between Westbeech and Coillard but perhaps the trader considered the Protestant option the lesser of two 'evils'. In any event, history seems to have decided that it was George Westbeech who swung Lewanika's decision from the Jesuits to Coillard. A question left hanging in the air is the extent to which West-beech's Freemasonry might have influenced the situation.[36]

A delightful irony in the whole Catholic, Protestant, Westbeech triangle is that in 1888, on his way down from Barotseland to the Cape Colony, Westbeech became seriously ill. The nearest place of help was a mission station in the western Transvaal and it is here that Westbeech lies buried. He died in the arms of a Jesuit Brother![37]

4 Count Caprivi's Folly

MANY international boundaries in central and southern Africa are less than 100 years old. Often, they resulted from hastily agreed lines drawn on maps in distant places with no concern for the people such boundaries divided, nor for the territories sometimes illogically dissected. There are many curiosities associated with the delimitation of such boundaries: the circumstances surrounding the creation of the Caprivi Strip in Namibia are a prime example.

The strip, as it is locally known, must be one of the most unlikely results of boundary negotiations that can be imagined. Not less than 30 km in width (but in some places very much more) and more than 400 km in length, it points like a finger from the north-east of Namibia into the heartland of central Africa. A long and narrow corridor, it squeezes between Botswana on the south and Angola and Zambia on the north. The corridor ends at the banks of the Zambezi between Katima Mulilo in the west and Kazungula in the east.

Ubiquitous is the grey-white blanket of once windblown sand that proclaims the region to be part of the Kalahari system. It is well wooded: tall trees with open canopies create an impression of lightness and airiness. The lack of deep shading favours the growth of shrubs but the tall grass of the African tree savanna is the dominant ground cover. Adapted to the sandy, rapidly drained soil, it is quick to establish itself as the summer rains begin.

Like so many other parts of the Kalahari system, it appears to be flat — yet it is not. It is crossed by three major rivers whose direction indicates a consistent tilt towards the south-east. In addition, there are traces throughout the Caprivi of those same fossil dune systems that are to be found elsewhere in the Kalahari. As much as 20 m high and nearly 2 km apart, these long lines of parallel sand dunes (called alab dunes) are a reminder of much drier climates in the relatively recent past, when true desert conditions prevailed. Today, they are slowly being reduced by the forces of erosion but retain their original shape because they are fixed in place by the vegetation they support.

Superimposed upon this gently undulating landscape are two other geomorphological features of interest. The first is a series of remnant beaches that speak of a now non-existent but once vast lake. The other is the presence of salt or clay pans, common within the Kalahari. Of the beaches and a remarkable story they have to tell, more will be said in the following chapter.

The so-called pans are dish-shaped hollows, naturally formed, which vary from just a few metres to a kilometre or more in diameter. The surface of a pan is generally quite flat although it does sometimes slope very gently towards the centre. It may consist of bare and firm grey clay or be overgrown with salt-tolerant grasses. The distribution of pans is highly correlated with the sand country of the Kalahari: they are found on either side of the Zambezi, from Barotseland down through southern Zambia, the Caprivi and northern Botswana.

Pans play an important part in the ecology of the semi-arid regions in a number of interesting ways. Being areas of depressed topography, they are the end point of local drainage systems. As such, they collect and concentrate the usually sparse rainfall. With a high clay content the pan has an impervious surface so that run-off is retained in what is, in effect, a mini-reservoir. Averaging 2 m or more a year, evaporation is high, so the water does not last. Nevertheless, it is retained for as much as three months beyond the end of the rainy season. In this way the pans make it possible for game animals to exploit the grazing resources of an area they otherwise would have to abandon for lack of water.

Pans have a further important part to play in the lives of the area's wild herds. Just as they are a collecting point for rainwater, so are they a collecting place for vital salts and minerals. Dissolved in the water with which they are annually flooded are a great many of the trace elements necessary for animal health. As the water evaporates so the salts are left behind and collect in the clay surface of the pan. Each pan probably reflects in a subtle way the unique chemical signature of its own particular drainage system.

Game will frequent those pans where the salts available meet the animals' particular needs. In such cases they lick whatever rocks or stones protrude from the pan surface or, more frequently, simply eat the salt-laden soil. Some pans are so popular with game that large holes are found, usually at the lowest elevation, where the animals have literally eaten the surface away.

Little or no game exists in the Caprivi today although it was once renowned for the elephant and antelope found there. Early German reports from the Caprivi[1] speak of the unrestricted slaughter of game animals, including elephant and rhino. Today, no rhino are to be found and elephant are rare; they have been poached out of existence. Frederick Courteney Selous, the famous hunter and naturalist whose writing has left us with vivid pictures of the late 19th century, hunted in this area. He tells the tragic story of the death of his companion, French.[2]

The African bush looks deceptively benign, yet it can and does kill in a remorseless way. It is the antithesis of the fictional jungle. In most cases, reality is far removed from the dripping and green-shrouded gloom, filled with man-eating animals and snakes. On the great savannas and in the sandveld, the country is open, the trees are widely spaced and the often park-

like nature invites exploration. But it also demands respect and the obser-
vance of simple rules. Failure to obey them can be fatal, as French discovered.

On 25 September 1879, Selous with his companions Miller and French came
across a small herd of cow elephant, not far from the Chobe or Linyanti River,
somewhere in what is now the Caprivi Strip. Six were downed and two got
away, both wounded. It was still quite early in the day and French, against
advice, decided to follow the injured animals. He took with him two bearers
while his companions returned to the camp less than 5 km away. Barely had
they arrived when they heard two shots from the direction in which they had
last seen French. It was near midday and they expected him to return with
the bearers at any moment.

French did not appear; in fact, he was never seen again. Selous, concerned,
had fired two shots in the evening, and again some time later. At about 20h00
a distant shot was heard from the direction of the river but then there was
silence. Almost immediately a grass fire was seen to start in the direction from
which the shot had sounded. Selous investigated, got to the site of the fire but
found and saw nothing. He returned to the camp. At midnight, Selous fired
the last of his signal shots.

I can so easily imagine the consternation and growing concern that must
have been gnawing at the confidence of both Selous and Miller. In these circumstances no plan remains fixed. Flexibility is everything as nature cannot
be dictated to. Many things could have kept French away from camp and the
concern of his companions would have been dictated more by their knowledge
of his personality than the mere fact that he had not returned. After all, they
would have reasoned, the Chobe River lay about them in a semi-circle to the
south and nowhere more than 25 km away. French carried a compass, he
knew how to find south with the Southern Cross and so there could be no
possibility of getting lost. In addition, he had the two bearers with him, one
of whom was a most experienced hunter, and *they* certainly would make no
error. It was only necessary to turn to the river and follow its banks to where
a well-worn path, known to them all, started out for the camp itself.

So much for reason. Eight days passed before the gun-bearer and the water-
carrier returned to camp. French was dead and they had survived the most
incredible ordeal.

As Selous and Miller had predicted, the spoor of the wounded elephant had
quickly been lost. About to return to camp, French came across a giraffe,
which he killed. This explained the two shots heard at the camp. French then
insisted on leading the way back to the camp. His assistants quickly saw that
he was mistaken in his direction and pointed this out but French would have
none of it. The course he set zig-zagged so much that soon the two other men
also lost their sense of direction to the camp — although, of course, they still
knew the way to the river.

Eventually, French realised he was mistaken and gave the two men the lead.
At once they set off for the river and at once French disagreed with them and

took back the lead. So it continued until late into the night. Temporarily admitting defeat, French fired the shot that Selous heard in the distance and ordered that the grass be set aflame. Instead of waiting there, however, his impatience impelled the small party onwards on their crazy course once more. Soon the water was finished. The following day the madness continued. Without pause, through the extreme heat of the day, they zig-zagged onwards, French never allowing his two assistants to help him, never making for the river which was still within reach.

By nightfall they were all exhausted, French more so since he was less used to the rugged life. They had been trudging through the thick Kalahari sand, almost without break, for two or perhaps three days. For at least a day they had been without water. The final tragedy might still have been avoided but, as they walked on into the night, French started to cough up blood. This suggested some other complaint which was aggravated by his condition, but it was enough to so sap his remaining strength that his death that night was unavoidable.

French drove himself on remorselessly, stopping for a short pause, then forcing himself on again. The bleeding and the coughing continued and worsened. Late that night he could go no further and rested against the bole of a tree. By the light of a blazing bundle of grass he inscribed on the butt of his rifle the words, 'I cannot go any further; when I die, peace with all.' After his death, his escorts did what they could to protect French's body from scavengers by covering it with branches. Then they continued walking for the remainder of the night — this time in a direction of their own choosing — and reached the river in the early hours of the morning. From there, they made their way along the bank and returned to the camp. French's body was never found.

The close proximity of the river is proof enough of how unnecessary French's death was. That he died seems fairly attributable to nothing more than his own stupidity and arrogance. The African bush is a harsh mistress. Played by its rules life within it is safe, comfortable and wonderfully free. If the rules are ignored the price can be high. That French would not listen to his assistants is incredible, especially when they had the experience that he clearly did not. That they stayed with him for so long is a tribute to the patience, tolerance and loyalty of the African people.

In the decade that began in 1880 those events that we now call the scramble for Africa — a rather undignified rush for African real estate by European powers — were at their greatest intensity. Germany, for example, a latecomer to the game, acquired within the space of just four months in 1884 South West Africa, Cameroon and Togoland.[3]

The frenetic apportionment of Africa was powered by a complex series of motives that varied from national pride and a quest for glory to security needs, new supplies of raw materials, new markets and even personal ego. It reflected as much the complexities and difficulties of European politics as it did any considered and logical plan of territorial acquisition. Huge tracts of the continent were acquired by future colonial powers, often reluctantly, and occasionally by the efforts of a handful of visionary individuals who dragged a reluctant government into agreeing to some form of protection or guardianship.

Inevitably, the possibility of conflict between powerful states over zones of influence and continental aspirations became a pressing issue. Under the deft hand of Otto von Bismarck a meeting in Berlin from November through to February 1885 was called to settle the issues. Attended by 13 European nations and the United States, its aim was to lay down ground rules for the commercial and political exploitation of Africa. What emerged was a mutual acceptance of those territorial claims already made, and, as guidelines for future acquisitions, two misleadingly simple concepts: the hinterland doctrine and spheres of influence.[4] As Robin Hallet so neatly explains, 'the Berlin Conference did not, as is sometimes supposed, bring about the "scramble for Africa"; it served merely to lay down the rules for a game already begun'.[5]

Germany had established herself in and laid claim to the coastal regions of present-day Namibia by 1884. However, the hinterland was unexplored and largely unknown to the country's new claimants. Certainly it was not all mapped and such maps as existed were of questionable accuracy, but some years were to pass before the importance of these facts made itself felt. By December 1886, however, an agreement with Portugal was entered into which delineated the border with Angola. From the village of Andara on the Kavango River, it read, the boundary ran 'due east to the rapids of Catima, on the Zambesi.'[6]

This agreement is interesting for it is the first clue to Germany's eastward aspirations and desire to have access to the Zambezi. The reasoning behind this eastward extension is obscure. One suggestion, often put forward, is that the German administration in South West Africa was seeking access to the Zambezi so that it would have a trade route to the sea. This is most unlikely. Not only does it completely ignore the presence of Victoria Falls, but it also ignores David Livingstone and another of his discoveries. Amid great publicity and public awareness, he had shown that, in addition to the falls, the rapids and cataracts at Cahora Bassa were an impenetrable barrier to navigation.

A more likely explanation seems to have been a German equivalent of the British 'Cape to Cairo' idea. Germany was already established in South West and in East Africa and the possibility of a link between the two existed. What would become Northern Rhodesia was as yet 'unclaimed' and might have been seen as the area through which such a connecting corridor could pass.

Events moved at incredible speed during these years and the situation changed almost weekly. What happened on the Zambezi was influenced, as frequently seems to be the case, by matters apparently quite unconnected and geographically far removed. In East Africa, Britain and Germany were

PRECEDING PAGE
A crowded harbour on the island of Lealui in Barotseland.

ABOVE
Two heads in a hat are better than one, they say!

RIGHT
Gerard's striped burrowing snake (Chilorhinophis gerardi). A preserved specimen from the Natural History Museum, Bulawayo, shows how the legend of two heads might have arisen.

fast approaching a state of conflict over rival claims. The immediate focus of British concern was the country that would become Uganda. Ultimately, however, the real issue was concern over the safety of the route to India through the Suez Canal.

This concern for India underlay much of British foreign policy in East Africa at this time and gave rise to a chain of conclusions hard to justify and accept today. For it made Egypt, Sudan and the Nile important and gave an unnatural eminence to Uganda. Ultimately, it was fear for the safety of India and the possibility of losing Uganda to the Germans that brought Britain and Germany to negotiate.

The negotiations became an opportunity to settle a number of smaller issues and as a result, on 1 July 1890, Britain and Germany made up their differences. Germany won what would become German East Africa, later Tanganyika, now Tanzania. Britain secured Uganda and the embryonic state that one day would be called Kenya. The agreement created, at the stroke of a pen, entirely new countries. It also created the Caprivi Strip. For German negotiators used the occasion to pursue their claims for access to the Zambezi from South West Africa. And they won.

With the words 'under this agreement Germany shall have free access from her Protectorate to the Zambesi by a strip of territory which shall at no point be less than 20 English miles in width', the Caprivi Strip came into existence.[7] As a sweetener and in addition to the strip — named in honour of Count Caprivi, Bismarck's successor — Germany acquired the tiny island of Heligoland in the North Sea at the mouth of the river Elbe. Britain received the island of Zanzibar and confirmed her control over the port, and some 750 km[2] in the vicinity, of Walvis Bay.[8] This little anomaly of history may yet create further complications since technically, Walvis Bay is not part of Namibia and, legally, is a possession of the Republic of South Africa!

The present-day problem of Caprivi is intriguing — for the question must be asked, what should be done with it? It is hardly likely to be of any benefit to the Namibians. Exceedingly remote, just a little over 30 km wide, it would be nice if it possessed some redeeming feature that would justify its continued existence — but there is none. It has no mineral resources, such game as it once possessed has long since been shot out, populations are low and are restricted mostly to the river banks. Its furthest outpost, Katima Mulilo on the Zambezi, is 400 km further from the state capital than the main body of the country. It has, of course, great strategic benefit to South Africa — but that is only of a temporary nature. It seems to me that the most sensible step for an independent Namibian government would be to give the strip away — either to Botswana or to Angola and Zambia! It surely would be a most cost-effective move!

It was after the signing of the 1890 agreement that the lack of knowledge of the interior and the poor maps available to administrators made their impact felt. The 1886 agreement between South West Africa and the Portuguese of Angola established a border from Andara to Katima Mulilo as already described. Coincidentally, of course, it was also the northern border of what would become the Caprivi Strip. The agreement with Britain in 1890 not only sought to establish the Caprivi Strip by defining its southern boundary, but it also demarcated the boundaries of the Bechuanaland Protectorate which lay to the south.

Here an anomaly was unwittingly created for, strictly speaking, the southern boundary of the strip as defined in 1890 was actually, at one point, further north than the northern boundary established in 1886![9] Any confusion that this might have caused was compounded by the fact that none of the borders was marked on the ground. These irregularities were not resolved until well after the First World War. This did not in any way prevent the nations concerned from adhering to the spirit of the agreement but the aberration allowed for the exploitation of the Caprivi Strip by those who lived outside the law.

For some years, especially after the First World War, it was known as a kind of no-man's-land. Ostensibly it was administered by the Union of South Africa under a mandate from the League of Nations. In fact, that responsibility had been delegated to the Bechuanaland Protectorate, which had neither the resources nor the will to be concerned. In this way, from about 1918 until 1929 when the South West African authorities accepted responsibility for its administration, the area became a refuge for poachers, thieves and vagabonds — yet another of so many 'crooks' corners' which appear to be a legacy of southern African history.

As a refuge of the lawless, Caprivi might have remained almost unknown were it not for the series of deaths that occurred in 1922 when a murder and a horrific suicide shocked people of the region. The two central characters in these events were Harris Johns and Ben Johnson. There are several versions of what happened. Although they differ somewhat in detail, the general outline of events seems to have been as follows.[10,11]

Harris Johns was a Cypriot Greek who had taken an English name. He lived as a recluse near the Caprivi on the Kwando River. He cultivated quite a large acreage which he irrigated by a canal and he ran a trading store. His main source of income, however, was from hunting elephant and hippo. For the latter he could get £20 for its fat and hide and it was nothing for him to take six a night — quite an income for those days. Harris Johns was known to be a thief, ruthless and extremely violent.

Ben Johnson lived on the same river, about 50 km downstream. He had come to Africa as a boy and had lived in several countries, including Angola. He had been running a store in Livingstone but during the First World War had become a 'scout' for the British military for whom he worked in South West Africa. Some of his reports were found in Zambia's National Archives; he was an embittered man and claimed that he had never been rewarded or recognised. He took to a life of poaching in Barotseland and Angola. Living as he did in the remoteness of Caprivi he still managed to quarrel with his neighbours.

There are conflicting opinions as to Johnson's character. Much of the evidence comes from Colonel J.C.B. Statham's book *With my Wife Across Africa*. This unlikely witness to these tragic events 'happened' to be crossing Africa with his wife when, in the early 1920s, he came by chance across Johnson's camp on the banks of the Kwando and spent a day or two with him. This alone is a remarkable coincidence when one thinks that they were two of but a handful of Europeans who might have been in this vast and largely uninhabited part of Africa.

Clearly it was a traumatic time, if not for Statham, at least for his wife. Statham came away with the certain conviction that, had they not been continually on their guard, Johnson, whom he claimed was mad, would have murdered them both. Paradoxically, Johnson is said to have wept when they left and then to have written a series of threatening and abusive letters. Statham does not hesitate to describe Johnson as a moody recluse with a reputation for unpleasantness and aggressiveness. Others did not see him like this at all.

Several people of repute claimed a knowledge, and had a high opinion, of Johnson. He was described by one as a well-educated man who, despite living in the wilderness of Caprivi, contributed poetry and prose to some of the leading English periodicals. Others spoke of his courage and of being generous to a fault. It was said of him that he scorned mere money-making and chose to throw off the shackles of civilisation to live free of all convention.

With two such opposing views of the central character, it is difficult to know now where the truth lies. His most ardent supporters speak, however, of Johnson's fierce pride and it may have been this that lay at the root of all that followed.

Johnson and Johns knew of each other, of course, and ocasionally met. They had quarrelled on a number of different occasions — mostly about trivia and, specifically, about who had shot a particular elephant. Johns believed that Johnson was reporting him to the authorities and telling them not only of his poaching but also of his cattle rustling. He decided to face Johnson with an accusation and set off to visit his camp with this purpose in mind. Somehow, Ben Johnson had been warned and was ready.

The confrontation took place, angry words were exchanged and these quickly led to blows. Johns allegedly struck at Johnson with a hoe, but the latter warded off the blow, drew a revolver and shot Johns dead.

There followed a period of confusion which owed its origins to a number of factors. Nobody, including presumably Johnson, was quite sure in which country all this had taken place. Johnson wrote out a report and sent it to the nearest representative of Portuguese authority in Angola, a half-caste who lived more than 200 km away. In the meantime, in a manner inexplicable and yet typical of Africa, a quite unknown Northern Rhodesian half-caste who purported to be of French royal blood and to carry the title of Count d'Artois, appeared on the scene. He made the unlikely claim of being a relative of the murdered Harris Johns and demanded from Johnson his 'relative's' possessions. Johnson was not fooled and refused to hand them over. In response, the good Count broke into the store that night and removed them all, threatening to shoot anyone who followed him, and made his escape.

Neither the Portuguese, the Northern Rhodesian nor the Bechuanaland Protectorate officials seemed terribly enthusiastic about taking an active role in this affair and for some time nothing appears to have happened. Indeed, it is said, the authorities rather inclined to the view that Johnson was a 'good influence' in the region and John the Greek an evil one. If true, this may have explained official inertia even as the events themselves appeared to have developed a fateful momentum of their own.

One account claims that a half-caste son of the murdered man reported to the post at Schuckmannsburg, which would then have been manned by a police representative from Kasane in Bechuanaland. We shall never know whether it was the rumoured approach of justice or the dictates of his own conscience that led Johnson to act as he then did and cued the final act in this chain of melancholy events.

One evening, at his camp on the Kwando, Johnson was sorting through his possessions, when he began methodically to destroy or dispose of them. He called his native wives and half-caste children about him and divided among them all his cash. Every one of his animals was destroyed and all his other possessions burnt. Such metal objects as would not be consumed by fire were thrown into the river. He stripped naked and those clothes too were burnt. Finally, carrying only his rifle and a single cartridge, he walked breast deep into the Kwando River. There he blew his head off.

In the years that followed this event there was much claim and counter-claim as to the roles and responsibilities of the two principal characters. Far too much time has passed for us ever to know the truth. One writer,[12] with some authority, helps flesh out the story with a location for Johnson's camp. This, he says, was not in the strip at all but in southern Angola where, when he wrote in 1940, the Portuguese were said to have had their outpost of Luiana.

I have not travelled far enough along the Kwando to have reached where Johnson's camp might have been. I am sure, were I able to do so, that there would be scant trace of it. Such places were temporary, made of natural materials locally available. When left on their own they return quickly to the soil from whence they came and leave little sign of their passing. It would only be in the sense of a presence that the old camp might be experienced. In the cool shadows, beneath the trees that line the Kwando, perhaps the murmuring of the evening may be more than just the whispering of the breeze by the riverside.

Although in 1890 they acquired title, as it were, to the Caprivi Strip — or as they preferred to call it, the Caprivi Zipfel (meaning tassel) — the Germans did not occupy it with any serious administrative intent for 18 years. It was not until 1908 that the decision was made in Windhoek to establish an administration in the Caprivi Strip. Herr Hauptmann Streitwolf was sent to do the job. He took with him the grand title of Imperial Resident and a number of officials, including a sergeant of police and a medical orderly, to bring the strip more securely into the grasp of the German eagle.

As we have seen in a previous chapter, from the point of view of the native people the Caprivi definitely fell within the domain of the Lozi. Germany had ruled South West Africa for nearly 24 years — more than long enough for the rulers and the ruled to have made up their minds about each other. There had been a series of savage wars fought by the Germans against the Herero and the Hottentots in which no quarter was asked or given on either side. The German reputation for brutality and for demanding absolute obedience, reinforced by severe punishment in its absence, had gone far ahead of them. The Lozi reaction to the rumoured arrival of the German administration was telling. To a man they got up and left the strip, taking their cattle with them! (They also took with them all the cattle of the Basubia, a subordinate tribe whom they regarded as serfs.)[13]

One of Streitwolf's first tasks, when faced with hundreds of starving and deprived Basubia, was to try to persuade the Lozi to return, preferably with their own and the stolen cattle. In fact, it was only after long negotiations and British assistance that any cattle were returned at all — and they came without the Lozi. Not an auspicious start for German administration.

A pressing need was to establish a centre in which the administration could be based. Streitwolf, evidently, was not especially skilled in the art of founding cities. For the site on which he located the capital of eastern Caprivi could hardly have been chosen with less imagination.

The Zambezi floods annually, sending long fingers of water between the lines of forgotten dunes. On one of these ridges of sand, at least 3 km from the river, the future town was founded. Named in honour of the then governor of South West Africa, Schuckmannsburg seemed to have nothing whatever to commend it. It had no view of any kind, it was not in sight of the Zambezi and, indeed, was only connected to it at times of flood. For the rest of the year it baked in the sizzling heat and succumbed to incessant waves of flying insects, notably mosquitoes, that bred year-round in the dank pools of murky water left by the receding floods. Schuckmannsburg was monumentally forgettable, yet in five years it would gain for itself a unique, if tiny, place in the annals of war history.

In the meantime, the German administration slowly established itself. It was largely indirect and worked mostly through the existing chiefs and tribal leaders. Yet the German penchant for discipline made itself felt and if nothing else remained of their time in the strip, the memory of their punishments lingered painfully, long after their departure. One such sentence will serve as an example. Awarded in a case of witchcraft, the offender was expected to survive 25 lashes every week for a total of three months. I make that out to be some 300 lashes![14]

On 4 August 1914, in response to the invasion of Belgium, Great Britain declared war on Germany. As is often the case, the Zambezi was again about to be affected by events far removed from it. It would be nice to say that Schuckmannsburg, in consequence of the war, was suddenly torn from its place of obscurity in the sand near the banks of the Zambezi and hurled into the pages of history. In fact nothing happened at all. At least, not immediately. But plans were afoot.

In Salisbury, the capital of Southern Rhodesia, Schuckmannsburg was looked at in a very serious light. Ignoring its unimaginative and unhealthy location and the fact that there were probably not more than four Germans and 100 native people stationed there, it was seen by the military authorities as a threat! As such, it had to be seized — and seized quickly.

A troop of British South Africa Police was organised within a very short time and by 12 August 1914 was at Victoria Falls. There, under a Major Capell, the BSAP Mobile Column was formed. At this point, some of the early haste evaporated and after digging trenches for the defence of the railway bridge that crossed the Zambezi just below the falls, time seemed to hang somewhat heavily. Some of the policemen were recalled to Bulawayo while the others were sent off to nearby Kazungula to erect a fort there.

The fort was completed by 13 September and the troop responsible for its construction was split in two. Half remained as a garrison; half returned to Victoria Falls, arriving there in the afternoon of 14 September 1914. Here they were told of the intention to attack and seize Schuckmannsburg.

Joining forces with a number of Northern Rhodesia Police the column left the town of Livingstone on foot and horseback, with five wagons. As they passed Kazungula they were joined by men from the garrison and the entire force made its way to the riverside village of Sesheke (now Mwandi) which was the nearest British post to the target town of Schuckmannsburg, across the river in German Caprivi Strip.

It is difficult, working from some of the available reports,[15] to know now exactly who and how many were involved in this incident but it seems that there were not more than 25 white police officers and perhaps 12 native police, a mere 37 in total. One can understand their apprehension. Serious fighting had not yet broken out in Europe and white men in Africa were not accustomed to fight one another. Moreover, this was not just a fight, this was war and I can imagine very mixed emotions among the men of the Mobile Column as they neared their destination.

On their arrival they were met by Major Capell who had gone ahead. He had decided to take Schuckmannsburg without delay and, to avoid bloodshed, intended under a flag of truce to seek a German surrender. Lieut Stevens was selected as emissary and, in company with a Corporal Vaughan who carried the flag and a Native Corporal-Bugler by the name of Kapambue, the three set out in a leaky boat across the wide Zambezi — intent on conquest.

Knowing the kind of boats in use, I imagine that the crossing itself might have been something of an experience. I can see the three police officers wondering if they were ever going to make the other side, let alone being able to deal with the might of whatever German forces were waiting for them on the far bank. In the event, they need not have worried. After all, this was Africa, and anything could happen.

Two German sentries had watched their approach and before the landing, one had set off to base to report the imminent arrival. The other, outnumbered three to one, greeted the arrivals and asked if they wouldn't mind waiting, which they agreed to do. Irritation at delays is not a new a phenomenon, apparently. The visitors began to get restless (and the remaining sentry more nervous) but an incident was avoided by the return to the riverside of the sentry's companion.

He extended his master's greeting and the three British personnel, escorted by two armed native guards, walked the sandy 2 km to Schuckmannsburg and the house of the German Imperial Resident. To his great relief, no doubt, Herr Streitwolf had long since been transferred and his place had been taken by Herr von Frankenberg. This gentleman, seeing that he was outnumbered, wisely decided to hand over the place without resistance. On paper, at least, Schuckmannsburg had fallen. But so momentous an occasion could not pass unmarked and preparations for its proper execution were begun immediately.

Back on the Northern Rhodesian bank, the 'fall-in' sounded and the men marched to Susman's drift where boats had been arranged. Lieut Hornsby of the Northern Rhodesia Police was the first across with some native constables. He encountered a slight difficulty on the German bank in the shape of an innocent and well-meaning sentry who had not been told what was happening and who, courageously and somewhat understandably, took exception to this obvious invasion of his country. He was soon disarmed; the remaining men landed and the whole party marched to Schuckmannsburg. The arrival of British forces at sundown did not leave much time for ceremony but several centuries of tradition and 'form' could not be overlooked, whatever the excuse.

The troops were formed up into a square and the German Resident was called upon formally to surrender. With the Resident accounted for, it was the turn of the British Sergeant to arrest the German Sergeant and the British Native Police to arrest the German Native Police. Once this had been done to everybody's satisfaction, all were released again — on parole — except for the unfortunate German Native Police who seemed to have done very poorly out of the whole show and who spent the night under guard! It was too late to raise the Union Jack so this vital piece of ceremony was postponed to the following morning. The accounts, regrettably, do not relate how the evening was spent.

At the nearly civilised hour of 8h00 on the following day, 22 September 1914, the troops were once more drawn up in the form of a square, facing the flagstaff. The British flair for pomp and ceremony was irrepressible and made the best of the occasion. The troops were facing the flagstaff with the BSAP Maxim Section, under Lieut Tribe, to the right. The Northern Rhodesia Police with their Maxim stood on the left. The BSAP under Lieut Stevens took the centre while opposite, behind the flagstaff, stood the magistrate and several residents of Sesheke, imported from across the Zambezi specially for the occasion! On the dot of eight, Lieut Castle broke out the Union Jack and Major Capell called three cheers for King George V. The Germans, whose 'defeat' was the cause of all this ceremony, were nowhere in sight. Not a single shot had been fired and history had been made, for the taking of Schuckmannsburg was the first Allied occupation of enemy territory in the Great War!

After its brief rise to glory, Schuckmannsburg was quick to fade from prominence — but not without creating a tale or two for posterity. The captors suffered more seriously after the occupation than during it. It was six weeks before they were relieved by more conventional forces and during that time almost all of them went down with serious bouts of malaria.

Once the evacuation had been completed, the task of overseeing the occupation and ensuring that the Germans did not return, something rather more easily said than done, fell to the District Commissioner on the Northern Rhodesian bank at Sesheke. It was some time before the simple answer struck the DC. Returning to Schuckmannsburg he removed the two items upon which any returning forces would most surely depend: the cattle and the station water cart. The latter was put to good use at Sesheke where, for the next 20 years, the German Imperial Resident's water cart carried water daily from the Zambezi River to the British DC's compound![16]

At first sight the expedition to capture Schuckmannsburg seemed a little melodramatic, to say the least. The seizure of a minuscule post containing a handful of German officials in an otherwise vast and mostly uninhabited area of Africa hardly seemed to make sense. Yet when the circumstances become known,[17] it made excellent sense.

For reasons deeply rooted in South African politics of the time, General Maritz, who commanded Afrikaner troops on the border with South West Africa, at the outbreak of war had joined the German forces. At the same time, there was rebellion against the Union government in both the Free State and the Transvaal. The Germans were well aware that, if the rebellion failed, their position in South West Africa would be untenable. Accordingly, they issued a general instruction to the effect that, in such circumstances, all German troops were to make their way across Africa, via the Caprivi Strip, through Northern Rhodesia, in an effort to link up with the German General von Lettow Vorbeck in East Africa. The British view was that, if the rebellion were to be successful, there would be the risk of a German attack from the strip into either Northern or Southern Rhodesia. Even the news of General

Francke's surrender in South West Africa, as the Schuckmannsburg plan was being put into effect,[18] made little difference to the reasoning. In either case it made strategic sense to eliminate the Caprivi Strip as an option — and hence, Schuckmannsburg had to fall.

Despite its capture, Schuckmannsburg lived on. As the administrative centre for the eastern Caprivi Strip it was sensibly abandoned in 1935 with the move of the government to Katima Mulilo. Somehow, though, something kept it alive and it is still occupied today. I went there recently and found no road leading directly to it — just unsignposted and seemingly aimless tracks through the sandy veld. A clinic, a police post and a small number of huts are all that mark the site today. As to its place in history there are few reminders. Left standing is a small square brick building with a corrugated iron roof and, in the sand not far away, part of the carriage and one wooden, steel-rimmed wheel of what is said to have been a German field-gun. Nobody knows the purpose of the building — nor can anybody say for certain that it is German.

I could not leave Schuckmannsburg without paying my respects to its part in our history and so, with the reluctant help of the small party with me I made my obeisance to the past. Some 73 years, six days and a few hours after the event, I raised again three cheers to King George V. White people in the more remote parts of Africa are often regarded as eccentrics. When, at 14h00 in the heat of summer they suddenly and without warning burst into pointless cheering, invoking the name of a long dead king, they are regarded by the local witnesses as being more than eccentric. They are thought to be mad. I suppose I can understand why!

With the establishment of Katima Mulilo, administration of the region was, for the first time, placed on a firm footing and a succession of loyal and dedicated officials followed. The most outstanding of these — at least in terms of the reputation he left behind — was Major Lyle French W. Trollope. A descendant of South Africa's 1820 settlers, he was first posted to Katima in October 1939 as Magistrate and Native Commissioner. He continued in the post of senior administrator with a break of two years until December 1952. On his retirement he stayed in the area, running, among other activities, a series of stores on the Northern Rhodesian bank. He died of a heart attack while travelling on a barge on the Zambezi and lies buried in Katima Mulilo.

Like many of his kind, Trollope grew to become a legend in his own lifetime. He was physically striking, with a mass at one time of more than 136 kg, and he was by nature of his position a dominant person. So long was he in his post that he acquired in the eyes of many a god-like status and was often referred to as the king of Caprivi. There are many stories about this man. One relates how he shot at the aircraft that brought his successor to relieve him, driving it away. Another describes how he threw into the wastepaper basket all correspondence from his superiors, ignoring it completely, safe from interference in his austere and distant isolation.

It is strange how such tales become part of the lore of a region, especially when the individual concerned is controversial. I was fortunate in having the opportunity to verify them — and found them completely exaggerated. Trollope's successor was A.B. Colenbrander and he puts the myths to rest with charming ease.[19] As the individual concerned he points out that he arrived overland, not by aircraft! He goes on to say that Trollope was an extremely efficient administrator, highly regarded by his superiors. He was much respected, erudite, and an excellent conversationist with a wonderful sense of humour. Almost certainly, it was Trollope's manner, his success and perhaps one or two small eccentricities that gave rise to his reputation and the stories that have persisted about him.

It is time now to leave the Caprivi Strip. During this interval the river has rested and has crossed the area in a rather languid and lazy fashion, rolling gently by between banks of gleaming white sand. Its course has changed and continues to change frequently, as dictated by the presence or absence of large islands of sand, which the river itself creates and destroys. There have been no rapids to bar its way. The last were at Katima Mulilo and have given their name to the centre. The language is Silozi and the words mean 'to quench the fire'. It is an allusion to an ancient practice of carrying burning embers on long journeys by canoe to save difficulties in lighting fires at night. In rapids such as those at Katima the waves, or an upset, could easily quench the fire.[20]

After the calm below Katima, the river encounters the huge plateau of basalt that will lead it to Victoria Falls. The entry to this area is at the southern boundary of the strip and is marked by the rapids of Mambova and Kasai. These are not spectacular but they are of great significance for they provide evidence of the role this river played in the evolution of a great inland sea.

5 Where Angels Gaze

THE great falls of water on the Zambezi that David Livingstone named after his queen remain as beautiful today as they were when he first saw them. Hundreds of thousands of people have seen them now and have come away touched by their beauty. I seldom miss the chance to visit them and I am drawn by the fact that they are never the same. The vegetation changes little but the subtle shifts of Africa's seasons are reflected vividly in the cascading curtain. Its colour and volume follow the year round through blue, brown and green and from thin lacy veils to a phalanx of broken white that rolls in slow motion over the lip of rock.

Rightly, a great deal is made of the falls as an attraction worth visiting. Much less is said about the remarkable beauty of the jagged gorge that the Zambezi has cut. Extending from the base of the falls for about 130 km, its upper reaches are easily viewed from the Zambian side and are well worth the effort. For reasons that we shall return to later in this chapter, it zig-zags abruptly close to the falls and has almost perpendicular walls. As it progresses it becomes less severe but no less an example of some of Africa's most rugged and impenetrable country.

The river, of course, is seasonal but its floods do not coincide with the time of local rain, for it has already travelled over 1 300 km through a region of higher and different rainfall. Its lowest flow at the falls is usually in November and December. Thin trails of water slip vapidly over the crest and into the chasm below. In separate veils they seem barely to have the energy to fall. Even the angry thunder of the Devil's Cataract is muted to a whisper of its former self. At such times it is easily possible to walk almost the entire length of the crest from the Zambian side.

I wish I had been there in the floods of 1958, however. It must have been an elemental and moving experience. The dam at Kariba was being built at the time and the Batonga people were waiting for Nyaminyami, their river spirit, to strike it down. He attempted to do so in two successive years and the resources for those assaults were marshalled here, at Victoria Falls. (See also Chapter 8.)

The falls are said to be the widest curtain of falling water in the world. The distance from one side to the other is 1 690 m and the average drop is 92 m. There is a dramatic change in the flow of water between December and March, for in those three months the river rises from the lowest to its highest level. When the water is high is normally not the best time to visit the falls. They are impressive and beautiful still, it is true, but there is so much spray it is difficult to appreciate them fully. In March 1958 a visit must have been positively frightening.

On the third day of that month, in the second year of Nyaminyami's attack on the dam site, some 350 km downstream, a record and unimaginable flow of 722 million litres per minute powered down into the gorge below![1] The river height on that day helps us to grasp the sheer magnitude of the flood: it rose to 4,86 m. This means that across the entire 1,5 km of the falls, the water was 4,86 m deep at the crest! The narrow and sheer-sided gorge below the falls confines the river in such a way that the level of water within it rises five times higher than the water above. Thus at the height of the flood, the water in the gorge rose an additional 16 m.[2] The average maximum flood level for any year is 550 million litres per minute, so during the river spirit Nyaminyami's attack on Kariba, the volume of water going over the falls was nearly half as much again.[3]

What a sight that must have been! Nearly 5 m of water, foaming and curling, clawing at the edge before plunging down through solid sheets of spray into the chaos of white water that half-filled the chasm, hurling itself onto the smooth black rocks that lay somewhere below. A tremendous updraught is created in the gorge as the falling water punches air upwards under pressure, carrying with it sheets of water skywards before they collapse back into the wild white mêlée. The earth shakes, the sound is deafening and a deluge of spray drowns everything within reach.

For at least six months of the year when the water level in the river is high, the whole of the Victoria Falls area vibrates. On any still evening in the houses there, you may hear the countinuous rattle of a window or a door. It took me some time to realise that the houses respond softly to the echoing thunder of the falls themselves.

David Livingstone, during his trip across Africa, understandably lost track of time and he was a day out in his reckoning when he reached Victoria Falls. Thus it was that for many years, until just before the centennial in fact, 17 November was regarded as the day of Livingstone's discovery. In the nick of time, the London Missionary Society found a hitherto unknown copy of one of Livingstone's original note books. In it was an entry clearly showing that he arrived there the day before, on 16 November 1855.[4]

This revelation saved the embarrassment of the wrong date appearing on the statue of David Livingstone that was proudly unveiled on the Zimbabwean bank, 100 years to the day after his discovery. A greater embarrassment that has not been explained to me is why the statue is there at all — since there is no record that Livingstone ever set foot on the Zimbabwean side of the falls.[5] (Indeed, there is no direct evidence that he stood anywhere on Zimbabwean soil!)

In the years that have followed, there have been a number of attempts to discredit Livingstone's claim to have been the first European at the falls.

Prospective claimants have not fared well. The Portuguese fail through lack of records — although we do know that they were at Khami in the mid-1600s (see Chapter 13).

A strong case has been made for a young man called Carolus Trichardt. His achievements were quite extraordinary for, in 1838, from what is now Maputo, he explored the East African coast and much of its hinterland. He kept no written account and what is known today came from interviews recorded 50 years after the event. Nevertheless, there is good reason for believing that he reached Somalia, visited Ethiopia where he met the Emperor, paid calls on Zanzibar and the island of Mozambique before travelling up the Zambezi as far as Cahora Bassa Gorge. All this was done alone, without fanfare or report. Trichardt took a passage on any convenient vessel and hired porters where he landed.[6]

It has been suggested that the falls he reached on the Zambezi were those at Livingstone, but this is erroneous. He did not have sufficient time to make such a journey for he was only away for 13 months, during which he also visited Madagascar!

Claims that the Victoria Falls appear on early maps can easily be refuted also. The largest collection of such maps in southern Africa is in the hands of the fascinating and kindly Dr Oscar Norwich, who lives in Johannesburg and who gave me access to his collection.

The 'Clouet' map of 1727 clearly shows the Zambezi River and marks upon it the 'great cataract' at a point on the continent and river so out of scale that it is impossible to be sure where the cataract might actually be. A copy of this map, produced in 1749, repeats the information but adds the location of Chikova and its silver mines — which are upstream of the cataract. Clearly, therefore, the cataracts referred to must be those of Cahora Bassa, not Victoria Falls.[7]

There are two other claims to challenge Livingstone but neither of them stands on very firm ground. Henry Hartley's is one, but few people take it seriously; William Cotton Oswell's is the other. Like many others, I pondered long over this last claim, but, on balance, I do not think it valid. The claim is not made by Oswell himself, who accompanied Livingstone on his early journeys, including the one to Linyanti and Sesheke, but by his relative, Maj.-Gen. Baden-Powell. The critical words are, 'the Falls were first made known . . .' Oswell published a sketch map, much of it admittedly hearsay. On it he had mentioned the falls and their spray, of which he had been told. He never claimed to have visited them. The question is, how should 'first made known' be interpreted?[8]

A string of visitors followed Livingstone and there is the inevitable list of 'firsts'. William Baldwin was the second European to reach the falls but he was the first to get into trouble with the authorities there. He had walked from Natal, using a pocket compass as a guide, and arrived just before Livingstone's second visit.

A Kololo representative of Chief Sekeletu deemed that a fine must be paid in recompense for Baldwin's use of water, firewood and grazing for his horse, as well as his foolhardy act of swimming in the river. In the event, 6 pounds weight of beads were paid, subsequently to be returned to Baldwin by the chief, perhaps because of Livingstone's intervention, for he arrived the next day.[9]

There was evidently, in the eyes of some at least, considerable status to be attached to having visited the falls in those early years. Before he was knighted, Ralph Williams, as Resident Commissioner of Bechuana-land, took his wife and seven-year-old son there, arriving on 14 August 1883. It is all reported in his book, *How I Became Governor*, the title of which says a great deal about the man before you've read a single page.[10] The book expresses his pleasure at his wife being the first Englishwoman to see the falls but then we share his agony of doubt when he learns that possibly a Mrs William Francis might have been there earlier. In the end, he graciously gives Mrs Francis the benefit of that doubt. Not only is the manner in which he does this — publicly — amusing, but the incident illustrates his undoubtedly innocent but transparent arrogance. Williams himself was the 81st recorded European visitor and his wife the sixth, if not the seventh, European woman![11]

When I was a youngster, cutting your name into the bark of a tree was a hair's breadth short of a hanging offence, but most youngsters never-theless did it. Not much has changed since then except that the aerosol can seems to have taken a large slice of the pen-knife market — and in any case, we don't seem to have so many trees left. With the wisdom of greater age it is possible to think you know the reason why such strictures are important. I found buried in the literature on the falls, a delightful cameo that illustrates the point.

David Livingstone reached by boat an island on the lip of the falls which now bears his name but has also been called Garden Island and was known locally as Kaseruka and as Kempongo.[12] When Livingstone met Baldwin at the falls, he told Baldwin that in the bark of a tree on this small island he had cut his initials, the only place between the coasts where vanity had allowed him to do so.[13] (I must admit to thinking this statement a little pious for I know of at least two other places where Livingstone's initials appeared.)

Baldwin evidently had already noticed this, for according to his account his initials now appeared below those of the celebrated Doctor, on the same tree. In the light of such eminent examples, Charles Livingstone, who was with his brother on his second visit, added his initials to the other two.

Thomas Baines visited the island two years later and records that 'D.L. 1855' and 'C.L. 1860', together with the broad vertical arrow of the government, cut beneath them, were still visible. He says nothing about

Baldwin's name although he notes that the garden, wishfully planted by the Doctor, was overgrown and that the fence had been trampled by hippo. There was no trace of the 100 peach and apricot stones or of the quantity of coffee seed that he had planted.[14]

A year later, in 1863, Sir Richard Glynn and his party of four arrived at the falls. He noticed that the initials of the two Livingstones and of Baldwin were nearly grown out and so re-cut them, inscribing Glynn 1863 by their side.[15] There were now four sets of initials on the tree! I wonder if this was the point my parents were trying to get across?

In 1928, Sir Reginald Coupland paid a visit to the island and examined the trees there. 'Livingstone's tree' was pointed out to him but he found no trace of initials on it or any other tree.[16] I carried my ever-present and long-suffering Jack Russell companion Gypsey, quivering, through the torrent as I waded to the island in 1986 and, likewise, found nothing. However, I am delighted to say that tourism has not faltered at the loss of this priceless piece of Livingstonia. I have a brochure from 1963 which contains a picture of a suitably fezzed guide with a suitably vacant expression on his face, pointing to a perfectly unscarred section of a tree's trunk. The caption suggests that if you are lucky, you too can have a look at this particular piece of tree on which Livingstone's initials would have appeared had they survived 120 years of growth!

In contrast to the plunging chaos below the lip, the section of river above the falls is broad, dotted with islands and very beautiful; it is a part of the river steeped in history.

Here among the islands is one called Kalai (now Queen Elizabeth Island). It was claimed in the 19th century by Sekote, a Tonga chief who controlled the shallow fords across the Zambezi at this point. His father was buried on this island and, as was the Batonga custom of respect for important men, his grave was surrounded by 70 large elephant tusks.[17]

Kandahar, one of the most beautiful islands, is said to have been named by the British General Frederick Sleigh Roberts, who took part in the suppression of the Indian Mutiny, relieved Kandahar, the then capital of Afghanistan, and played a prominent role in the Boer War. He is probably better known as Lord Roberts, First Earl of Kandahar.

Ray and Nadia Stocker, two friends of mine, are, I think, the only couple to have celebrated a marriage ceremony on this island.

There is a long, deep and silent stretch of river between Kalunda island and the shore. It was here that the flying boat service used to land. In 1948 and 1950, BOAC and South African Airways flew 'Solent' flying boats from the Vaal Dam near Johannesburg to Southampton via Victoria Falls. It was an innovative and exciting concept in travel.

The aircraft carried up to 30 passengers and was a double-decker. One could stroll about from the upper to the lower deck where there were three passenger cabins, luxuriously appointed powder and dressing rooms, and

a promenade with wide deep windows through which one could watch
the scene below. Lady Ruth Khama travelled on this flight and tells of the
low altitude at which one flew, compared with today's aircraft, so that you
could see interesting sights on the ground below.[18]

Because the craft flew only during the day, large reaches of water were
required at the end of each flight. Thus the journey became a magic carpet
flight over Africa to exotic places which included Lakes Malawi and Victoria, the Nile at Khartoum, Luxor and Alexandria as well as Augusta,
Valetta or Marseilles. An early arrival earned an afternoon's excursion to
the Sphinx or the pyramids, sometimes a boat trip on the Nile or a visit
to the Dinka. The nights would be spent in a luxury hotel.

Between 1946 and 1947, Ian Dixon flew as a supernumerary purser on
other flying boats that followed the coastal route for part of the way from
Durban. He speaks with pride of the airline's years of outstanding service
on this route and unequalled safety record. He also remembers the inspired promotional efforts of the sales department with passengers being
presented with matched suitcases when they purchased their tickets. In
addition, ladies received a silk scarf and a box of toiletries and gentlemen
a Yardley pomade or shaving soap. Where have those gentle days of
leisurely, comfortable flight gone?[19]

Can you imagine arriving in southern Africa, circling the falls in your
aircraft, watching the spray turn to a pillar of light as it catches the
afternoon sun? What a magnificent sight it must have been to see the falls
and gorges spread out beneath you.

Lifting a flying boat off the water is a little more difficult than one might
think. As a layman, I would have ordered smooth water and no wind for
such an occasion — and I would have been completely wrong. The
smoother the water, the longer the take-off; a well-organised airline
always had a small motorboat on standby. If conditions were too good,
so I am told, the boat went out and motored through the take-off zone. The
wake created a pattern of wavelets that broke the 'grip' of the water upon
the hull and helped the aircraft into the air!

The geology of the falls area is at once simple, fascinating and extremely
ancient. We have already seen in Chapter 1 how southern Africa came to
be covered with huge tracts of deep lava beds and how, over time, these
had been partly removed by erosion, tending to remain as a filling in
ancient valleys and troughs, temporarily protected from the elements. A
geological map of the Zambezi in the vicinity of the falls shows the river
flowing across an example of such an ancient, filled valley.

Like a prehistoric stone arrowhead, pointing down the river, the visible
portions of this vast field of lava measure some 170 km from east to west
along the axis of the river's flow. The sides of the arrowhead are initially
bounded by faults, reaching back into Zambia and Zimbabwe, themselves
an extension of the network of major faults that create the Gwembe

Trough. On the Zimbabwe side it is most dramatic, extending for 115 km and being traced on the ground by the Deka River which follows it closely for the entire distance.

The surface of the basalt is practically flat and it is over this that the Zambezi flows. Located on the eastern periphery of the Kalahari sand, the basalt in the area of Victoria Falls and its approaches is covered with sand but only to a limited extent. As one travels further west, however, so the depth of the sand increases and the extent of Stormberg lavas becomes less certain as they disappear beneath it.

We, however, are concerned only with the basalt over which the river flows. To appreciate the geology, it is easiest to imagine a flat, table-like area of harder rock, embedded on the downstream side in softer material and with the Zambezi beginning to flow across it. As the river gets to the furthest side, it flows onto softer material which it quickly erodes, thus lowering its channel in that section and creating a steep fall from the more to the less resistant rock.

There is a limit to how far the river can cut down into the soft rock and when that limit is reached, the only direction for further erosion is backwards, along the course of the river. In the case of the Zambezi the cutting back process carved out the present gorge. A river cutting down through such hard material as basalt will do so vertically and the resulting feature will be remarkable because of its relatively smooth face and its perpendicular sides.

This is best illustrated near the falls themselves where the gorge is youngest and where a glance into it clearly shows the near vertical sides. It also shows something else of great interest. If one looks carefully, one can detect distinct layers in the rock face. Depending upon where you look in relation to the falls, three or four of these will be noticed, each of which represents a different lava flow event.

Imagine very liquid lava flowing from some great rent in the primeval earth's surface and spreading out across the land. Eventually the flow stops, as if the earth's interior has paused to gather strength for the next assault. The lava is filled with gas and, like gas in any liquid, it rises to the surface in the form of bubbles. Some of these bubbles reach the surface and escape. Others are retarded by the surface tension and begin to collect near the upper portion of the flow. Still others slowly ascend in a losing race against time for, as the lava cools and solidifies, so escape eventually becomes impossible.

The air spaces trapped within lava in this way are called vesicles. A geologist with a good knowledge of local conditions can tell the proximity of a flow's ancient surface by the number and distribution of vesicles. The more there are, the closer the top of the flow. In some localities, given the right conditions, chemicals are deposited within the vesicles, often filling them completely. When the surrounding rock is eroded the filling is exposed and lies on the surface. They are called amygdales and are the source of the beautiful and highly varied agates.

The exposed surface of the cooling flow is at once attacked by the elements and its pitted nature accelerates the process of degradation. In each tiny pocket, the rain collects, ice can form or seeds can shelter, sprout and grow. Faced with this ceaseless assault and burned by the sun, the uppermost part of the flow discolours and its nature changes as soil begins to form. The longer the time interval between flows, the more marked the effect. Eventually another flow follows the first and a sea of molten rock engulfs the previous surface, searing the top metre or so and, in a process of metamorphosis, changing it yet again. These zones of degradation, discoloration and increased numbers of vesicles clearly demarcate the separate flows.

A point of interest concerning the gorge is the change in its shape from one end to the other. I have already pointed out that near Victoria Falls the gorge is 'young', freshly cut, and so the sides are sheer. As one progresses further downstream it is fascinating to note how the profile changes and the once sheer walls that hemmed the river in, increasingly fall back to form less impossible slopes. This phenomenon graphically expresses the passage of time in degrees of more advanced erosion.

Not only do the sides of the gorge become less severe as one progresses downstream, but the depth increases also. At the falls, the depth to mean water level is 110 m; it is more than 330 m at the mouth of the gorge where the basalt abruptly ends and is replaced by sandstone.[20]

Geoffrey Bond, a wonderfully warm and interesting man with a special skill for popularising science, was Zimbabwe's leading authority on that country's geology and took a particular interest in the Victoria Falls region. He observed that there is at least as great a thickness of basalt beneath the river bed as there is above it. So it proved to be, for Zimbabwe's Geological Survey suggests that depths of basalt at the falls may well reach 1 000 m.[21]

It is easy to imagine how such great depths of basalt, spread over vast areas, would be subject to considerable internal stress due both to cooling and to regional tectonic activity. The effect of these stresses is to cause deep fracturing and lines of weakness and it is these that the river preferentially exploits. The best example of this is the zig-zag pattern of gorges, followed by the progression upstream of Victoria Falls itself, which can be vividly seen in its immediate vicinity.

The valley cut in the basalt by the Zambezi above the falls is extremely shallow. On average, the river has not incised more than 15 m to 20 m down into the basalt and this over a width of between 2 km and 5 km. Characteristically, at different elevations on the sides there are deposits of river gravels that mark old riverbeds and in these are to be found large quantities of distinctive Stone Age tools.[22]

It is a reasonable assumption that the tools are there in such quantity because man found it a convivial place to be: he was able to hunt and fish and, above all, had easy access to the river. He is unlikely to have lived on the edge of a precipitous gorge.

It is a telling fact that the distribution of these tools extends down either side of the Zambezi for about 18 km below the present falls — and then stops abruptly. If the assumption is valid, an obvious conclusion is that when man first arrived on the river in this area, the falls were then located that distance further downstream.[23]

If it were possible to date man's arrival at that early waterfall, then one could work out the average rate of regression of the falls to their present position. With this established, it might be possible to extrapolate that information and to arrive at a general conclusion as to when the Zambezi first started to flow in the region, across the basalt.

Attempts to do this have been made but there are considerable difficulties. For example, we can date the emergence of certain types of stone tools with only approximate accuracy. In addition there are many potential inaccuracies in extrapolating a date derived for a short distance of gorge to the whole gorge length. There may be variations in rock hardness, for example, changes in rainfall and the sediment load, which would alter the cutting power of the river; the effect of the presence or absence of fissures and fracture zones could also be considerable. Despite these limitations, an approximate age has been arrived at and the conclusion is that the Zambezi has been flowing along its present course for approximately two million years.[24] This may sound a long time indeed, but compared to the perspective of geological time, it is very recent.

Getting messages across the great spaces of Africa was always a problem for the colonialists but it was solved long before by the indigenous people of the continent. The workings of 'bush telegraph', as it came to be known, have never been satisfactorily explained — but I must admit to being drawn by Sir Percy Sillitoe's attempt. He suggests that 'the bush and the veldt are both great whispering galleries, where every native would seem to cock his ear into the wind and tell you news accurately from a hundred miles distant'.[25]

Bush telegraph was not enough for the early missionaries and so, in the absence of a formalised system, the more remote correspondents were forced to depend upon traders and hunters. The missionary John Smith Moffat was stationed at Inyati in Matabeleland and in the 1860s corresponded with his brother-in-law, David Livingstone, who was at that time leading the Zambezi expedition and was somewhere on the lower river. Less than 500 km separated the men but the letter travelled south to Cape Town and then by sea to the mouth of the Zambezi. One letter took a year to get from the Lupata Gorge to its destination and another, to Mrs Livingstone from Emily Moffat in Bechuanaland, took eight months to be delivered. To me, it is not the length of time that is remarkable, but that such an informal system worked at all.[26]

An organised mail service across the Zambezi was installed by 1897 and relied almost entirely for its effectiveness upon native runners. Coaches in the 'wild west' style were employed by several companies to provide a passenger and mail service but they were not the postal pioneers, representing rather the second step of development that continued and expanded the initial service until railways superceded them.

Despite their secondary role, the coaches of a man named Zeederberg are worth a longer look. American made and imported into southern Africa, they carried 12 people and were usually hauled by mules. A typical journey was that from Mafikeng to Bulawayo, a distance of about 750 km which was completed in ten days. Such a journey was expensive and cost £45 — far more than one might pay today for a very much faster train journey.[27] Zeederberg's coaches followed the runners and the postal service northwards. For two years from 1903 coaches operated in the steadily diminishing gap between the railhead from Bulawayo and Victoria Falls[28] and after that date moved across the river into Northern Rhodesia, extending the service from Livingstone to Kalomo, a distance of 160 km. Zeederberg was always experimenting to find better and cheaper ways of hauling his coaches. He had enjoyed no success with zebra but on the section to Kalomo he used trotting oxen with great effectiveness![29]

For me, however, the fascination really lies with the runners of the early post office. A network of these men spanned huge tracts of central Africa and, with a punctuality and reliability only empire builders would have insisted upon, provided a remarkable service to distant outposts.

The route to the north lay through Francistown in Bechuanaland. Here mail from the south and from Bulawayo was collected and taken by runner via Pandamatenga to Victoria Falls. Mr Dobson's post office, which was opened in 1898, was not located at the site of modern Livingstone but further upstream at the Drift. The arrival of the post on the opposite bank was announced by a bugle call which occasioned great excitement and a flurry of hurried canoe activity to fetch it.

At the falls the post was divided to follow two routes, one to the north-east and the other to the north-west, along the Zambezi to Lealui in Barotseland and as far north as Kalene Hill near the source of the river.[30]

A typical runner carried between 15 kg and 18 kg of mail and could average 40 km a day although there are plenty of references showing that in emergencies this figure could be dramatically increased — one report speaks of a runner covering over 150 km in 24 hours![31] Runners usually travelled in pairs and on the Barotseland run carried a Martini Henry rifle and a few rounds of ammunition.

The runner service lingered for many years. In 1940, one of these energetic people was still active and, after 30 years' service, was calculated to have walked nearly 200 000 km and to have carried some 30 000 kg of mail![32] My research on the Zambian side of the Zambezi Valley took me several times along a lonely bush track there. It led through almost uninhabited country to a remote farm house and twice along that road I met the postman. Uniformed and with the traditional postman's bag slung over his shoulder he nonchalantly pedalled an incredibly antiquated bicycle along his rutted round, apparently heedless of the numerous game animals whose spoor showed in the dust around him. He does 70 km down one day, 70 km back the next — and this was 1987!

There is a lovely story told by the District Commissioner at Mongu in Barotseland, well worth repeating. It alludes to the special status that was attached to carriers of mail, a status that almost guaranteed them protection, food and shelter wherever they went.

On this particular occasion, in about 1900, the DC was 'on safari' in the far west of Barotseland, close to the Portuguese border. There he came across (to their mutual surprise I am sure) two Portuguese African policemen. Each carried the traditional cleft stick with an official envelope firmly clamped in its grip. They replied somewhat casually, in answer to questions, that they had come from Benguela on the west coast and were carrying letters from the Commandant there to the Commandant in the east. This news struck the DC as somewhat odd and his suspicions were aroused. He knew that it was far quicker to send a letter round by ship than to despatch it overland, a distance just under 3 000 km.

An examination of the letters revealed the fraud. Both envelopes were empty and had blue pencil scrawls across the front but no address. The two men had been transferred from east to west against their will and had decided to walk back home, using the protection of the 'white man's letter'![33]

Although, by 1904, many hundreds of people had visited Victoria Falls, it was the arrival of the railway that really put the place 'on the map'. That the line passed that way at all is the result of a curious set of circumstances.

In the era of empire building, Rhodes's dream of a Cape to Cairo link was still in vogue and inspired the idea of a transcontinental railway. As early as 1898 a small party of surveyors made their way to Kariba Gorge overland, following by just a few weeks the heroic struggle of Major Gibbons's group through that same fearsome gorge by water (see Chapter 17). The party's objective was to survey a route by which the intended railway could cross the Zambezi. In those years, the expectation was that the line would bridge the river somewhere in the north of Zimbabwe.[34] For its present route, we have to thank Mr Albert Giese.

Giese is the man who discovered Hwange coalfields in western Zimbabwe and it was because of this discovery that all plans for the great northern railway were eventually changed and the line rerouted from Bulawayo through Hwange and from thence northward via Victoria Falls.

Albert Giese was a young German immigrant and made his discovery in 1894. Analysis of samples clearly showed the coal to be of extremely good quality and Giese, who had pegged the claim, was set to become a wealthy man. However, he had to contend with tsetse fly, raiding parties of Matabele warriors and rinderpest, so when the Mashonaland Agency approached him, he expressed his willingness to sell. He was given a choice of a single payment of £1 000 or a royalty of a penny a ton. He took the former. When Giese died in September 1938, Hwange Mine had produced more than 18 million tons of coal which, at his royalty rate, would have earned him approximately £75 000![35]

The train service of 1905 was not quite the sophisticated means of travel it later became. There were no dining cars and there were no corridors. Travellers took their servants with them and when tea or hot food was required, the servant jumped out of the train at the next stop and made a fire.[36] A witness described a typical hazard faced by the trains of the day. One locomotive passed through a herd of elephant, knocking several down and so enraging the beasts that they attacked the train, smashing great gaping holes in the sides of the trucks.[37]

The railway line arrived at Victoria Falls on 1 June 1904. Miss Pauling, the contractor's daughter, and a friend drove the locomotive the last kilometre into the town. A small romantic touch that appeals to me is that the engine was the same one as had hauled the first train into Bulawayo seven years earlier, in 1897.[38]

The real excitement of those days at the falls was only partly the arrival of the railway line; I suspect it was the work on the bridge that caught people's imagination more. Rhodes decreed that the bridge should span the great gorge immediately below the falls and should pass so close that spray would moisten the carriage windows — as indeed it does.

Work on the bridge began sometime after May 1903 with the clearing away of the approaches and the cutting of the great steps in the chasm's wall on which the main supports would rest. Erection of the steel was completed in just under six months. An interesting method was employed: the bridge was built from both sides simultaneously and as the great mass of steel-work edged out from either side across the gaping chasm and the river 130 m below, it was anchored to the bank by a set of 12 giant steel hawsers.[39]

The closing was a triumphant event. It was timed for 6h00 on 1 April 1905 and took place without a hitch. So precise were the calculations that the engineer responsible had allowed for the fact of spray on the girders which would have slowed heat absorption and, therefore, expansion of the metal. There was great consternation just a few minutes after dawn that day when it was seen that, unpredictably, the wind had shifted and the bridge had remained dry.

In the event, concern was unwarranted for the two great steel semi-arches were perfectly joined by the centrepiece which matched first time the rivet holes waiting to receive it.[40]

The location of the bridge, where it is frequently saturated by spray, demanded the inclusion of some rather interesting design features. To ensure that rust would never become established there is no portion of the bridge that cannot be examined by the human eye and no place that is not accessible to the painter's brush. There are no 'cups' or hollows that might hold water and all the important members of the structure can be entered by a man who can crawl through them.[41]

Wallie Walters was one of many who benefited from the new bridge — even if the manner in which he did so was somewhat unorthodox! Wallie was an inveterate gambler and was present when one of the last girders to be placed into the steelwork of the bridge fell into the river. By chance he had also seen the telegrams ordering a replacement part. He knew the name of the ship on which it was travelling and its expected date of arrival and was therefore one of the few people who knew it would be in place before the scheduled opening day.

Thus forearmed, he could not resist taking bets that the official day would remain 12 September 1905, as arranged. Knowing of the missing girder and the difficulties of transport and communication, many people took him on. Wallie stood to lose £2 000 or make £500. Of course, the girder arrived in time, the opening day went ahead as scheduled and Wallie Walters walked away a richer man by £500![42]

The bridge was formally opened by Professor Darwin, great-grandson of the famous Charles Darwin. Many dignitaries of Empire were present, among them scientists and distinguished academics. History has it that one of them, a member of the British Association, thought to test the depth of the gorge below the bridge. He picked up a stone and drew out his pocket watch with which to time the descent. Absent-mindedly, he dropped his watch into the gorge and found himself timing the event with the stone in his hand![43]

A great regatta was organised to celebrate the completion of the bridge. Four clinker-built fours had been sent from Oxford for local crews while four teams came up from South Africa. The Barotse added much excitement by attending in their light, dugout racing canoes. The Litunga, the Lozi king, was present as a guest of honour — in a grey flannel suit, hat and hunting crop, binoculars over his shoulder.

The same course, which picked its way among hippo and crocodiles, was later used for a World Sculling Championship event. This took place in 1910 when the British champion defended his title against a New Zealand challenger — and lost — over a 7 km course.

The railway line quickly changed this part of Africa. Suddenly, it all seemed tamed. Gone were the Matabele raiding parties, game was shot

and began to disappear, farms and roads were established and the administrators moved in. Even so, there was still excitement and adventure around.

Arthur Harrington, one of the great pioneering characters of Livingstone, had yet to walk into the local pub, demanding credit, meaningfully
lifting his pet leopard onto the bar counter to get it![44] It is also said of him
that he frequently fired revolver shots through the screen in the local
open-air cinema whenever he had consumed sufficient liquor to make him
feel strongly about the rights and wrongs of what he was watching. Ted
Spencer had yet to fly his aircraft into the pages of local history by being
the only one to pass along the gorge under the bridge! All of which says
that the wild life around Victoria Falls is far from dead and forgotten . . .

6 Stone and Iron

I am always amazed when I compare the age of our own species with the lifespan of our earth — we have been here for such an incredibly short time. Planet earth has existed for some 4 600 million years. A little more than a quarter of that total passed before the first living single cells emerged 3 200 million years ago. Multicellular life did not appear until as late as 600 million years ago.[1] Hominid types, of which we are descendants, first walked the earth about 3 million years ago and it was in Africa that the slow and hazy transition from primate to tool-making hominids must have taken place.

The Stone Age in Africa is thought to have begun more than 2,5 million years ago[2] although very recent finds in Zaïre tentatively suggest a new date of 3,2 million years.[3] Based on the method of manufacture of Stone Age tools, three broad divisions emerge and to those are given the names of Early, Middle and Late Stone Age. Sometimes, the broad categories are seen as being divisible into smaller subgroups, each of which is also named.

In different regions the categories may overlap, with Early Stone Age tools still being made as recently as 75 000 years ago while tools of the Middle Stone Age may have started about 130 000 years ago and continued until 30 000 years ago. Late Stone Age tools began appearing some 28 000 years ago and continued to be made in various places until about 200 years ago.

The criteria employed to differentiate the hominid tool sequence are straightforward. The prime characteristic of Early Stone Age tools is that they were made by removing flakes from a rock to leave a core, which was the required article — although the flakes may also have been used. Such crude and simple, hand-held tools were used for chopping, pounding and cutting, and were made from cobbles and pieces of rock. Tools from this category, often called pebble tools, are found in the high level gravels in the Victoria Falls region of the Zambezi.[4]

The latter part of the Early Stone Age is characterised by a much higher degree of skill in the manufacture of the tools. This fact is held as the first indication of the emergence of man's sense of aesthetic appreciation. The period saw the evolution of beautiful hand-axes and axe-like cleavers that depended on the invention of what is known as the 'soft hammer' technique.

This technique involved using as a hammer with which to chip off flakes, not a rock, but something softer, such as a bone or hard piece of wood. The effect was to take off much thinner and more accurate flakes so that finer workmanship was possible.[5]

The Middle Stone Age is identified by a new method of tool manufacture. Instead of removing flakes from a core and using the core as a tool the new technique was to use the flakes instead — but with an important difference. The would-be flakes were first prepared 'in situ', while still in place on the core. Only when detailed preparation had been completed as far as possible, was the flake then struck from the core to yield the finished tool. The Middle Stone Age was a period in which increasing adaptation and specialisation were reflected in the range, variety and quality of tools. The heavy duty tools of the past were less in evidence and scrapers, blades and finely flaked points became more common. From this time, also, tools began to be mounted on handles and 'retouching' techniques began the sequence of finer tools that led into the Late Stone Age.

The Late Stone Age proper lasted from over 15 000 years ago to the very recent past.[6] Late Stone Age tools were the most varied and creative in the long history of man's production of such implements. Some are exquisitely made and are quite delicately beautiful. New tools for new uses appear in this time. Examples include edge-ground stone axes as well as stones with holes bored through them which were probably used as weights for digging sticks.[7]

Small size and the fact that most tools were mounted on sticks are the distinguishing characteristics of the Late Stone Age. The tiny stone ovals that were used for scraping come from this period, as do microlithic lunates and bladelets associated with the bow and arrow and the hunting of large game. Too light to inflict a mortal wound, these small barbs are thought to be linked to the discovery of some of the lethal plant poisons that abound.[8] Indeed, there is a suggestion made by some that the arrival of bow and arrow technology may have spurred the Late Stone Age into existence or, perhaps, refined still further its skills and craftmanship.[9]

Diminutive, curved scrapers were probably used as tiny hand adzes for paring down bow-staves and arrow-shafts. This period's tools from bone and shells are the first to be regularly recovered at archaeological sites.[10] Almost certainly, such tools had been in use for millennia but, unlike stone ones, they had not been preserved.

Attempting to understand and piece together what life in Stone Age times was like is frustrated by the lack of material remains. In a culture that depended entirely upon natural materials, few artefacts persist through time and only in a few locations are the floral and faunal remains preserved to broaden the picture somewhat. Limited remains of man himself survive from those times — which perhaps explains the importance attached to those specimens that are preserved. Although not directly associated with the Zambezi, the so-called Broken Hill man is undoubtedly of interest as a representative of Stone Age times.

Homo rhodesiensis, as he is more correctly called, was probably a Middle Stone Age man of the Neanderthal type, a lineage that did not give rise to modern man for it apparently died out. There has been some confusion over the age of this fossil which was discovered in a cave some 30 m below the surface during mining operations at Broken Hill (now Kabwe) in central Zambia in 1921. The fossil is variously said to be 30 000, 40 000 and 60 000 years old, while a more recent finding suggests an older date of 110 000 years.[11]

The nearly complete skull presents a remarkably primitive appearance and graphically illustrates the great changes in *Homo sapiens*, even in as short a period as 100 000 years. The skull is unusually large; behind massive eyebrow ridges lies a low forehead. In the side of the skull is a small rounded hole which could have been made by a wooden spear, for example. We cannot say that the man died of this injury for he certainly lived for at least a short while after it.[12] The teeth are also particularly large and, interestingly, all show severe signs of decay.[13]

Clearly, this African Neanderthal had not yet learnt a habit recently proved to be common among his contemporaries in Stone Age southern Europe. There, two American researchers have been studying the teeth of ten such individuals. The presence of grooves on the side of the teeth strongly suggests that these early men were no less addicted to the use of toothpicks than we are today![14]

In many localities along the river, stones and rocks have acquired a remarkable — and sometimes beautiful — varnish-like finish, commonly, and mistakenly, called a patina. Strictly speaking, the word patina implies a process of chemical change that takes place *within* a given surface. The 'desert varnish' that gives rise to the shiny surface is not that. Rather, it is an accretion or addition to the original surface: a brilliant polish, giving a depth and lustre to the stone's appearance. It also adds the softness of subtle colours, with pale browns and vivid orange fading into hues of luminous rusty reds. Stone tools often acquire this same varnish and a locality especially well known for this phenomenon is the river valley gravels in the vicinity of Victoria Falls.

As early as 1905, the brilliance of the varnish on tools in this area was attracting attention and it became the subject of considerable interest. Early investigations eventually concluded that the varnish comprised a smooth layer of silica deposited on the rock in the form of chalcedony and was the result of biological, chemical and capillary action. It was believed that low humidity for long periods each year may also have had an effect on the rate and how the varnish formation actually took place.[15]

Today, this view is no longer accepted. Modern research has shown that the varnish is not made up of layers of silica and is not dependent on low humidity for its formation. Instead, the coating consists of clay minerals, iron and manganese oxides as well as trace elements. It occurs in many climatic environments but its formation seems most favoured in deserts and semi-arid areas.[16]

Desert varnish is a well-known phenomenon which occurs worldwide and the possibilities it offers for establishing the age of artefacts has not been overlooked. A group of researchers in California has recently been able to date the carbon that forms part of the minute mass of the varnish itself. Although successful, the method has two disadvantages: first, it cannot be applied to landforms or cultural artefacts beyond the limit of the radio-carbon method, which is just over 50 000 years. Although a long time, this span is not really significant when considering the whole of the Stone Age, nor when examining landforms, for example. A second drawback is that the amount of organic matter present in rock varnish is very small indeed, forming less than 1% by mass. For this reason, large areas are needed for a successful test, anything between 0,5 m^2 and 2 m^2.[17]

A more sophisticated test has, however, been developed by the same team of researchers. Called the cation-ratio dating test, it is based on the differences in the rates at which minor chemicals are leached out of rock varnish, some of which can be readily analysed by X-ray emission techniques. This test not only covers a much greater span of time but requires nothing like the same quantities of material for testing purposes.[18]

Armed with this exciting technique, David Whitley, one of the people involved in developing the test, visited southern Africa in 1988. In America, in the Mojave Desert, Dave and his colleagues were able to establish dates for 13 rock engravings.[19] His hope is to date rock engravings and Stone Age tools in southern Africa in the same way as he has been able to do in America.

The art of making Stone Age tools has been rediscovered; in some American universities, such a skill forms part of an archaeological undergraduate course. A professor responsible for such courses happened to notice that he could tell apart tools made by those students who were right-handed and those who were not. In this simple observation lies a fascinating tale.

Man, the human animal, is the only species on earth exhibiting a preferential right-handedness. Right-handed individuals make up about 90% of our population and the characteristic is one that seems to be genetically based. Our nearest relatives, the chimpanzees, exhibit more or less equal numbers of left- and right-handed individuals.

Given our antecedents, it appears then that we must once have come from equal left- and right-handed stock. If that is so and as we are 90% right-handed now, the great question is, when did the change take place?

Scientists have been trying to answer this question for decades and there has been much speculation based mostly on rock paintings and skull injuries to hunted animals. Our talented professor, however, may be the man with the answer. Having satisfied himself and others that he could indeed tell apart tools from left- and right-handed people, he then, over a period of seven years, carried out an extensive study of stone tools found in Kenya and in Spain. The tools he examined covered a range in time from 1,9 million to about 300 000 years ago.

Nicholas Toth's findings suggest that somewhere between 1,9 and 1,4 million years ago, the critical change took place. In that time span, there was profound lateralisation of the human brain and our species moved from being equally left- and right-handed to mostly right-handed.

The implications of this discovery are fascinating, for the right hand is controlled by the left side of the brain, the same side that controls speech and language and logic. And this, of course, begs the question — did the development of logic and language, for instance, lead to a domination by the left side of the brain which was partly manifested in right-handed-ness? Or did the need for greater precision and skill in tool-making and tool-using lead by chance to the domination of the right hand, and con-sequently the development of the left brain, through evolutionary selec-tive pressures?[20]

As a coincidental aside, it is interesting to note that new fossil skeleton finds from East Africa suggest that either two hominid species were coexisting or abrupt changes took place in the size and anatomy of our ancestors somewhere between 1,8 and 1,6 million years ago. It seems that *Homo habilis* was much less human and more like an ape than was originally thought and certainly very different from *Homo erectus* — our immediate predecessor — who appears in the fossil record only some 200 000 years later.[21]

To add further to the complexity of our palaeolithic past, mention must be made of another recent and thought-provoking discovery. Molecular biology has made such strides that it is now possible to examine and compare the DNA in cell nuclei. A characteristic 'signature' can be read and this can be used to determine how closely related two specimens might be. For example, this 'signature' has allowed biologists to verify the time of divergence of apes and humans and has shown when other groups of mammals, including horses and donkeys, lions and domestic cats diverged from common ancestors.[22]

Following the mitochondrial DNA trail of *Homo sapiens sapiens,* re-searchers have concluded that we are all descended from a single African female — whom they have christened Eve — who lived between 285 000 and 143 000 years ago. Given our present bigger and better brains, this has enormous implications for the significance of, and the way we inter-pret, the various divisions within the Stone Age.

The scientists involved in this remarkable work, which is rapidly gaining widespread acceptance, stress that Eve was not the only woman alive during her time. She was merely the only woman of her age whose descendants have included some females in every generation since.[23]

Evidence of Stone Age man's occupation of the Zambezi's valley occurs sporadically throughout its length with areas of local concentration. These reflect as much the opportunities for sampling as the actual distribution of population. Nevertheless, Early Stone Age evidence is rare, occurring almost exclusively in the vicinity of Victoria Falls and in the Gwembe Valley. This is probably because there were relatively few such people and it made more sense to live in the cooler climate of the highveld, where game was abundant, as opposed to the hot and uncomfortable valleys.

In contrast, Middle Stone Age sites are common along the entire length of the river and even the hot valleys have their share. This, suggested Professor Bond, is because populations had grown, but the mode of life remained unchanged. Groups of pre-historic man lived as hunter-gatherers and, like such people all over the globe, they had areas or territories that they exploited. Sooner or later, even a primitive population can fill all the available space and soon marginal areas begin to be utilised.[24]

Late Stone Age sites are abundant, a fact due both to their relative recency and to much larger populations. Numerous sites have been recorded from many points along the river although in the upper reaches, in Barotseland for example, they tend, as with all Stone Age sites, to occur close to rapids, because of the abundant stone there.

This does not mean that man lived only where the raw material for his tools could be found. In many cases he carried suitable rock for considerable distances and examples of 16 km, 25 km and as great as 65 km have certainly been established.[25]

Thanks to the generosity of my good friend Paul Connolly and his company Canoeing Safaris, I had the experience of travelling by canoe for several hundred kilometres down the Zambezi. I took with me a list of known Stone Age sites on the southern bank of the river between Kariba and Kanyemba. There were fewer than 20 of them. Whenever convenient, I spent a few moments searching for more, and easily and quickly found four new ones. This fact reflects not my skills, but the great abundance of such sites and the lack of resources to seek and record them.

Although, in one sense, we are all descendants of these Stone Age men, suprisingly few people in southern Africa are aware of the much more interesting fact that the immediate, lineal descendants of the Stone Age people still live and are known locally as the Bushmen or the San.

Before the great Iron Age migrations, the whole of southern, central and eastern Africa was inhabited by hunter-gatherers known as the Khoesan. (Note that this word refers to a language complex. It is sometimes spelt

Khoisan but this is an outdated spelling, Khoe being phonetically more correct.) Survivors of the Khoesan still live today and we know them now as either the Khoe (Hottentots) or the San (Bushmen). The San are the living descendants of Stone Age man and, in certain parts of southern Africa, were still making stone tools as recently as perhaps 200 or 300 years ago.[26] The San are also believed to be responsible for much, but not all, of the magnificent rock art that abounds in the region.

Rock art falls into two distinct categories: engravings, which are cut into the rock with sharp stones, and paintings. Unlike rock artworks in Europe, none here occur deep in caves, beyond the reach of sunlight — so all are subject to weathering. The oldest dated rock paintings in southern Africa are those in the Apollo II cave in Namibia. They were painted about 26 000 years ago. Because paintings in southern Africa fade, there is no reason to suppose that the longest surviving picture dates the first appearance of rock painting. More probably, the picture is much younger than the art itself, which some believe in southern Africa may be as old as 50 000 years.[27] Others support less ancient origins and prefer to equate the emergence of such art to the beginning of the Late Stone Age, not more than 30 000 years ago.

Along the Zambezi, rock art is scarce. There are a few rock engravings on the Zambezi/Congo watershed in the Mwinilunga District and also in the Zambezi Valley between Kariba and Feira. Paintings are totally absent in the Kalahari sand country of western Zambia where rare rock outcrops are unsuitable. Along the remainder of the river there are very few paintings, if any. This may reflect the point made by Professor Bond about the Stone Age people who had no reason to live in the hot and uncomfortable valley of the Zambezi until relatively recent times.

Khoesan life and history were radically altered by Bantu-speaking peoples who came from the north. The word Bantu comes from the stem of the word for 'people', which in most languages is 'ntu' or something similar. As the Bantu-speakers expanded into their present range, so the Khoesan were displaced, absorbed into the new populations or annihilated. They survived longest in places where the Bantu preferred initially not to go and so are still found in the great sand reaches of the Kalahari where their populations are actually increasing, although their traditional way of life is rapidly disappearing.

Along the Zambezi, therefore, there is little room now for the San and it is only in that portion where the river crosses the Kalahari sands, in western Zambia, that these direct descendants of the Stone Age are still found at all. There, small groups of Hukwe San still live a hunter-gatherer life but a life that is rapidly being changed through contact with Bantu-speaking people and Western influences.[28]

Although the names we have for the different Stone Ages are merely convenient labels for comparatively distinct portions of one continuum, the same cannot be said of the Stone Age and the Iron Age: they do not form a continuum. The transition is abrupt. The Iron Age represents a totally different technology and a culture belonging to an entirely different people.

What do we mean when we talk of an Iron Age culture and what are its essential characteristics? In southern Africa it is said to mean the culture of a food-producing, probably Bantu-speaking people, which was imported into the region as a fast developing but alien entity and which is marked by certain distinguishing characteristics. These were the possession of stock; agriculture; living in villages consisting of semi-permanent dwellings; the technology for smelting and manufacturing iron implements and the making of a characteristic style of pottery.[29]

Iron Age archaeology is a vigorously dynamic subject and some have questioned these assumptions. It is possible, for example, that a small number of stock, probably sheep or goats, had been introduced into southern Africa before the arrival of Early Iron Age Bantu-speakers, through Late Stone Age people, some of whom also used and made pottery. However, the Bantu-speaking newcomers most certainly knew how to work iron and copper and they did make and live in thatched, pole and mud huts with dagga (mud and straw) floors.[30]

Where did these Bantu-speaking people come from and why did they move? This has been the subject of much speculation and investigation and only in relatively recent times has a fairly coherent picture emerged. The Bantu-speaking people who now occupy most of southern, central and eastern Africa came originally from the western side of the continent, probably from a region near present-day Cameroon, in a movement that started between 2 000 and 4 000 years ago.

The cause of their geographical spread is hard to determine but there are at least two suggestions. It is well known, for example, that the Sahara had been much more savanna-like than it is today, and therefore probably supported relatively large populations. Between 4 000 and 6 000 years ago it became increasingly arid with the result that large numbers of people would have been driven southwards, compelled to find new places to live.

A second reason has to do with increasing productivity of agricultural methods. At least one authority believes that improved agricultural techniques for growing yams, sorghum and millet and making use of oil palms fuelled a population expansion that in turn led to the gradual diffusion of Bantu-speaking people first towards the east and then in a southerly direction across the African continent.[31]

It was once thought that the possession of iron-making technology may have been at the root of this expansion but evidence shows large-scale farming existed before there were iron-making skills.[32]

So where, then, did iron smelting come from? One view is that iron technology diffused out of the region of modern Egypt, probably from the

PRECEDING PAGE
Lozi children stand and wonder at the photographer's fascination with the Zambezi's evening light.

ABOVE
A moth from the Zambezi's valley — one of many species yet to be named and identified.

RIGHT
A young green pigeon (Treron calva).

centre of Meroe on the Nile in Sudan, about 800 BC. However, recent evidence suggests that, much earlier than this date, there was a well-established iron smelting culture living to the south-west of Lake Victoria in modern Tanzania. Dr D.W. Phillipson, for example, considers this as evidence that the invention of the skills necessary for working iron is probably indigenous to Africa and not 'imported'.[33] This is a contentious view, however. Some claim that the Lake Victoria dates will be proved wrong, while others speak of iron-working skills reaching West Africa from the northern coast, near Carthage.

The precise routes by which Bantu-speakers spread through the continent are the subject of continuous debate and are far from settled or agreed upon. We can say, however, that Early Iron Age Bantu-speakers were established in Natal by AD 250 and in Zimbabwe by AD 300, and had passed through Botswana as early as AD 350.[34] The possible manner of their arrival is a fascinating story.

The early Bantu-speaking people, originating in the west of Africa, approached the obstacle of the great equatorial forests in two different ways. Some probably passed round to the north of them, swinging south on the eastern side and entering the area we call East Africa. Others may have moved into and through the forest areas in a southerly or south-easterly direction, coming from the forest fringes, certainly from tsetse fly infested areas.

It may have been this division that accounts for the present-day distinction between the Bantu languages spoken in eastern and southern Africa, and those spoken elsewhere. Research has shown that this distinction is extremely old and that the Western Bantu-speakers occupied the equatorial forests long before the Eastern Bantu-speakers spread onto the savannas of eastern and southern Africa. The distinction is important because today archaeologists speak of Eastern and Western-speaking Bantu — a concept quite different from the ideas of eastern and western 'streams'.[35]

In describing the occupation of southern Africa, most archaeologists speak of 'streams' as a means of splitting up into smaller units the broad movement of Eastern Bantu-speaking, Early Iron Age people who settled in the subcontinent. For example, Dr Phillipson names two streams, the eastern and the western. Both groups are Eastern-speaking Bantu and are divided, rather confusingly, into eastern and western streams to indicate the routes through which they penetrated the eastern and central part of the southern continent.

Phillipson's western stream Bantu-speakers share with the eastern stream the same language and distant ancestry in Cameroon or Niger, but in the immediate past, prior to their appearance in central and southern Africa, came from the forests of the north and west, not from the open savannas of the east. These people, says Phillipson, were agriculturists who, although they possessed stock in the form of sheep and goats, are unlikely to have had cattle, because of the presence of tsetse fly in the areas from which they had recently arrived.[36]

According to Phillipson, the vanguard of this western stream may have been responsible for the early introduction to the western and southern Cape of sheep and pottery. Remains of both are found at archaeological sites that date from the 1st century of the Christian era. However, as already mentioned, others believe that the introductions so far south, so early, must have been through the agency of Stone Age pastoralists. The point has yet to be resolved.

Professor Huffman follows Phillipson's stream idea and has adapted it by dividing the eastern stream into two parts, both having their origins in eastern Africa but penetrating the southern part of the continent as two separate entities. The movement implied by these streams must not be thought of as a mass migration but rather as a steady but slow movement of people from a point of common origin.

Of Huffman's two eastern streams, one follows an essentially coastal route, halting in the vicinity of modern Natal, the southern limit of cereal production. The other took an inland route through Malawi and the western side of Mozambique, probably following the Zambezi westwards as far as Victoria Falls. Typically, according to Professor Huffman, the eastern stream were agro-pastoralists who may have practised a patrilineal system and arranged their dwellings according to a particular pattern.[37]

There are other views, of course. Dr Jim Denbow, an archaeologist who has worked extensively in Botswana, believes that both eastern and western stream were matrilineal when they first came to southern Africa. He believes that they remained so until they grew rich in cattle. It was this wealth that led, from as early as AD 750, to the emergence of the male-dominated patrilineal system of inheritance.[38]

In southern and central Africa, the Iron Age is traditionally divided into two portions, known as the Early and the Late. The division between the two does not take place everywhere at the same time, but it is generally agreed to have been completed between AD 1000 and AD 1200. The greatest single indicator of this transition is the occurrence of regionally separate but simultaneous events in the ceramic record — the pottery record at many archaeological sites shows significant and abrupt changes. Numerous attempts have been made to explain this marked discontinuity and much controversy has been caused.

One current, and novel, suggestion relies on a proposed intrusion or series of intrusions from the Western Bantu-speaking area at about the turn of the millennium. Moving eastwards from the vicinity of the Congo and Zaïre, these population movements set in motion a domino effect so that, like the hunter-gatherers they once usurped, the Early Iron Age

Eastern-speaking Bantu settlers were either absorbed or annihilated, or moved on.

'Moving on' invariably meant moving east or south, which would have caused a gap in the pottery record. These initial moves may have set in motion an entire series that would eventually have resulted in a major redistribution of peoples throughout the subcontinent. Migration hypotheses such as this have never been popular with archaeologists as a whole but it remains to be seen if an idea can be produced that better fits the facts currently known.

Evidence to support invasions of Western Bantu-speakers in explaining the division between the Early and Late Iron Age comes from very marked differences between the Western and Eastern Bantu-speaking cultures. Apart from speaking a fundamentally different language, Western Bantu-speaking colonists, being matrilineal, followed a different method of kinship succession. They were without large numbers of cattle and arranged marriages differently, accepting service instead of the payment common among Eastern Bantu-speakers. Perhaps because of a reduced dependence on cattle, the Western Bantu had a more diverse economy, incorporating fishing and hunting as well as root crop and grain agriculture.[39]

There are also marked differences in the way the two groups smelted iron, the craft that gave its name to this long period of time. The fundamentals remained the same and were followed by all metalsmiths, regardless of whether they worked in iron, copper, tin or, after about AD 950, gold.[40] The differences in iron smelting technique paralleled the two groups' differing views of procreation.

The matrilineal Western Bantu-speakers believed that in the act of procreation a man simply activated a woman who then carried out the remainder of the process on her own. Patrilineal people believed that after conception, a man had to continue to 'strengthen' the embryo. These ideas were repeated in the methods of smelting. Both groups saw the procreative symbolism of the bellows but the Western group, who considered the male's contribution as relatively unimportant, minimised the use of the bellows, relying instead on a very tall chimney and a natural draught. Eastern Bantu-speakers' techniques required a short chimney and relied heavily upon the use of bellows.[41]

I have seen a photograph of a particular Eastern Bantu furnace in which the close parallels between the role of the female and the production of iron were obvious. The low, squat furnace had two large, breast-like shapes incorporated as part of the superstructure while the symbolism of a single orifice into which the bellows were placed was obvious.

Metalsmiths from any cultural group in Africa were usually respected and feared and considered men of status and standing in the community, especially among Western Bantu-speakers.

Perhaps because of the link with the female and reproduction, two injunctions during smelting are common throughout Africa. One is an abhorrence of the presence of menstruating women and the other the requirement that individuals involved abstain from sex during the period of smelting.[42] Often, furnaces are in secluded places, outside the settlement, just as a woman is placed in seclusion when giving birth.

There are numerous accounts of the magical-ritualistic associations with smelting. One, common among the Tonga people of Zambia, is that a piece of afterbirth in the furnace will improve the smelting. Among people in Zimbabwe, it was widely believed that goat skin was the only proper leather from which bellows could be made. The very best bellows came from a goat that had been flayed alive and the most efficient instruments of all came from a goat that had survived such treatment all day until nightfall, a practice which, happily, was outlawed in 1897.[43]

This account emphasises the close association of Bantu-speaking peoples with goats. Also from Zimbabwe comes even more unusual evidence of this connection. There, among some of the people, it was the practice to delay naming children because child mortality was so high: unnamed, the child was not a 'person' and therefore the traditional grief demanded by a death was eliminated. During the nameless period, the child was carried on its mother's back, wrapped for protection — in a goat skin![44] Goats have probably criss-crossed Africa with their owners from earliest times. Their ability to acquire a level of immunity to the bite of the tsetse fly has added to their great value as domestic stock.

Early Iron Age and Late Stone Age peoples apparently coexisted in reasonable harmony for many centuries. Throughout the range of Iron Age sites there is abundant evidence of this: stone flakes and abandoned and broken stone tools are found in the village refuse and remains. Among the Stone Age sites can be found limited evidence of iron and pottery. Clearly, these two peoples lived in close association with each other.[45] There are reports from eastern Zambia that the San may have continued living there among the Iron Age villages until as late as the 17th century, a fact confirmed by both folk-memory and archaeology.[46]

Throughout southern Africa there is abundant evidence of this harmonious coexistence, the basis of which is easy to understand. The San were superlative hunters, had an outstanding knowledge of wild plants and were craftsmen in the making of stone tools. The Bantu-speakers had cattle and grew crops and probably took the San women as second and third wives.[47] Between the two groups there was an excellent basis for exchange and barter. This ought to have made it possible for San populations to flourish, yet there are relatively few about today (although their numbers are now increasing again).

I cannot say why this should be so, but I wonder whether part of the solution may not be found within the San themselves and the psychology of their situation. In many ways, it is a question of success or failure in adapting to change.

Specialists in hunting, some San may have been unwilling to foresake it for another skill — such as cattle keeping or agriculture — about which they knew nothing and at which others, the Bantu-speaking people, were already expert. Some of course, would have made the transition and gone on to become the pastoralist Khoe (Hottentots) we know today. Some would only make that transition once they came to realise that their way of life was threatened.

The threat to this wild food based lifestyle might have taken many centuries to appear and would only have followed so great an expansion of Iron Age populations that open, unoccupied land was significantly reduced. Then, the San would have seen their future threatened. By that time, however, they would have had little choice but to become part of the Iron Age community. The only alternative would have been to move to a 'refuge' area where there would be few people, high game concentrations and no competing San — and no such places existed.

It is remarkable how many San or Khoe words and genes are distributed through the Bantu populations of southern Africa. Not all peoples like to admit it but the San's genes are widely spread and the tongue-twisting clicks of their language are shared by many others.[48] I believe that this may be partly because the San, always relatively few in number, had been almost totally absorbed into the Bantu population, and that this had generally taken place where Bantu and San coexisted, during the Late Iron Age.

The Early Iron Age can be seen as a period of growth and consolidation in which cultures and traditions became established, sometimes over considerable areas. Slowly, small surpluses were acquired and trade began, as the following chapter shows. This trade was of two kinds: internal and mostly between villages, and external, reaching to the coast and beyond. Until recently, it was considered that trade alone, in gold, ivory, skins and iron, underlay the emergence of the great Late Iron Age states. Latterly it has been suggested that the creation of cattle wealth may also, in some cases, have been an important factor.[49]

Until fairly recently, it was the belief of many that the 1 800 years of southern Africa's Iron Age was largely a vacuum of time filled with little more than the directionless activities of agro-pastoralists. This is far from true: during that interval, a succession of powerful African states arose, each reflecting increasing wealth, some based initially on the ownership of cattle.

The first in this succession was Toutswe in eastern Botswana. Dating back to as early as AD 900, it was a substantial settlement of cattle-herding people. Perhaps not quite a 'state', Toutswe was a large central village with a number of surrounding subservient settlements under its suzerainty. Toutswe shows evidence of an economy based on cattle as well as signs of considerable cattle wealth. At Toutswe are found the best documented indications of a hierarchical settlement pattern, a theme that is embellished at later Iron Age sites.[50]

By AD 1300 the Toutswe site had been abandoned,[51] but well before that time, and perhaps contemporaneous with Toutswe, other settlements had been established. A cluster of these occurs near the junction of the Shashe and Limpopo rivers in the northern Transvaal. One, known today as K2, was large enough to enjoy a substantial trade in ivory and gold with the east coast.

In immediate succession came Mapungubwe, a short distance away and a direct continuum of the same tradition. Mapungubwe saw the establishment of an élite who took up residence on a walled hilltop. This is a vitally important development for it is the first evidence of an evolving ruling class. In this succession of major villages, evidence of ever greater wealth is apparent in at least two forms. Cattle numbers steadily increased and trade in ivory and gold, exchanged for exotic goods, evidently made a considerable contribution to the economy.

As we see in Chapter 13, Mapungubwe was abandoned by about AD 1270 and was succeeded by an African state, centred on Great Zimbabwe, which lasted from AD 1270 to 1450. The Zimbabwe culture represented a considerable degree of sophistication compared with the smaller entities that had preceded it; nevertheless, it was a continuation of the same evolutionary trend of an elevated royalty, a ruling élite and a hierarchical settlement pattern supported by a cattle economy and trade. This same trend continued in the Zimbabwe state's successors; the Mwene Mutapa empire, the Torwa state and Changamire's Rozvi kingdom, all of which are considered in some detail in Chapter 13.

The Iron Age chronology, briefly described above, refers only to the region to the south of the Zambezi. Clearly, however, the history of the Iron Age was not the vacuum many have been taught to believe. On the north side of the river, constant change with the infiltration of new people and new blood is the hallmark, at least of the Late Iron Age.

From the end of the first millennium onwards came waves of Western Bantu-speakers who engulfed, first, the western parts of Zambia and moved steadily eastwards, displacing, replacing or absorbing the Early Iron Age populations. Exactly how is not certain. It seems that small Western Bantu-speaking groups challenged and replaced existing rulers, dominating smaller tribes and coalescing them into larger groups. Their precise origins are uncertain but they definitely crossed over the Zambezi/Congo watershed.

In the following centuries there came from the north and west many of today's major tribes. The exact date of each arrival is, of course, uncertain, being based as much on oral tradition as on archaeology. Despite this, it is probable that the Ila-Tonga arrived from the north by 1500, inhabiting the Gwembe Valley and the heights to the north of it. At about the same time the Maravi were moving eastwards to their modern home in Malawi. The Luba people settled in the north-west of Zambia by the end of the 16th century and the Lozi into Barotseland by the middle of the 17th century. The Bemba followed into northern Zambia, perhaps 100 years later, and the well-known Lunda empire, not adjacent to the Zambezi but near its watershed, was settled in eastern Katanga by the mid-1750s. The Late Iron Age on the north side of the river saw a constant succession of new peoples and was a time of great change and, perhaps, conflict.[52] The Lozi controlled a substantial part of the Upper Zambezi for nearly 300 years. The headwaters formed part of the Lunda and Luba states which, between them, dominated the area for more than 400 years.[53]

The cause of these extensive and significant second millennium migrations of Western Bantu-speakers has not accurately been determined. Many suppose it was due to improved agricultural techniques and new food plants becoming available (see Chapter 11), which led to abundant food and perhaps more rapidly increasing populations. The migrations could also be due to escape from conflict — much the same as the Mfecane described in Chapter 2 — although this seems unlikely.

The Late Iron Age along the central and southern reaches of the Zambezi saw enormous conflict and bloodshed, much of which forms the subject of Chapter 13. In the 19th century the Lozi kingdom fell into foreign hands, the once great state of Mwene Mutapa was controlled by a Portuguese puppet and Changamire's great state was toppled by rampaging Ngoni. By the middle of the 19th century the peace and tranquillity of 1 500 years of Iron Age was at an end.

As we saw in Chapter 2, the Mfecane sent several waves or groups of Ngoni people northwards through Mozambique and Zimbabwe in the 19th century. Their destructive effect is difficult to ascertain precisely but they brought about the downfall of the Changamire empire — which may already have been rent by succession disputes. One claim is that a Ngoni group brought Changamire to battle and, on defeating him, flayed him alive on a high hill known as Thaba zi ka Mambo.[54]

Of interest to me is the manner in which one group of Ngoni is said to have crossed the Zambezi. It is widely known that under their chief Zwangendaba, they accomplished this on 20 November 1835 in the vicinity of Kanyemba. The date of the crossing is accurately fixed by the occurrence of an eclipse and the fact that the chief's wife was so frightened by it that she was prematurely delivered of her son.[55]

What is less well known are the fascinating details of the story. For example, according to one account the water had been divided on being struck by the staff of the spirit medium![56] Others say it was Zwangendaba himself who struck the water with a spear, whereupon it miraculously parted for him to take his men across dryshod.[57] Now that's a story we've all heard before and I wonder at its repetition in Ngoni oral history. Missionary influence? Perhaps; what else could it be?

7 Beads, Bangles and Barter

IF we could view the Early Iron Age landscape through which the Zambezi flowed we would be surprised at its many differences compared with today.

The obvious things would be gone, of course: the towns and cities, the roads and bridges, the airports, pylons and dams. The rectilinear shapes of monotonous greens would be replaced by a natural mosaic of trees and grass. There would be far more trees than now and settlements would be hard to find. An occasional large village, perhaps, with several smaller villages in the same area; a handful of thatched huts surrounding an open space of bare ground, the hub of a radiating complex of ribbon-thin paths that are soon lost in the distance. Nearby would be much smaller fields than those we are accustomed to. Millet and sorghum, not maize, would be standing on tall stems inside a surrounding palisade of thorn-tree crowns — the only protection against animals far more numerous and widespread than today. As a token of resistance and protection against such marauders, a small boy might be sitting in the shade of a tiny, open-sided thatched square that leaned on higgledy-piggledy legs on a convenient mound or an abandoned ant-heap.

Within the village itself, everything would be made of natural materials — the pots for drinking, storing and cooking, the thatching, hut walls, grinding stones, wooden headrests and gameskin covers that added comfort to the night; the drums, xylophones and gourds that helped make music and the seats carved from a single piece of wood on which the elders or honoured guests sat. Nature provided all that was needed, it was there to pick up, cut or shape — all, that is, except iron.

Iron provided a better means to cut, to dig and to hunt but it possessed a unique characteristic that, in a fundamental way, set it apart from all other materials used by people of the time: the means of its production were not universally available.

Iron smelting required a skill and a technology known to relatively few. Possibly to protect that knowledge it came to be surrounded with magic and mystical beliefs which had the effect of making it more difficult for the common man to reach, to understand and to learn about.

Conversely, those who owned or controlled the smelting of iron acquired power as a result of their knowledge. They possessed something that others wanted and were thus in a position to give it in exchange for a service or item they required. I can think of only one other item, salt, that offered such a powerful incentive for internal trade between villages, separate communities and tribes.

I suggest that the knowledge of iron smelting in a society whose needs were otherwise totally and equally met by nature may well have done more to encourage the concept and practice of trading than any single other item, including salt, for which there were many alternative sources and methods of extraction.

In the natural world of the Iron Age, housing, clothing, food, animals, skins, all came from the same source and all were of the same colours, the natural hues of nature. How could such people have resisted the glass beads of early commerce, in their blue, red, black, white and other colourful varieties? How could they not have reacted to the opalescent depths of the tinged glass whose reflective qualities could otherwise be seen elusively only on the surface of ponds and puddles? What must it have been like to hold in their hands, for the first time, the blue of the sky, the ember of the fire or the translucence of water?

It is small wonder that such trinkets became the mainstay of centuries of exchange. After all, what is value? A practical application in performing a task is only part of the answer. The rest lies in the unquantifiable realms of aesthetic appeal, of desire, want and the satisfaction of rarity and ownership. Value is what something is worth to someone. So it is possible to understand how glass beads, comparatively worthless to the manufacturer, could have enjoyed a value beyond words to a person from the Iron Age of central Africa.

Although the Zambezi did not prove to be the highway to the heart of Africa in the manner that Livingstone had hoped, it certainly was a route to the interior. Along its course, tribes and nations have, since earliest times, been involved in a fascinating network of exchange, not only between themselves, but with the outside world.

I have made reference elsewhere to the Eurocentric world in which we live — a world that would happily leave us with the impression that nothing much took place along the Zambezi or the African coast until the Portuguese arrived. A little research shows that this is far from the truth and reveals an unexpected world of anecdote and interest.

Perhaps the oldest reference to Africa and its coast is a surprising story of possible circumnavigation achieved in a three-year marathon by a small group despatched by the Egyptian king Necho in 610 or 600 BC. The tale contains a statement by the men that, when sailing west, they had the sun on their right hand.[1] To people in the northern hemisphere who have never lived south of the Cancer Tropic and who do not understand the celestial mechanics of the sun's annual migration, such an experience would be unthinkable.

It is on the basis of one's willingness to accept or reject the group's statement that their credibility is usually founded. Personally, I do accept it and the reason I do so is this. Assuming that those early sailors did not understand the principles that govern the sun's movement in the sky, there is no reason for them to have known that such a reversal as they described was actually possible. To me, their accurate reporting of an event so strange and inexplicable that they could not understand it lends considerable credibility to their claims.

An ancient Arabian document known as the Periplus of the Erythraean Sea, a book of instructions for Arab pilots sailing off the east coast of Africa, was written in about AD 60. Some scholars seem willing to accept that it speaks authoritatively of places we know as Dar es Salaam, Bagamoyo and possibly Kilwa.[2]

The evidence is hazy but there appears to be a strong suggestion of a string of Arab trading posts gradually extending southwards along the east coast with the occasional spurt of growth reflecting a wave of immigration. This happened during the 8th century, for example.

There is a much repeated story that dates from somewhere between the 8th and the 12th century of a boat from Mogadishu travelling along the coast and being caught in a storm which blew it far off its course. As a result, it landed at a place called Sofala or beyond, some 250 km south of the Zambezi mouth. There its crew heard tales of gold inland, which eventually led to the establishment of a trading post, perhaps at Sofala, or possibly further south, beyond the Save River near Inhambane. There is every reason to believe this account for it is supported, as we shall see, by archaeological evidence.

Several Arab geographers wrote extensively about the coast, and from their works comes confirmation that Arab occupation there began in about AD 740. One of these reporters, Ali Masudi, completed a 30-volume work published in AD 947. From its pages comes a much clearer picture of the extent to which the coast was known and the type of trade that was carried on there.[3]

Madagascar was well known even at that early date; it had apparently been seized by Muslims at the same time as the capture of Crete, in AD 674. North of the Zambezi and south of it along the coastal plain as far as Sofala, there lived the Zanj, possibly a reference to the native Bantu-speaking people. The surroundings of Sofala itself were known to be fertile and produced an abundance of gold. In the hinterland behind there lived a people whom Masudi called the Waq-waqs, a name commonly believed to refer to the San.

Al Idrisi, who lived between 1100 and 1166, has been described as the most brilliant Arab geographer of all. He too wrote extensively about the eastern coast of Africa. Although he did not visit it himself, he often despatched special messengers to gather information for him. Again, there are references to Sofala and its gold and to the Zanj people whose principal products were game skins and iron. Indian traders are mentioned and it seems that China, at a time of rebellion and trouble at home, was also trading with the east coast of Africa and with the many islands off the shore.[4]

A succeeding Arab chronicler was Ibn Batuta, who in the mid-14th century travelled down the coast himself, although no further south than Kilwa. Reporting both on what he saw and what he heard, he reinforced the stories linking gold and Sofala.[5] To Batuta is attributed one of the few passages that could possibly be construed as a reference to Great Zimbabwe, which was at its height between 1300 and 1450.

The passage states that the gold dust went to Sofala from Yufi, in the country of the Limis, which was one month's journey from the port. 'Yufi was said to be one of the largest negro towns, and its ruler exercised the widest power. It could never be visited by white men, for they would be killed long before they approached the town.'[6]

There has been much disagreement over exactly what is meant by the obscure names in the text, for they are not otherwise known. There have been some suggestions that Batuta was, in fact, referring to a place in Niger. Others have pointed out that he is normally very accurate with his distances, which is taken to suggest that he was so in this case also. If that is correct, archaeology knows of no other more likely place in the region to which the description might apply than Great Zimbabwe. In any case, it would be ridiculous to imagine gold from Niger being carried to Sofala for the sake of port facilities.

The purpose of this extensive review of early coastal history is to establish several important points. Historical records did not start with the Portuguese. Arab people knew of the whole coast, the people and its products from earliest times. Arabs were living on the east African coast from about AD 740. Not very much after that date, Sofala or ports to the south of it were established. Trade was the object and was linked to the hinterland to which the Zambezi was unquestionably a major route.

The volume of traffic may have been considerable. Three Arab chroniclers wrote about the coast in the years between AD 950 and AD 1350. Sofala, south of the Zambezi mouth, and its gold were the subject of comment and speculation. It is clear too that the coastal traffic was not confined to traders from Arabia or the Middle East alone but also from India, China and Indonesia.

The last may surprise many people, as it did me, but there is apparently little doubt that the island of Madagascar is a mix of Indonesian and African blood and heritage. For example, 93% of the basic vocabulary today consists of Indonesian words although Bantu-speaking people migrated to the island in steady waves from about the 9th to the 16th century.[7]

There are many ideas about the origins of Malagasy. Of the explanations currently on offer, one links Madagascar's historical origins to the 8th century rise of the Sumatra empire. This produced a nation of skilled navigators who established an east-west seasonal trade between Africa and the Far East. As a trade, it was based on coastal ports, the most southerly of which could have been Sofala.

The demise of this association was partly brought about by the collapse of the empire and partly by the arrival on the African coast of the first Muslims in the 8th century. They ousted the Sumatrans, who fled to inhabit the Comores and Madagascar.

Evidence to substantiate this interesting assertion is centred mostly on Madagascar and is therefore not part of the Zambezi story. However, sewn boats and canoes with outriggers found on the coast are both strong evidence of Indonesian influence. So too is the growing of wet rice in Madagascar.[8]

I mentioned that there had been extensive coastal trade with China, and if there be any doubt about this, an amusing anecdote may help to put your mind at rest. There are many references to Chinese travel to Africa, which may have reached a peak in the first millennium. The scanty detail makes it tantalisingly difficult to pinpoint visits, especially in the earlier times. Despite this, it seems that Chinese made direct visits to the east African coast in the 7th, 8th and 9th centuries and we have some detail of a visit to Malindi, near Mombasa, in 1060.[9]

Obviously profitable and enduring relations had been established by Africans with their Eastern friends, for, in 1414, the citizens of the small town of Malindi sent as a present to the Chinese Emperor, accompanied by their ambassadors, one giraffe![10] This took place durng a period of intensive Chinese maritime expeditions: in the years between 1417 and 1431, three major fleets visited the eastern coast of Africa, the earliest one returning the African ambassadors! Of interest is the enormous size of the Chinese fleets, one report describing 62 vessels carrying 37 000 soldiers.[11]

The implications are clear: the eastern coast of Africa was not an isolated entity, existing in a commercial and historical vacuum, but a willing and able participant in a vibrant, energetic trade that embraced not only the coast itself but was trans-oceanic in extent and had probably been so for nearly 1 000 years before the arrival of the Portuguese in 1498.

Given this, who were the traders, what were the goods being traded and how was the trade effected? None of these questions can be answered with complete accuracy but much has been elucidated and we can perhaps make intelligent guesses regarding the remainder.

At one end of the scale were the Bantu-speaking Iron Age immigrants who had established themselves during the first millennium in eastern, central and southern Africa. At the other end were the consumers as far afield as China, Indonesia, India and the Middle East. Between them stood the middlemen. Precisely who these may have been we cannot exactly say. They may originally have been Sumatrans, as has been suggested, or, however unlikely, Indians, as another claims.[12] For most of the time and certainly in the 600 years before the advent of the Portuguese, they were probably people of Arab descent or association. Whoever they were, they were likely, because of their dominance at sea, to have held a position of strength or power on the coast.

Nothing I've read makes me think that *pure-blooded* Arabs are meant in this connection. The impression is that the terms Arab, Moor, Muslim and Mohammedan are all used loosely and interchangeably to mean, generally, a person who may or may not share Arab blood, who is essentially of a Swahili or Bantu-speaking culture and who has adopted the Muslim religion. These, in my understanding, were the people who established and ran, as middlemen, the trade networks of Africa.

Trade along the Zambezi probably began in the Iron Age and took two forms. The first we could call internal trade: the exchange or barter economy that existed between adjacent villages, chieftainships or tribal confederations within the continent. The other form of trade is external: usually long distance and involving the importation of exotic goods via the coasts. Examples will show that, just as the coast was part of a dynamic trading system, so were the distant parts of the hinterland involved much more than we might have thought.

The two kinds of trade are not separate activities, of course, and merge into each other so that they are difficult to distinguish. For example, there is evidence to show that goods acquired by external trade were often redistributed by the internal network, so that sea shells discovered in the Kalahari are not necessarily indications of direct trading links with the coast. Nevertheless, it is convenient to consider trade separately as internal and external.

There are numerous examples of internal trading in the Early Iron Age and some of the best are reported from sites near Victoria Falls. Here, at Kumadzulo were recovered, among other items, fragments of copper bars, pottery and a small piece of greenish glass, all of which dated from the 7th century.[13]

The copper is interesting because none occurs locally. The nearest known source is more than 100 km away at Hwange, in Zimbabwe, where the style of manufacture is far different from that found at the site. Copper bars of similar mould are known only from the well-known Katangan and Zambian deposits far to the north. It cannot be definitely said that this is where the copper came from, but we can conclude that it was imported into the region and probably from some distance away.

The same is true of the glass, which is considered to be a piece of crude window glass. Iron Age dwellings not having glass windows, this fragment is clearly ex-continental in origin. In its unbroken form, or as fragments, it could have been passed on from one person to another, finally coming to rest thousands of kilometres from the sea near Victoria Falls.

Several pieces of pottery were found at Kumadzulo. From their shape, style and pattern it is plain that they too had been traded, or were the substance of gifts, perhaps, although their origins were more local. This evidence, together with that of the glass and copper, demonstrates the existence, early on in the Iron Age, of internal trade and communication networks that extended locally and for considerable distances within Africa.

Other evidence of internal trading is found north of the Zambezi, on the Batoka plateau. On the cool and pleasant heights, isolated finds of cowrie shells at the base of the Kalundu mound again indicate internal trade at the time of the earliest period of settlement. Had larger quantities of shells been found one might have suspected large-scale direct trading, but their rare occurrence indicates they have arrived indirectly from the coast.[14]

The Batonga people were probably among the first of the Late Iron Age immigrants of about 1500 to be in the area still today. They occupied the land north of the Zambezi between the Kafue River in the east and Barotseland in the west. Research has shown that they eventually became well established as local middlemen in an extensive subsistence level trading network. They routinely dealt with about 30 different items which they exchanged with as many as ten groups of neighbouring people over distances approaching 500 km. Some of the items they regularly dealt in were salt, fish, ochre, hoes and bamboo shafts as well as a number of imported items.[15]

Obviously, trading was as natural a part of the African Iron Age as anywhere else in the world. The people understood its advantages and how to go about it. It was, therefore, a simple matter to adapt to different goods and different people when, from coastal ports, they first appeared, which we must assume would have been with the arrival of the first Swahili traders after AD 800.

It is apparent that the trading system originated on the coast, developed and progressed inland from there. A series of coastal bases were first established and, as the growing volume warranted it, so more were created further inland.

The obvious and earliest are the well-known coastal ports: Lamu, Malindi, Mombasa, Zanzibar and Kilwa. Much mention has been made of a port called Sofala — the name dates from the 8th century and means 'sandy shoal', which does not help fix the locality. We have already seen that a port of Sofala was established in the 8th century, together with another trading post to the south of it, Chibuene. It is possible that they were one and the same: the 8th century Sofala being the modern archaeological site of Chibuene while the 16th century references might mean the fishing village not far south of Beira.

Probably at different times all the ancient ports from Kilwa in the north to Chibuene in the south, including places such as Mozambique Island, Angoche and Quelimane, were involved in trade which drew extensively upon the Zambezi hinterland.

Chibuene is located about 5 km south of modern Vilancoulos in Mozambique and was first occupied in the late 8th or early 9th century. It appears to have been abandoned in the 13th century. Archaeological evidence from the site — Persian pottery, burnished bowls and glassware — underlines its trading nature and suggests, partly because of the time period it occupies, strong links to the K2 and Mapungubwe sites on the Limpopo, referred to in Chapters 2 and 6.[16]

Mapungubwe is not part of the Zambezi story, except distantly. However, I have included mention of Chibuene to emphasise again the extent and antiquity of the Arab coastal trade and to suggest that it was usual for the large African states to maintain trading contacts with the Indian Ocean.

On the Lower Zambezi today the towns of Sena and Tete dominate the river. It is generally said that they were founded by the Portuguese in the 1530s in response to the realisation that trade was not coming to them at Sofala and that they would have to go out and get it. I believe that this might be Portuguese history manipulation. There is strong evidence in the early Arab chronicles that the Zambezi had been navigated upstream for a considerable distance and that Arab towns had been established along its banks.

From the time of Al Idrisi onwards, about the middle of the 12th century, several Arab writers speak of towns on the Zambezi that were Arab trading posts. One, Seyouna, was said to be the capital of the land of Sofala and was located at the junction of what is assumed to be the Zambezi and the Shire, within sight of a high mountain. It is difficult to imagine how this could have been anywhere but at the site of the modern town Sena.

One can speculate that the locality described in about 1320 by Abu-el-Fida as Dendema might well have been Tete.[17, 18] If these suggestions are true then Tete and Sena, which the Portuguese claim they founded, had already been in existence for at least 200 years by then.

As interesting is the report that Arab boats sailed up the Zambezi for a distance equivalent to 500 km. This would have taken them to the mouth of Cahora Bassa Gorge and the impassable rapids in it (see Chapter 16).[19]

The persuasive circumstantial evidence of widespread Arab trading posts 400 km to 500 km up the Zambezi at least 200 if not 300 years earlier than is commonly said implies a much more sophisticated system and one

LEFT
The natural range of the whitenosed monkey touches only the most northern reaches of the Zambezi.

BELOW
Close encounters of the wild kind await those who venture through the wilderness areas of the Zambezi Valley.

PRECEDING PAGE
The state barge of the Lozi people,
carrying their leader the Litunga, sets
out on the annual journey of
Kuomboka from the inundated islands
of Barotseland's floodplains to the
mainland.

RIGHT
Bushbabies are still common along the
Zambezi, but near the source they are
trapped and taken as food.

BELOW
Maoma, the Lozi Royal Drums, usher
in the dawn and the day of the great
Kuomboka ceremony.

that was much better established than early Portuguese historians would have us believe. It also helps explain why the Moors were so successful, compared to the Portuguese, in the early days of their commercial rivalry, before the Portuguese used force.

The so-called Arab traders knew the African people, lived among them, identified with them and were part of them. Each understood the other and they had enjoyed several hundred years of, presumably, harmonious relations. The Portuguese lacked this experience and tact, as they found to their cost.

Within 100 years of their arrival in Mozambique, the Portuguese, ever in pursuit of Ophir, their fabled land of gold, copied the Moors and they too established distant trading centres which were intended to act as a magnet for trade and a collecting point where numerous small transactions could be consolidated.

Along the river, as we have seen, the Portuguese occupied former Arab settlements such as Tete and Sena but in the interior, with the permission of the appropriate chiefs, they established on the Zimbabwe plateau numerous small 'market villages' such as Dambarare, Bocuto, Chitomborwizi, Luanze, Masapa and Masekesa, otherwise known as Chipangura. These fairs, as they were known, suffered great fluctuations of fortune and were not always entirely successful. That they did not work was due more to the way the Portuguese conducted the policy than any flaw in the idea itself.

At the end of the 17th century, as Chapter 13 explains, the Portuguese were driven off the plateau by Changamire Dombo, at which time they opened the trading post at Feira and Zumbo at the Zambezi/Luangwa junction. These were maintained sporadically for nearly 200 years. Henceforth, with the exception of Chipangura, official Portuguese trading was restricted to the line of the Zambezi River. Evidently, however, the Portuguese were neither the first nor the only people to establish bases for trade so far up the Zambezi.

On a hot September afternoon, deep in the Zambezi Valley, my sons and I stared through the haze of heat at a cluster of baobab trees that crowned a low rise. Beyond them was another tree, some distance away, recumbent. Its massive grey bulk looked exactly like a sleeping cow, which may explain the name, for Ingombe Ilede means exactly that. The site is on a distinct 'S' bend in the Lusitu River which, in the rains, carries water into the Zambezi just a few kilometres away.

Ingombe Ilede is an extensive and most remarkable archaeological site. It was discovered in 1960 and investigations quickly revealed that it had been occupied twice. The first occupation was not especially noteworthy although it is thought to have lasted from the 7th or 8th century to the end of the 10th. The succession in that time is confused and difficult to follow. It is the second occupation that has caught the imagination of archaeologists.

Ingombe Ilede's occupation during the 14th and 15th centuries was dramatically different from the first. From this period, 11 richly decorated skeletons were discovered with abundant evidence of both wealth and trading. They wore ornaments of iron, copper and, in one case, gold. The copper had preserved several pieces of cotton cloth, most of which were of local manufacture but one particularly fine piece, if not local, may have come from India.

Other ornaments included sea shells, some with a backing plate of hammered gold, gold beads and tens of thousands of imported glass beads. In the graves were other items that showed the extent of internal trading for, in a region where no copper occurred, there were bundles of thick copper wire, bars of copper, cross-shaped copper ingots, wire drawing equipment as well as iron hoes and iron gongs.[20] Clearly, Ingombe Ilede was an important link in an extensive trade network that may well have included Great Zimbabwe and the copperbelt on the Zambezi/Congo watershed.

One discovery at Ingombe Ilede of particular interest was that of two amulet holders — the only ones of their kind reported from southern Africa. Professional opinion is that these holders were of a kind commonly worn by Arabs.[21]

Evidence from pottery and from the numerous finds of cast copper at the site links Ingombe Ilede strongly to the Urungwe area of the Zimbabwe plateau on the south side of the river. Urungwe is a well-known area for metal production and, along with the Zambia/Shaba copperbelt region far to the north, may well have been the source of the copper found at Ingombe Ilede.

Several interesting conclusions can be drawn from the evidence at Ingombe Ilede. The considerable quantity of exotic trade goods indicates that, from at least 1350 onwards, just as the Arab historians suggested, trade with the interior of Africa was well developed. The location of Ingombe Ilede near the banks of the Zambezi emphasises the idea of the river providing an arterial route to the interior, if not by water in the higher sections of the river, then on foot with the river in sight, perhaps.

Ingombe Ilede also clearly played a central role in the regional trade network which extended at least as far as the Zimbabwe plateau in the south and the central African watershed with its huge deposits of copper in the north.

These observations have led at least one researcher to suggest that Ingombe Ilede's rise to trading prominence and evident success may well have had an important part to play in the collapse of the Great Zimbabwe state. The penetration of the continent via the trade route of the Zambezi in the 14th century was so successful, argues Peter Garlake, that it may have gradually replaced the one along the Sabi River on which Great Zimbabwe's prosperity had depended.[22]

Great Zimbabwe virtually ceased to exist after 1450 and archaeologists have been at a loss to explain satisfactorily the event. Many possibilities have been suggested, ranging from disease to environmental collapse and political disintegration. One idea was that competition from Ingombe Ilede helped destroy Great Zimbabwe's economy and might have hastened its decline.

It seems much more likely, however, that Ingombe Ilede might have shared Great Zimbabwe's trade — not been a competitor for it. This suggestion is strengthened by the fact that its apparent decline seems to be contemporaneous with that of Great Zimbabwe.

Over the course of one and a half millennia, an amazing variety of items has been brought into and taken out of the lands of the Zambezi. Imported items include glass beads from India and to a lesser extent Indonesia. In the National Museum in Bulawayo is exhibited a brass cup, manufactured in India in about the 15th century. It was found in an ancient gold mine near the Angwa River, not too distant from where it flows into the Zambezi.

Sea shells, cowries mainly, glass, glassware and plate were other popular imports but undoubtedly the demand was greatest for cloth. It is possible that the weaving of cotton cloth along the Zambezi was taking place as early as the 13th century but dyeing techniques and skills lagged a long way behind weaving. This may be one reason why the brightly coloured imported cloths were in great demand. Local weavers were in the habit of unravelling the imported cloth and incorporating its coloured strands into work of their own which would otherwise have been the plain natural colour.[23]

Fireams were a highly coveted prize from the earliest date of their appearance in Africa and it was in exchange for these that the major trade goods changed hands.

The Portuguese made extensive use of the matchlock long after the flintlock was more generally popular. In Barotseland, for example, Lewanika still retained a matchlock in the 1880s which he was able to 'persuade' a passing traveller to exchange for a Martini-Henry!

The quality of firearms was often extremely poor and a cheap, Birmingham-made, 'female' trade gun (which got its name from early slaving days when it was exchanged for a woman) could be had for 7/6d in the 19th century. A 'male' London-made 'Tower' musket was far better quality and was a comparatively sound weapon, often surviving decades of use to become a priceless collector's piece today.[24]

Ivory and gold were the two biggest exports from Africa and the area of the Zambezi was no exception in this regard. The largest customer for ivory then and until 1960, at least, was India, and for good reason: only the ivory of Africa can be used for the making of bangles which have a special ritual significance in the marriage rites of Hindus. No one else is allowed to wear these items which are often cremated with the wearer. The ivory of the Indian elephant cannot be used because it is not thick enough.[25]

The Chinese were keen on importing ivory although, because of their sporadic links with the coast of Africa, China was probably not as consistent a consumer as India. Even so, there was a time when no Chinese official would dare appear in public unless he was carried in an ivory palanquin. These same people also had the unusual practice of burning ivory in their temples as an incense.[26]

Gold, certainly in the time of the Portuguese, was probably the most sought after commodity of trade. Little or no ancient mining took place in Zambia whose wealth is in copper, not gold. It was Zimbabwe, as rumour correctly told the avaricious Portuguese, that was the centre of the Zambezi's gold. Roger Summers has completed an exhaustive investigation of that country's gold production and his work paints a remarkable picture.

His research shows that the Early Iron Age miners were extraordinarily efficient at locating gold. So much so that in Zimbabwe between 1890 and 1899 when over 100 000 gold claims were pegged, almost all of them were found by following ancient diggings. Summers estimates that mining in Zimbabwe probably began in about AD 900, although there are different start dates for different areas. Over the period from then to 1890, he calculates, a total of between 567 and 709 tonnes of gold were extracted.[27]

Prior to the arrival of Portuguese traders in the 16th century, most gold production went to the Arab middlemen and the east coast. However, because of civil conflict within the country, there was a decline in Zimbabwean gold production just as the Portuguese arrived (see Chapter 13). Although mining recovered, gold production was subject to the constant vicissitudes of war and conflict. Overall, production figures fell.

Summers estimates that, before the Portuguese advent, Zimbabwe was producing and trading about 567 000 g to 850 500 g a year. This fell off dramatically from the 16th century, but even so the Moors continued to take the lion's share of production. By the end of the 1590s the Portuguese had traded only some 39 000 g, and in the following century, at 23 000 g had acquired even less. Evincing their better adapted trading methods and networks, the Moors consistently far outperformed the Portuguese efforts in the gold trade, right up to the 19th century.[28]

Among other items that regularly travelled the trade routes of the Zambezi were salt, ostrich feathers, game skins, smelted iron — which the Indians considered to be of exceptional quality — beeswax, copper, silver, rhino horn and, surprisingly enough, ambergris. This was found in considerable quantities on the shore of one of three islands at the mouth of the Sabi River where it reaches the coast, somewhat south of Sofala.[29] As Chapter 15 points out, slaves too became an increasingly important item of trade as the centuries passed.

The nature of trade was almost always barter, the exchange of goods. In some parts of Africa the cowrie shell served as a unit of currency but not in the hinterland of the Zambezi, although cowries were often highly valued items of exchange. Those shells that have been recovered there have been found in relative isolation and seem to be more items of curiosity or jewellery than symbols of an exchangeable currency.

In addition to cowries, conus and conch shells were also popular. Around the Zambezi they were mostly used as items of adornment: the upper portion of the shell was filed off and discarded; the base was the part retained and used. As an ornament, they were worn on the forehead or the arm and often confined only to chiefs. In Zimbabwe they were known as 'ndoro' and in Zambia as 'mpande'. One, in a gold setting incorporating a surround, probably of coloured glass, was given as a gift to the Mwene Mutapa king by Diogo Simoes in return for the Zambezi silver mines (Chapter 16).[30]

Where they were used as currency, their value tended to fluctuate wildly. In Uganda, for example, when the cowrie had only recently been introduced by traders and was still extravagantly valued, two shells would buy a woman. Quickly the currency devalued and by 1860, 2 500 were needed for a cow — and a woman was worth at least four or five cows. The shells remained currency in Uganda until 1901 when importation was stopped. By then, the shell was so devalued that 75 000, requiring seven men to carry them, were worth £5![31]

Trading under these circumstances would seem to be a highly profitable undertaking and, indeed, it often was. From the early 16th century figures of profits on goods imported from India by the Portuguese show that, in Sofala, the profit on cloth was anywhere between 12 and 17 times its original cost. Red beads could be exchanged for items worth 24 times their cost and gold was traded for between 10 and 15 times the value of the goods given in exchange. These figures are for the coast and may have been 20 times greater when the goods were traded again in the interior. It has been estimated, for example, that to purchase three pieces of calico, a miner might have to give as much as 285 g of gold which could take him an entire season to produce.[32]

While profits do seem to be extremely high, on occasion the costs could be so too. For example, Vasco da Gama's extraordinary voyage of discovery from Portugal via the east coast of Africa to India, between the years 1497 and 1499, achieved fame and success at incredible cost.

It is said that, after deducting all the expenses, the balance of income exceeded the total investment by 60 times, but such wealth came at a price. Da Gama had set out from Lisbon with 160 men. Only 55 survived the journey to see their homes again. The rest died of disease or in combat.[33]

There are few written records with details of the routes followed by traders in pre-Portuguese times. It seems reasonable to suppose, however, that if well-established tracks to the interior existed at all — and the extent of Arab trading activity suggests that they must have — then the Portuguese are likely to have followed them.

By the middle of the 16th century, reflecting the dominance of gold, the Portuguese were using four well-known routes onto the Zimbabwe plateau. One went west from Sofala, following the Buzi River, through the lands of the Manykia to Massekesa. Three others followed the Zambezi from Tete. One of these turned up the Mazoe River and reached almost to what is now Harare. A second scaled the escarpment of the Zambezi Valley, probably following the Musengedzi River, so that it emerged near modern Guruve (formerly Sipolilo). The third route continued up the Zambezi to the point where it begins to turn south, near Chirundu. From here, the Portuguese turned to the south-east, passing through Urungwe to the centre of the plateau near Chakari and the Zimbabwe midlands.[34]

The Portuguese crown attempted to maintain a monopoly of trade but was not successful. Much of the trade was carried out by private individuals who, because of the circumstances, seldom broadcast information about where they were operating or how they got there.

There is little doubt that the Luangwa was a major route into the central and north-western parts of Zambia but it seems that trade with the deep interior was largely indirect until relatively recent times. In 1862 at Sena, Senhor Isidore, who befriended David Livingstone during the Zambezi expedition, regularly sent parties of men to trade with Mzilikazi in south-western Zimbabwe.[35] No details of the route are given but we can guess that it might have followed the Zambezi. We know, for instance, that in 1867, in the Gwembe Valley two days' walk downstream from the Gwaai, a Portuguese trading post for ivory and slaves existed beside the Zambezi and may have been there for some time.[36]

External trade in Barotseland and the upper portion of the Zambezi remained indirect and probably linked more to the east coast than the west, at least until the Portuguese became established in Luanda in 1576. There are few records of early Portuguese contact with the hinterland but it seems reasonable to suppose that, as their influence expanded, that of the Swahili coast would have declined. Despite this, contacts with both coasts were maintained by the residents of central Africa's heartland.

As we saw in Chapter 3, Livingstone encountered far more evidence of trans-continental traffic than he might have liked. Silva Porto from Angola was trading firearms and slaves in the 1840s in Barotseland. Before him, da Silva Teixeira and Assumpcao e Mello had been trading in north-west Zambia and the higher parts of the Zambezi in the 1780s and 1790s (Chapter 17). The Kwena people in Botswana claim that they were in trade contact with the Portuguese (from Angola?) towards the end of the 18th century and the Ngwato say that they knew of white people at Lake Ngami long before Livingstone, in about 1820.[37]

In this chapter I have tried to show that, from earliest times, the Iron Age people who lived along the Zambezi were not isolated communities without trading contact. The Swahili Arabs were established on Africa's east coast by the 8th century and rapidly created a trade network that reached to the heart of the continent, whereby, directly or indirectly, goods flowed in two directions.

Evidently this trade was flourishing long before the Portuguese arrival and we have seen that the coast was a place of great trading activity, maintaining long-range contacts that spanned the entire Indian Ocean.

8 Kariba

OF the many early portents at the village of Binga, it was the rats that
were most dramatic: first in tens, then hundreds, finally in thousands. It was as if the fields themselves had come to life and had suddenly
started to ooze and flow in an undulating, brown and furry motion.
Always upwards, always away from the valley, the movement was not
a panic but an ordered retreat. Millions of rodents were leaving the fields
of the Batonga people, for something dramatic was happening in the lower
reaches of the valley.

On 2 December 1958, man had sealed the last remaining gap in the wall
that spanned the 600 m across Kariba Gorge. The dam was filling and the
valley behind it would never be the same again. Floods there had been
aplenty in the past, but never had the water risen with such speed or so
far. The valley's rodents, exhibiting those remarkable instincts that we
have come not one wit closer to understanding, for all our study and
research, knew that the time had come to leave.

Food increasingly became a problem as the animals moved out of the
cultivated areas and into the bush where the carrying capacity was far
lower and which, in any case, was already fully stocked. Kevin van
Jaarsveldt, who was there at the time, says it took the rats nearly three
months to settle down and find new homes. During that time, the food
situation was so desperate the rats would eat anything — including vehicle tyres![1]

The rising waters created problems not only for the rats. Larger animals
and people also had to be moved. With regard to animals, there are few
people who have not heard or read or seen something of the famous
Operation Noah. There were many heroes of that epic, animal and human.
A publicity programme that seemed to have an impetus of its own took
the contractors and governments concerned completely by surprise.
Heart-rending stories of drowning animals and brave men reached to the
farthest corners of the globe which, in return, gave up its laddered nylon
stockings for making nets and ropes.

In all great sagas there are those events and participants for whom recognition, although deserved, never comes. It is more than 30 years now since
the dam began to fill, and time for some of those stories also to be told.

On the then Northern Rhodesian bank beside the fast-rising waters, an
enthusiast was quick to notice something that sent tremors of horror

through the ranks of the fishing fraternity. The tigerfish were dying. Tigerfish are regarded by many as the finest fighting fish of African waters and a threat to them is a threat to the fisherman's very existence. Top men in their field, Federal Fisheries officers included, rushed to investigate. Patrols brought in the floating bodies of the dead and these were quickly dissected in search of the truth. It was not long in being revealed.

Tigerfish are voracious feeders and, rather like Jack Russell puppies, have no idea when to stop. As the river topped its banks and began to spread out across the valley, so were the homes of ground crickets inundated. Unable to do very much about it, these hapless creatures simply floated in the water and awaited their end. It came in one of two ways. Either they expired from exhaustion and sank beneath the waves or they were gobbled up by a rampaging and bloated tigerfish. The tigerfish were dying from a surfeit of crickets!

There were lots of success stories in Operation Noah and they, of course, always made the news. The failures weren't talked about so much. Taed Edelmann worked from the north bank and he tells the sad story[2] of trying to rescue three elephant cows and two calves. Marooned on an island, the five somehow had to be taken to the mainland.

Thunderflashes had failed to persuade the family to move and so the calves were captured and released on the shore. But they could not fend for themselves and, strangely, their mothers would not follow. They had to be recaptured and returned to the island. Then, tragically, one of the adults was killed by a warden in self-defence. Sensibly, it was decided to leave the island alone for a week. When Edelmann returned a sad scene awaited him. The two remaining adults had gone. The two calves lay dead on the shrinking island. An examination showed that they had been badly knocked about. We shall never know if the adults killed them and, if so, why.

There were winners and losers, of course, but luck played its part. Once, Edelmann encountered an island of trees where the ground seemed to be just covered with water. Anything on it was presumed dead — an assumption justified by the discovery of 25 impala carcasses. Then luck stepped in. For no accountable reason, Edelmann investigated the back of the island. He saw enough through the vegetation still standing above the water to suggest to him that there was a part of the island not yet quite drowned. A line of beaters was formed and two tiny islets were located, neither more than 15 m^2. On each, the soil was already sodden and they were only hours from being submerged. Rescued from beneath the beaks of the waiting marabou storks who patiently perched in the branches overhead were five antbears, four impala, one bushbuck doe and her calf, two hares, two mongooses and some francolin!

There were many lessons to be learnt in Noah, but some discoveries had to be made by trial and tragic error. There were also good opportunities to study animal behaviour in this unique situation. The treatment of shock under these circumstances is a good example. In the early days of rescue operations, captured animals were taken to the shore, carried out of the boat and released on dry land. Usually they lay exhausted for a few moments before moving off slowly into the bush. Gradually it was learnt that the experience of capture and close proximity to man was extremely traumatic and that a manifestation of this trauma was a condition of deep shock accompanied by a dramatic rise in temperature. This discovery led to the practice of lowering the animals into the water when an appropriate distance from the shore. As a result there was time for their body temperature to fall during the short swim to shore and for them to overcome the immediate effects of contact with man. The result was startling. As the creatures landed they shook themselves off and moved quickly away. The signs of exhaustion and apathy were gone.

Doctor Graham Child, whose Ph.D. is based on research he was able to conduct on the south bank during Operation Noah, records the curious phenomenon associated with shock in impala.[3] He found no way of predicting whether or not it would occur in any particular group of animals, but once initiated it spread like mass panic and antelope would start to struggle and die in as little as one minute. Mortality once shock had set in was, in one example, as high as 80%. The bushbuck was another antelope prone to panic. In all cases, as the teams on the other bank had found, shock was associated with high temperatures, shallow respiration and a rapid heartbeat. Dousing the animal with water or putting it in the water often saved its life.

There is a magnificent irony associated with Operation Noah. With all the people, the heroics, the money and the public support, somewhere between 4 000 and 6 000 animals were rescued over a period that is variously recorded as running from December 1958 to June 1961[4] or February 1959 to June 1963.[5] The discrepancy in the number of animals rescued is due partly to counting methods (smaller animals were disregarded and so too, sometimes, were those only herded to the shore) and partly to the fact that north and south banks both appeared to operate as separate entities and joint totals are not clearly stated. Whether Operation Noah lasted for two and a half or four and a half years and whether there were 4 000 or 6 000 animals rescued, at best somewhere in the region of 2 500 animals a year were given a new lease of life by being saved from the rising waters. The irony is that in Southern Rhodesia, in 1958 alone, a total of 14 911 animals were shot as part of the Tsetse Control Hunting Programme.[6] The figure is for the whole country but most of the animals would have been taken in or around the Zambezi Valley; many would have been shot within 100 km of Operation Noah.

Alan Simpkins, a surveyor, is one of those whose job it was to trace out the maximum food level contour line from the wall at Kariba to the upstream end of the dam.[7] Given that Lake Kariba's total shoreline is 2 164 km long,[8] Alan probably walked more than 1 000 km of it: a thankless task just before the rains break, when the trees, the sky and the hills are grey and everything dances on shimmering waves of heat. The valley is hilly and the hillsides are covered with a fine veil of thin, reedy, parched, white grass, just enough cover to conceal the round pebbles on which to slip and fall. To meet the precise requirements of surveying under such conditions is a considerable achievement. After it had been surveyed, the contour had to be physically cleared and what are called benchmarks constructed. It was exhausting work.

There was more than a shoreline to be marked: 1957-58 was the International Geophysical Year and the construction of Kariba dam provided scientists with a remarkable opportunity to measure the depression effects of such a great mass of water on the earth's crust. For this to be done it was necessary that a number of precisely surveyed points be established on the bed of the new lake as well as in the country around it. Alan placed five of these, all to be covered with water when the wall was closed.

He describes them as being triangular steel platforms, set in concrete and located in a horizontal plane to within a centimetre accuracy. Since it was depression effect that was to be measured in the years ahead, the exact height of the plate was vitally important and here the accuracy was expected to be to three decimal places of a metre. It was the intention that the plates, placed in the deepest portions of the future lake, would be located by a magnetic grappling iron lowered by tape from a boat.

The Batonga people who inhabited the Gwembe Trough, as that portion of the Zambezi from Devil's Gorge to Kariba Gorge was known, were not all moved, literally or metaphorically, by the prospect of the dam. Alan worked among a number of them. They were particularly memorable to him because even in the late 1950s he was struck by how untouched they were by the 20th century.

Sensibly, for the climate suggested nothing else, the people still went about naked or half naked, including the women. However, a rather enterprising Greek storekeeper had established himself in the Binga area. In his several stores his principal line, so I am told, was imaginative, if not too colourful. He sold to the good ladies of the valley a range of Maidenform brassières, a load of which he had acquired. They came in pink and white and suddenly, as Alan describes, the entire district seemed at once to be peopled by neopolitan ice creams!

The mass of the water in Kariba has, since the survey work in 1958, been calculated and it stands at the colossal figure of 160 000 million tonnes. At the time, it was the greatest load that humankind had ever placed on the surface of the earth.[9] This great mass is not distributed evenly along the length of the lake. Kariba is divisible into five distinct basins of which the largest and the deepest is at the end near the dam wall; it is in this vicinity that the greatest load is borne.

Thanks to accurate measurements it was possible, in 1969 and again in 1975, to compare what change, if any, there had been. The results were quite dramatic.[10] Of the five circuits that had been carefully levelled the most easily remeasured was the profile along the Makuti road and this is the one for which information is currently available. Extending for 74 km, the Makuti road is a magnificently scenic drive, taking one from the high edge of Zimbabwe's central plateau at 1 168 m to the humid heat of Kariba 600 m below. Along this road, 30 benchmarks had survived the years and some reconstruction of the route. Measurement of these in 1969 showed considerable movement and proved conclusively that the mass of Kariba dam has caused a marked depression in the region.

At a distance of 36 km from Kariba there has been a fall in the level of the earth's surface of 23 mm. As the dam is approached more closely, so the fall increases. About 10 km from the shore the fall is approximately 50 mm and on the lake shore it is 120 mm. What is more remarkable is that not all measured points have moved downwards. Some have actually increased their altitude by a small figure; this especially applies to benchmarks some distance away from the lake as well as one on the island in the lake. Redcliff Island has risen by 57 mm.[11]

More surprises were in store when further levelling took place in 1975 and the results were compared with those of 1957 and 1963. No additional depression was noted, and this suggests that such movement as was going to take place had now occurred and a new balance been struck. Of interest, however, was that three benchmarks quite close to the lake had risen substantially. All three were in Karoo Sediments — basically sandstones — and it has been suggested that rather than crustal movement, the uplift here was local and due to the sandstone absorbing more water than other substances and expanding in the process.[12]

It is one thing to measure the small amounts by which the earth's crust is misshapen by humankind, but it is quite another to understand why and how this happens. I had always thought of rocks as something solid and ungiving, hard and brittle, not capable of flexing or bending without fracturing. It seems that this is not so. Rocks are far more pliable than we think, especially on a regional scale. Although the mechanism of deformation may not be completely understood, it does seem certain that it is primarily the result of the elastic bending of the stratum as a result of loading.[13]

The knowledge that such a great mass of water is stored in Kariba with such measurable effects on the earth's surface also prompts questions about earthquakes. Has there been any increase in earthquake activity? The short answer is definitely yes.

When the levelling survey was being carried out in 1957 and 1958, two seismic networks were also established. It was considered that crustal deformation and earthquake activity might well be two sides of the same coin and interpretation and understanding of one would be aided by knowledge of the other. At the same time, investigations were made into the history of earthquake activity in the Gwembe Valley.

There is a well-known fault line in the Binga area where there are several hot springs. The Batonga people living in the valley there have clear recollections of earthquakes and such events have become incorporated in their traditions. Eric Thomson served near Binga in 1934 and he well remembers the tribesmen speaking of earthquakes and attributing them to a great snake that lives underground, moving from time to time, shaking the world as it does so.[14] Victoria Falls is not generally known for its earthquake activity yet quite strong shocks have been recorded there.

In 1910 Piet Erasmus, a brickmaker who lived in Livingstone, had a clamp of 80 000 bricks in the process of baking one night when there was a violent tremor — it left not a single whole brick in the entire clamp. The tremor was so severe that the railway bridge was closed until engineers had had a chance to examine it and declare it safe.[15]

Research showed that although there was a considerable history of earthquakes and tremors in the south-west, where they were quite well known, there was no evidence whatsoever of such activity in the north-east — where the dam wall would be built and where the deepest of the new lake's five basins would be located.

The wall was closed in December 1958 and the first recorded earthquake occurred in June the following year when the water level had risen to 60 m.[16] A low level of constant background seismic activity became established and continued until the middle of 1963. At that point, there was a marked increase which culminated in a series of strong shocks and 'swarms' of earthquakes between September and November 1963. This was the peak of earthquake activity.

It is significant that this peak coincided with the filling of the lake to its maximum level for the first time. Interestingly, most of the shocks and all of the larger ones had their epicentres located, not in areas of known activity, but in the Sanyati basin at the north-eastern end of the lake. (The epicentre is the point on the earth's surface directly above the centre of the earthquake.) Despite this, the upper end of the lake had its moments. In Binga, for example, over the fault line, 192 minor earthquakes were recorded: 180 of them occurred in the space of four days![17] After the burst of activity in 1963, the number and magnitude of tremors returned to the low background level of previous years. Since then it appears to have 'pulsed' in a moderate way, with periodic resurgences of activity. One of these was recorded between May and October 1979 after a period of quiescence from 1975 to the middle of 1979.[18]

Scientists can calculate the energy released in any particular earthquake and it has been established that 87% of all the seismic energy released in ten years of records to 1968 was released in just two days at the peak of activity, starting on 23 September 1963.[19]

In the three years while the new lake filled, the seismic network recorded some 2 000 separate tremors. Of these, the epicentres of 159 could be located in the down-faulted rift valley of the Middle Zambezi, which, as Professor Gough has indicated, strongly suggests that the lake has reactivated the ancient fault lines that are part of the area's complex geological history and may date back as far as the late Precambrian Period, perhaps 1 000 million years ago.[20]

The three largest earthquakes recorded in the Kariba region are two measuring 5,8 and one measuring 5,5 on the Richter Scale. All three occurred in September 1963. Well within the design capacity of the dam wall, in no way did they represent a danger to it.[21] Although many tremors have been recorded, most are too slight to be detected by humans and none are so severe as to threaten life or cause damage.

Undoubtedly, the existence of the dam and the great mass of water imposed on the area are causative factors in the tremor activity. We have seen that the crust of the earth has a certain elasticity and that it 'gives' in response to the mass put upon it. This 'give' involves movement and the movement accounts for some of the recorded earthquake activity. It reflects the 'stretching' of the crust as it tries to accommodate the load. There are a number of examples of this elsewhere in the world. In the highly seismic region of the continental shelf off the coast of Alaska, for example, one researcher has shown that the 'unloading' of the tide is sometimes sufficient to trigger a minor tremor or earthquake.[22] Such activity, the earth's surface rising and falling in a regular rhythm reminiscent of breathing, is strongly suggestive of the Gaia hypothesis — the idea that the earth itself is a living organism.

In some places, one assumes, the limit of elasticity is exceeded and at these points, notably the ancient fault lines, the fault is reactivated. Interestingly, it is not considered to be just the mass of the water that is responsible for this movement. It is also the water itself. Under great pressure, it is forced down into cracks and fissures in the rocks and there acts as a lubricant. In this way it makes possible and encourages movement that might not otherwise have taken place.[23]

Lake Kariba is more than 250 km long and has a surface area that varies, depending on the water level, between some 5 000 km^2 and 6 000 km^2. Evaporation rates are close to 1,85 m of water a year.[24] In such circumstances, one would think that the dam should have a significant effect on the climate in the region. It does, but not in quite the way one might expect.

If it were possible to contail all the water that evaporated from the lake in the course of a year and let it fall evenly on a country the size of

Zimbabwe, the total fall would not amount to more than an additional 25 mm. In this way a lake such as Kariba has limited potential to affect a large region significantly. Of course, it is not possible to hold the moisture; the wind carries it away and even then, the countries downwind do not necessarily benefit. The evaporated moisture is dispersed over a wide area and also, probably, to a high altitude. So very few lakes can affect the climate of a region. Even the Caspian Sea, which is 85 times the size of Kariba, is not big enough to affect the pressure systems — and hence the rainfall — over the Asian Continent. Nevertheless, there are reports of increased rainfall as a result of Kariba. How can these facts be reconciled?

The answer is that a lake can have a considerable local effect up to 30 km to 50 km from its shores and mostly, but not always, in the direction of the prevailing wind. At Kariba the wind tends to blow from the north-east and east. Thus, if one is seeking evidence of changed rainfall patterns one needs to look at western Matabeleland and eastern Zambia.

Several people in the Hwange area in Zimbabwe's Matabeleland told me that the rainfall has been higher there since Kariba filled, but I did not get official figures to verify this. Instead, I was intrigued by the work of Dr Peter Hutchinson, formerly the chief meteorologist for the Department in Lusaka, Zambia.[25]

The Zambian side of Kariba is normally the lee side and it receives moisture-laden winds from across the lake. Dr Hutchinson's work shows that over an area of Zambian lakeshore measuring some 32 km by 250 km (or 8 000 km²) the rainfall has increased by an average of at least 50 mm a year. He also found that the increase has been greatest close to the lake, one shore station recording a rainfall increase of 337 mm or nearly half as much again as its usual figure. Two other stations, for which only limited data exist, suggest increases of 500 mm or nearly 70%. Further research shows that the additional rainfall comes not from an increased number of rainy days but from the greater intensity of each individual fall.[26]

One might not be surprised to learn that, in a lake the size of Kariba, lunar tides are observed. In so far as they can be measured accurately the maximum range is between 3 cm and 4 cm at the north-eastern end of the lake and slightly more at the upper end.[27] It is difficult to measure the tides accurately because of an extraordinary and fascinating range of complicating factors.

When a strong wind blows across a lake, it will 'pile up' the water at one end. The effect is much the same as tipping a bath: when the wind stops, the water returns to its original position. Of course, being fluid, it 'overshoots' and a periodic oscillating motion, tide-like but quite independent of the moon, is established. Gradually, the oscillations will slow down and, in the absence of any more wind, will stop. But the wind does not stop for long periods, although it may change direction and intensity, and each time this happens, a new wave is set in motion, complicating the pattern already established by the waves before it.

Such a periodic, oscillating, wave-like motion is called a *seiche*. The name comes from French and, specifically, from Lake Geneva where large seiches have been recorded, the largest, in 1841, being 1,87 m.[28] The highest seiches observed at Kariba over an eight-year period showed ranges between 0,30 and 0,43 m — much less dramatic than their European counterparts, but significant nevertheless.[29] A seiche makes the task of measuring tides in lakes much more difficult than it might originally have seemed. There are still greater complications, however.

Everyone knows that water near the top surface of a lake is warmer than that below. Often, because of the difference in temperature and therefore in density, two distinct bodies of water are formed in this way, one above and one below. In certain circumstances, when the wind has created a seiche with the warmer surface waters, an internal seiche may also be established. This will be formed by the colder and deeper waters moving in the opposite direction to the warmer ones above.

To complicate matters still further, these different waves superimposed upon each other are all equally affected by drag due to the earth's rotation. Known as the Coriolis effect, it is related to the spinning of the earth and tends to influence the direction of a seiche.[30] Surprisingly, at Kariba, the one factor that has no effect on tides or seiches is earthquakes. An examination of measurements made during and after each of the major quakes, including the large ones of September 1963, showed no abnormal fluctuations at all.[31] Finally, seiches are affected quite considerably by the nature of the lake bottom. In the case of Kariba, only some 18% of the flooded area was cleared of trees prior to filling. In the remaining 80%, trees still stand, and the tree canopy offers considerable resistance to the movement of water, thereby slowing down those parts of any seiche that come in contact with it.

The clearing of vegetation in the pre-filling days was an impressive, if costly and controversial exercise. It was the intention that the cleared areas would be used as fishing grounds. The bush clearing techniques varied from men wielding axes in the inaccessible places to sophisticated machinery on the open flats. Alan Simpkins during his survey work along the valley often watched these teams in action. One team consisted of three D9 bulldozers, yellow giants that dragged themselves across the veld, hauling destruction in their wake. A pair of them pulled a 2 m steel ball on battleship anchor chains and cleared a swathe through the bush about 50 m wide. A third bulldozer followed behind, clearing snags and odd bits missed, pushing the debris into piles so that it could be burnt.

ABOVE
A monument to an imaginative district commissioner at Katima Mulilo in Namibia.

LEFT
The famous flying boat service recalled in stamps.

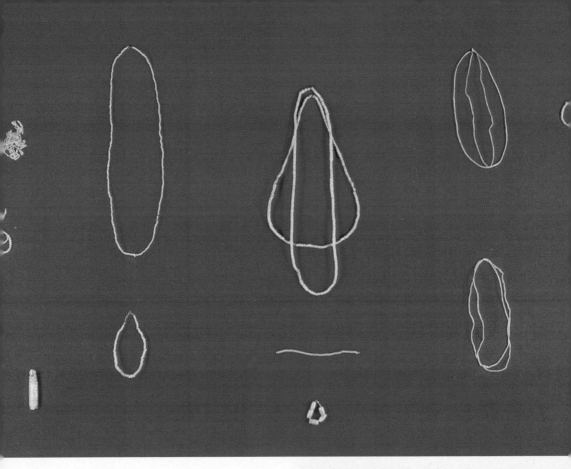

ABOVE
A selection of gold-wire necklaces from
archaeological sites in Zimbabwe (used
with permission of the Natural History
Museum, Bulawayo, Zimbabwe).

RIGHT
In the rain forest at Victoria Falls.

At a good walking pace a team could clear about 14 ha an hour. But the cost in money and time was high.

In total, 954 km² of bush was cleared, 510 km² in Zambia and the remainder in Zimbabwe.[32] This figure represents about 18% of the total area of the lake but it is just over half (52%) of the area within the 20 m contour line. In other words, it represents half of all the shallow water in the lake where, it was thought, most of the fishing would take place.[33] It took more than two years to do the clearing and one unexpected problem was that the vegetation started to grow again, often so quickly that the first areas cleared were substantially regrown by the end of the operation.[34] Although the stripping and burning technique was effective, the regrowth problem meant that few areas eventually went under the water devoid of anything that would snag a net. And that was the object of the exercise for which six million US dollars had been paid![35] Perhaps it is no surprise that bush clearing did not take place when Cahora Bassa dam was built.

All life forms need a place to live, a habitat. A greater range of habitats leads to a greater diversity of species and a healthier and more productive ecosystem. One of the unforeseen advantages of only partial tree removal was that those trees remaining have provided a remarkable array of habitats which otherwise would not have existed.

Kariba is well known for the great stands of gaunt grey trees marooned in the shallows. Dead since the lake waters deprived their roots of oxygen, they have stood leafless in the sun for 30 years and are baked as hard as iron. They have about them an air of permanence which is only a little misleading. There is evidence from Lake Windemere in England that tree trunks under water may never decay, for specimens there remain from 4 000 years ago.[36]

There are two categories of trees at Kariba: those so deep in the sublittoral zone that the widely fluctuating lake level never exposes them, and those that are periodically exposed. Although in time the former may lose their crowns and smaller branches, the trunks are likely to remain and may fossilise as those at Windemere have done. The latter group occupies what is known as the littoral zone and they are exposed to much greater change. Dr A.J. McLachlan earned his Ph.D. from his studies of this habitat and his work is fascinating.[37]

He discovered, for example, that the ratio of tree surface area to bottom surface area is just over two to one. This means that dead trees provide much more space than they occupy, offering a different habitat to benthic (bottom dwelling) fauna. The nature of the shoreline affects how much use is made of submerged trees. If the shoreline is being rapidly eroded and the water is discoloured by a high silt content, the trees are usually blanketed by silt and support little life. Where the water is clear the trees are often festooned with conspicuous growths of algae.

An interesting extension of habitat occurs in trees in the littoral zone. As more of each tree is exposed by falling water levels, so the new wood is attacked by terrestrial borer beetles. Two species are particularly responsible and they both specialise in boring tunnels between the bark and the xylem. When the tree is resubmerged a new and highly specialised microhabitat is thus available for use. There are other borer beetles which drill more deeply, frequently at the minimum water level. Their activities structurally weaken the tree, which future storms will break. Slowly the woodland littoral zone is diminishing.

McLachlan demonstrated the usefulness of trees as a habitat in the lake by measuring the mass of the faunal 'standing crop' and comparing it with that of two other substrates: the mud and aquatic vegetation. Both supported a much higher faunal mass than trees, which trailed sadly by comparison. However, the contribution by trees is significant: they form an additional habitat when vegetation is present and may partly substitute for it in its absence. Trees also provide anchoring points for floating mats of vegetation; this is an important aspect in the ecology of aquatic weeds, for instance. They also offer perches, roosts and nest sites for birds as well as serving as frames for photographers' endless pictures of sunsets on Lake Kariba!

The story of Kariba dam is well known, but there are several anecdotes that I think are worth repeating. One relates to the question of access to Kariba. The route from Makuti, on the main Great North Road through Zimbabwe and Zambia, is just under 80 km long and drops 600 m. No start could be made on either the dam or the future township until this road had been completed: an all-weather road that had to be constructed within five months, before the rains began. If the construction teams failed, the whole project would be set back, for it would then not be possible to reach Kariba until the rains ended.

Those whose task it was to know said the job could not be done — and they were probably right, for they were looking at it as professionals.

A Mr J.H.R. Savory, an official of the Department of Irrigation, offered to undertake the work and claimed he could finish it in time if he were allowed to ignore the surveys and follow the instincts of the elephant whose traditional routes traversed the same ground. He was given the go-ahead and was successful — thanks to the elephant in whose tracks he took the new road.[38]

Anyone who has walked extensively in the wild country of Africa where elephants are still to be found will know of the elephant trail. There are at least two varieties: the elephant version of the local commuter track and the long-distance migratory trail. The latter is distinct, well worn and always, with incredible skill, follows the best possible route from one locality to another. These trails are used by humans and other animals as well as by the elephant. Migratory trails extend in a network for hundreds of kilometres and may be centuries old. This timelessness and antiquity add an eeriness to the following true story.[39]

In the late 1970s, Graham Hall was the warden in charge of the national parks at Kariba. At about 17h00 one day the boat driver of one of the local hotels reported that he had seen three elephant swimming in open water out from Spurwing Island towards Kariba. Kariba looks 30 km south across the huge and beautiful bay to the Sanyati Gorge and the Matusadona Game Reserve. Spurwing is one of several islands just off the Matusadona shore and is at least 25 km from Kariba.

Graham told me he knew the report was nonsense: no sane elephant would attempt to swim such a distance and, indeed, would have no reason for doing so. But his confidence diminished as he questioned the driver who had taken his boat to within a metre of them and could not possibly have been mistaken. Graham took the driver and a National Parks boat and went to have a look.

The report was true. There were three young bulls, all about 20 years of age. They had already covered a third of the distance. Despite his many years of experience Graham had never seen or heard of anything like this and he was at something of a loss. His instinct was a mercy killing — the animals, he thought, would never make the distance and would die a horrible death by drowning. Better to kill them now, was his reaction. He loaded his rifle and then thought, instead, to try and turn them, to make them go back to the shore they had left. He fired seven or eight shots and was successful. In the growing darkness he saw all three together, heading back safely for the shore. He returned to Kariba.

The next day, just after midday, the Lake Safety Officer reported two elephant in the middle of the lake swimming strongly towards Kariba. Graham was incredulous but the report could not be denied as the officer was looking at them through the station telescope. (Graham later checked for the third elephant. It was not seen in the water, nor was any carcass ever found. It is presumed to have returned safely to the game reserve.)

With two boats and plenty of rope the two animals, now well over two-thirds of the way, were approached. Both were swimming strongly and steadily and certainly did not seem to need the help of National Parks personnel who tried to assist by passing ropes underneath them. In the end, the parks staff rode 'shotgun', not interfering in any way, keeping the animals company and making sure they would not be molested when they landed.

In the water the elephants rested in turn by the one at the back placing its forelegs on the haunches of the animal in front. They made for the same point on the shore at which they had been aiming for more than 24 hours.

They climbed out of the water without any sign of weariness and paused briefly on the shore. Graham noticed that the soles of their feet were a bright white after so long in the water and that both animals were lean. One ate a few leaves from a nearby tree and the other had a drink! Soon they walked away, up the hill onto the nearest elephant trail, and disappeared into the trees.

The story is remarkable. It is an extraordinary feat for an animal to have swum so far for so long and there are very few, if any, records of a similar event. What is more remarkable is that these elephants made the journey in the first place. Mr Hostes Nicolle walked this area in the days before the dam and knows it intimately. He says that there used to be an old elephant migratory trail that crossed the valley from the present game reserve to the vicinity of Kariba. He believes the elephant were following it. So do I — but I cannot overlook the fact that Kariba dam had then been filled for about 25 years and that the elephant were only 20 years old. How does one explain that?

The exact meaning and origins of the name Kariba are difficult to pin down. The two oldest references I can find both date to the 1930s and, because of their close agreement, I have some faith in them. Eric Thomson[40] was told that, earlier than the Batonga people can remember, there was a shelf of rock at the head of Kariba Gorge that completely overhung the river. It was exactly like one of those basket traps for catching birds: the basket is supported by a stick with a liberal sprinkling of seeds about, and a string leads to small boys who pull it when there is a chance that the basket will catch a bird when it falls. Eric was told that the name of such a trap is 'kariwa'. The name was applied to the gorge because of its basket-like rock overhang.

At about the same time Col Essex Capell[41] was given much the same information except that the trap he was told about featured not a basket but a slab of rock to do the killing, but was otherwise operated in the same way. 'Kariba' is the name for the rock. The name also suggests 'to fall like a stone' — an allusion to a legend that all canoes going through Kariba Gorge will sink 'like a stone'. Capell's informants said the word is from the Makorekore language, not from that of the Batonga. This reassures me still further because, when I spoke to some Batonga, they said they knew of the word but it was not their language. The Batonga have never lived near Kariba Gorge; they have always been much further upstream. The gorge was Makorekore country.

The first suggestion that a dam should be built at the gorge appears to have been made in 1912 but many years were to pass and a great many surveys carried out before there was any prospect of the dream becoming reality.[42] Not until June 1955 was the first contract awarded for various preliminary tasks. One of the early ones, once the problem of access had

been overcome, was to provide accommodation and all the resources necessary to sustain a population which, at its peak, would number 8 500
people. This meant building an entire township: the present settlement of
Kariba was constructed as a result. Work on the town started on 14 March
1956 and was virtually completed 18 months later, by September 1957.
The main civil contractor began work in August 1956 and the first skip
of concrete for the wall was poured on 6 November 1956, 17 months after
the original work had started. However one measures it, whether in terms
of human achievement, engineering skills, planning or logistical support,
it was a mighty achievement.[43]

A little over two years and seven months passed before the last skip
of cement in the dam wall was tipped by the then Prime Minister of the
Federation of Rhodesia and Nyasaland, Sir Roy Welensky, on 22 June
1959. In the meantime, the wall had been plugged on 2 December 1958 and
Lake Kariba began to fill.[44] Initially, in the south bank station, there were
six 111 MW (megawatt) generators and the first electricity was generated
in December 1959.[45] Improved technology has made it possible to increase
the efficiency of the existing turbines and by 1990 each of these reached
125 MW. Since Kariba was opened, the north bank power station has also
been brought on stream with four turbines, each of 150 MW generating
capacity. In 1990 the total output of Kariba stood at 1 350 MW.

The bald facts of Kariba are not especially interesting. The real excitement of Kariba's story lies in the devastating floods that for two successive years hurled unprecedented volumes of water at the incomplete
dam and twice threatened to obliterate it, precisely as the indigenous
people of the valley had predicted.

The catchment area of Kariba is 663 820 km² and today it is monitored
by a network of warning stations that give accurate and advance warning
of rainfall and flood conditions. There are 15 of these stations in all, six
of which are radio-controlled and automatic with the remainder operating
by telephone, telex or letter. A flood in the upper highlands of the Zambezi
catchment usually takes abut 30 days to reach the dam but a local one,
in the tributary rivers of the lake itself, is much more dramatic and can
reach the lake within hours.[46] These facts go a long way towards explaining what happened in 1957 and 1958.

There are two separate flood regimes on the river: one has its origins in
the distant headwaters, the other is much more local. In a normal year these
two floods do not overlap although one may supplement the end of the other.
Also, because of the distance over which the river has already flowed by the
time it reaches the lake — more than 1 430 km — there are significant climatic differences between the high watershed and Kariba. Thus, good rains
and flood conditions in one do not necessarily mean the same in the other.

In 1957 there were exceptionally heavy rains over Barotseland and
these coincided with a high flood — probably the highest for many years

— arriving from the uppermost reaches of the river. This colossal quantity of water was delivered over Victoria Falls and down to the mouth of the gorge at Kariba. The flood was a little earlier than usual and it managed to tag on to the last of the local floods.[47] Thankfully, it did not overlap with them but did damage enough, threatening the road bridge across the gorge and flooding the cofferdam, setting the work schedule back.

At least the contractors could take comfort from the fact, when it was all over, that it could not happen again — or so they thought. Such floods were a once in a lifetime event and the odds against a recurrence were thousands to one.

All the calculations went out of the window the following year with floods that greatly exceeded those of the previous year. Earlier and heavier rains had fallen in the upper reaches, as they had over Barotseland, as well as between there and Victoria Falls. The same had happened locally so that everywhere normal volumes of water had been far exceeded. Run-off was also probably greater because the water tables were still high and the ground saturated from the previous year. The potential for disaster at Kariba was multiplied enormously by the two floods coinciding and striking the dam site simultaneously.[48]

The effect at Kariba was devastating and the work was set back many months. For the second time the cofferdam was flooded; the road bridge was lost; the foot bridge barely escaped; severe damage was done to the banks; the underground works had, for a short period, to be sealed off.

In the event, the skills and perseverance of man prevailed over nature and the dam was completed without further complications, on schedule. It is hard, however, to ignore completely the superstitions of the local people and to disregard their belief in Nyaminyami.

Like many African people, the Batonga maintain contact with a large number of powerful spirit forces all linked deeply into their traditional way of life and culture. One of these is the spirit of the river, misnamed today the river god. He is not a god and, in a definite but subtle way, represents more than a simple river spirit. Known as Nyaminyami he is, perhaps, a personification of the Zambezi itself and, by analogy, of the life force and the will to survive.

In the days when the Batonga were being moved from the valley and relocated to areas that would be clear of the future dam, the name of Nyaminyami was invoked in a spirit of resistance. He never became a political symbol but it was widely rumoured that he 'disapproved' of the white man's plans and that he would destroy all the white man's work in the gorge. After the 1957 floods, many locals nodded knowingly, appreciating Nyaminyami's power and waiting for the final destruction of the dam. As we have seen, it very nearly came in 1958 and elders today claim that only their intervention saved the dam and placated the river spirit.

Rainos Tawonameso[49] is an enterprising Mshona, based at Kariba, who has established something of an international reputation for himself. An accomplished woodcarver, he retains a small staff who, under his direction, carve walking sticks in the shape of a particular, elaborate and symbolic design. Rainos created (and registered) the design himself and honestly points out that, although it is topped by a carving of Nyaminyami and is known by that name, it is not traditional. What he has done is to incorporate in it motifs and symbols that are traditional and are closely associated with the Zambezi Valley and its inhabitants. The demand for his product is, to me, not only a tribute to its quality and imaginative creation, but also an indication that even the casual visitor to Kariba is more than a little touched by the tale of Nyaminyami and unwilling to dismiss it entirely.

There is one last story of Kariba that must be told before we move on. It concerns a remarkable and little-known feat of engineering and courage all the more noteworthy because the work involved took place beneath 40 m of water in a confined space. There are six water intakes on the south bank at Kariba. Each is a concrete-lined tunnel, 6 m by 5 m, and leads water through a right-angle bend to the turbines. At the bend there is a radial gate which controls the flow of water. In front of it another gate, the stop beam, can be lowered into place along rails through a small aperture from above.

A combination of operator error and design fault made one of the stop beams inoperative. The concrete holding the rails had broken, the gate could not be lowered and, as a result, there was no emergency back-up for the radial gate which itself could now not be maintained, due to lack of access.

The job was a tremendous challenge to both engineers and underwater specialists: nothing like it had ever been done before. Part of the difficulty was in deciding how to solve the problem. The obvious solution of placing a cover over the outside of the intake cover would not work because the surrounding concrete was not designed for and would not carry the inward loading that this would create. Eventually, an innovative solution was decided upon. The plan was to build a 35 tonne steel gate inside the intake tunnel, supporting it with beams resting on the closed radial gate. The fit would have to be precise and rubber seals would be used to make it watertight. Once in place, the shaft and the space between the two gates could be pumped dry and the railings could be repaired. Appropriately, it became known as Operation Bulkhead.[50] It was a grand idea, but who could do it?

Already well established at Kariba was a commercial diving firm that carried out maintenance work in the stilling pool immediately below the dam wall, led by a remarkable American whose heart had been stolen by Africa and a young lady he had met there. Conrad Blackadder Wilson was himself an engineer and a man in every way equal in terms of his technical skills and leadership ability to tackle this dangerous task.

The finished gate was first completely assembled in the yard of an engineering works in Salisbury, now Harare. I have a vivid memory of seeing it there, all 35 tonnes of it, waiting to be carefully checked before being taken to pieces and shipped to Kariba. At Kariba, other problems had to be solved. Apart from the simple logistical constraints of working with compressed air below 40 m, there were also problems with lighting and, more especially, with getting the pieces of the gate to the assembly point down at the bottom of the shaft.

A mass of 35 tonnes represents a great deal of material to move and most of it was lowered down the stop beam shaft, which although nearly 6 m long, was only 1 m wide and did not allow much room to manoeuvre. The gate itself was lowered in one piece but all the supporting steelwork was taken down bit by bit.

The day came when the gate was finally installed, the seals were in place and the pumping began. At that depth, a mass of water in excess of 1 350 tonnes was being forced up against the seals and the bulkhead. But they held, and there was no leakage. Contractors were able to get down to the damaged area and work dryshod inside the shafts. It was a worthy achievement and recognised as such by colleagues who had been watching progress with interest. They showed their appreciation in telegrams of congratulations, which came in to Kariba from all over the world. All that mars the memory of that proud achievement is the tragic death of Conrad Wilson, who was killed in a diving accident at sea just a few years later.

9   Matters Aquatic

MUCH, rightly, is being made of dams as discrete ecosystems and one can readily see the sense of this if one looks at a lake, such as Kariba or Cahora Bassa. Such a dam, especially in its early years, is not a naturally balanced environment. Its natural systems, its flora and fauna have not adapted or are still adapting to the change from a riverine to a lacustrine environment. Such dams are much less ecologically stable than we might like to think. A little research brings some interesting information to light in this regard.

The origin of the water in Lake Kariba, for example, has an important role to play in the ecology of the lake. Over 78% of it comes from the Zambezi itself, via Livingstone and the Victoria Falls. Another 14% arrives from the tributary rivers between the falls and the dam wall. The remainder comes in the form of rain on the lake surface.[1] Each of these waters is distinctly different, as one might imagine. Each type of water has its own, unique chemical make-up and, more importantly, bears a different sediment and nutrient load.

Water carries, dissolved in it, the basic chemicals necessary for life, in the same way soil does. Like soils, there are waters that are nutritionally rich or poor. The quantity of nutritional chemicals, of which the phosphates and nitrates are among the most important, has a direct bearing on the amount of life the water can support. The richer it is, the more productive it will be. Chemicals dissolved in water are used first by what are called the primary producers. These are the aquatic plants and phytoplankton that, by photosynthesis, initiate the food chain, meaning that they are consumed or by their death provide food for the secondary producers.

The nutritional load of water can be estimated by counting the ions in it, a measure that is called its conductivity. We need not try to understand the chemistry of this concept but use it only for comparison purposes. Thus we find that the water of the Zambezi has an extremely low nutrient status and its conductivity ranges from 40 to 121 units while that of a tributary river such as the Sanyati varies from 60 to 300 with a mean of 155.[2]

The significance of chemical content, and hence conductivity, is readily to be seen when the effect of its productivity potential is measured. For example, Dr Brian Marshall of the University of Zimbabwe was able to show that growth spurts in populations of the well-known Kapenta sardine in Kariba are related to inflows of the highly nutritious water from local rivers, like the Gwaai and Sanyati.[3]

The quantity of chemicals brought into Kariba by inflowing rivers is quite staggering. Despite the poor nutritional quality of its water, the Zambezi alone brings in nearly two million tonnes a year. This includes about 800 000 tonnes of bicarbonate, 460 000 tonnes of silica and 150 000 tonnes of calcium. On top of this, the secondary rivers — those that flow into the lake downstream of Victoria Falls — bring in another 400 000 tonnes, while the rain adds a further 42 000 tonnes.[4] In the days before the dam, most of this flowed down through the valley, but now the river is impounded and there is an opportunity for various life forms to make use of the chemicals in a way that was not possible before.

It is important to understand that in an ecosystem such as a lake there is a finite quantity of nutrients and life-supporting chemicals in the water. The quantity of nutrition available can change and, in man-made lakes, it invariably does. It is usually extremely high to begin with, but declines over a period of a few years, eventually settling at its natural level. Whatever the nutritional level happens to be, it can only support a fixed biomass, a limited quantity of living material, and there is no means of exceeding that amount. Another way of looking at it is to recognise that, like people working for a salary, there is a budget and you cannot, for long, spend more than you earn. Every lake has a fixed energy budget and productivity depends entirely on how that energy is used. In a simple sense, for example, more of one species may mean less of another. The implications of this are fascinating when it comes to considering the growth and decline of the so-called 'Kariba weed' and the success of Kariba's money-spinning sardine, the Kapenta.

Any opportunity to increase the nutrient level of a lake is obviously going to be of benefit. An excellent source of nutrients for primary producers in an aquatic environment is animal waste. Thus one solution to the relatively low nutritional status of the Zambezi would be to encourage the towns of Livingstone and Victoria Falls to pour their untreated sewerage into the river! As this is not acceptable to us and unlikely to happen, we have to rely on animals to do the dirty work for us and some interesting research has been done in this regard.

A characteristic of Lake Kariba's shore is its gentle shelving in many places. A small drop in lake level exposes relatively large areas of land. Certain grasses have adapted themselves to this environment and quickly sprout on the exposed flats. Soon the game animals crowd the area, removing the grass and leaving their own waste in its place. Eventually, when the water rises, the dung is submerged and releases its nutrients into the water. Research has shown that conductivity — and hence the water's nutritional status — starts to rise within an hour while pH and oxygen content fall. Experimental results show conductivity ratings increasing from 80 units to 830. As one might expect, some dung is better than others. Topping the charts is the dry dung of impala followed by dry buffalo and elephant dung. Dry grass is next, followed by fresh dung, headed by that of the elephant. Dung from grasses releases nutrients much more quickly than grass itself — probably because the grass has been partially digested. Hippo dung was not measured but it is likely to be a most significant contributor of nutrients, especially as hippo eat on land and defecate in the water.[5]

Not many years ago, the bad boy of the African lakes was an aquatic weed, *Salvinia molesta,* popularly known as Kariba weed. The story of its rise and fall is an excellent example of how a lake's nutritional status changes and how nutrient availability is the most important single factor in determining species diversity.

The weed had been a stable part of the Zambezi system for many years and had first been collected near Victoria Falls in 1949.[6] It did not become a problem until the new lake began to fill, at which point it burgeoned into a very serious ecological threat indeed. At its worst, in May 1962, about a year before the lake filled, *Salvinia* occupied 22% of its surface. More than 1 000 km² was covered in a thick green mat, nearly half a metre deep in places and so thickly packed that it was impossible to take a boat through it. Given the rate at which it had already expanded there were fears that it would completely engulf all the open water, killing off the fish and the embryonic fishing industry, rendering the lake unnavigable and threatening electricity production.

The fears were groundless, however, although some time had to elapse before this became plain. Wind action over the great expanses of open water that existed when the lake filled in June 1963 was sufficient to break up and destroy those mats of weed not in sheltered areas. Weed cover fell to about 15%, remaining between there and 10% until 1973 when it fell to 5%. By 1980, at 1% cover, it had ceased to be a problem.[7]

Salvinia is a small, aquatic fern of South American origin. Vaguely cabbage-like, it is green to yellow-green and its leaves are covered with densely packed, very fine hairs, each of which bears a tiny cap-like structure at its head. This allows the leaf to trap large quantities of air and gives the plant its buoyancy. Below each pair of leaves there hangs in the water a third leaf, so extensively modified that it looks like tiny rootlets. A characteristic of the plant is its huge capacity for rapid growth in favourable environments.[8] Doubling times for the plant are variously recorded in a range from a staggering 2,5 days[9] and 3,4 days under laboratory conditions to a more practical 8-17 days when tested *in situ* at Kariba.[10]

I described *Salvinia* as the bad boy of the lake but this is only partly true. It is fascinating to note how its role has been seen to change over the years since it was first reported on such an intimidating scale in the early 1960s.

Salvinia would choke up the rivers, create blockages, affect how floods occur and hamper fishing and boating. The thick mats, by excluding light, reducing oxygen and creating a rain of organic debris would affect water quality and this would lead to marked changes in aquatic life. Growth of other plants would be prevented, animal life would be reduced, as would the species diversity of an aquatic environment. This was the verdict, supported by extensive research, of one writer and fairly sums up the views of many.[11] To these can be added one or two others. *Salvinia* does indeed exclude light and, in doing so, prevents the development of rooted aquatic plants. Such plants, when they exist, support the greatest diversity of invertebrate life. In addition, large mats of *Salvinia* at river mouths gain first access to nutrients from this source, preventing them from becoming available to other users and, effectively, confining them to this limited part of the lake.[12]

The picture of *Salvinia* does not look too encouraging but, as with many things in life, there are two sides to the coin and researchers are now less hasty to condemn *Salvinia* than formerly. Although there is no doubt that dissolved oxygen levels are lower beneath a large and fixed mat of Kariba weed, beneath the smaller, marginal ones this is not a problem, especially near river mouths. Here the circulating water is constantly replenished along the shoreline.

It has also been found that there is a strong correlation between the total mass of fish in any given area and its vegetation. The highest figure, with up to 400 kg of fish per hectare, is under *Salvinia,* which is used by fish both as a nursery for their young and as a shelter during the day.

A further advantage of *Salvinia* is that it floats. Water levels in Kariba constantly fluctuate. With the drought cycle of the 1980s water has been lower in Kariba than for many years. Aquatic vegetation that is rooted to the bottom cannot follow the water level down, as *Salvinia* can and does. *Salvinia,* therefore, goes on providing a food source and shelter when other vegetation has been left stranded.

Of course the weed does itself become stranded and it was originally thought that this might inhibit the germination of other plants on the shoreline. In fact, this is only true for newly deposited *Salvinia* — the older material actually encourages growth, especially of the rich grass *Panicum repens* which is important as grazing for herbivores and for Tilapia fish during times of rising water levels.[13]

According to Dr Mitchell,[14] *Salvinia* mats in Kariba can be divided into three categories: the permanent ones that are sheltered from wind and wave, permanent mats with sudd cover and wind-blown mats. The last two are particularly interesting. Professor A.S. Boughey, of the University of Zimbabwe, in 1961 made a study of the growth of other types of vegetation which had been seeded onto permanent *Salvinia* mats. His results were amazing. In all, he collected no fewer than 50 flowering plant species which included the obvious aquatic and semi-aquatic plants but, in addition, such unexpected examples as a banana, some roadside weeds and a luffa![15] The wind-blown mats provide one final and rather surprising beneficial aspect of *Salvinia*. Sheltering in the protection of the fine curtains of hair-like roots beneath the matted vegetation, fish fry are safe from predation. When the mat, caught by the wind, begins to move, the young fish go with it and in this way are delivered to parts of the lake that they would never have been able to reach unprotected![16]

The benefits of *Salvinia* that have been outlined would probably not have weighed too greatly in its favour if it had continued its explosive rate of growth and occupied a quarter or more of the lake, but it died off; so, two questions must be asked. Why did it grow so suddenly and why, with equal rapidity, did it decline? There is much more certainty now about the answers to these questions than there was in 1963 and both answers have to do with the level of nutrition in the waters of the lake.

There is little dispute about the answer to the first question: it was environment, lack of competition and, above all, nutrition that made the weed grow so suddenly. As the waters of the new lake rose and flooded the lands of the Gwembe Valley, unimaginably large quantities of organic material were engulfed, providing a high level of nutrients in the water. *Salvinia* is an exotic plant and like many exotics competes successfully against local plants. In the case of Kariba, however, it had no competition and quickly filled a largely vacant ecological niche. Compared to other aquatic vegetation and fauna, *Salvinia* was quick off the mark. Its phenomenal growth rate left it without serious competition and its short-term success was assured.

The causes of the steady decline of Kariba weed are more difficult to determine. There are probably a number of contributing factors. As already suggested, wind and wave action as the lake reached its fullest extent may have been one of the first of the natural controls affecting weed populations and possibly accounts for the weed's remaining between 10% and 15% for the seven years between 1963 and 1970. Even at this early stage, however, nutrient stress may already have been having some effect. The frequent changes in lake level and consequent stranding of large areas of weed must also have worked against continued success. In these circumstances, however, the rapid growth rate would surely have made good the losses — unless the growth rate itself was now retarded in some way, perhaps due to insufficient nutrition.

The reduction in *Salvinia* populations between 1973 and 1980, when the weed settled at a 1% coverage, represents a victory in the battle to control it. That victory is attributable to either one or both of two probable causes. In 1970, biological controls were first introduced to the lake. In that and following years a grasshopper, *Paulinia acuminata,* imported from Trinidad, was released in a number of different localities around the lakeshore. It was not, however, until May 1973 that it was recovered in significant concentrations. Throughout 1973 and the following year, concentrations of *Paulinia* at approximately 20 per m^2 were common — at a time when *Salvinia* was noticeably decreasing.[17] It was tempting to link the two but difficult to justify doing so with absolute certainty. Later laboratory work showed that *Paulinia* at a density of 85 per m^2 is necessary to equal the growth rate of the weed. There are too many variables for these results to be applied directly and the likely explanation is that, even if there were not sufficient grasshoppers to eliminate the weed, those that there were helped to control it.

The second probable reason is simply a lack of food. The idea of a fixed energy budget has already been mentioned. The early days of the dam, when the waters were exceptionally rich in chemicals, had passed. Booming populations of every kind had utilised the excesses and species that were less capable of rapid growth than *Salvinia* had now had time to establish themselves. There was far more competition for resources than previously. So there was an energy squeeze. On the one hand, the nutritional status of the water itself was far diminished compared with what it had once been; on the other hand there was increased competition for what remained. Something had to give and it was the *Salvinia* that lost ground.

Huge increases in energy consumption had come from other species. There were no underwater plants when the dam was first created but by 1973 they were dense enough in some places to hinder fishing. An investigation of the mussel populations indicated *a standing crop* of about 16 000 tonnes and there was an estimated offtake of about 30 000 tonnes of fish in the lake.[18] All of this biomass was new and it all had to be paid for from a dwindling energy budget. *Salvinia* could not survive at its original levels against such competition. Whether its final collapse was due solely to only one of these factors or to more than one in combination is difficult to determine. The fact is that the weed problem in Kariba no longer exists.

If, in the long term, the decline of Kariba's troublesome weed was a function of the remorseless rules of energy budgeting, then the success of the Kapenta was, in some ways, the other side of the same coin. The basic source of life-giving energy in a lake is the sun and the chemicals in the water. But the chemicals are not everywhere evenly distributed and neither are the fish. We have already seen that conductivity and the nutritional status of the water are much higher nearer the inflowing secondary rivers than in Zambezi water alone. The productivity of a lake is also higher around the margins and in the shallow water. Most fish life occurs between the shallows and a depth of about 20 m and the highest catches come from an average depth of 5 m.[19] This being so, there will be a vast area of the lake that will have few, if any, fish in it at all — and this was indeed the case in Kariba.

When Kariba turned from a river into a dam, naturally enough it contained only river fish. Such fish are not accustomed to utilising deep waters and this ecological niche, with all its unused nutrients, remained empty. Two-thirds of Kariba's productive potential for fish was not being used. Clearly, however, no riverine fish could fill the open-water, or pelagic, niche and so some other species would have to be imported.

The fish decided upon was an excellent choice and has been highly successful. In 1963 an attempt at introduction was made with the freshwater sardine, *Limnothrissa miodon,* and 350 fry were imported from Lake Tanganyika. Considering the success that ultimately followed, this vanguard had an extraordinarily uncomfortable time of things. About 55% of them died on the flight in. Half of the survivors were transferred immediately to a lakeside storage dam where, within a few minutes, they were all dead! Of the remaining 80-odd, only 14 survived through the night to the following morning. They were placed in a keepnet in the lake where they continued to live for three months. Then a storm came, destroyed the net and the fish were never seen again. It was not an auspicious start![20]

In spite of these setbacks, further research confirmed that *Limnothrissa* was the right choice and arrangements were made for large-scale imports. These took place between July 1967 and September 1968. Although mortality rates were about 50%, slightly more than 360 000 live fry were placed in the waters of Lake Kariba. (So were 12 000 shrimps, which have never been heard of since!) All the researchers could then do was to sit back and wait.

Kapenta, as the new fish came to be known in Kariba, do not generally live for more than a year, so when reports of sardine shoals started to come in during October 1968, the fisheries officers concerned allowed themselves, for the first time, some hope that their experimental introduction might be working. They had to wait a nerve-racking ten months before they got final confirmation, in July 1969, when two tigerfish caught in gill nets were found to have been eating Kapenta. In the stomach of one there were 43 fish and in the other just a single Kapenta. Together, however, it was enough to show that the sardine from Lake Tanganyika had made it![21]

An extraordinary feature of the sardine's introduction was the rapid rate at which it spread. First recoveries were in 1969, yet within a year the fish was well established throughout the entire lake. Zambia began experimental fishing in 1969 but this was too early; widespread as they may have been, the sardine populations were not large enough and, by 1971, the attempt was given up. Pessimists were quick to condemn the effort as 'yet another useless deed of fishery practitioners', but they were wrong.[22] In the same year, the Zimbabwean side began their experimental fishing, which led to the awarding of the first commercial licences in 1973.

In the early days much had to be learnt about the biology and ecology of the sardine, and how to catch it. Normally the fish occurs in very large, dense shoals found throughout the lake. These small fish may eat continuously and consume huge quantities of phytoplankton, zooplankton and a few insects. Their population size is directly related to the amount of plankton available. The plankton, as a primary producer, is directly linked to the level of nutrients in the water.[23] The plankton rise and fall daily through a considerable vertical range in the lake and are followed in this pattern by the sardines which prey upon them.[24] The Kariba sardine is smaller than its ancestors in Lake Tanganyika and this is an interesting illustration of the importance of nutrition. The northern fish will average between 9 cm and 14 cm with a maximum length of 17 cm. In contrast, a Kariba specimen will not be longer than 13,5 cm and will average between 4,5 cm and 7 cm. This much reduced size is purely a function of diet. The average conductivity of Lake Tanganyika is in the region of 600 units while that of Kariba averages below 100.[25]

A number of different techniques were tried in order to make commercial catches of the new sardine. None was particularly successful until the special secret of such fishing was discovered. It lay in net design. The small-scale methods imported from Lake Tanganyika did not work and success only came after the adoption of larger nets and bigger vessels.

Light is also essential. All Kapenta fishing is now carried out at night; to attract the fish, powerful lights are suspended over the net or submerged in the water. With the lights on, the net is kept beneath the Kapenta at a depth between 20 m and 30 m until sufficient fish are gathered. At that moment, the net is retrieved as quickly as possible. The detail of the several techniques varies with the type of net used but the basic principles are much the same.

Originally, in Zimbabwe's Kapenta industry, the fresh fish were frozen and marketed in packets. But this is no longer important and most catches are sun-dried after being dipped in brine. This makes processing less costly and within 24 or 48 hours a nutritious, inexpensive product with a long shelf-life is available to the low-income consumer where the need for protein and variety is probably greatest.

Kapenta fishing focuses on several natural basins within the lake. The largest and most exploited is immediately south of Kariba township. I have sat many times on the high hilltop there, caressed by the warm breezes of a summer's night, and watched the lake below me. When there is no moon and the sky is clear it is as if the stars themselves, lured by the beauty of a thousand lighted boats, merge with them across the invisible horizon and surge towards one, bobbing on the silent swell far below.

Technology, human skill and natural growth have taken the tonnages of sardines caught from a bare 66 wet tonnes in 1973, the first year of experimental fishing in Zimbabwe, to a total Zimbabwean catch in 1981 of 11 131 tonnes. This catch was worth just over US$4 million, of which more than half went back in wages to about 2 000 people employed in the area by the industry.[26]

Figures for Zambia are somewhat lower that those for Zimbabwe: 872 tonnes were landed in 1981, 2 663 tonnes in 1982, 4 970 tonnes in 1983 and 6 198 tonnes in 1984.[27] The industry in Zambia is less advanced and is hampered by a shortage of raw materials, but it has the same potential, which will shortly be realised.

The size of the *Limnothrissa* resource in Lake Kariba is enormous. Estimates suggest that the total biomass of this fish may exceed 90 000 tonnes, implying that bigger catches are possible. It has been noticed in the past, however, that Kapenta populations are volatile and respond quickly to the presence or absence of floods and to river flow, for example. Catches are seasonal and tonnages are related to inflow patterns. Although there is no danger of biological overfishing, excessive commercial fishing is a possibility. This means that fishing pressure is unlikely ever to reduce Kapenta populations below a survival threshold but it is quite possible for catches to decline below a point at which they are commercially viable.

The Tanganyika sardine has been a complete success in its new environment. Biologically it has flourished; commercially it has earned money and provided jobs. It is interesting to recall that this was all made possible by the sensible exploitation of a vacant niche in the energy cycle and in the open spaces of a man-made dam!

The tigerfish has already been mentioned as one of the top sporting fish in Africa. In Kariba, on a diet of Kapenta, it has flourished and it is from there that the South African record of 15,5 kg was taken in 1962, at a time when the lake was at its most productive.[28] Mostly, however, tigerfish average about 3 kg but are renowned for the leaping fight they offer. Zimbabwe has turned the tiger to good account and, since 1962, has held an annual tigerfishing competition on Lake Kariba. In 1988 315 teams took part, involving over 1 000 people. Total catches during the years have varied but have recently averaged approximately 2 500 kg.[29] In a survey in 1978 it was noted that approximately US$33 were spent on each kilogram of fish landed in the competition. Since then prices have risen and it may not be unreasonable to say that the figure is now US$40.[30] If so, then US$100 000 are injected into the local economy with each competition — and all thanks to the tigerfish!

Without doubt, the greatest fishy mystery of the Zambezi is the presence of the African mottled eel in Lake Kariba. The mystery lies in that the eel must breed in the sea, but as young have been recorded above the dam wall it means they have found a way to bypass both Cahora Bassa and Kariba. There are no artificial ways around these dams and so young have either worked their way through the turbines or surmounted the walls. Both prospects are difficult to accept — and yet there seems to be no alternative.

There are two species of eel that have been associated with and collected in the Zambezi: the longfinned eel and the African mottled eel. The latter is by far the most common. All eels found in southern Africa breed off the north or north-eastern coast of Madagascar. The males spend between 10 and 19 years in fresh water and the females between 6 and 8 years before returning to the sea.[31] After breeding, the adults die. Eel larvae are delicate, transparent and leaf-like creatures that must drift for months or years on the currents before being transported from their birthplace to the coast.[32] The flat larva gradually changes shape and by the time it is between a year and 18 months in age it becomes an elver, no thicker than a match and about 5 to 7 cm in length. It is the elver that begins to make its way upstream.[33] There is no suggestion that young return to the river of their parents but it is probably true that they are driven by an instinct we do not yet understand to continue their passage upstream until further progress is impossible.

In migrating upstream, young eels will obviously encounter rapids and waterfalls of various sizes and a neat relationship that determines their ability to surmount these obstacles has been suggested by R.A. Jubb. He mentions three South African waterfalls, all of which are more formidable in height than either Victoria Falls or those on the Kafue. Eels have no apparent difficulty in bypassing the South African falls while they are seldom recorded upstream of the two on the Zambezi. Jubb suggests that the size of the eel and the distance of the obstacle from the sea are related. The greater the distance, the older the eel until, at last, they become too large and heavy to negotiate the hazard.[34] This reasoning is an attractive explanation for the scarcity of eels in the headwaters of the Zambezi and in the Kafue.

For the record, however, there is evidence of eels above both Victoria Falls and in the Kafue. A large eel was caught on the Zambezi above the falls in September 1962. That the fish was able to climb the falls is not, apparently, surprising. What is remarkable is that it was able to achieve this feat given the size it must have been after travelling 1 500 km from the sea and 2 500 km from its birthplace. A few kilometres upstream from where it enters the Zambezi, the Kafue cuts through a dramatic gorge. This too was held to be an impassable obstacle to the passage of eel. Today a dam wall also blocks the gorge and there are no reports to say what has happened to upstream eel populations. However, in the days before the dam, there are at least three accounts of eel being caught (and eaten!) in the Kafue above its falls.[35]

These reports show the tenacity and formidable climbing ability of young eels but they have another little-known advantage: eels are adapted to take in oxygen through their skin. In the water about 10% of their requirement is obtained in this way. But in the air as much as 66% of their needs can be met, the remainder coming via the gills.[36]

Kariba was sealed off in December 1958; any eel born after that date must have found some way past the wall. Eddie MacGregor was in charge of the pumps that drew water from the river near the Deka mouth, about 120 km downstream from Victoria Falls. He was present when an eel of just under 15 kg was caught near his house in May 1986.[37] There is no possibility that the eel was 28 years old. It had entered Kariba after the wall had been closed.

Dr E.K. Balon presents the most detailed and interesting evidence. He found populations of eel at three localities in Kariba and was able to investigate them thoroughly. An analysis of 67 specimens from one area showed that 57% had entered through the gorge while the remaining 43% had somehow bypassed the dam.[38] In another group, all seven had entered Lake Kariba between 1960 and 1968. Balon believes that eel juveniles would be between 6 cm and 10 cm long when they enter the dam in the second year of their lives. Not only is he convinced that the eels somehow cross the wall but his figures suggest they do so in large numbers. To sustain the density of eel populations in the grounds that he examined, approximately 300 juveniles would, he says, be required per square kilometre per year. As he estimates the grounds to be 1 357 km^2, this works out to be over 400 000 young eels getting through or over Kariba's walls every year.[39]

It cannot be disputed that eels have mastered Kariba, but before we examine how this might be possible, we must consider the problem of Cahora Bassa. This dam, in every way as formidable as Kariba and equally without facilities for migratory fish, closed the river in 1974. There should not, therefore, be any eel younger than that date either in the Zambezi above Cahora Bassa or upstream of Kariba.

For evidence of eels born after 1974 we have to return to Eddie MacGregor. In 1984 he drained a water tank that had not been cleaned for seven years. Flopping and wriggling in the mud at the bottom of the tank was an assorted and rather startling collection of fish — and an eel. The eel measured a fraction under 61 cm. The average length for one of 10 years is 68 cm. It is possible that this youngster was post-Cahora Bassa. However, in 1980, when the floodgates at Kariba were last opened, Dr Brian Marshall found eels below Kariba's wall.[40] They were 25 cm in length, which suggests an age of approximately 3 to 4 years. Unequivocally, they had managed to get past Cahora Bassa.

I cannot imagine any more than two ways round an obstacle such as a dam wall: over or through it! At least two people have reported watching eels trying to surmount the wall at Kariba. Frank Junor and some of the staff of Kariba Fisheries Research Institute saw young elvers nearly half-way up the wall. They did not watch them move higher, assuming that they would not negotiate the overhang, and noted that there have never been any reports of eels crossing the road on the top of the wall.[41]

John Minshull, the Keeper of Ichthyology at the Bulawayo Museum in Zimbabwe, watched eels early one morning in 1970. They were making their way up a series of step-like ledges at the south end of Kariba's wall, down which ran a trickle of water that kept the fish moist. They had climbed more than 110 m but John could see that it was impossible for them to progress further. The wall in front of them was smooth and sheer, the ledges had ended, they could not go on. John is firmly convinced, as I am, that this is not the way the eels used.[42] If Balon's figures are correct, on average more than 1 000 eels a day would have to pass across the top of the wall. As there has never been even one report of this happening, they must have found another way. If not over the top, then passing through the wall is the only alternative. That this is likely, however incredible it may seem, is suggested by the following report. In 1965, 55 dead eels were found on the upstream side of an idle turbine. They had been killed by a sudden change in water pressure which had sucked them against a metal strainer.[43] This is the best evidence I have found that it is possible for eels to make their way through the turbine although how this is physically possible is beyond me.

To me, the conclusion must be that, somehow, eels are getting through the turbines at both Cahora Bassa and Kariba. We can but admire and be amazed at the powerful drive that impels these fish, enabling them to find ways around these man-made obstacles, to colonise the river beyond.

There are, altogether, 156 different species of fish in the Zambezi[44] and included among them are some rather unexpected and unlikely creatures. Not the least of these is the shark, something seldom thought of when one is worrying about hippo and crocodiles! Known locally as the Zambezi shark, *Carcharhinus leucas* occurs throughout the world and is probably one of the best known and most ferocious of the killer sharks. It is extremely aggressive, frequents shallow waters off the coast and is the main species responsible for human attacks in East and South Africa.[45]

In the days before Cahora Bassa, it had been caught as far up the Zambezi as Kariba Gorge, over 1 000 km from the sea. It is, admittedly, rare in the river, only six specimens having been recorded, but it is nevertheless remarkable that it should have made its way so far upstream. In the sea these fish grow to some 200 kg and a length of about 3 m. The largest taken in the Zambezi, however, was only 1 m. Voracious and savage eaters, these sharks make fearful forays against shoals of fish and have been known to attack hippo as well as their own kind. It seems possible that incidents for which crocodiles have been held responsible may have been the result of shark attack.

Other unlikely inhabitants of the Zambezi include jellyfish, mussels, sponges, shrimps and prawns. Anyone familiar with African rivers will recall having seen the occasional mussel shell on the banks. The fact that freshwater mussels occur is not particularly unusual. What did surprise many was the work of Dale Kenmuir, who was able to show that in Kariba alone, the biomass of the four species there amounted to between 33 000 tonnes and 167 000 tonnes.[46] An attempt has been made to exploit this crop commercially but collection is difficult and the taste does not appear to be popular. Perhaps an opportunity awaits a more enterprising entrepreneur?

Sponges are ubiquitous in aquatic environments — although we may not always recognise them. There are plenty in Kariba and they take the form of a ball-shaped collection of matter adhering to reeds, ropes, wood and the like. So they are one of the many forms of life that benefit from dead trees in the Zambezi's dams. The largest recorded sponges measure about 21 cm in diameter; they are found between 1 m and 15 m from the surface.[47] Little research has been carried out on sponges with the result that their role in the ecology of the river can only be guessed at.

The same is true of the jellyfish, also found throughout the river, but most noticeably in dams. Typically 'jellyfish' in shape, these creatures are a pale grey to white colour, about 2,5 cm wide. They are most common in the winter months and have been known to undergo explosive bursts in population numbers.[48] Like most of their kind, they are equipped with nematocysts that can fire a barbed and poisonous dart.[49] These have been seen to kill young fish but I know of no reports of them affecting humans in any way.

A species of shrimp occurs naturally in the Zambezi (and there is a possibility that it has been joined by survivors of the 1968 Zambian airlift). No one has studied them sufficiently to discover if they will breed and shoal in such a way as to form the basis of a commercial industry but they are otherwise quite plentiful. If, for instance, you search a bed of *Salvinia* by torchlight you will certainly see the eyes of these tiny creatures reflecting redly in the light. They are easily caught on the weed but have a habit of flicking their body and will leap right out of your hand. Although they are small and only measure about 3 cm in length, they play an important role in the ecology of the river. They consume the detritus and algae that accumulate on the leaves of rooted aquatic vegetation, and in their turn are consumed by fish and birds.[50]

Although an exotic species, the freshwater prawn that has been imported into Kariba is a fascinating creature because of its remarkable life history. *Macrobrachium rosenbergii* is indigenous to and common in the big rivers of South-East Asia where it spends its life, except for the four or five occasions when it migrates downriver to breed in the saline estuaries. It is this aspect of its biology that makes it attractive: since it must breed in salt water, it cannot propagate or threaten a lake such as Kariba. Although some specimens have 'escaped', they can cause no harm and remain without breeding until they die. One was caught in a net in water 70 m deep some 80 km away from the prawn farm at Kariba. Its mass was nearly 0,5 kg and it was 0,75 m long.[51]

The prawn's breeding limitations, rightly seen as an advantage by the custodians of Zimbabwe's National Parks, are a major difficulty to the producer. Trying to duplicate, during the breeding season, the gradual change to the correct level of salinity without the benefit of natural sea water on tap is extremely difficult and expensive.

Despite this, the enterprise at Kariba has been operating since 1980 and has had considerable success. Its hatchery produces some 2,5 million larvae a year, which go to open, aerated ponds where the young are kept until they reach between 25 g and 30 g, the market size. About 8 tonnes are sold frozen in packets each year. Despite this success, rising import costs are squeezing the business and a change is envisaged, to farming carp. These fish have phenomenal growth rates, will not breed naturally if they escape, are ideally suited to conditions in Kariba and will do away with the reliance on imports.[52] Exciting as it may have sounded, the freshwater prawn does not compete with its marine cousin, so perhaps the change will be for the better.

Common in places and found throughout the entire length of the Zambezi downstream of Victoria Falls is the remarkable electric catfish, *Malapterurus electricus*. This is one of two African species and is extremely widespread, occurring as far afield as the Nile and West Africa. It is remarkable because of the extraordinary role that electricity plays in its biology and ecology.

The electric organs cover the whole body and consist of tiny cells known as electroplates. Under laboratory conditions, the catfish can give a discharge of 450 volts. It has been known for some time that catfish, which have small and weak eyes, use this ability to help them navigate and that they also employ the system to locate and kill or stun their prey. Studies have shown that the rate and duration of electrical discharges rises after dusk, their primary hunting time.[53]

There is some evidence that, in addition to assistance in finding its way locally, the ability to send and receive electrical impulses may also have a role to play in long-distance navigation. Exactly how this might work is not understood. There is also a strong belief that electrical sensing may help the catfish to find injured prey. This is because open wounds strengthen the direct current field that is generated so that injured prey can be detected at a greater distance than an uninjured organism.[54]

Stimulated by studies on electrical catfish, scientists have investigated other species and have discovered groups they call 'weakly electric' fish.[55] Unable to navigate and stun or kill their prey with electricity like the more powerful of their kind, these fish generate an extremely subtle electric field, no stronger than a volt or two. There are at least eight species of the Mormyrid family with this facility in the Zambezi.[56]

The Mormyrids emit small electrical impulses that are used for locating obstacles in the environment and for communication. It is in this latter regard that fascinating discoveries have been made. It appears that, by this means, one of these fish may be able to tell the sex, age and mating status of another; it may even be able to recognise different individuals.

An obvious problem with either kind of electric fish is how they avoid getting killed or confused by their own discharges. It seems that in the more powerful fish the nervous system has an unusually high degree of insulation. Tissues are often embedded in thick layers of fat and, in addition, muscles tend to have a high threshold of excitation which must be overcome before they respond.[57] In the Mormyrids, signal confusion is avoided by having two sets of receptors. One set is designed to recognise and filter out the fish's own signals, leaving another far more sensitive set to concentrate on signals from other fish. And we all thought the Japanese were best at this sort of thing!

No investigative studies have been carried out on the Zambezi's Mormyrids and there is every possibility of more remarkable finds when the work is done. It would be interesting to know if this level of sophisticated use of electricity is also found among the catfish. Perhaps we have been so intrigued by the power in the past that we have not looked for the subtlety? This reminds me that much of the interest and excitement in a river like the Zambezi is its size and diversity, and the certainty that there is much more to be discovered.

10   Gnat Chat

THE purpose of this chapter is to share the enjoyment I experienced in learning of the life histories and special adaptations of some of the insects and parasites that are to be found within reach of the Zambezi. The survey is by no means exhaustive, nor is it intended to be. Rather, it is a journey of discovery motivated by curiosity and a delight in the unexpected.

No one who spends a night or an evening beside the Zambezi, except at the height of the relatively warm tropical winter, can fail to be aware of the millions of winged, whining insects that cram the air and jam the airwaves with their ceaseless sound. Mementoes of such a night are often swelling bumps, raw red bites and a stream of invective aimed at the mosquito. This is a little unfair, for the mosquito is only one of the winged warriors out there, waiting to enjoy its share of your blood! Nevertheless, carrying malaria as it does, the mosquito can be very dangerous: even today with all our drugs, malaria still kills with frightening frequency.

The earliest records of malaria come down to us from Ancient Egypt where clear references to the disease are to be found in a papyrus dating from about 1600 BC. The Greeks were also well aware of malaria and Hippocrates left us with a description of the course of the disease that is sufficiently detailed for us to recognise the slightly different symptoms associated with various species of the parasite.[1]

So widespread and devastating has the disease been that it has unquestionably affected the course of history. It may well have hastened the collapse of both the Greek and Roman empires and at least one crusade was defeated more by the disease than by the Turks. Malaria, which is caused by a protozoan parasite of the genus *Plasmodium,* reached its worldwide peak in 1958 when an estimated 250 million people were infected with it.[2]

There are four species of *Plasmodium* that cause the disease in man, of which one, *falciparum,* accounts for about 95% of all cases, in Zimbabwe at least.[3] The parasite is transmitted in the bite of an infected female mosquito belonging to the genus *Anopheles.* I was surprised to learn that there are more than 100 species within this genus.[4] Not all the species are carriers, however, and in Zimbabwe, for example, where there are 30 species of *Anopheles,* only three transmit malaria.

The history of how malaria evolved is not known, but it is found in all major groups of terrestrial vertebrates in the Old World. This suggests that the parasite species concerned are likely to be exceedingly ancient and predate hominids by millions of years.[5]

In southern Africa malaria is now being treated with chloroquine but there are persistent stories of a malaria strain resistant to this drug. These stories have some truth in them.

Drug resistance occurs through gene mutation when a parasite continues to multiply despite the presence of the drug. The earliest record of this dates back to 1910, in Brazil, when *falciparum* developed a resistance to quinine.[6]

Chloroquine-resistant *P. falciparum* originated in Thailand about 25 years ago and has slowly spread in all directions, into south-east Asia, India, the western Pacific, east and west Africa. It first reached South America in Columbia and has now spread throughout the continent except for Argentina, Paraguay and Peru.

The first reports of chloroquine-resistant malaria in Africa came from Kenya and Tanzania in 1978. Subsequently, the strain has been confirmed in Comoros, Madagascar, Uganda, Zambia and the Ivory Coast. Mozambique is likely to have been infected with the resistant strain[7] and a small number of cases have been confirmed in Zimbabwe.[8]

There is a delightful story told about the control of malaria and the use of DDT, which is worth repeating. South Africa was the first country in the southern part of the continent to make use of DDT. She had seen evidence of its remarkable effect in two experiments that took place just before the Second World War. The first had been run by Professor Buxton of the London School of Hygiene and Tropical Medicine, when the use of DDT in controlling lice and mosquitoes in the Nile Valley had been demonstrated with astounding success to the British Middle East Command.

The second experiment took place shortly afterwards when General Fox and Major Woodward of the US Army Medical Corps again proved its value in controlling lice, when they applied it as a dusting powder to houses in Naples.

Beyond doubt, DDT was the answer (so it seemed then) and the Union government attempted to get hold of it. There was a snag, however. The formula for DDT was regarded as a top military secret and the authorities would not release it under any circumstances. It would have been stalemate and many lives might have been lost but for the fact that a Major Murray, of the Union Health Department, was also a keen handyman.

Murray's interests caused him to buy regularly copies of an American magazine called *Popular Mechanics*. There, in one of the back pages, were all the details of the secret formula, which the Union then began to manufacture![9]

Simple observation in the malarial zone of Africa shows plainly that people can acquire some kind of tolerance of malaria. Gene mutations in humans that can confer any degree of protection against the parasite would, by natural selection, increase in frequency. Such genetic adaptations would assist young children to survive the first year or two of life, during which time their immune system could begin producing antibodies which would take over the long-term role of partial protection against the disease.[10] Just such a mutation has occurred in some people and it serves now to introduce the remarkable story of malaria and the sickle-cell gene.

Just over 8% of black Americans carry a single gene for sickle-cell anaemia. For years this well-established fact was a cause of no concern, for such a characteristic was considered to be benign. However, research has shown that persons in America with the sickle-cell trait who undergo the rigours of basic army training run a risk of sudden death which is some 20 to 40 times higher than that for the normal young person.[11] What is sickle-cell anaemia and what does it have to do with the Zambezi and malaria?

A patient who has sickle-cell disease has inherited from *each* parent the same mutant genes which, together, produce abnormal haemoglobin. Haemoglobin is a protein — an iron complex — found in the red blood cells; its function is to collect oxygen from the lungs and deliver it to muscles and body tissue. Abnormal haemoglobin, called Hb S, can still accomplish this task, though with severe limitations.

Typically, blood cells are highly flexible and capable of slipping along the smallest capillaries, delivering oxygen as they go. However, under certain circumstances, such as low oxygen levels and increased acidity, the presence of Hb S can cause cells to stiffen and become rigid. As the cells do so, they assume odd shapes, one of which gives the disease its name. Instead of being able to squeeze through the tiny blood vessels, they get stuck and cells following along behind have to burrow through an even smaller space. If the blockage is complete, the tissue nurtured by that small blood vessel will be deprived of oxygen, the patient will experience pain and, after repeated episodes, may suffer from the malfunction of irreparably damaged organs.

In every blood stream, and especially the spleen, there are cells whose function is to scavenge. One of their roles is to seek out and destroy damaged and elderly red blood cells and invaders of many kinds. Called macrophages, these cells, in the case of a patient suffering from sickle-cell disease, consume irreversibly damaged red cells, young and old, which is the main reason why patients with the condition always appear so pale. Should one of these unfortunate people contract malaria, then the macrophages will be doubly busy for they will be removing both 'sickled' cells and those infected with the malaria parasite. Under these circumstances, patients become very anaemic and can die, especially if they are infants, too young to have developed their own immunity.

In a place like central Africa, where malaria is very common, one would expect sickle-cell disease to die out, as few children would survive long enough to pass it on. Why then does Hb S continue to survive in the populations? The answer is found with those people who have inherited one mutant gene from one parent and a normal matching gene from the other parent. These people are said to have the sickle-cell *trait*, as opposed to sickle-cell *disease*. They produce enough haemoglobin to live healthily like anybody else, without the terrible complications caused by sickle-cell disease. However, because of the Hb S gene they have inherited, such people produce red cells containing a mixture of normal haemoglobin and abnormal Hb S and these cells are slightly vulnerable to early removal by the macrophages, especially in someone with a fever.

Thus it happens that when a person with the sickle-cell trait is infected with malaria, any red cells containing both parasite and some Hb S may be quickly demolished by the macrophages. This can happen before the malaria parasite has had time to spread through the body, causing its sometimes fatal complications. The result is that people with the sickle-cell trait tend to weather malaria better than people with only normal haemoglobin. In other words, having the sickle-cell trait actually offers an advantage, especially to children, which helps them to survive malarial attacks.

In regions where severe malaria is very common, infants with sickle-cell trait have a slight advantage over other children and this explains why, instead of dying out, as one might expect, the gene for Hb S continues. The Hb S gene remains in the population at a level where the advantage to people with the sickle-cell trait is balanced by the disadvantage to people with sickle-cell disease and to people with only the normal haemoglobin.[12]

What, then, is the connection with black American servicemen, who served to introduce this story? It was in America, in 1910, that sickle-cell disease was first identified and the work was carried out on West Indians of African origin. Much controversy surrounds the origins of sickle-cell disease but current thought suggests that its present distribution originated from identical mutations in different areas.

These areas include Saudi Arabia, India and central and west Africa. The widespread presence of sickle-cell disease in both North and South America can be explained by its carriage there in slaves imported from Africa in previous centuries. It is a common misconception that the disease occurs only among people of negro descent. This is not so for it has been imported into Europe and is found in Italy, Greece and Turkey.[13]

Although the disease itself was identified in America, its role in offering carriers partial protection against malaria was not discovered until the late 1940s. The credit for this work must go to a Dr Beet, a government medical officer working for the Northern Rhodesia government and stationed on the Zambezi, at Mongu in Barotseland.

A more malarial region than the Zambezi floodplains in western Zambia would be hard to imagine and Beet had thousands of patients to work with. In a major paper he recorded his observation that malarial parasites occurred much less frequently in blood which could also be made to 'sickle' under laboratory conditions.[14] This led to intensive, and often controversial, investigations and the eventual elucidation of the strange relationship between malaria and sickle-cell anaemia.

It would take a vivid imagination to recognise the mosquito as a creature of beauty but the same does not hold for another flying insect that abounds along the Zambezi. In the warmer months dragonflies with their characteristic helicopter flight are everywhere to be seen. Two of the most common are perhaps the most striking, one a deep blue and the other a pillar-box red.

Typically, these creatures pause briefly in their flight to rest atop a reed or stem of grass and it is then that the exquisite beauty of their wings can be seen. Gossamer veined, translucent and prisming the sunlight, they shimmer and seem to spark, beautiful to watch. Part of the purpose of this gaudy display is mate attraction and it is in the mating that recent discoveries have revealed some extraordinary facts.[15]

As with many creatures, female dragonflies typically mate with a number of males in succession. Copulation takes up to 20 minutes and this is because, for most of the time, the male insect is busily removing sperm from the female so that any left by the previous mating male is safely disposed of and cannot compete with his own!

There are several methods by which this is done, as a series of scanning electron micrographs have shown. In one, the male pushes the head of the penis up into the female's sperm storage organs where its extensible head expands, scraping out the sperm and trapping it behind a flange. The base of the penis is covered with minute, backward-pointing hairs which further help to trap and remove the sperm.

Another method involves the male in pushing existing sperm further into the female organs so that it becomes inaccessible to her: she then uses sperm on the basis of 'last in, first out'. The penis of the male that does this has inflatable lobes which help to force previous sperm upward. Some males have a penis with horns and flanges that correspond closely to the internal shape of the female's reproductive organ. So closely does it fit that it works as an efficient scraper.

As I have mentioned, the purpose of these remarkable adaptations is to allow a male the best chance of ensuring that his genes survive into the next generation. Research of this type opens enormous new areas of interest for it encourages scientists to examine the factors that influence natural selection and, in this way, to obtain insights into the complexities of evolution itself.

There are a number of flying insect forms very similar to dragonflies but entirely unrelated. One of these is the antlion. Antlions have the same four

membranous wings and the same thin and elongated bodies as dragonflies. They are rather shy and secretive creatures that often rise in silently
fluttering clouds as you pass through rank vegetation.

Unlike the dragonfly, which has its legs far forward under the thorax,
conferring the advantage that it can eat and fly at the same time, the
antlion, in common with most other flying insects, has its legs under its
wings. This is one easy way of telling the two apart. Another difference
is that, while the dragonfly perches with its wings open and spread wide,
the antlion sits with them tented along the length of its long body.[16]

The most striking difference of all is to be found in the larval stages.
Dragonflies always breed near water and their larvae are aquatic. Antlion
larvae are quite the reverse: they build the tens of thousands of tiny
conical pits one encounters in areas of dry sand and soil that are nowhere
near water at all.

The antlion larva is a rapacious predator. It builds its tiny pit-trap and
buries itself in the bottom. The idea is that prey falls into the hole and,
unable to gain any purchase on the slippery slope, tumbles to the bottom
and into the jaws of the waiting larva, which has helped the descent of
its prey by flicking particles of sand at it.

The larva has no mouth and subsists by sucking the body juices from
its prey, along grooves in the partially hollow and fearsome jaws with
which it is equipped. Very few of the many antlion species dig the pit-
traps with which people in Africa are familiar, but all spin cocoons and
bury themselves in the ground from which the showy adult eventually
emerges.[17]

I never cease to be astounded by some of the extraordinary sequences
that life forms follow to ensure the perpetuation of their kind. Not only
are the cycles sometimes complex and, to us, perhaps, risky, but I am invariably at a loss to know how they could have evolved in the first place.
The life-cycle of the lungworm is a good example.

A species of lungworm is found in impala antelope in several localities
along the Zambezi. Lungworm are not uncommon, nor are they necessarily a threat to the animal's health and condition unless present in overwhelming numbers. Their interest to us lies in their life-cycle.

First-stage lungworm larvae pass out of the animal in its faeces. Impala
often defecate in fixed places known as middens, where considerable piles
of dung can accumulate. Unlike many nematode species, the larvae remain in the dung, awaiting the arrival of a suitable host. They can remain
viable for at least nine months.[18]

In Zimbabwe, where research on this subject is being conducted, only
two slug hosts are known. The lungworm larva remains in the faecal
pellets until such a slug should pass immediately over it. In a manner that
is not yet understood, somehow the slimy mucus that the slug exudes as
it travels activates the larva. When this happens, the larva penetrates the

'foot' of the slug and remains there through two more larval stages, pausing then in its development.[19]

At this point, if the system has worked the way it should, the slug gets eaten by an impala as part of a mouthful of grass or shrubbery. Slugs are known to aestivate during the dry season and when the rains do come both the slugs and impala move on to the fresh green shoots of grass to feed.

By this means the third-stage larva arrives back in the intestines of its mammal host. As a lungworm, however, this is not really where it wants to be and so it migrates through the lymphatic circulation to the lungs were it grows into an adult![20]

In the lungs the adult lungworm lays eggs which, in time, are coughed up by the host animal and swallowed. Reaching the impala's intestine, the eggs hatch and the first-stage larvae pass out of the animal to begin the whole extraordinary cycle again.

I remember very well an occasion some years ago, standing with a good friend overlooking the saline marsh at Cape Cod, Massachusetts. We had agreed, as a challenge, to take a direct line through the marsh to the distant seashore. As we waded through mud, swam murky channels and tramped through sodden reed beds I was suddenly struck by how different it all was from Africa. There were no snakes to fear, the water held no such hidden terrors as bilharzia, crocodiles, hippos or leeches and there were no malaria-laden mosquitoes, centipedes or any of the other unpleasant things one comes to take for granted at home.

I also realised with amazement how complacent one can become as a resident African. In a kind of 'conditioned forgetting' one loses sight of the many dangers facing those who move out of the towns and cities and into the continent's wild places.

A mild example of what I mean is a common fly known by various names throughout southern and central Africa: the name 'tumbu' or 'putsi' fly will be recognised by most. The female putsi lays her eggs in sand or soil that has been contaminated by urine or faeces. However, she is just as likely to choose clothing on a washing line as a suitable site, provided it is not damp and is in the shade. Babies' nappies that have been poorly washed are a particularly favoured target for egg laying.

Hatched larvae that are brought into contact with human or animal skin can penetrate it very quickly. On a rat or guinea pig, this can take as little as 25 seconds. Once embedded, the larva grows, consuming the flesh about it and creating a boil-like swelling, which is about as painful. If undisturbed, the maggot drops to the ground after eight to ten days. Burying itself, it remains there for a further ten days during the pupal stage before the adult fly emerges.[21]

Many newcomers to Africa meet the putsi fly the hard way but the inconvenience of it can be avoided. Clothing in the sun will not have eggs laid on it and proper ironing destroys the eggs. If maggots do develop in

the skin, they are easily removed once the trick is known. The most unpleasant aspect of the experience is the thought of the larvae consuming
living flesh. Dogs are very common victims of the putsi fly and I recall on
one occasion taking 14 of the maggots from my dog Gypsey's chest and
belly.

Myiasis is a term used to describe the infestation of live animals by 'bot'
or 'blow'-fly larvae which feed on the host's living or dead tissue.[22] I had
no idea, until I began this research, how many species of such flies there
are, nor the wide range of animals that fall prey to them. It occurred to me
that, while it might be easy for humans to iron clothing or remove the
maggots, animals don't have these options. I wondered how many instances of animal aggression might be explained by the agonies of blow-
fly infestations.

An example of flesh-consuming larvae among humans comes from the
Punjab in India. There, a young boy had been circumcised by a native doctor and the wound had become infected. Two weeks later, when the boy
was admitted to hospital, the entire penis was a foul-smelling ulcer, the
soft parts at the end had been destroyed and several hundred maggots were
removed from the remaining flesh.[23]

A remarkable aspect of blow-fly biology is its degree of specialisation.
One fly, for example, which infests horses, donkeys and zebras, lays its
eggs on the head hairs near the jaw. When the larvae hatch, they migrate
to the lips and invade the spaces between the teeth below the gum line. Ne-
crosis often results in the formation of pockets of pus in which as many
as 12 larvae have been found.

Another specialist fly was first reported by Dr James Kirk, a member of
David Livingstone's Zambezi expedition. He discovered the larvae of the
'blue elephant stomach bot-fly' in the stomach of an elephant shot near the
Zambezi. Research in later years showed that the adult fly lays its eggs
near the elephant's mouth at the base of the tusks. The newly hatched
larvae crawl into the mouth and down into the stomach where they grow
to maturity. At that stage, they crawl back up into the mouth and the
elephant spits them out while feeding. Another species spends its larval
life attached to the wall of the elephant's throat before escaping in the same
way as the stomach bot-fly. Finally, there are bot-fly larvae that live only
in the nasal mucosa of the elephant's trunk. Each can grow to 1,5 cm in
length and there may be between 20 and 50 in one animal.[24]

Almost all of the antelope are, in one way or another, victims of
specialising blow-flies: hartebeest, wildebeest, roan and tsessebe seem
particularly vulnerable. The consequences of this dipteran predation can
be far-reaching. For instance, the larva of one of the nasal bot-flies that
occurs widely in many antelopes leaves the host through the nasal passages. A heavy infestation will cause the animal to sneeze continuously,
walking along with its head down. In such circumstances, its vigilance is

greatly reduced and instances have been reported of such animals being easily taken by carnivorous predators.[25]

One of the less easily overlooked irritations associated with Africa is the tick. Apart from the unpleasantness in having to pick them off oneself occasionally, there is also the risk of disease, notably tick-bite fever. How many hundreds of species there are, I cannot tell you, but the family is extraordinarily diverse. Like the blow-flies, some ticks have specialised in the most amazing ways. Some not only restrict their choice to a single species of animal on which to feed but often further confine themselves to a small and specialised locality on that animal. An example is *Ambylomma tholloni*. The adults of this species live almost exclusively on elephant and hippopotamus. On elephant, *tholloni* are found widely distributed over the entire body and, surprisingly, inside it also, for they have been collected from the roof of the mouth and from underneath the tongue. In hippos, life is a little more difficult for the tick because of the animal's aquatic existence. However, it solves this problem in a unique if somewhat unpleasant way. *Tholloni* on hippo enter the nostrils and attach themselves to the skin far up them, out of sight.[26]

Tholloni adults, when engorged, can measure up to 2 g, slightly bigger than a thumbnail. The effect of a heavy infestation of these creatures on any animal can be imagined, especially when as many as 100 might be found at a single site. Reports of atypical aggression in normally placid male elephants or hippos, for example, are much easier to understand when considered in the light of the constant nagging pain or irritation caused by ticks.

Along the length of the Zambezi, black rhino occur naturally only in the Zambezi Valley. Inextricably linked to the rhino's survival is the fate of another specialist tick of the *Ambylomma* genus, *rhinocerotis*. *Rhinocerotis* is found on no other animal and so, if the natural populations of rhino should be exterminated (see Chapter 12), the tick will become extinct also. Too little is known about the biology and ecology of tick species for us to say why a species would make itself so vulnerable by dependence upon a single host.[27]

One animal that suffers terribly from tick infestations, because it cannot groom, is the tortoise. Those ticks that have come to specialise on the tortoise as a host can measure up to 4 g or 5 g each and be as large as half a squash ball. Andy Norval, a tick specialist from the Veterinary Research Laboratory in Zimbabwe, tells me that a tortoise sometimes carries so many of these gruesome creatures that it can no longer retract its head. Under these circumstances it quickly falls prey to a hungry predator.

Ticks are more complex than one might imagine and an hour or so with Andy Norval is enough to make one forgive them a great deal, such are his interest and enthusiasm.

PRECEDING PAGE
David Livingstone's statue at the town of Victoria Falls in Zimbabwe. Ironically, some researchers claim that the explorer never actually stood on the Zimbabwean side of the river.

ABOVE
Mangane, a Batonga village in Zimbabwe.

RIGHT
A monogram, claimed to be that of David Livingstone, carved on the inside of a hollow baobab tree on the banks of the Zambezi in Mozambique. (Photograph by Quentin Keynes from B.W. Lloyd (ed.) 1973. Livingstone 1873 – 1973, Struik, Cape Town. The author has been unable to contact Mr Keynes, but gratefully acknowledges his work.)

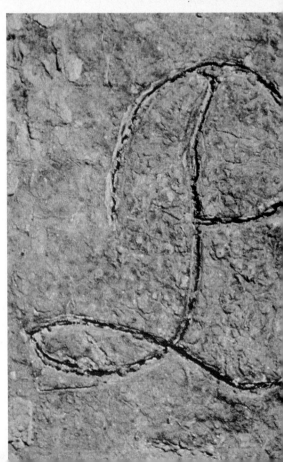

In a manner we do not fully understand, ticks have a facility always to locate themselves on that part of an animal's anatomy where it is most difficult, by ordinary grooming, for them to be removed. By means of a pheromone release, they also have the ability to attract others of their kind to a particular site. This explains why these pests are often found concentrated in small groups on an animal.[28]

For reasons also not understood, the three stages of a tick's life-cycle are sometimes spent on different hosts. This makes for a complicated and apparently high-risk survival strategy, yet it must have some advantages that, as yet, we have not been able to see.

The primary problem created by ticks is that they are vectors of innumerable diseases. One might therefore ask what useful role they play in the natural order of things.

It seems that there are two answers to this question. Firstly, ticks help weed out the weak and unhealthy in any given population. An animal that is out of condition will have a higher tick and parasite load, part of a fatal spiral that leads to such debilitation that the animal either dies or is killed off by a predator.

Secondly, as a route of infection, ticks are the initiators of the process of natural immunisation. Host animals build up antibodies to various diseases as a result of low-level infections introduced by ticks. The host animals also build up resistance to the ticks themselves, in two interesting ways.

Through the constant attachment of the parasite to their skin, animals become sensitised and this leads to an increased level of grooming. They also develop an antibody to the ticks because of the way in which the tick attaches itself to the animal's skin. Once aboard, so to speak, the tick bores a hole through the skin. At the same time it secretes a cement-like substance which hardens into a hollow tube and holds the tick to the animal while allowing it access beneath the skin.

Securely attached, the tick releases quantities of anticoagulant and enzymes into the bite, consuming the host's blood and body fluids, returning its own waste into the host. Tick antigens, which are part of this waste, stimulate the host's immune system to produce antibodies which become the basis for an acquired low-level immunity to the tick.[29]

Such a method of acquiring immunity would also form the basis of a vaccine against ticks, but at the time I spoke to Andy, such a vaccine did not exist although he firmly expressed his belief that it would be developed. He explained that the tick antigens would come from the gut and that a vaccine based on this would enter the tick from the host's bloodstream and attack the surface cells in the tick's gut, causing the blood there to diffuse through the tick's body. It would drop off the host and die.

Since then, Andy's prediction has come true, for a vaccine has now been developed in Australia, although it is some three years from being commercially available.[30] The market for such a vaccine is colossal, for hundreds of millions of dollars are spent every year in combating tick-borne diseases. A successful vaccine will benefit cattle owners wherever they are, from Australia to America, from Europe to Africa.

Before leaving the unlikely subject of the tick, there is a life-history of one about which I must tell you, for it stretches credibility to the limit and rivals the most bizarre. To appreciate it, we need to know a little about a small but delightful antelope, the klipspringer.

Widely distributed throughout Africa, klipspringers are commonly found in pairs and always in rocky places, preferably koppies, to which environment they are specially adapted. The males are territorial and mark their territories with secretions from a gland near the eye. Typically, the male will choose a convenient twig, some 60 cm from the ground, and will manoeuvre the twig so that he can cover it with a black tarry substance from his eye gland.[31]

An unusual tick, Ixodes Afrixodes) matopi, occurs in association with the klipspringer, which is its sole host. Adult Ixodes lay their eggs in the leaf litter between the rocks. Hosts for the larval and nymph stages are occasionally the klipspringer itself but more commonly the hyraxes and rock hares that typically share the same rocky environment. A problem arises for those ticks not lucky enough to be attached to a klipspringer in the first place. How are they to find their highly mobile host and attach themselves to it?[32]

The answer is simple; studies in Zimbabwe show that they climb bushes marked by the territorial klipspringers and wait in ambush on the ends of the tarry twigs!

Amazing as this explanation is, it leaves us wondering how the ticks know which bushes to climb. It is true that ticks were found on bushes that had been marked as well as bushes that had not been marked by klipspringers. However, there were twice as many on the marked bushes as on the unmarked.[33] How do the ticks tell the difference?

As klipspringers are specially adapted to life on rocks, one would expect that bushes passed by them would be close to, or overhanging, rocks. Out of a sample of 102 twigs on which ticks were present, 84% were directly over rocks and only 16% above litter. How the ticks know which bushes to climb remains a mystery.

The scourge of trypanosomiasis, carried by the tsetse fly, is too well known to need a detailed introduction. It has two forms: one attacks cattle and domestic stock (nagana) and the other affects humans (sleeping sickness). Both forms can be fatal. The upper parts of the Zambezi are virtually free of the menace of this fly but it does occur along the river in Angola and also in the south-west of Zambia. Mainly, however, it is found on the south bank of Lake Kariba and on both sides of the river, in varying intensities, downstream from Kariba dam to the sea.

Trypanosomiasis is one of the great economic diseases of Africa: millions are spent in trying to control or eradicate it and in dealing with the consequences of it. Over the centuries it has taken a huge toll of human life, accounted for the deaths of innumerable animals and undoubtedly has done much to shape the history and development of the continent.

One local example of the tsetse fly's historical role is seen in the largely treeless Barotse floodplains. These have never been fly-infested and so have allowed the Lozi people to own cattle and reap the benefits of the status and wealth that such ownership gave them, compared to their neighbours. Much of the remainder of the region harbours the fly; cattle cannot survive there and surrounding tribes, therefore, are without them.

Along the Zambezi it is in Zimbabwe that the greatest effort is being made to understand, control and eradicate this dangerous pest. In many respects, the research being undertaken leads the world and is the product of some of the finest scientists in the field.

Predictably, methods of fly control have reflected our understanding of the biology and ecology of the fly itself. In the first half of this century, for instance, such efforts were unrefined and concentrated on eliminating parts of the fly's habitat in the hope that this would destroy the fly.

Thus, for example, in one approach, large areas of woodland were cleared. In another, host game species were eliminated. This was a major programme undertaken in Zimbabwe and Zambia. In Zimbabwe tsetse hunting, as it was known, began in 1919 and continued until 1961. In those 42 years, a total of 659 334 game animals were shot. Included in that total were 374 black rhino![34]

The tragedy of this game killing, well-intentioned though it undoubtedly was, is well illustrated by research in the 1970s in western Zimbabwe. By that time it was believed that only certain animal species were hosts to the fly and the prevalent idea was that if only these animals were eliminated, the fly would go. Of these 'key' species the most important was the warthog.

In the experimental research, an area of 11 km^2 of woodland in the fly zone was enclosed and the warthog removed. The tsetse switched their feeding to antelopes (mainly kudu) and elephant. When the elephant were removed six months later, the antelope then formed 90% of the tsetse diet for the next year. The tsetse did show some stress at being denied their usual diet and being forced to depend on antelope, but they survived easily, however. Clearly, the flies were highly adaptable and thousands of animals, such as warthog and elephant, had died unnecessarily in the years of game culling.[35]

Numerous different methods of tsetse eradication have been tried in recent years. Some have proved impractical, others have been abandoned in favour of something better. The side effects of spraying the chemical dieldrin, an otherwise effective killer, make it ecologically unacceptable.

In an infamous 1958 experiment 800 ha of Florida's coastal marsh were sprayed with dieldrin to eliminate sandflies. Apart from exterminating all the crustaceans, an estimated 20 tonnes to 30 tonnes of fish were also killed![36] Dieldrin is not host-specific: it kills mammals, birds, insects and reptiles indiscriminately. Not only is it unselective, but it also seems to kill in the most horrible manner imaginable. The description of the death agony of a snake in Viv Wilson's paper on the subject is not for the squeamish.[37]

In 1960, the elimination of screw-worm fly in Florida by the repeated release of males rendered sterile by exposure to radiation raised great hopes for the same success with tsetse. Much work on suitable techniques has been carried out in Zimbabwe but there are practical problems yet to be overcome.[38] Sterilising is expensive and it also requires that flies first be captured. Devising techniques for doing this successfully has created other options which look a little more attractive.[39]

Spraying is unquestionably the currently favoured mass technique and takes place over huge areas from aircraft using endosulfan, a host-specific, short-life insecticide. Aerial programmes are usually backed up by ground teams spraying a peripheral or barrier area with 4% DDT wettable powder.[40]

Despite their success, aerial spraying programmes are expensive and, like many other methods, do not guarantee complete elimination of the tsetse. Some flies always escape and a major worry is the size of the remaining tsetse population and its ability to recover from just a few individuals.[41]

For these reasons much hope lies with the odour-baited trap, now in an exciting stage of development. The idea of traps is not new, nor is the idea of baiting them with a smell attractive to tsetse flies: both probably originated in the 1940s.[42] Oxford-trained Glyn Vale has followed the long and exhaustive development steps to bring his trap designs to their present level of success and sophistication.

In devising a good trap, Vale had two problems to solve: how to attract the fly in the first place and what to do with it (and how to do it) when it arrived.

The tsetse has extraordinarily good eyesight but, as Vale discovered, for long-range identification of a host species, tsetse rely primarily on their sense of smell, using their eyesight only for close-range 'finetuning'. The trick in producing a good bait, therefore, was to discover which smells attract the fly.

A large covered hole in the ground, containing a cow, quickly showed what kind of smell attracted the fly but then began the long and arduous task of identifying which particular elements of cow odour were actually responsible. In time the three important components of acetone, octenol and carbon dioxide were discovered; this was followed by a period of testing the relative proportions to find the optimal mix before field trials finally began.

An island in Kariba was chosen for one such trial. Just 4,5 km^2, it was stocked with cattle and deliberately infested with two species of tsetse fly which were allowed to breed for two years, the population growth being monitored. By May 1981 there were about 11 000 tsetse flies on the island, when six odour-baited traps were introduced. Experimental, these traps either captured and killed or captured, sterilised and released the flies.

In 24 months, one fly population had declined by 90% and the other by 99%. At the end of that time, 20 odour-baited targets were introduced. The targets themselves were nothing more than inexpensive, shaded, triangular cloth shapes impregnated with insecticides designed to kill flies as they alighted. Vale modified his bait by removing the carbon dioxide which was both expensive and inconvenient. In 11 weeks, one species of fly had been eliminated, and the other followed after a total of nine months. It was a triumph for Vale and his belief in attractants and traps.[43]

Following this success, the next step was to try the method out in the Zambezi Valley. An area of 600 km^2 known as the Riva triangle was chosen on Zimbabwe's side, beginning at the end of Kariba Gorge. Over 2 000 targets were placed in position, four to every square kilometre. Not only was the fly within the experimental area eliminated, but there were fly reductions for a considerable distance outside it.[44]

· No system of fly control is ever likely to be perfect. The threat of re-invasion is always present and there is, increasingly, a tendency to move away from pesticides towards non-chemical means of control. Reg Allsopp, who works with the Tropical Development and Research Institute in London, acknowledges the effectiveness of insecticides and large-scale aerial applications but looks towards an integrated approach involving chemical and non-chemical methods.[45]

A pointer to future methods of control lies in recent work associated with the tsetse fly's immune system. Interest in this research was stimulated by the knowledge that only some 10% of flies actually carry the trypanosomes that cause the disease. Evidently, some tsetse's immune systems reject the parasites. How, we don't understand, but the possibility of breeding a strain of fly that would not carry the dreaded disease is there, somewhere in the future.[46]

Before leaving this chapter, the tsetse fly and all this science and technology, I should tell you that as early as 1867 a method of preventing nagana in cattle was well known to some Victorians. It's all there, in *The Field, The Country Gentleman's Newspaper*. The fine print tells you that you need only smear your animals with the kidney fat of certain Viverridae (a family that includes the civet cats and mongooses) to be sure of protection. For the doubting Thomas, a mild solution of carbolic acid was offered![47]

11 A Bird in the Bush

GREY and grotesque, the baobab tree is synonymous with the drier parts of Africa. Often massive and not everybody's beauty, this sometimes squat giant is found from the Kalahari in the south to Sudan in the north, from the coastal regions of east Africa westwards to Senegal.[1] Along the Zambezi it flourishes from the coast to Barotseland. It has always fascinated humans because of its size, its reported age and its many uses, including the provision of water; this fascination is reflected in the many myths associated with the tree. It is of particular interest at present because it is being destroyed by elephants.

Humankind has had a long association with the baobab. The fruit is edible and provides a refreshing drink, the bark makes cloth and twine, the leaves produce a good tea and the tree has many medicinal uses. Often, a hollow tree will contain water for many months of the year. In the Sudan the trees are registered as personal property and are inherited, passing down through generations.[2]

Their age is in dispute. Only relatively recently, thanks to the work of Graham Guy, has it been accepted that the baobab, which consists of an extremely fibrous material with a water content of 79%, does have identifiable annual rings. Small trees of known age have been dated by this method with an accuracy of 2%.[3] Larger trees are more difficult to deal with as they are often hollow. At least one attempt has been made to date a baobab using carbon-14 techniques. This was done on material taken from a tree in the Kariba area of the Zambezi and yielded interesting results.

The tree was just under 3 m in diameter and had a circumference between 10 m and 12 m. Three samples were taken from the radius, one at the core, one half-way and a third from near the bark. As we shall see, the tree was relatively small as baobabs go, but the trunk was intact. The heartwood sample gave the greatest age of just over 1 000 years. A larger tree could be very much older: the investigators suggested as much as several thousand years.[4]

At first sight, this figure may seem a little high but when one is familiar with the enormous girths possible for these trees, such ages are quite conceivable. One tree, reported as the world's largest, is on the south-east slope of Mount Kilimanjaro and has a girth of over 28 m, perhaps three times the size of the measured tree from Kariba.[5] However, I have recently been given evidence of a baobab in the north-eastern Transvaal that is evidently colossal and is certainly much larger than the Kilimanjaro specimen. The new 'world's largest baobab' is in South Africa and has been registered and carefully measured at 33,4 m at breast height.[6] Clearly, then, ages ranging from 1 500 to as much as 4 000 years are possible.

Along the Zambezi River the baobab is ubiquitous but in areas of wildlife concentration — on the north-western and especially the northern borders of Zimbabwe — the tree is coming under considerable pressure. Its massive size quickly catches the eye and the often symmetrical boldness of the fat grey tree with its smooth and shiny bark is a familiar sight. Increasingly, as at Kariba for example, trees are discovered with the bark hanging in torn tatters, like a cheap thorn-ripped skirt shading the soft white heartwood, now unprotected from the drying wind. Elephants tear at the bark, leaving it limp and shredded all the way round the tree, in a manner that will certainly kill it. In the Ruhaha National Park in Tanzania, where this elephant behaviour also occurs, it is estimated that at the present rate all baobabs will be eliminated between 30 and 170 years from now. Why do elephants do this? The short answer is that nobody seems to know.

Some educated guesses are being made to understand this problem, which is widely reported from other parts of Africa. It is known, for example, that elephants require between 150 kg and 300 kg of food a day and that this is drawn from some 165 different plant species. The baobab is one of these but normally comprises only a small percentage of the elephant's diet. Often the tree is rich in salts and necessary acids but it has not been established to be the only source of these. There is no dietary reason why the baobab should suddenly be singled out for this unusual — and fatal — attention.[8]

A detailed survey of baobab damage was carried out at Mana Pools National Park, the results of which are more than disturbing. The researchers established a number of separate sampling routes and examined trees along them over a period of time. Route one was 26 km long and ran roughly parallel to the river, about 4 km from it. Along this route, 84 individual trees were monitored for a period of six months. In that time, 13 trees, or 15,5%, were killed by elephant damage.[9]

It was noted that as the dry season progressed, elephant concentrated in the area closest to the river and this was accompanied by a significant increase in the number of baobabs damaged or destroyed along route one. To a lesser extent this was true too on route four, which also passed through areas of high elephant concentrations, but far away from the river front. Routes two and three, which were in different parts of the valley, sustained much lower levels of damage so that the extrapolated mean figure for the whole of the area gave a mortality rate of 4,9%. These results support the horrifying possibility that the baobab extermination rate in the valley is worse than that quoted for Ruhaha.

A final observation gives some possible clue as to the cause of this strange behaviour. Although routes one and four both had equal densities of elephant along them, the damage to trees on the former was much greater than that on the latter. It was noticed that the vegetation on route one was much more heavily utilised and the suggestion is that there is a relation between elephant numbers, the state, condition and quantity of food and the amount of damage that is done to baobab trees. I hope this research is going to lead us in the right direction —the Zambezi would never be the same without its baobab trees.

Herbivores can be divided into three groups by the manner in which they take their food. The grazers eat only the ground-growing plants; the browsers consume the leaves and tender shoots of trees and shrubs; other species do both. Trees, therefore, are an important food resource. At first one might think of them playing a passive role in this food relationship, but amazing recent discoveries show that this is most definitely not the case.

Kudu are essentially browsers and prefer savanna woodland where water is available. They are a favoured game meat animal and are often kept on fenced farms in southern Africa, having considerable commercial value. In 1981 reports were received from the north-eastern Transvaal of kudu dying in the wild and on commercial farms. It was a problem that offered no immediate solutions and came to intrigue Professor Wouter van Hoven of Pretoria University.[10]

The dead kudu were emaciated, clearly dying of starvation. It was noted that on enclosed farms the percentage that died was very much higher than in the larger nature reserves where, nevertheless, deaths still occurred. A curious fact was that, although the grazing was poor, it was not so poor that it would not support the kudu. The question was, then, why were they dying?

Numerous investigative dead ends were followed before tests on the food and dung revealed that large quantities of proteins were passing through the animals undigested. They were dying of starvation but the cause was not a lack of essential foods; instead it was an inability to digest them. What was the cause of such bad digestion?

The next clue was provided by the decision to test tannin levels in the leaves of some of the trees eaten by kudu. 'Tannin' is a somewhat misleading term since it applies not to a single chemical but to a complex series of them. The tannins we are familiar with are used to preserve hides. They do this by combining with the protein molecules in the hide, making an insoluble compound that cannot be destroyed by microorganisms. One of the functions of tannins in plants is to protect them against infection and injury.

A component of tannin, conveniently called tannin-C, was isolated and found to exist in high concentrations in the surface cells of leaves. There were different concentrations in different kinds of trees. In a series of experiments tannin-C was extracted and mixed with lucerne which was fed to captive kudu. Here the first breakthrough was made for it was discovered that the higher the level of tannin-C in the lucerne, the less efficiently was the lucerne digested. When the tannin-C is eaten, it combines with protein molecules in the food, making them indigestible. If the concentrations of tannin are high enough, the food becomes almost completely indigestible; the animal starves to death. The tree has this method of protecting itself but why do the animals eat it?

Beating the trees with sticks and ropes and measuring tannin-C levels before and after the operation provided the next startling revelations. Results showed that, incredibly, tannin-C levels rise dramatically when the tree believes it is being browsed upon. Both the rate and duration of response vary with different trees. The fastest could double its tannin-C level in 15 minutes, while another took an hour to raise it 2,5 times. A further important discovery was that as long as the tree was left undisturbed, tannin-C returned to normal within 50 to 100 hours. One cannot escape the conclusion that the tree was using tannin as a defence mechanism, increasing the levels of this substance in its leaves to make them unpalatable to browsers, so causing them to move on to other trees.

This remarkable response from the tree also explains behaviour commonly noticed in both browsing and grazing animals: they frequently move on when clearly there remains more that they could eat where they started. One suspects that further research will soon show that almost every plant has the ability to deter predation in this way.

By means of some exciting scientific investigation, the problem of dying kudu has been solved. Kudu density was sufficient to cause hungry animals to return to feed on overbrowsed and stressed trees in which tannin-C levels were still dangerously high. Tannin was ingested in such quantities that it impaired the digestion process and the animals died of starvation. It was brilliant work and, as is often the case with such discoveries, revealed at once not only how little we know, but also suggested further lines of investigation that may lead to new discoveries.

Wouter van Hoven has not stopped at answering the question of the kudu deaths. His experiments with beating trees and showing how their tannin count rose revealed another avenue of research. During those experiments it was discovered that not only did tannin-C levels rise in the experimental tree but it did the same in adjacent trees! These neighbours were not part of the experiment and had not been touched yet, clearly, they were responding to the experience of the first tree. How did they know?

Much work still remains to be done in solving this new and intriguing problem. Researchers have been aware for some time that trees can and do communicate with each other but the mechanism by which they do so is something of a mystery. Professor Van Hoven has discovered that ethylene seems to be the messenger for some species of trees. His recent work suggests that ethylene is liberated from damaged leaves and is carried through the air to other leaves. It enters the leaf cells and its presence then changes the permeability of these cells. This begins the sequence that leads to such a spectacular production of tannin.[11]

The methods that trees and plants employ in self-protection are only beginning to be understood and I suspect that there are a great many surprises still in store for us. Indications of one came to me from time spent with a fascinating young man. Kim Damstra is an exciting and an excited scientist. He works at the University of Zimbabwe and is one of those gifted people who have, and can communicate, enthusiasm for their subjects. I use the plural because I came away from several afternoons in Kim's company with the distinct impression that he pursues interests in several fields at once. In between discovering more about the permeability and colouring of the dermis of a frog, he seems also to be expert on butterflies, moths and trees.

By Kim I was reminded of a good old-fashioned skill that today, in the age of push-button technology, is all too easily forgotten: the art of observation that underlies much of good science. In the valley of the Zambezi, on one occasion, Kim happened to notice a young *Kigelia* tree. He observed tiny appendages, what he thought were common stipules, in the leaf axil. At first he thought little of this observation until, a year later, he came across three specimens of the same species growing close to the university, where he was able to study them more easily. Detailed examination showed the stipules to have many crater-like glands; they seemed to be exuding a sticky substance in minute but discernible quantities.

Kim then noticed that ants were climbing the young trees and making their way to the leaf junctions, sticking their heads into the gland and apparently consuming the secretions. In time, he discovered that the tiny stipules or glands disappeared from the plant as it matured and grew larger, leaving him with the problem of explaining it all.

He has much work still to do on this little project but an interesting hypothesis is being tested, for Kim believes this to be part of the plant's protection system. When it is young, the tree, with relatively few leaves, is vulnerable to attack from caterpillars. By offering a palatable attractant to ants, the tree draws them onto its branches and, by hosting such voracious predators, deters female butterflies or moths from choosing the plant as a nursery for their young.[12]

One of the many delights of the natural world is its exciting dynamism. It is a world of constant change, a testing world of evolutionary challenge where survival is the prize. A bat, for example, hunts using echolocation and moths fall victim to it. In their turn, moths develop a scrambling system that distorts the bat's return signal and allows the moth to escape.[13] A further illustration of this dynamism shows that trees don't always have it their own way either.

Along the Zambezi's banks there are at least five species of trees that are members of the Rutaceae, or citrus, family. On one of these, the wild citrus (Citropsis daweana), the beautiful swallowtail butterflies (Papilio demodocus) choose particularly to lay their eggs because their caterpillars have a defence system uniquely adapted to and depending upon this particular kind of tree for its operation.

Behind the head of the larva is an extrusible gland called an osmeterium which is a sac-like invagination of the skin. Into this the caterpillar has the most extraordinary ability to concentrate citrus oils which it obtains from the leaves it has eaten. Threatened by approaching ants, the caterpillar lowers its head, extends the gland, which looks rather like two wavy feelers, and offers them to the ants. The end of each 'feeler' is covered with the volatile oils, which have a strong and unpleasant smell and repel the ants![14,15]

Mention has already been made of the Kigelia tree but I want to return to it, for the most fascinating stories are associated with it.

Properly called Kigelia africana, it is popularly known in English as the sausage tree because of its fruits. These are large, sausage-shaped as the name suggests, and up to a metre long by about 18 cm in diameter. Each can be up to 10 kg in mass and is filled with a fibrous pulp in which are embedded many seeds.[16] At the appropriate time of the year the fruits fall without warning and the loud sound as they strike the ground has often caused consternation. I need hardly say that one takes a serious risk camping beneath such a tree!

The tree occurs all along the Zambezi, from the sea to Barotseland, and is of use to humans in many ways. One specimen, a very large one on the east bank of the Zambezi at the point where Caprivi, Zambia, Botswana and Zimbabwe meet, has given its Sisubiya name 'Mzungula' to the town Kazungula which has developed there. David Livingstone and F.C. Selous are among the many hundreds who have camped beneath it; in recognition of its historical importance, it was declared a national monument by the Botswana authorities. The tree is said to have been damaged by rifle fire during Zimbabwe's independence war, to have been burnt by honey seekers and to have been assaulted with explosives to make a bunker for the military. Despite that, some reports claim there yet remains a flicker of life in the tree stump. Others are sceptical.[17,18] Although its wood is useful, mostly for making dugout canoes, the fruit has attracted more attention.

The unripe fruit is said to be poisonous but small quantities can be taken as a remedy for syphilis and rheumatism. The ripe fruit is inedible but is sometimes baked and added to beer to help fermentation. Dried and powdered fruit is used as a dressing for ulcers and sores and is also rubbed on babies to make them fat — but not on the head as this induces hydrocephalus.

On one particular journey in the Zambezi's valley, I chanced to meet Dennis 'Bomber' Harris, who has spent a lifetime in the wild and knows it well. He claims to have cured himself of skin cancer using the fruit of the sausage tree. This is how: he took a small, ripe fruit and cut three or four discs from it. He pounded them, adding water as he thought necessary to the pulp, the seeds and the skin. This was simmered slowly until a jelly was formed, which he applied to the cancerous spots on the back of his hands and wrists. Today there are no marks there at all. He says the sausage tree had cured him.[19] This claim is known to the medical profession but has yet to be verified. Tests so far are said to have yielded 'variable results'.[20]

In Zimbabwe there are many tribal superstitions associated with the sausage fruit. It is known that in some areas of the country a concoction of it is applied to the penis in the belief that this will cause it to emulate the fruit in size and in shape! Women apply the same preparation to their breasts to make them grow.[21]

Rubber is not something one readily associates with the Zambezi: today there is only a tenuous link. There was a time, however, when northern Zambia exported considerable quantities of rubber and the story of its brief boom is interesting.[22]

Rubber is the name given to the milky juice of certain plants; the name was acquired from the first use to which it was put in Europe, as an eraser. Its existence was reported in the early 16th century by Christopher Columbus, who saw the natives in Haiti playing with a rubber ball. However, rubber was not introduced to Europe until the beginning of the 19th century when it was used in the manufacture of waterproof overboots — wellingtons — and Charles Macintosh's celebrated raincoat.

Rubber was not, initially, terribly successful as a product because of its thermal instability. In high temperatures it became sticky and in low temperatures it went hard. Its full potential awaited the inventive genius of Charles Goodyear from Connecticut who, in 1844, added sulphur to rubber in a process called vulcanisation. To judge by the persistence of the Goodyear name, Charles and his heirs seem to have done fairly well out of it!

Improved manufacturing methods increased the demand for rubber, but for many years wild sources were the only supply. The great estates of the Far East did not exist then for the rubber tree on which they were based is not indigenous there; it is a native of Brazil. There are a number of good rubber-producing trees, including one from west Africa, but the two best are Brazilian and, in the early years, the government there would not allow the export of either seeds or seedlings. In 1876, however, the enterprising Sir Henry Wickham smuggled seeds of *Hevea braziliensis* out of the country to Kew and from those every one of the great Asian plantations is descended!

Not until 1910 did significant quantities of commercial rubber begin to appear on the market; even in 1916, wild rubber was still supplying a third of the world's needs with a contribution of 55 000 tonnes. By 1940, however, wild rubber was no longer commercially significant.

The export of wild rubber from east and central Africa probably reached its peak in about 1910 although Zambia's share of the total was very small. In its best year, 1912, Zambia produced a little over 7 tonnes.

Four plant species along the Zambezi produce rubber. Two are vines that can be tapped and two are plants that yield rubber from their roots. They are found mainly in the headwaters in the Mwinilunga district and also in Barotseland in the west and along the Zambezi in the south of Zambia. Collection was slow and labour-intensive and the future of rubber production as a commercial enterprise depended upon successful introduction of the Brazilian species. Unfortunately for Zambia, this did not happen. The trees did not take to conditions there, as they did on the shores of Lake Malawi, and the great expectations of the early farmers came to nothing.

The peculiar qualities of the latex in both *Landolphia* and *Carpodinus* were well known to the natives of Barotseland. When David Livingstone passed through there in the 1850s he found the people playing with a rubber ball, as Columbus had seen in Haiti. He also reported a well-established trade in rubber with the west coast from where it was despatched to Europe.

A suitably tropical addition to the flora of the Zambezi River are a number of different and beautiful palm trees. Among the most common, and certainly well known to visitors to Victoria Falls, is the wild date palm. Properly called *Phoenix reclinata*, its name reflects its distinctive characteristic of leaning over. This lovely palm is often found along the banks of the Zambezi, gracefully arching out over the water, its slight form and light crown creating exquisite silhouettes against the evening sky.

A much more common palm found throughout the middle and lower portions of the river is the Ilala or vegetable ivory palm. *Hyphaene benguellensis* has been turned to good use by humans and animals. Its fruit is spherical and 4 cm to 5 cm in diameter; as many as 2 000 are borne by a single tree. The interior of the seed is white and extremely hard: this earns the tree one of its common names.[23] A number of game species consume the fallen fruit, notable among them the elephant.

I have heard it said that viewing the area of Victoria Falls on the Zimbabwean side from high altitude in an aircraft, one notices long lines of Ilala palms reaching out from the river and disappearing into the blue and distant haze towards the game reserves. These lines of trees mark the traditional migration routes of elephant. They eat the vegetable ivory which passes through their digestive systems; the seed gets deposited in the wilderness, neatly left in its own pile of manure. In this way, over time, are the lines of palms created. I remember once being told that the old slave trading routes from the coast to far inland in Tanzania could be traced in a similar way. They are marked out by long lines of mango trees, a fruit on which the slaves were fed and the seeds of which they discarded as they walked.

Africa is full of all sorts of weird and wonderful cures for warts. The surprising thing is that so many of them work. One comes from the vegetable ivory palm. Apparently the leaves from a small palm are finely chopped and roasted until they turn to ash. The wart is trimmed down to a point just before blood level and the ash rubbed into it.[24]

Like many palms in Africa the Ilala can be tapped. It slowly yields a delicious opaque fluid which is most refreshing when first drawn and turns into an extremely potent brew after a few days of fermentation. Unfortunately, the local techniques developed for its production involve the removal of the growing head of the small palms that are used and hence signal their certain death. This kind of destruction is, to my knowledge, prevalent both in the Caprivi Strip and in northern Botswana. This is a pity for in north Africa, palms have been tapped for up to 40 years without loss and have yielded in that time between 250 *l* and 1 100 *l* of fluid.[25]

Far less common but singularly striking where it occurs, in the lower reaches of the Zambezi and on some of its tributary rivers, is the remarkable Raffia palm. This beautiful tree has the distinction of bearing the largest leaf in the floral kingdom, a leaf for which a record length of 21 m has been recorded.[26] Another record holder is found in the Lower Zambezi, especially in the delta, where *Hyphaene* is also common. This is the towering Borassus palm, unusual because of the great height it attains. Some have been recorded as reaching up to 27 m.[27]

Palms have several features of considerable interest, which make them highly distinctive as plants. They have a limited number of water-transporting vessels in the xylem and so only a restricted number of leaves can be supported in the crown. They lack the ability, except in one or two exceptional cases, to thicken the trunk as the tree grows. For this reason they tend to develop a full crown first and only when this has been achieved is it raised up into the sky on the pillar-like trunk.

All roots require oxygen to survive, yet many of the palms found along the Zambezi, especially in the low-lying areas of the delta, have their roots at least periodically waterlogged. *Phoenix reclinata* has the remarkable ability to produce special breathing rootlets called pneumathodes. These allow the diffusion of oxygen from the water into the plant at the same time as allowing carbon dioxide out of it. After 16 years of immersion, stands of *Hyphaene* were still alive at Kariba after their roots were flooded and so it must be assumed that these palms also have some, as yet undiscovered, ability to survive in water.[28]

The idea that certain fruits and seeds must pass through the digestive tract of an animal before they can grow into trees is quite well established. Generally in the African savanna, trees such as the *Acacia* produce large quantities of seed. Research has shown that as much as 96% of these seeds fail to germinate because they become infected with larvae of the bruchid beetles. When the seeds pass through an animal the seed coats are softened and the bruchid larvae are killed. As with the vegetable ivory, the seed is deposited in its own packet of manure and, freed of infestation, has the best chance of survival.

Recently, however, there have been changes, as research in Uganda is showing. Poachers have killed off the browsing animals and, as a result, there are fewer savanna trees than formerly. However, possibly because of poachers' carelessness, perhaps aided by the absence of trees, there are now more bush fires. Seeds on the ground get burnt by the fires and experiments have shown that those taken from a burnt area have a 65% germination rate compared with only 10% for those taken from unburnt areas. The heat of the fire apparently splits the seed coats, killing the larvae and thus increasing the seed's chance to survive.[29]

All this is important because a sad truth in Africa is that outside the game reserves, there are fewer and fewer wild animals but probably also an increased number of fires. It is reassuring that nature has alternative methods for tree generation. Few life forms in Africa are as threatened as trees; anything that helps them germinate and survive is good news.

Thoughts of survival bring me to the subject of food and from the world of plants there are some interesting observations concerning the origins of certain items. If you have lived in Africa as long as I, you become accustomed to thinking of certain foods as 'African', suggesting that they originated on this continent. Immediately to mind come such plants as maize (the Americans call it corn), cassava, ground-nuts, beans, avocados, guavas, paw-paws and pineapples — and yet every one of these is an exotic introduced at various times from the Americas. Added to this American list should be chilli peppers, sweet potato, potato, cocoa, rubber, sisal and tomato,[30] as well as cashews, pears, sunflowers, passion fruit and vanilla. These are but a few of some 80 plants introduced from America![31]

Asia has also made contributions to Africa's food list: banana, taro, Asian yams, citrus, rice and sugar-cane.[32] Other Asian imports were mulberry, mango, barley, ginger, peach, soya bean and loquat, while Europe may have contributed rape (*Brassica napus*) and oats.[33] The Portuguese also added items, among them pepper, wheat, tobacco, manioc, haricot beans, lentils and onions.

Quite a remarkable list, but I am glad to say that the trade was not entirely one-way. Africa's indigenous food is sorghum and pearl millet and both of these have been exported to Asia where, for many, they have become a staple diet. Nevertheless, one does get the impression that the continent was not overly blessed with a wide variety of food resources or, and this is perhaps more likely, it had not exploited and developed them as other nations or continents have been able to do.

The purpose of this chapter was twofold: to look at some of the trees and plants associated with the Zambezi and to introduce a few of its birds. There is so much of great interest associated with the flora of the river that it warrants several chapters of its own, if not a book. Nevertheless, I must move on, for among the birds in the bush beside the Zambezi there are as many equally absorbing facts to relate.

No one has counted the different species of bird that may be found on the Zambezi. Probably no one ever will, but if they could the figure would be close to the total for central Africa, such is the wealth and diversity to be found upon and beside this river. From among this enormous range it is difficult to choose the few examples for which there is space, but surely the hunting behaviour of the black egret and the greenbacked heron is worthy, at least, of a mention?

Many people know of, and have seen illustrated, the interesting fishing technique of the black egret. Found throughout the Zambezi, this entirely black bird is a solitary feeder which prefers to stand in shallow water with its wings partly stretched and held together a little forward of its head. Staring down between them, into the water, the bird gives the impression of a small black umbrella left stuck in the river bed! The shaded area either improves the egret's vision or attracts the small fish on which the egret feeds. It is a most unusual technique, fascinating to watch, but for originality cannot compare with the method used by the greenbacked heron.

Wherever one goes on the Zambezi this bird is surely to be found but one needs to be sharp-eyed to spot it. In this regard I was lucky, for on the river above Victoria Falls I had as a companion Paul Connolly, a successful businessman and a talented amateur ornithologist. He showed me this elusive bird and told me of its remarkable method of hunting.

It seems that this species of heron is of the contemplative kind — an occupation perhaps not unusual for a bird that spends most of its time sitting and waiting — and, in consequence, it has been able to make some rather penetrating observations regarding the behaviour of those fish to which it is partial. The greenbacked heron appears to have noted, for example, that fish are rather stupid. It has also observed that they tend to be curious.

Putting these two observations together led to the evolution of the heron's remarkable fishing method. It first chooses a suitable stretch of

FIRST PAGE
The chasm at Victoria Falls as David Livingstone might have seen it from the island now named after him.

PRECEDING PAGE
Victoria Falls on the river Zambezi.

ABOVE
One of the many hot springs that suggest the tectonic origins of the Zambezi's great valley.

RIGHT
This is the view Baines and Chapman would have seen from Logier Hill where they struggled, eventually without success, to assemble the copper canoes brought from the Cape and intended to take them down the Zambezi to the sea.

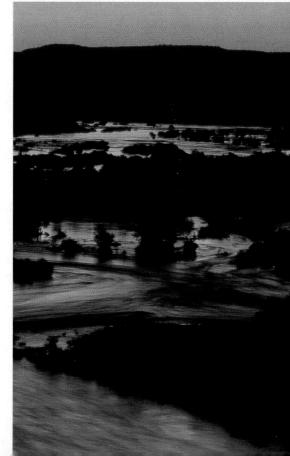

water — clear, with a slow current and smooth surface, shallow and with eddies only in the right places. Next it seeks out a suitable grain of cereal or a single small seed. Finally a vantage point is selected. The seed is carried on the wing to a point somewhat upstream and dropped carefully into the water at a predetermined place. The heron returns to the vantage point from which it knows, by dint of careful practice, it will be able to watch the grain gently come down the current towards it.

The silly fish, ever curious, playful and without care, tug and bob at this new toy. In increasing numbers they join in the game, heedless of the growing danger as they approach ever more closely the poised beak of the motionless and thoughtful heron! This, at least, is the idea, and it does apparently work. If it fails, the heron retrieves the grain or seed, returning it to the starting point upriver. This is most unusual behaviour which, it seems to me, must be placed in the same category as those other, more famous, examples of tool-using animals: the Galapagos finch, the chimpanzee, the vulture that drops stones on ostrich eggs to break them and the otters that use stones to break open mollusc shells.

There is another unforgettable bird of the Zambezi whose hunting method is fascinating to watch. It consists of a combination of patience and, if one can apply such a term to a bird, good common sense. The technique is obviously practised and is evidently adjusted as learning takes place. The hunter is that beautiful, large and stately creature we call the goliath heron.

This huge bird, by far the largest of the herons, is found throughout southern and central Africa and is by no means restricted to the Zambezi. It is found wherever there is permanent water and the fish or frogs that are its diet. The herons are often found in Lake Kariba and I have watched them there, peering intently along their long and narrow beaks, spearing the water with their glance.

Mostly alone, the goliath fishes the shallows and has learnt to make fascinating use of floating mats of weeds. The bird seems to be aware that such weed mats are a source of food to young fish, as well as offering them protection. At the same time, the heron has an opportunity to see through small gaps in the vegetation, allowing it to estimate what fish, if any, hide beneath a particular mat. Researchers have been able to show several other interesting advantages that accrue to the heron that makes intelligent use of floating aquatic vegetation.

Firstly, water in the vicinity of floating macrophytes is generally clearer, often with visibility increased between 17% and 28%. Secondly, the mass of vegetation helps keep the water calm in its lee. It was noted, for example, that a wind of only 15 km/h was sufficient to ruffle the surface so that it was no longer possible to see below it. Yet, sheltered from the wind by the weed's edge, there is a small 'ripple free' zone and in this, visibility is much improved. Such weed mats also give the heron a table on which to place its prey prior to delivering the final, fatal blow. It was noticed too that cunning birds, when seeking a new hunting site, often landed on large weed mats. These sagged gently under the bird's mass, lowering it into the shallow water without the normal splashing violence of entry.[34]

Goliath herons are unhurried hunters. One study showed that they made an average of slightly less than one strike an hour. This is assumed to be evidence of a deliberate feeding strategy in which the bird chooses to forego a frequent number of smaller meals in exchange for fewer but larger fish. Interestingly, unlike other herons, the goliath spears or skewers 86% of its prey (usually in the gill region) while most other birds of that kind grasp their prey in a scissor-like fashion.

There must be disadvantages to being one of the most conspicuous fishing birds about. An obvious one is that a significant number of lazy predators will be prepared to sit about and let the goliath do their fishing for them. Worst among the offenders are fish eagles. They have been recorded to watch goliaths and, as a strike is made, to fly down, harass the bird and make off with its catch.

There are many reports of this nature but two are sufficiently unusual to be worth repeating. The goliath is a tall and powerful bird that does not hesitate to defend itself or its prey when attacked. Usually, as we note frequently in the animal world, real aggression is not resorted to — but there are exceptions. In one incident, a goliath had landed a fish and was about to swallow it when a fish eagle swooped down in attack. The detailed circumstances cannot be explained for, within seconds, both birds were dead. It seems, however, that the heron pierced the eagle right through with its beak at the same time as the eagle's talons tightened round the heron's neck.[35]

The second incident is amusing and demonstrates that birds, like humans, have definite 'off days'. On this occasion the heron, once again, had landed a good-size fish and was about to devour it. As it began doing so a pelican floated into view, not making a direct effort to steal the fish but being close enough, evidently, to threaten and to put the goliath 'off its stroke' for it made repeated efforts to swallow its meal with no success. Undoubtedly frustrated, the heron saw more irritation appear in the form of two fish eagles, obviously intent on an easy meal. To deal with them, the goliath had to put its meal down on the weed mat; then, keeping a watchful eye on the nearby pelican, proceeded to deal with the eagles. At this point, unseen by all the participants, a young crocodile surfaced by the weeds, snatched the dead fish and disappeared from view! The witnesses to this event did not record the heron's reaction . . .[36]

One can hardly write about a major African river without mentioning something more of the fish eagles, for these beautiful birds are to be found wherever there is water. Always in pairs and highly territorial, they are for many a symbol of Africa's waterways. Dressed in a striking russet brown coat with bright white head and shoulders, this eagle sits on a prominent branch overlooking its particular stretch of water. Few who have experienced it will ever forget the sight and sound as the bird throws its head back and fills the valley with its strange echoing and haunting call.

The accumulation of persistent pesticides in the food chain has been seen by many as a possible threat to the continued existence of these and many other waterbirds. The example of Lake Kariba is a case in point. Zimbabwe continues to use DDT both in its malaria control and tsetse fly eradication programmes. As early as 1972 and 1974, researchers were reporting pesticide residues in fish-eating birds and crocodile eggs from the lake.[37, 38] By 1978, as a result of long-term monitoring programmes, it was concluded that the threat, at least to fish eagles, was not as severe as had at first been thought.[39]

This three-year study had monitored fish eagle nests along a 200 km stretch of the lake's coastline. In this distance 67 nests were recorded, giving a spacing of about one every 3 km. Only 50 of the nests were used, suggesting a population of some 100 birds. The study showed, however, that the population and its breeding rate was quite normal.

Regrettably the same cannot be said for another threat that has recently been reported. Kit Hustler, a professional ornithologist who works at the University of Zimbabwe's Lake Research Station, was in 1988 handed the bodies of two fish eagles collected at Sanyati Gorge. One had been picked up dead, the other showed signs of having been poisoned and was destroyed. Brain, fat, liver, kidney and muscle samples of both birds were sent for analysis. The disturbing results showed that both birds contained high levels of inorganic mercury: 175 mg and 395 mg per kilogram of liver respectively.[40]

This is the first such report about birds from Kariba. It is not cause for unnecessary concern but immediate investigation is being undertaken. In the past, low mercury levels have been detected in crocodile eggs; the mercury was evidently coming from fish eaten by the reptiles. Now, through the same route, presumably, it is reported in birds also. As Kit points out, the concentrations do seem very high but there are no baseline data available for comparison: no conclusions can be drawn. The source of the mercury remains a mystery. The catchment drains Zimbabwe's industrial heartland and a highly productive commercial agricultural region. The area also has many abandoned gold mines in which extraction processes may sometimes have used mercury. There is also the possibility of an ore body over which tributary waters flow, carrying the mercury to the lake. At the moment there are no answers.

Space, again, demands that we move to other subjects, but before leaving birds, I do want to quote a most remarkable list of materials taken from the nest of a particular bird. The hamerkop is a solitary but very common bird of Africa's rivers and streams. Its heavy bill and peculiar crest give the head its characteristic shape, hence its name.

It builds an enormous nest of twigs and branches which, rarely, may be used in successive years but generally is nested in only once. This makes the nest all the more extraordinary for it may contain as many as 10 000 separate items and take as long as six months to construct. Typically, a pair of hamerkops will collect and place in their nest anything unusual that they find, but usually only in the topmost layers.[41]

The following list is not an inventory of a Zambezi nest — it is of an urban one — but it serves to illustrate the range of the bird's curiosity. In the nest was a pan brush, a broken cassette tape, a glove, a plastic dish, a plastic cup, two peacock feathers, chicken feathers, two socks, rabbit fur, 45 rags, four mealie cobs, one piece of glass, four bits of wire, a plastic comb, one pair of underpants, a typewriter ribbon, a piece of leather belt, four bits of stocking, two bits of tin, two bits of foam rubber, seven bits of hosepipe, nine bits of electrical pipe, six bits of asbestos, 11 miscellaneous bones, 12 pieces of sandpaper, four bits of insulation tape, ten plastic bags, nine pieces of paper, 56 scraps of tinfoil, six bicycle tyres, six lengths of insulating wire and more than 100 kg of twigs, sticks and grass![42]

12 The Zambezi Menagerie

IT was dawn in the great valley of the Zambezi River. The first fingers of sunlight crept silently between the tangled mass of jesse bush and slid across a clearing into the greyness beyond. Some were interrupted in their journey and cast low squat shadows onto the grey mosaic. A heavy foot thumped once upon the damp earth and a muffled snort briefly broke the silence. Six animals stood stock still in the open space. Heads raised, ears pricked, noses questing the damp, river-smelling air; they were nervous. Their eyesight is poor but there is little that their ears and sense of smell cannot detect. Some deep and instinctive feeling persisted with its warning of dreadful danger but neither scent nor sound confirmed the fear and the group lingered a fatal second too long. On a silent signal, 16 men rose as one and emptied the magazines of their automatic rifles at them.

Terrified panic erupted as the hail of lead stitched criss-cross patterns through the clearing, striking earth and flesh with the same sickening thud. The great beasts, despite their size, were knocked to their knees and before they could rise, were felled again with savage fury. One animal, with more than 60 bullet holes in it, spraying blood like a colander, ran 20 m before it dropped. Another, perhaps because it was so small, miraculously escaped the first wave of fire. For a moment it stood, stunned, bewildered by the carnage that lay about it. Seconds before its companions had been together, alert, concerned but alive. Now they lay choking their last on the blood-soaked soil. Two magazines snapped into place; 29 more bullets took this last life with ease.

So began the present phase of Zimbabwe's rhino war. On this day, in February 1985, the gang of poachers, all armed with automatic weapons, killed an entire group of six black rhino. Their sole objective was the rhino horn, but of the animals killed, three were too young to have any.[1]

When I spoke to him last, Glen Tatham was the Acting Chief Warden of Zimbabwe's Department of National Parks and Wildlife Management. At that time, he was fully occupied with leading and organising Operation Stronghold, the codename for Zimbabwe's determined effort to save this last viable stronghold of Africa's black rhino.

There are a number of black rhino populations in Zimbabwe but by far the biggest — and the most threatened — is found in what in Zimbabwe is called the Zambezi Valley, that part of the Zambezi along its northern frontier. Along its great length, there are few more spectacular reaches than this part of the river. Between the great gorge after Kariba in the west and the narrows of Mupata in the east lies the valley, hemmed in on north and south by the towering walls of the ancient rift. Within this area, divided between Zambia and Zimbabwe by the river itself, the rhino have their home in the 12 000 km² of uninhabited bush on the Zimbabwean side. This is the stronghold that is being assaulted by poachers from across the river, seeking the horn for export to the Middle and Far East.

In this great area there are reckoned to be between 750 and 800 black rhino. They are the last population of their size in Africa. From a breeding point of view, population density is important. Although black rhino are occasionally found in small groups, this is not usual: the animals generally tend to be solitary. If they become too thinly spread, however, mating does not take place and the entire population is at risk.

Poaching of rhino for their horn has always been a problem in Zimbabwe but, for many years, it remained within acceptable levels. In July 1984 this began to change as increasing evidence of cross-river poaching was discovered. The trade did not become organised until the first six months of 1985. What began with the dreadful massacre of six, continued thereafter at an average rate of one rhino a day.

Glen admits that the authorities were caught by surprise. No one could have imagined an onslaught of such ferocity and it took time to understand the nature of the threat, to organise and to react. In the war now being waged the latest figures I have are that some 600 rhino and more than 78 poachers have been killed; 45 poachers and considerable quantities of arms, ammunition and equipment have been captured. By November 1989, 312 rhino had been translocated away from threatened areas to safer game reserves in Zimbabwe, but this initially attractive alternative is not without risks. Poaching has started at Ghona-re-zhou in the south-east and two rhino were recently taken from Matetsi in the west.[2]

The picture is not entirely negative and, in all wars, there are heroes. People have rallied at every level — in the threatened area, in the towns and cities of Zimbabwe, and internationally. Appeals for help have eased the tremendous shortages of equipment and spares, of aircraft, vehicles, radios and camping equipment. Public figures have openly declared their support and, perhaps most important of all, the Presidents of Zimbabwe and Zambia have stated their determination to see the rhinos survive.

In the meantime, the battles are still being fought but the nature of the fighting has changed. Whereas in the early days large groups sought to find and kill the rhino, today this is no longer so. Now the groups are smaller: individuals or two people working as a team and practising great stealth, move into the valley. These are trained men, masters in bushcraft, skilled in anti-tracking — and ruthless. Gone are the cumbersome rucksacks and bulky equipment; boats are summoned from the other side, not hidden: now the killers travel light and fast. The enemy has become more formidable.

I asked Glen the same question that everybody must ask him and smiled at his tolerant reply. He knew the answer so well that it was evident he had given it many times before, yet this busy man displayed no irritation, showing only his deep commitment to saving the rhino. I asked if it would not be sensible simply to capture the rhino and remove their horns which, being made of hair, would one day grow again. Perhaps the poachers would be discouraged and the rhino problem solved. But Glen outlined six good reasons why such a plan would not work.

No matter how a rhino is de-horned, some horn will always be left behind and that remainder is enough to kill for. As the February incident shows, poachers are inclined to shoot first and look afterwards; in these circumstances, removal of horns would not be a deterrent. It is an impossible task to count all the rhino in an area the size of the valley. Thus, if a hornless rhino corpse is encountered, the authorities would never know whether or not it had been de-horned prior to its death unless a permanent and reliable system of marking had been devised. No work has ever been done on the social and behavioural role of a rhino's horn. Removing them without a proper understanding of this role could have very serious consequences — especially in a population that is already at risk and nearing its breeding threshold. In the Zambezi Valley, it could take as long as four years to complete 90% of the de-horning operation. Many people feel that the money expended, for so little guarantee of success, could be better spent in trying to protect the animals more effectively in the first place.

Along the great length of the Zambezi, it is surprising that so little land set aside for the protection of wildlife abuts onto the river. In Angola there is none at all, but Zambia has created the International Game Reserve in the Zambezi Valley. In Mozambique, as far as can be established, the only portion of the river that has been granted any wildlife protection status is the south-eastern side of the delta. There was a proposal that Cahora Bassa's south shore should be similarly protected. Given the present unfortunate state of the country one cannot but guess what has happened to these areas.

In effect, the majority of land adjacent to the Zambezi in which game animals receive some form of protection lies within Zimbabwe. The status of that land varies from national parks to game reserves and safari areas but it all comes under the administration of Zimbabwe's Department of National Parks and Wildlife Management. Of these protected places the most beautiful is Mana Pools National Park in the Zambezi Valley.

As we have seen, for aeons past, the Zambezi has been steadily removing the sandstone that once filled the present valley to its brim. The process is far advanced but there still remain great thicknesses of sand-stone. Impediments to this removal exist in the form of great bars of rock that traverse the valley in several places. In exactly the same way as in Barotseland, these rock bars slow erosion so that the great rift which is the Zambezi Valley, custodian of alluvia past and present, has a markedly flat floor. These flat and low-lying so-called floodplains give Mana Pools its special character.

One of 13 World Heritage Sites, Mana Pools is an area of deep alluvial soils some 80 km² in extent. It is graced with tall spreading trees and open park-like vistas with views across the Zambezi to Zambia and the mountainous north wall of the valley. The beautiful and unique nature of Mana is believed by many to depend upon its adaptation to a flood regime. Before the con-struction of Kariba dam, the Zambezi came down in periodic floods which inundated Mana, leaving new deposits of rich sediments and thoroughly soaking the soils. As the river subsided, so pools of floodwater remained behind in old, abandoned drainage channels, giving Mana Pools its name.

Mana has been the subject of two major controversies in recent years. The first has to do with Kariba, its control of the Zambezi's flow and hence its effect on Mana. The second is linked to Zimbabwe's need for more power and the possibility of a dam at Mupata Gorge which, if it were constructed, could permanently flood the Mana area. Mupata dam is no longer an immediate prospect and the future possibilities for such a dam are discussed in Chapter 18. To better understand Kariba's threat to Mana it is as well to see both sides of the argument.

Roelf Attwell, in 1970 Chief Research Officer for National Parks, was concerned for the future of Mana.[3] He believed there was a general ecological deterioration attributable to three factors. Firstly, the outflows from Kariba matched neither in volume nor in timing the natural river flow. He cited a number of out-of-season floodings and described the deleterious effect they can have. Secondly, because of impoundment there was a reduction in the quantity of silt, which caused increased erosion as 'silt hungry' water carried soil away, rather than adding it as alluvium. Thirdly, unnatural and rapid alterations in river levels were causing river-bank erosion and different channel patterns. These factors, com-bined with heavy utilisation by game, were leading to a change in the com-position of vegetation.

Of particular concern were the beautiful *Acacia albida* trees. These giant *Acacias* lend a special ambience to Mana because of their shape, size and spacious appearance. They are also of great ecological importance because they produce a highly nutritious fruit. Each hectare of well-established *albida* will yield more than 1 000 kg of seeds a year and this at a time when other food sources are scarce.[4] *Albida* trees are slow-growing, and, although their ecology is still poorly known, it is believed that they are reliant upon floodwaters for the dispersal of their seeds.[5]

Attwell concluded that, unless Kariba made a more successful effort to emulate the natural flow patterns of the Zambezi, evidence of increasing desiccation at Mana would continue, species diversity would decline and there would be a general lowering of biological productivity.

Now, 20 years later, Mana Pools appears to be alive and well, unchanged. Were the experts wrong? The short answer is nobody is sure! There is no doubt that the area is evolving but in which way and what the long-term effects will be remain a controversial issue. An 11-year study showed, for instance, that over a distance of 40 km of river bank, approximately 1 030 ha were lost to erosion while 210 ha were added in the form of semi-permanent sandbanks.[6] P.R. Guy, whose work this was, acknowledged that such erosion certainly took place in the days before Kariba but he also showed that the rate has since accelerated. He gives three reasons for this, all due to Kariba dam: out-of-season flooding, abrupt fluctuations in water level and the silt-free water.

Because of four major rock bars across the river within the valley, it cannot easily down-cut its course. The removal of sediment, then, instead of deepening the river, widens it.[7] River bank removal is a major problem today and many stands of riverine trees, including *Acacia albida,* are threatened. A further threat to the *Acacias* and probably many other species of tree is the elephant.

There is good evidence to suggest that elephant density in the Zambezi Valley — today regarded as a major elephant sanctuary — was extremely low at the turn of the century and may have reached its nadir after 200 or 300 years of exploitation by Portuguese ivory seekers.[8] This would explain the present crop of *albida*; for, as several authorities point out, there are few or no young trees at Mana Pools today. Elephant and other game eat them long before they grow out of reach.[9] Presumably, existing trees were seedlings at a time of low elephant populations. If this is the case, we can expect to see the relatively short-lived *albida* quite quickly pass, for they are not being renewed.

One remarkable fact that raises fundamental questions about the origins, nature and ecology of Mana Pools was unearthed by the research carried out by Raoul du Toit. Raoul came professionally into contact with the Zambezi when he was asked to complete environmental impact assessments on the effect of hydro-electricity schemes at Mupata and Batoka Gorges.

Raoul's investigations showed that there appear to have been only four major floods of the Zambezi Valley this century: those of 1916, 1934, 1957/ 58 and 1975.[10] This comes as a complete surprise in the face of what is generally accepted. Everyone, including scientists, speaks of Mana and its floodplains. There are photographs of flood-stranded debris[11] and references to periodic floods to a depth of 5 m.[12] How can this conflict be reconciled?

Could it be that the photographs and the references to depth both refer to the same evidence, which itself was merely traces of the last flood (probably 1957 or 1958) before the pictures were taken? Or is it, perhaps, just a matter of semantics with the answer depending on what everybody means by a flood. Is it possible that a depth of 5 m at Mana Pools, virtually on the river bank, may still not be described as a 'major' flood in terms of how much of the entire Zambezi Valley it engulfs?

Such contradictions seem to characterise the study of Mana Pools. There appear to be few certainties and much conflicting evidence. As recently as 1981 one authority stated that 'the alluvial systems of the Lower Zambezi are vibrantly alive and well'[13] and there is no doubt that outflows from Kariba are much less problematic than formerly: now they approach more closely the pre-dam pattern of monthly flows.[14] If this is so, then perhaps Mana has reached a period of stability, a new state of equilibrium. How long it will remain is questionable, for changes at Kariba have seen the construction and recent opening of Zambia's north bank power station. Now twice the volume of water flows through Kariba and down the Zambezi with, as yet, unstudied effects.

Whatever the complications surrounding Mana Pools itself, it is true that the Zambezi Valley, between Kariba and Kanyemba, is an enormous riverside menagerie. The south side of the river is divided into two game reserves and three controlled hunting areas. No people live within this region and the entire area is reserved exclusively for animals. It contains many thousands of game animals but, surprisingly, some are absent.

Not present in the Zambezi Valley are giraffe, hartebeest and wildebeest. This is something of a puzzle for all three occur in Zambia's Luangwa Game Reserve, not a great distance away, although on the other side of the river. Conditions may not be quite right for giraffe, which seem to prefer the more arid environment further west, but both antelopes are common to the east and south. It is a mystery why they have not recolonised the valley.[15]

I have already mentioned the extent of protected wildlife areas along the Zambezi's banks. Much has been said about the Zambezi Valley and Mana Pools, downstream of Kariba. Now I want to talk in more general terms about the entire length of the Zambezi within Zimbabwe's border. Within a distance of some 700 km from west to east, and in the area between the river and the southern crest of the escarpment, there are more than 2,5 million hectares of protected land, either in the form of national parks, game reserves, safari or forest areas.[16]

Total game populations in this region are estimated to be 22 000 elephant, 56 000 buffalo, 2 000 lion, 230 000 impala and 50 000 warthog. A fascinating observation reveals that game areas carry an average of 223 kg per hectare while the figure for domestic livestock is 103 kg. These two figures may not be strictly comparable for a number of reasons; nevertheless, they give a strong indication of wildlife's potential. Indeed, on some of the rich commercial farmland in Zimbabwe, game profits per hectare have exceeded cattle profits by 3,5 times.[17]

The vital import of this kind of information is its message of hope. Zimbabwe still has vast wildlife resources. The land has been set aside and methods of protection have been established; it remains only to make the wisest use of them. Zimbabwe is one of the few African countries where wildlife is seen as a renewable resource that must be used on a sustainable basis.[18] There are encouraging signs that the message is well understood. For example, local authorities in the Gokwe area approved more than 50 development projects that were to benefit from a million Zimbabwe dollars, received as a result of district elephant culling operations in the previous three years.[19]

Before the rhino recently took top slot, at least in this part of Africa, the number one target for poachers was elephant with their ivory. The trade, of course, is centuries old and highly organised. This alone makes it difficult to control, for substantial interests are involved, along with a great deal of money. Take the case of Burundi, for example. This country, in which there remains just one live elephant, exports 140 tonnes of ivory and accounts for a third of the world's annual ivory trade, valued at US$50 million! The country earns vital foreign exchange by placing a tax on re-exported ivory.[20] According to Esmond Bradley Martin, the volume of the world ivory trade has fallen from 800 tonnes to 500 tonnes in the last decade. This is partly because there are fewer elephant to kill.[21] For example, within the last few years Tanzania has lost 100 000 elephant from her remote Selous Game Sanctuary[22] and elephant from Zambia's Luangwa Game Reserve, estimated in 1973 to number over 80 000,[23] were in 1980 being shot at the rate of 100 a week.[24]

An intriguing point about ivory has been made by two researches. They show that world 'ivory numbers' — the number of tusks, the mass of ivory, the number of elephant killed, etc. — are chaotic and exceedingly unreliable. Despite this they can demonstrate a startling fact. A minimum estimate of the African elephant population is 1 343 000. The average number of tusks per beast is known to be 1,88. Mortality rates are about 7% per annum of which 50%, being youngsters, carry no tusks; the average mass of usable ivory can be placed conveniently at 10 kg. Those of you with a mathematical bent will already have observed that the supply of natural ivory — that is, from elephant that have died of natural causes — is sufficient to substantially exceed the current world demand of 500 tonnes per year![25] Perhaps we should be encouraging poachers to look for dropped ivory instead of killing elephant.

The commercial value of elephant is not restricted to their ivory or to the price that hunters pay to kill them. The skin and trophies also contribute to the substantial worth of one of these animals; however, what

I might easily have overlooked is the worth of the live animal itself, as this example shows.

Graham Hall, who also appears in Chapter 8, did many things before becoming a game warden: some he hasn't told me about and others he wouldn't like me to tell you. He has led an exciting life — and has turned his hand to some unusual tasks. One, in 1957, was to capture, pack and export by sea, in a single batch, 3 000 crocodiles from Caprivi and Kasai to America. But it was elephant I was talking about. Much more recently, in July 1984, Graham was charged with collecting and despatching, again to America, 64 young African elephant. This time they went by air, in one lift, and I must confess that I could not forbear asking the aircraft make. It was a 707 cargo carrier, not a Jumbo jet![26]

To continue with elephant a moment longer: there are similarities and differences between African and Asian elephant that are generally quite well known. I came across two recently that few will have heard of.

Musth is a well-known phenomenon periodically exhibited by male Asian elephant. It is accompanied by high testosterone levels and its most obvious manifestations are frequent or continuous discharges of urine and copious secretions from a temporal gland. The animal also becomes much more aggressive. This is obviously important for these are domesticated creatures and work with humans.

Musth does not occur in African elephant — or so it was thought. Now a strong case has been put forward to show that it does and, as with the Asian species, is also linked to the onset of temporal secretions in males. After five years of work in Kenya, researchers are satisfied that in males over 30 years of age, these secretions have the same implications: there is a positive association with female herds and an increase in aggression.[27] I wonder if hunters in Africa have observed this?

Few will have noticed that the skin of an African elephant has more wrinkles than that of the Asian species. I certainly had not and, if I had, I might well have done nothing about it. But one scientist was curious enough to investigate the question and came up with an interesting explanation.

The skin of an Asian elephant is rather like an open honeycomb while that of the African elephant, although similar, is pitted with deeper but finer channels. Experiments show that the skin of Asian elephant holds between five and ten times more water than would remain on a flat surface and the African elephant's skin holds about half as much again. This has everything to do with cooling and the environments in which these animals live. The Asian elephant spends most of its time in forests where humidity is high and there is little exposure to direct sunlight. The African elephant lives in quite different conditions: out on the great savannas, day after day with little relief from the sun.

The African elephant must rid itself of excess heat. It does not sweat, for this would use far too much water, and so it seeks to keep itself cool by splashing water and dust over its body whenever it can. The way in which its skin surface is structured ensures that it retains as much of this water as possible. This slows the drying of the mud and therefore tends to keep the animal cooler for longer, with less water. As an additional advantage in such arid conditions, higher skin surface humidity probably serves to prevent or delay drying out and cracking.[28]

In Chapter 8 is the unusual account of two elephant swimming the Sanyati bay. Not all elephant take so to water and there is a sad story to confirm this from the Zambezi near the Deka River mouth.

On an island there, in 1978 or 1979, an elephant was stranded. It had probably reached the island with others of its kind, for at this point the creatures regularly cross backwards and forwards over the river. When the time came to leave, evidently it chose to remain. Nor would it leave, and local residents became increasingly concerned.

The river rose and fell periodically, so that the small island was practically under water and the elephant sometimes stood for long periods with its feet in the river. Three weeks passed; the animal would long since have died of starvation but residents fed it bales of hay. At the end of that time, the herd returned, but when they left, the lone elephant again remained. By now it was possible to see from a boat that its feet were rotting.

Finally, two elephant went back to the island and appeared to try to coax their companion to safety. They made several attempts and each time, painfully, it started out, reached a point nearly half-way to the shore and then returned alone to its island. Clearly, it would never leave. Its condition deteriorated and it was shot by a game warden.[29]

Stories of this kind always leave me with two thoughts. Firstly how little we know about other animals and how their mental processes work. The elephant had crossed the river once — why would it not return? Had something happened on the way over — had it slipped, fallen, hurt itself, been hurt? Was it therefore frightened to return? Was it so frightened it would choose to die? How much we have yet to learn.

Secondly, such stories make me think of the remarkable bonding of which animals are capable. I have a report from a game scout whose duty it was to shoot a marauding female elephant.[30] He found her with a group of females and shot her dead. He was chased for some distance but made good his escape and returned shortly to the fallen cow. She lay where she had fallen but all the females in the group were trying to raise her. The report does not say how many elephant were involved but it describes vividly how they tried at once to lift the dead cow's legs, tusks, trunk and body. One of her tusks was broken in the attempt and this was thrown away. The group stayed at the same place for four hours, knocking trees down. It is anthropomorphic and unscientific but I cannot suppress the strong sense that those elephant felt something.

Elephant, of course, are entirely at home in the Zambezi. The majority seem to have an affinity with water and when they have leisure and food in abundance, they linger. Like all animals, they are generally patient at the waterhole. Their right to water is not disputed; I suppose their size and strength guarantee this, for there are few creatures big enough to challenge them. One is the hippo.

Hippo can be exceedingly aggressive. Indeed, it is an oft-quoted statement — although I have never been able to verify it — that they account for more deaths in Africa than do snakes. At no time are the males more aggressive than during the mating season. The females are equally dangerous when they have calves.

When I canoed the Zambezi River with Gypsey, my Jack Russell terrier, for company, I watched the hippo closely. On one occasion, I saw a male run through water about 1,5 m deep, just deep enough to cover the animal. Anybody who has tried it will know that it is almost impossible to make progress at speed when one's whole body is in the water. To the hippo it seemed to make no difference at all. Its pace slowed not one whit and as it submerged, a black and menacing bow wave continued at the same speed without pause. It was the most powerful display of sheer brute strength I have ever seen.

There is a report from the Gwembe Valley, now occupied by Lake Kariba, of a fight between a hippo and an elephant. The latter came down to the river's edge to drink when, according to the witness, its trunk was seized by a hippo. The elephant retreated a little, followed by the hippo, and both gave battle on the bank. Each died from its wounds — an extremely unusual occurrence of animal violence.[31]

Separate testimony to the strength of hippo bulls comes from an account of two fighting. One was injured and clearly flagging. The other, sensing victory, managed somehow to get under the injured one and to lift it nearly a metre into the air, throwing it up so that it crashed back into the water with a gigantic splash.[32] A male hippo has a mass of about 1,5 tonnes!

All along the Zambezi from Angola to the sea, the hippo is a common sight. Generally they forage at night, sometimes travelling as much as 30 km or 40 km; they rest in the water during the day, punctuating the river with pink-brown humps, snoozing and dozing half weightless in the shallows.

It is then that one is likely to witness a hippo gape and see the enormous length of its incisors and canines. The former are the principal weapon of attack and, seeing them, one might suppose that the thick covering of fat many believe hippo to have is partly a defence. In fact, hippo have little subcutaneous fat, even on a well-nourished animal. The skin is not as thick as one might imagine and, at its thickest, on the flanks, does not exceed 35 mm.[33]

One might not be surprised to learn that hippos sweat. Interesting, however, are the forms this secretion can take, for it does not appear to serve the same function as in humans. Always slimy, the liquid varies from being colourless to shades of pink or red or dark brown and it is this that gives rise to the story that hippo sweat blood. The fluid's thickness also varies: sometimes it flows easily, sometimes it oozes onto the skin in fat red beads. Not a great deal is known about the function of this secretion except that it does not appear to be related in any way to stress.[34]

I believe it a mistake to think of wildlife only in terms of big animals. The smaller creatures are often much more interesting. Some examples come readily to mind: a frog-eating bat, mice, a centipede-eating snake and a snake with two heads!

Bats occur in great number and variety throughout Africa but there is only one that eats frogs and fish (and other bats too) in central and southern Africa, and it so happens that it is found along a portion of the Zambezi. At Mana Pools National Park, Dr John Hutton has been part of a research project involving these creatures.[35]

Nycteris grandis, or the large slit-faced bat, occurs along the Zambezi from the vicinity of Tete, as far west as Kariba Gorge. It is notable for its large ears and for the physiological adaptations that accommodate its echolocation system. The bat earns its unappealing name from a slit in the skin of the face that gives access to a cavity in the skull. Set in this cavity, which the bat can open or close at will, are small bony structures called noseleaves. They are associated in a way not completely understood with the mechanics of echolocation.

Five bats were studied and each was fitted with a tiny radio transmitter of just 1,5 g. With the aid of radios and powerful night vision equipment it was learnt that, most commonly, these bats hunt from perches by making low-level flights of short duration, usually attacking prey on the ground. Food consists of insects, frogs, fish and, occasionally, other bats.

There was no opportunity to discover the way in which the bat caught fish and I am absolutely intrigued as to how this might be accomplished. As far as frogs are concerned, there are two possibilities. Frogs and toads call from numerous ponds and frogs are frequently seen moving through the woodland. There is thus an opportunity for the bats to locate their prey either by sound or by movement.

Bats are not as blind as is commonly supposed. In fact, many of them have good eyesight; in this regard, some extraordinarily interesting work from America is worth mentioning. Large-scale bat tagging programmes in the northern hemisphere have shown that some bats make long-distance, seasonal migrations at night. As always in such cases, the question of navigation is raised. Two American workers have strongly suggested, as a result of their experimental work, that the eyesight of these bats is so good that they are actually able to see and to navigate by the stars![36]

Given the evidence, it is perhaps not surprising that *Nycteris grandis* is such a competent hunter. Even so, it seems to me probable that good eyesight, hearing and highly developed echolocation all play an equally important role in snatching frogs off the ground in the darkness.

Perhaps because many of them have good eyes, not all bats use echolocation, while there are other animals, surprisingly, that do. Although no work of this nature has been carried out in Africa, it has been shown that North American shrews employ echolocation to help them navigate in the dark tunnels they often enter when hunting. The system is not as sophisticated as that of the bat: its range is limited and it is not used to help in finding food; nevertheless, it is a most useful support for the other senses.[37] The tenrec, a large insectivore from Madagascar, is another animal that unexpectedly makes use of echolocation, but the biggest surprise comes from the rat.

Rats, it seems, also employ a means of echolocation although the details of this are not clear yet. A rat was placed on a small platform high above the ground in a darkened room containing sensitive audio recording equipment. As the rat cautiously explored its novel situation a series of audio signals were recorded. These had been noted in similar previous experiments and are believed to be part of an active echolocation system.[38]

Small rodents play an important role in the food ecology of the wild. In the Zambezi region, research suggests that they form a significant part of the diet of at least 20 other mammals — mostly mongooses, jackals, genets and cats — and some 34 birds have been recorded as taking rats and mice. A number of African tribes enjoy such rodents as delicacies, particularly the Gwembe Tonga along the Zambezi who relish the tiny fat mouse; the giant rat is enjoyed by Africans of Mashonaland and Manicaland in Zimbabwe.[39]

The fecundity of rodents is legendary and they are capable of great explosions of population. Reay Smithers told me once of a collecting trip he made to Maun in northern Botswana. There a great surplus of food had triggered a massive increase in the number of multimammate mice. So numerous were they at one stage that it was not possible for him to complete the laying of a trap line — those at the beginning were filled before he could get to the end.[40]

The broader ecological significance of such dramatic increases is wonderfully well illustrated in the following case, reported by Vivian Wilson who then was working for the Department of National Parks in Zimbabwe. Over the course of 11 months, Viv recorded the breeding history of a pair of barn owls living in an area which, during that time, was experiencing a population explosion of multimammate mice.

Staggering as it may seem, this one pair of owls raised 32 young in that period! There were four clutches of eggs, averaging eight at a time, and all the young survived to leave the nest. The importance of the abundant

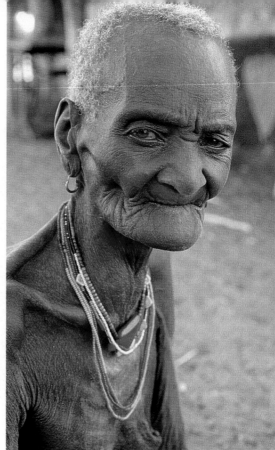

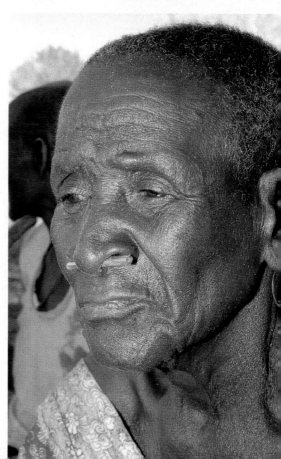

PRECEDING PAGE
The gorges downstream of Victoria
Falls are at once magnificent and
forbidding.

ABOVE LEFT
The traditional pipe of the Batonga
people is called an 'Nchela'.

ABOVE RIGHT
An aged Batonga woman, Cholobwe,
waits out the passing of her days.

RIGHT
A woman called Bachelo wearing a
'chisita'. This stick through the septum
is ornamental but its popularity is
waning.

food supply can be seen in some of Viv's observations: 24 mice delivered by the two parents working toegether in 17,5 minutes; 16 mice in 25 minutes.[41]

I've never been overly fond of snakes, although, of course, like any young man who attended a 'bush' school in Africa, I kept them as pets. I recall no trauma associated with them and I have no fear of them now. Nevertheless, at a fairly early age I parted company with snakes — to go on to more interesting things (I think girls came after snakes!). Now I am interested in anything unusual and different and at least two of the Zambezi's snakes qualify on these grounds.

The first is an example of specialisation, for this snake, commonly known as the reticulated centipede-eater, specialises to the remarkable extent that its sole diet is centipedes. It occurs along the entire Zambezi, but for reasons unknown is very common at Mana Pools and occurs there in a chestnut colour phase not known elsewhere. It is back-fanged and poisonous to centipedes, which it kills within 30 seconds.[42]

A second curiosity from the valley of the Zambezi is Gerrard's striped burrowing snake.[43] This black and yellow striped creature with a bright orange belly must be one of the most unusual snakes in the world. Not only does it have two heads, but, when alarmed, keeps its heads down and in that position can travel backwards![44] Don Broadley of the museum at Bulawayo is the source of this startling piece of information. As he is one of the great reptile experts in southern Africa, perhaps I should tell his side of the story.

The striped burrowing snake does not, of course, have two heads. However, the tail is so coloured and shaped as to look remarkably similar to the head. Less than 0,5 m in length and little thicker than a knitting needle, it has probably felt somewhat bullied in the past and has now become secretive and unusually cautious in its dealings with humans. Threatened, it raises not its head, but its tail in the air! This cunning strategy draws attention away from the vulnerable head and explains the strange phenomenon of its apparent backwards motion. It is not going backwards at all but has acquired the skill of locomotion while holding its nether regions in the air and giving an exact impression of backward movement.

In Africa, reptiles have an image problem. This is probably because they are so common and, outside the cities, so much part of our daily lives. We are generally afraid of snakes, we shoo out lizards, ignore chameleons, consider geckos a nuisance and know nothing at all about turtles. For this reason, many people may be surprised to know the extent and monetary value of the so-called reptile trade in the northern hemisphere.

Sales of turtles in America in the 1970s, for example, are said to have exceeded 15 million turtles a year, of which at least one million were imported! It is estimated that some 60 million American homes kept a turtle, the average lifespan of which was, regrettably, only two months. Yugoslavia exported live tortoises at the rate of 300 000 to 400 000 a year until none were left. Thailand exports pythons, lizards, monitors and geckos and in 1971 a total of 62 000 specimens of these species left the country, including more than 8 800 pythons. Mauritius is a more recent source of exotic reptiles and there the brilliantly coloured day-geckos and the ground iguana are coming under pressure.[45]

Nowhere along the Zambezi is there commercial collecting on anything like this scale. It may one day come and, if it does, we may be confident that the heartland of the Zambezi's menagerie is reasonably secure. Unfortunately, all that is of interest or worth to collectors is not restricted solely to the protected areas of the river and there is one particular gem that will be especially vulnerable.

In the lower reaches of the river, downstream of Cahora Bassa whose rapids restricted its distribution long before the dam was built, there is a rare and remarkable turtle. Known as the Zambezi soft-shelled turtle, it belongs to the family Trionychidae, the only reptiles in the world capable of breathing underwater. This amazing feat is possible because the animal is able to pump water in and out of its mouth over the surface of the pharynx which is richly supplied with blood vessels and by means of which an exchange of gasses can occur. In this way it can stay under water for considerable periods of time.[46]

This chapter began with a not very pretty account of man's attitude to Africa's fast diminishing wildlife. I'd like to end on a different note and one that appeals to the emotions in quite another way.

This story comes from a young game scout who was unarmed and patrolling, on foot, part of the reserve in which he worked. The man was amazed when suddenly, out of the bush, a full-grown kudu bull appeared and ran straight towards him. Kudu are among the most beautiful of Africa's large antelope; although widespread in their distribution and numerous they are, like all animals, wary of man.

The kudu was being chased by a pack of wild dogs, it was tired, its tongue was hanging out of its mouth and, most certainly, it would have been killed by the dogs. It ran right up to the scout and stood within a few metres of him. Nonplussed, the wild dogs also stopped and watched, not daring to approach closer than about 20 m. Some circled the pair in the centre. Fifteen minutes passed and the kudu moved closer to the man, almost within touching distance. Eventually, the scout threw clods of earth at the dogs which then all began to circle before running off into the bush. The kudu stayed a moment before he too left. The scout remained, standing alone in the grass, strangely moved by this remarkable touch with the wild.[47]

13 Great Zambezi Myths

THERE are a number of great legends closely associated with the Zambezi and this chapter will look at three of them. Like many legends, they have their feet in fact but with time the body becomes detached, drifts a little from reality and floats into the realms of romance. There are often reasons for this, as we shall see. To understand the first of these legends, we need to go back a long way in history.

The Portuguese, preparing to settle, arrived at the fishing village and trading station of Sofala on the Mozambique coast in 1505 and soon built a fort there. Their objective was trade and their interest gold and ivory. They quickly understood the link between what they sought and the far interior and soon resolved not to sit, waiting passively for it to come to them. A man by the name of Antonio Fernandes was chosen to carry out a reconnaissance and, to this end, he made three journeys westwards between 1511 and 1514.[1]

When, in 1511, he passed through a narrow gap in the dry stone wall at the foot of Mount Darwin in what is now northern Zimbabwe, Fernandes made history, for he became the first European to set foot in the court of what the Portuguese would later call the Empire of Monomotapa but which is more correctly called Mwene Mutapa. (The state is Mwene Mutapa, the ruler the Mutapa.) In making this contact, Fernandes revealed to the Portuguese the existence of this central African kingdom. He also initiated, unwittingly, 450 years of misinformation.

From the moment of its entry into the pages of history, accounts of Mwene Mutapa and the 'empire' have been exaggerated, belittled, misunderstood, denied, distorted or obscured. It is little wonder, then, that today there is so much confusion and uncertainty as to the truth. There are several reasons for this state of affairs. In earlier centuries the Portuguese were the only people who recorded written history; such recording was often biased. Events were not necessarily recorded when they happened, nor were they written down by people who had been closely involved with them. Often they were recorded by historians in state employ and were designed to reflect what the administrators wished to be seen. This, for example, explains a persistent theme in Portuguese documents, which tend to exaggerate the size and importance of the Mwene Mutapa empire when convenient to do so.

A further complication that awaits those who would understand Mwene Mutapa is that such fragments of history as have reached us from the African side have arrived by one of two routes. Either they have come through Portuguese hands or via oral history. In the first case, the bias of Portuguese distortion lies heavily upon the evidence. In the second, the passage of time, the frailty of human memory and the effects of an opposing bias have conspired to produce a foreshortened, different and no more accurate view of events.

Finally, in some cases, difficulties of interpretation are eclipsed by a complete absence of any historical evidence. In others, they are caused by the slow process of assimilation and counter-checking that follows new information from other fields of investigation, notably archaeology. Slowly, from this welter of confusing fact and fiction, research has established, in broad outline, the major events and is constructing a framework on which, in time, the details of the Mwene Mutapa story will more easily be placed.

In so far as any single event, taken in isolation from the great flow of history, ever has a 'start', the Mwene Mutapa empire had its origins in the state of Great Zimbabwe. This entity was itself a successor to the culture expressed by a site known today as K2 and its near neighbour, the hilltop town of Mapungubwe. Close to the junction of the Shashi and Limpopo rivers in the western Transvaal, these famous Iron Age sites had been occupied from about AD 1000 to 1270.[2]

For reasons at which we can only guess, Mapungubwe was abruptly abandoned in about 1220. Shortly afterwards, the state of Great Zimbabwe began to emerge. From AD 1240 to somewhere between 1420 and 1450 a state centred on the present-day Great Zimbabwe ruins held sway over a considerable portion of central and southern Africa. Its boundaries remain speculative but, at its height, Great Zimbabwe's influence certainly spread as far as the edges of the Kalahari in the west, the Mozambique coast in the east and parts of what is now northern Transvaal in the south, and probably included much of present-day Zimbabwe, even at that early period possibly reaching the banks of the Zambezi.[3]

By 1450, it was all over. As abruptly as its predecessors, Great Zimbabwe was apparently abandoned although the reasons for its sudden demise remain speculative. It could have been simple environmental collapse caused by the demands upon local resources of between 11 000 and 18 000 people.[4] It might have been due to some natural disaster such as a drought, or the causes could have been economic. Gold and ivory, both important trade goods, may have become more difficult to acquire, trade itself could have been threatened or trade routes cut. It is also possible that dissident factions were pulling the state apart. One certainty is that the end of Great Zimbabwe had nothing whatever to do with the Portuguese; it was over at least 50 years before they arrived.[5]

There were at least two successor states to Great Zimbabwe, one due west at Khami (about 20 km out of Bulawayo) and another far to the north on the edge of the escarpment, overlooking the Zambezi's valley in the north and north-east of present-day Zimbabwe. The former was the seat of the Torwa state and the latter that of Mwene Mutapa. It is not certainly known exactly how these two states came into existence nor how the transfer and division of the former Great Zimbabwe's power and influence were effected. However, they were both immediate chronological successors.

It is possible that Khami was the seat of a former provincial governor under Great Zimbabwe, to whom the succession fell and who, therefore, simply remained where he was, picking up the reins of government. This is not likely, however. Such an explanation would require archaeological evidence of an earlier Zimbabwe-type settlement at Khami, and none exists. It is more likely instead that Khami represents a geographical shift and a continuation of the same material culture. Whether the ruling families remained the same is much less certain.[6]

According to one of Zimbabwe's eminent historical authorities Mwene Mutapa was already in existence before the fall of Great Zimbabwe.[7] This suggests that it had originally been part of the Great Zimbabwe state and had probably been a provincial capital. Either it may have seceded, or acquired by default quasi-independence, probably due to the difficulties of control imposed by the distances involved.

Possibly, conflict and civil war were associated with the fragmentation of Great Zimbabwe and the establishment of Mwene Mutapa. Professor Tom Huffman, now Head of the Department of Archaeology at the University of the Witwatersrand and formerly with the National Museums of Zimbabwe, has spent time at the supposed site of the early Mwene Mutapa court near Mount Darwin in northern Zimbabwe. He makes an interesting point:[8] although there are a few stone-walled enclosures at the bottom of the hill, by far the most extensive works are on the heights — a tiring and difficult climb. This suggests that they were built during a time of conflict, adding to the idea that Mwene Mutapa may have been born out of violence.

The myth of Mwene Mutapa's origin has it that a chief or 'Mambo' by the name of Mutota led his people out of Great Zimbabwe away to the north. There they subdued the Batonga and Tavara people along the Zambezi. So great in number was the Mutota's army that the local people referred to his soldiers as KoreKore — which means 'the locusts' — and is a name still applied to the people of that part of Zimbabwe. Mutota himself came to be called the 'master pillager', for which the words were Mwene Mutapa, and hence the name of the empire that followed.[9]

Compared to the extent of the Great Zimbabwe state, both Torwa and Mwene Mutapa were very much smaller. In no case did boundaries ever remain fixed, of course, and the dividing line between a vassal, tributary and 'friendly' state is often hard to define. For these reasons it is not easy to describe the size of the Mwene Mutapa empire. However, its core lay roughly within the triangle north of the Mazowe River, east of the Manyame River and south of the Zambezi. At times it was larger than this and at times it shrank to little more than an enclave on the hills of what is now Cahora Bassa. The influence of Mwene Mutapa persisted through to the 1890s when the Portuguese in Mozambique were still backing various claims by reference to treaties they had with the state of Mwene Mutapa.[10]

The nature of Mwene Mutapa as a state is disputed. The Portuguese consistently referred to it as an empire, while others describe it as 'less an empire than a confederacy of Karanga chieftainships'[11] or contend 'that there never was a kingdom such as Mwene Mutapa save in the minds of the Portuguese'.[12] The truth appears to lie somewhere in between these statements.

Certainly there was a significant and vigorous state established in present-day northern Zimbabwe at the end of the 15th century. Without interference, this might have rivalled its peers and predecessors. Instead, it seems slowly to have succumbed to the corrosion of Portuguse influence and missed the opportunity for both empire and greatness. Beyond the 18th century Mwene Mutapa, in the sense of a large, centralised political unit, existed only in the form of a much reduced chiefdom.

The history of Mwene Mutapa is inextricably intertwined with that of a dynasty named after its leader, Changamire, the origins of which are uncertain. Most writers suggest that the first Changamire himself was a member of the original Mwene Mutapa élite who may have held responsibilities either as a provincial paramount or as an army commander.[13]

Suffice it to say that Changamire was seen as a threat by Mwene Mutapa and in this connection Portuguese records contain this interesting anecdote: the Mutapa of the time, Mukombero, sent a cup of poison to Changamire. In circumstances where the king suspects treachery, tradition requires him to do this. The guilty party may choose to drink it or throw it aside. If he elects the former, he dresses in his best clothes, publicly consumes the contents of the cup and dies. His sons and kin then inherit all his possessions. If he chooses not to drink, he is beheaded or strangled and his heirs inherit nothing; his estate goes to the king.[14]

Changamire declined the invitation to drink and sent, instead, four barrels of gold to the Mutapa, hoping thereby to placate him. In this he was not successful and, having been called out, Changamire marched on the capital, seized it, killed the Mutapa and all but one of his 22 sons and is believed to have reigned for four years, from 1490 to 1494. At the end of this time, he was overthrown by the remaining son and the dynasty disappears from the pages of history for nearly 200 years.

To piece together the next parts of the puzzle of Mwene Mutapa's past, it is necessary to look at Khami in the south-west. Here the ruling Torwa dynasty retained the power they had held since about 1450. By the early 1600s, however, it seems that civil war was in the offing and centred on a succession dispute between two brothers. Battles had evidently taken place, for history identifies a loser, and it was this individual who appealed to the Portuguese for help.[15]

The primary purpose of the Portuguese in Mozambique was trade and profit and, in their opinion, there had not been enough of either. Their trading policy was to work through Mwene Mutapa and they had hoped, by this means, to extend their trading to the south-west and the Torwa state, which they knew as Butua or Guruuswa.[16] This had not worked and so, when appealed to for help, they were quick to see an opportunity ultimately to open new trade links. The first step in successfully doing so was to become involved in the succession dispute and make sure they backed the winner.

One account explains that a wealthy Muslim trader, who had settled at Khami, had married his daughter to a young brother of the chief. Using the chief's unpopularity as an excuse the trader had arranged for his overthrow and for his son-in-law to take his place. The Portuguese version of this story claims the defeated ruler came to them at Luanze in Manica for help.

In the 1640s an expedition led by Sisnando Dias Bayao accompanied the deposed ruler and, in an incredible journey for the times, marched right across modern Zimbabwe to Khami where, it is claimed, they ousted the pretender and replaced the original chief.[17]

Modern historians have reservations about this interpretation. The account is partly truthful, however. Radio-carbon dates show that occupation at Khami ceased in the 17th century, when the site was abandoned. The town was attacked with cannon and those areas where the ruler lived were destroyed by fire.[18]

Far from the 'rightful' ruler being placed back on the throne, it seems that the Portuguese intention was to attack and destroy Khami. However, the original ruling dynasty appears to have escaped and moved to one of the smaller centres of Dhlo-Dhlo or Regina, both within 80 km to the north-east. In this way, the shaken Torwa state continued to survive.

There is an interesting anecdote associated with the arrival of Portuguese forces at Khami. Just a little beyond the former king's area of the present ruins, there is what is known as the 'cross ruin'. This ruin takes its name from a large stone Maltese or Dominican-type cross, laid on the flat granite and made from a mosaic of smaller stones. To preserve the feature the stones were cemented into place in about 1938. A common explanation for this unexpected evidence of European culture at the seat of a great tribal African ruler is that it was placed there by Portuguese missionaries.[19] Professor Huffman has pointed out that no ruler of a Torwa state would allow a foreigner to live so close to him. He believes that the cross was placed there in the 1600s to commemorate the Portuguese victory and destruction of Khami.

The absence of the Changamire dynasty for nearly 200 years was explained by earlier modern historians who simply said that Torwa and Changamire were the same and claimed that, after the first Changamire's 1494 defeat, he moved south and conquered the Torwa state. We now know that this was not the case: Torwa and Changamire were two entirely separate entities.

During the 'years of silence' the Changamire dynasty had continued to exist, not in opposition to the Mutapa apparently, but in loyal service to him. According to early Portuguese documents, Changamire was the keeper of the Mutapa's cattle herds and, in recognition of his services, had been granted land on the borders of the Mwene Mutapa state.[20] Towards the end of the 17th century, however, Changamire had grown sufficiently powerful in land, wealth and followers to establish a state of his own and he did so by turning south.

In about 1684 Dombo, who was then ruler of the Changamire dynasty,[21] led his armies south, invading and capturing the now weak Torwa state and establishing his capital at Dhlo-Dhlo.[22] From this point onwards the word Rozvi appears in Shona history. It was a generic name applied to the 17th century followers of Changamire and would henceforth refer to the new Rozvi state that had now come into existence following the collapse of Torwa.

After the defeat of the first recorded Changamire in 1494, Mwene Mutapa's relationship with the Portuguese slowly deteriorated, punctuated by a series of incidents. The first was the murder of a Catholic missionary — Dom Goncalo da Silveira of the Society of Jesus — about whom more will be said in Chapter 14. This tragic event was used by the Portuguese as an excuse for an attempt at conquest, which failed completely.

Despite failure, the attempt cowed the Mutapa into suggesting a treaty, which was signed in 1575 and which began the slow process of reducing his powers. By its terms, the treaty allowed the Portuguese to trade freely, mine gold, build churches and expel Muslims within the realm of Mwene Mutapa.[23]

To achieve and monopolise the trade they sought, the Portuguese considered control of Mwene Mutapa the key. To this end, by manipulation and interference, they worked constantly towards maintaining the structure and the myth of empire at the same time as aiming for total control over the so-called emperor. In all their dealings with African polities along the Zambezi and in Mozambique, the Portuguese missed few opportunities to further their aims.

Thus, when military threats against the state arose from Mwene Mutapa's neighbours, it was to the Portuguese that the Mutapa turned for help. Invariably, help was given — but at a price — and so in 1607 another treaty was signed by the reigning Mutapa, Gasti Rusere. This agreed that the gold, copper and iron mines of Mwene Mutapa would be handed over to the Portuguese and that two of the Mutapa's daughters and three sons would have a Portuguese education and be raised in the Catholic faith.[24] It was about this time that a 'personal guard of 30 Europeans and half-castes under the command of a Portuguese captain' was attached to the Mutapa. This small force was maintained by the Portuguese for the next 150 years.[25]

Like any agreement signed under duress, it was doomed to work with difficulty. Rusere, caught between rivals and Portuguese pressure, was aware that his power was slipping away and so fought a rearguard action, prevaricating in every way he could. He was successful in preventing Portuguese access to the mines of Mwene Mutapa.

Rusere's successor, Kapararidze, was aggressive towards the Portuguese who caused his dethronement and put in his place the first puppet Mutapa, Mavura. Installed in 1629, Mavura signed a treaty that made him a vassal of the Portuguese king, acknowledged the Portuguese ownership of the gold and silver mines and did away with a number of civilities demanded of visiting Portuguese by the Mutapa.[26] In exchange Mavura received from Philip IV of Portugal the gift of a European-style crown and throne![27]

The Portuguese made a strategic error in dethroning instead of decapitating Kapararidze, for in 1631 he inspired a revolt in the lands along the river from modern Cahora Bassa to the sea. Hundreds of Portuguese and thousands of Africans died in the uprising before the authorities regained control and when they did, it was an uneasy peace that prevailed.

Puppet followed puppet while Portuguese demands and arrogant disrespect for the Mutapa increased. As this happened, so the internal ties that bound Mwene Mutapa into a unitary state were loosened and the process of Balkanisation, begun three generations before, continued with new vigour as distant chiefs, at an increasing rate, withdrew and established their own independence.[28]

In 1669 the Mutapa Mukombwe died and the Portuguese expected that his son Mhande, groomed for the position, would succeed. However, Mukombwe's brother Nyakambiro seized the throne and managed to hold it against Portuguese wishes.

At some time during the following years, either for hatred of the Portuguese or for fear that they might depose him, he invited the current Changamire to help rid him of the Portuguese.[29]

The Changamire, Mambo, had his own reasons for wishing to attack the Portuguese. They maintained several trading posts or 'feiras' within his realm and there is every reason to suppose that direct trade with the Portuguese formed an important part of the state's economy.[30] Feiras had been sending Mambo an annual present in lieu of customs dues, but in the 1680s they unilaterally stopped this practice. Envoys with requests for its reintroduction were returned to Changamire insulted and mutilated, their ears cut off. Several minor skirmishes followed until 1693 when Mambo attacked in full force.[31]

The fury of Mambo's assault has certainly been exaggerated but at least two feiras were razed to the ground; Portuguese accounts are full of the savagery with which this was done. The feira of Dambarare, a little north of modern Harare, is a case in point. Portuguese accounts explain how all the Portuguese there were killed, the church destroyed, the dead disinterred and their bones burnt.[32] Excavations at Dambarare have shown no sign of any desecration of the church, nor of any fire.[33]

Word of Mambo's action rapidly spread and those Portuguese remaining on the Zimbabwean plateau quickly retired to the safety of the lowlands around Tete and Sena. Unopposed, Mambo swept on, driving all Portuguese before him. Nyakambiro was secured on his throne as Mutapa of Mwene Mutapa and the Changamire Mambo stood poised at the boundaries of Tete. Here he died and at once his cause lost impetus as potential successors became embroiled in disputes over succession.

Seizing his opportunity, with the inevitable Portuguese help, Mhanda was at last able to claim his throne by ousting Nyakambiro. The latter went again to Changamire for help, but this time to no avail. Meanwhile, Mhanda had consolidated his position but he did so within the confines of a much reduced 'empire'. Just as Mambo had swept the Portuguese from the highveld of Zimbabwe, so too had he taken possession of that portion of Mwene Mutapa. Later the former state was still further reduced in size, restricted to the lowlands between the escarpment and the Zambezi. From here it shrank towards the east and the steadily diminishing shadow of its Portuguese protectors.

For the next 150 years, until the 1830s, there was to be relative peace on the Zimbabwean plateau in the Rozvi state ruled by the Changamire dynasty. In the lowlands of the river the myth of Mwene Mutapa's greatness was perpetuated by the Portuguese. Although its name lived on for another 200 years the 'empire' had vanished. Like water spilt upon the parched earth of the valley to which history and the Portuguese had relegated it, Mwene Mutapa was no more.

This, then, is briefly the story of Mwene Mutapa, an important part of the Zambezi's history. Another character in the Zambezi's story, much less well known, is a so-called iron god that for several hundred years 'lived' in the Zambezi Valley and is still widely revered today. As examples of the awe and respect in which 'Chimombe' is held, the following were told to me by the people involved as true stories.

A young man of 20 walked through the Zambezi Valley in the footsteps of his guide, an African man called Mubayiwa. Hunting was the young man's life and he had already spent six years in the business. As they approached the junction of the Chewore and Zambezi rivers the man became aware of the number of wild animals about him. Strangely, he could not see them — he could only hear them calling — but he was amazed at their number and the volume. So loud were the sounds and so close, but still unseen, were they that despite his experience, he grew afraid. His guide reassured him, calmed him and told him not to be frightened for, he said, the animals were guarding Chimombe; they were his.[34]

In the intense heat of the Zambezi Valley, not far from the Chewore River, stood 14 lorries. Their drivers sought the nearest shade, patiently waiting for the villagers to finish loading. The villagers knew it was hopeless and had said so; but the young white District Officer did not understand and hurried them on. Finally, the last load and all the people were aboard. The engines started but the trucks would not move, it seemed they were all stuck in the sand. The vehicles were unloaded, tested and found to move freely, loaded again and once more they refused to move. Mystified, the official began asking why. The reason was simple: Chimombe had not agreed to the proposed move and would not allow the vehicles to drive away.[35]

Who or what is Chimombe and what is its strange power? Often referred to as a god, Chimombe is not, as will be seen. The name is applied by people to a stangely shaped piece of iron which they regard with great reverence and claim represents a spirit person through whom they can communicate with the spirit world of their ancestors. The name Chimombe, according to tradition, was that of the group's original leader who led his people south across the Zambezi to the vicinity of the Chewore River between 250 and 200 years ago.

Chimombe is kept in a small hut of its own which it shares with nothing but the paraphernalia associated with its rituals. As the African cattle tradition demands, the hut is located up-slope and behind the chief's residence.[36] In addition to having a private residence, Chimombe is attended by two permanent officials. One is Nyawundo, a servant, who looks after the dwelling and is responsible for maintenance. The second is Mubayiwa, a hereditary position in which the incumbent has the special skill of being able to communicate with man and spirit and thus fills the critical role of intermediary. The chief, Chundu, is traditionally appointed as ultimate custodian of Chimombe and the present holder of that office claims he is the eighth since the death of the man for whom Chimombe is named.

Chimombe is remarkable for a number of reasons. It is the only example in the region of this particular kind of ancestor worship where a metal symbol takes the place of the spirit. Chimombe has a long and fascinating history attached to it and, perhaps because of this, is still regarded with awe and respect by both its own and other tribes.

Only a few white people have had the privilege and opportunity to visit Chimombe. I was most fortunate in being able to spend three days at its village in 1987 and there learnt first-hand the story of the 'iron god' from Chief Chundu. One may not see Chimombe without making certain traditional gifts and I well remember the extraordinary situation on the evening of my first meeting with the chief.

I was camping in the bush nearby and while waiting for the chief, lay on my bed looking up at the early night sky. Finding Chimombe and discovering what I needed to know to meet him had been a long chase and now the final prize was almost within grasp. I was excited and thought of what little I then knew of Chimombe's history: of the murder and the deaths that followed, of the strange tales of magic and of the awe with which this piece of iron was regarded. I had with me the gifts ancient tradition required and I thought, as I watched two satellites cross the heavens above, of the strange juxtaposition of old and new, of past and present, that had somehow come together in this place and time. I reflected again on Africa's ability to offer the unexpected.

This is what Chief Chundu told me: in the beginning the man, Chimombe, was chief. He and his original followers came from the Kankomba area of Zaïre and eventually settled among the Vasori on the north bank of the Zambezi in the valley. Later they crossed the Zambezi onto the Zimbabwean side and there began working salt deposits they found.

This brought them into conflict with the Mutapa of Mwene Mutapa who claimed both the land and its salt. An army of Korekore was sent under the command of the state's most able commander — Nyamapfeka — to drive Chimombe and his people out.

The more closely Nyamapfeka's army approached Chimombe's kraal, the greater the difficulties they experienced. They were attacked by animals, stricken by disease, overtaken by natural disasters and found great difficulty in even locating Chimombe or bringing his people to battle. Faced with failure they adopted a cunning stratagem.

Semwa, a pretty young Korekore girl (some say she was Nyamapfeka's daughter[37]) was given certain instructions and left by a pool used by Chimombe's villagers. As Nyamapfeka had hoped, Semwa was found and taken to the chief. He liked her and took her to his hut. That night when he was asleep, she drew a knife and slit his throat.

Immediately, the blood gushed forth and a river was formed, the Masikote, which still flows today. Terrible events then fell upon all the people of the valley. The sun 'went out' for two days, there were floods, it became very hot, the Korekore could not escape from the valley and were losing men daily to disease and wild animals.

The distraught villagers were in despair. But one of them, walking along the banks of the Zambezi, came across certain items lying by the river: a rifle barrel, an axe, a round item of headwear called a Ndoro, a drum and a curiously twisted asymmetrical piece of metal. The metal object spoke to the villager who, fearing bewitchment, threw it into the river. But it emerged from the water and presented itself again to him, declaring itself to be Chimombe who was returning after his murder in order to look after his people, but in a guise that could not be destroyed.

Nyamapfeka, faced with increasing deaths in his much diminished army and desperate now for help, appealed to the new chief who had been appointed (and whom Chimombe decreed should be called Chundu). Chundu, in turn, was told by the spirit Chimombe that Nyamapfeka would find the relief he required only by offering his firstborn son to be the spirit's guardian. In this way did the first Mubayiwa come to be chosen from among the Korekore — from among the very people who had been responsible for Chimombe's death.

This strange twist has a corollary in traditions that survive to this day. There are two tests for any person who believes he is the one in whom the spirit of an immediate past Mubayiwa has chosen to reside. Firstly he must find the drum and the headdress which will have been hidden somewhere in the bush at a place known only to the chief. For confirmation that he is the right person, the applicant who has successfully passed the first test must travel to the old Mwene Mutapa in the Dande communal lands of north-east Zimbabwe. There he must seek out Nyamapfeka's spirit which will confirm the choice or render it invalid. This is still done in the 1980s and, indeed, the Mubayiwa during my visit was only acting in the position, as a new incumbent was being sought following the death of the previous Mubayiwa.

It is also true that, still living in the guilt of their ancestor's murderous act, no true Korekore today will go anywhere near Chimombe for fear of being struck blind or being killed.

Having reached an uneasy truce with the Korekore, Chimombe and his people lived in peace until the Matabele raided the valley, probably between 1840 and 1870. They succeeded in capturing Chimombe but immediately experienced so much bad luck that they threw it into the Zambezi. It re-emerged and faced them, whereupon they threw it once more into the water. Again Chimombe came out of the river and an attempt was made to destroy it. Half of the shape was broken off and the two separate pieces were discarded. Again Chimombe returned, minus the missing piece (which is still missing today — see photograph), and so terrified the Matabele that they fled, never to return.

There is a great deal more to this fascinating legend, but I want to pass now to Chimombe's origins.

The Mubayiwa would not permit me to touch Chimombe although he allowed me to approach it closely and take photographs. These clearly show it to be man-made. My guess at the time was that Chimombe was a Portuguese artefact that had been dropped or lost by the river and subsequently found by the tribesman. With photographs and as much information as possible, I enlisted the aid of the British Museum.

In the meantime, further research revealed an earlier suggestion that Chimombe might have been a kapanda or metal bow-stand. These are used by the Bemba people in northern Zambia and are a symbol of chiefly authority. With a single pointed stem which is pushed into the ground and an ornamental top branched rather like a candelabra, a pair of kapanda outside the chief's house provide a support for the chief's bow, arrows and spears which are laid horizontally between them.[38]

A comparison of Chimombe with examples and pictures of bow-stands shows that, while not precisely the same, they are all similar in design and shape, strongly suggesting that Chimombe, too, was originally one of these. That such items are associated with the office of chief strengthens the case for Chimombe, we know, was the chief. The British Museum also suggested that the search for Chimombe's origins be focused on Bemba bow-stands.[39]

A chance meeting with Professor Phillipson, an authority on Zambian ethnology and archaeology, provided the next piece of the puzzle. He pointed out to me that Bemba royalty (the 'Bena Ng'andu', the crocodile clan) came originally from Zaïre about 300 years ago, bringing their material culture with them. Other groups in Zambia also have Zaïrese roots.[40] This helped explain a link with Zaïre claimed by Chief Chundu.

David Beach's fascinating study of the history of Zimbabwe's Shona people describes Chief Chimombe and his followers as a group of the matrilineal Soli tribe from north of the river.[41] This is particularly interesting because a Soli chief's burial site was discovered and excavated near Zambia's capital Lusaka. Among the preserved remains was an extensive collection of Soli ironwork which included one bow-stand. Although more elaborate than Chimombe it is generally similar.[42] More interesting still is that the Soli tribe are known to be a branch of the Luba people who entered Zambia (from Zaïre in the west) south of the Luapula River and arrived in the Lusaka area between 150 and 200 years ago.

I am convinced that Chimombe is what remains of one of a pair of handmade bow-stands. I believe it was a traditional symbol of Chief Chimombe's authority while he lived and was transformed by the tribe into a symbol of his person when he died.

The last of the great Zambezi myths I want to talk about in this chapter concerns a tribe of valley dwellers who have haunted its legends for 100 years or more. Tales of men that run like the wind, climb trees like monkeys, flee from contact and are seldom seen persist in the stories of the valley but the source is hard to trace.

Much of the evidence comes from vague sightings and, above all, from strange two-toed spoor. The name Vadoma is repeated in bar-room conversations but few can add much more to the mystery than speculation. Who are the Vadoma and what is the truth about these supposedly two-toed people?

The Vadoma or Vadema are remarkable in that among their number there are some (not all as legend has it) who exhibit a genetic deformity of the hands and feet. The hand may have additional fingers or existing digits may be fused. The feet usually lack the normal arrangement of toes and have, extending from the stump of the ankle, two large toes which may stand at right angles to each other or be otherwise misshapen. It is because of this abnormality that the Vadoma have been called by some the 'ostrich people'.

According to Dr James Jijide at Harare's Queen Victoria Museum,[43] the Vadoma (they apparently prefer Vadema) came originally from the vicinity of Tete in Mozambique. A different account suggests an origin in the north.[44] A group of 200 to 300 people entered Zimbabwe about 250 years ago, settling in the lands of Mwene Mutapa. They split into two parties, one centred on the Chewore and Kanyemba area, the other on the Angwa, about 75 km to the south.[45] According to Dr Jijide the chief resides with the latter group. She is extremely powerful and is also the ancestral spirit medium, the rainmaker and medicine woman.

The spirit she represents has always insisted that the Vadoma may not leave the valley to find work, nor may they marry outside the tribe. The limitation on marriages, if truly traditional, may be important, for by restricting the size of the gene pool, a genetic defect is less likely to be dissipated. In modern times both these strictures have tended to be ignored.

While reading the material on the Vadoma queen I discovered a fact of singular curiosity. As we have seen, Chimombe's people dwelt in the Chewore region for 200 to 250 years. The Vadoma likewise dwelt in the valley in the same area for approximately the same time. We have seen that Chief Chimombe was murdered by a girl called Semwa. I did not mention that she was also known by an alternative name — Chiguwa.[46] The name of the Vadoma Queen is also Chiguwa.[47] This seems too much of a coincidence to lack significance and I hope, one day, it will be investigated.

The Vadoma myth always refers to their agility and speed. Those Vadoma I have questioned all claim not to experience any limitations of movement. This is hard to accept when the condition is seen and when victims of it walk. I suspect it is something they merely say, not wishing to be different from others, but further questioning does elicit that 'the deformity is a slight handicap in movement, and running in particular is difficult'.[48]

Near the Zambezi I met only one person exhibiting this condition. Karuma Nyakutepa, or Maharabani as he is known, is now 48 and has markedly ostrich-like feet, although his hands are normal. He knew of others who had the condition and all but one are now dead, he says. Karuma's wife is a Korekore woman who is not affected and he has six surviving children, all without a sign of the condition. His own mixed parentage of Vadoma and Korekore indicates the degree of deviation from Chiguwa's strict marriage rule.[49]

Traditionally living in tsetse fly areas of poor agricultural potential, the Vadoma have always been hunter-gatherers, living of honey, plants, roots and hunting wild animals, therefore tending to live in small isolated groups as dictated by the carrying capacity of the land. This factor may partly explain their elusiveness. It is a policy of the Zimbabwe government now to feed, educate, resettle and politicise the Vadoma.[50]

Another group containing six people suffering from the same condition is to be found near the border with Zimbabwe in north-eastern Botswana. I was intrigued when visiting this group to learn they were part of a related group over the border in Zimbabwe that contained 16 affected individuals.[51] Their oral history shows that they moved to this area from the Zambezi Valley in two waves: first a slow infiltration before 1839 and then more rapidly as foreign recruits to the Ndebele 'Mpande' regiment, which allowed them to settle in their present home.

So we see that there are at least four separate groups of Vadoma-related people in the region: at Kanyemba, on the Angwa, in south-western Zimbabwe and in Botswana. It is difficult to assess precisely the number of afflicted individuals but certainly not all the Vadoma are, as myth would have us believe. Nor is it likely to be 'about 100' as David Barritt suggests for one region alone.[52] The southern populations are said to contain as many as 22 affected people of whom I have seen and photographed six. Of 400 or 500 individual Vadoma in the north, only three so far have been found to display the condition,[53] giving a total of 25. It seems unlikely that this figure will be substantially exceeded.

Medical research has shown that this condition is genetic and therefore hereditary. Loosely known as ectrodactyly, it occurs universally and has been recorded in Europe, Iran and America; it is not restricted solely to the African continent.[54] The condition has been variously named and the list includes such tongue-twisters as perodactyly, oligodactyly, hypodactyly, aphalagy, cleft-hand and cleft-foot, clawpincers, crayfish claw, crab claw and lobster claw.[55]

The first documented report, in 1770, came from a director of the Dutch East India Company who complained of this condition in a slave from central Africa who was working in Dutch Guiana. He was one of a small group of Negro slaves all of whom had only two thick digits on both feet and hands.[56] With no pun intended, I am sure, the Dutch called them the Touvinga tribe!

14 Woollen Hats and Brass Potties

I am not sure that anybody really knows why the Portuguese occupied Mozambique. It would surprise me if they themselves were completely sure. The literature today tells us that the reasons had to do with religion, trade and glory.

If it were religion, their occupation was singularly unsuccessful. If it were trade, they had to learn to bring something more desirable to Africans than the goods they landed so hopefully at Sofala in 1505. Nobody, they found, wanted sailor's hats made from brightly coloured wool or brass potties from Germany.[1] If it were glory, their expedition and occupation could hardly have started less auspiciously. That little, if any, glory accrued should surprise no one.

The Portuguese did not land 'cold' at Sofala in 1505. Vasco da Gama had pioneered the route around the Cape of Good Hope in 1498 and although he did not visit the tiny port of Sofala, he learnt of its existence from the Muslim pilots on Mozambique Island. As a result, three years later in 1501, Sancho de Toar paid a formal visit. On that occasion he gave presents of crimson silk, mirrors, hawk trappings and little Flemish bells to the sheik from the king of Portugal. In return, the crown received a string of gold beads of handsome value.[2]

Vasco da Gama was not depending entirely on faith when he explored the African coast: he was privy to confidential reports given to the king of Portugal. These reports arose from a series of quite incredible and little-known journeys of exploration which themselves are a subject worthy of a book.[3]

In May 1487 King Joao of Portugal, in great secrecy, briefed Alfonso de Payva and Pero da Covilha — the latter's special knowledge of Arabic uniquely qualified him for this task — to explore beyond Jerusalem, find the spice lands and the routes to them and unravel the mystery of Prester John. Incognito, these two travelled and acquired knowledge that was priceless to the Portuguese.

Via Barcelona, Naples and Rhodes they reached Alexandria, where an illness detained them. From there it was Cairo, the Red Sea and Aden where they separated, de Payva returning to Africa and the quest for Prester John. Covilha took a dhow to the Malabar coast of India. Here he travelled extensively and discovered that pepper and ginger were grown locally and that cinnamon and cloves were traded from afar. He visited Calicut and the northern port of Goa before returning via Hormuz and Oman. It was here that he heard of the east African trade and learnt the secret of travel by the monsoons. Donning one of his many disguises he set off to explore by dhow the east coast of Africa.

Covilha certainly stopped at Mombasa and later described the great buildings he saw at Kilwa. We know that he called in at the island of Mozambique and paid a visit, at the most southerly point of his journey, to the sheik at the town of Sofala. Here he was told of the great quantities of gold that came from the kingdom of Mwene Mutapa which lay on the south bank of the Zambezi. He enquired about the possibility of sailing on and was told that 'the whole coast to the west could be navigated and its end was not known'.

We tend to have such a Eurocentric view of history that we are often surprised at what others knew of the world before we did. Covilha's discoveries clearly showed that the inhabitants of the Indian Ocean's coasts were known to each other and that trade was well established. His discoveries must also have reassured and motivated da Gama's fleet as they worked their way southwards down the west coast towards what would otherwise have been a totally unknown future.

While he has nothing to do with the Zambezi, I cannot leave da Covilha there. He intended to return with news of his discoveries to his king but he found messengers waiting for him at Cairo with new instructions and news of his companion's early death, before he had discovered anything about Prester John.

He was not able to return to Portugal. As instructed, he conducted two minor missions during one of which he became the first Christian ever known to have visited Mecca (another of his disguises) and then, after writing a long report on his first expedition, started out for Ethiopia. He successfully penetrated this kingdom and became a confidant of the emperor to whom he proved so useful that he was not allowed to leave. He acquired wealth, land, status and a wife and was still there 30 years later when the next Portuguese arrived![4]

While the outward signs of crusading zeal might have been fluttering from the top gallants, I cannot accept that lust for the storied Muslim gold was not a greater draw to the fleet of occupation that sailed from Portugal in March 1505. Indeed, avarice seems always to have been the underlying theme of Portuguese policy in Africa and India. Of itself the search for gold motivated many a colonial venture by nations from across the world. In this regard, the Portuguese were no exception. What made them different was that no others seemed to go to such lengths as they to pretend that it was Catholicism, not commercialism, that spurred their adventures.

Portugal in 1500 was a tiny nation of about a million people; resources for the empire inspired by dreams of wealth were simply insufficient. There were not enough trained sailors for Dom Francisco d'Almeida's fleet. As the ships were going down the river, the pilots called out the traditional Portuguese equivalents of starboard and port and unexpectedly created total chaos. None of the steersmen knew the terms and so, as the story has it, instructions were given that appropriate new terms should be coined. For the rest of the journey, garlic in bunches tied to the rigging on one side of the ship and onions on the other avoided further confusion as, I imagine, cries of 'Garlic six points!' or 'Whale to onions!' rang out across a stunned ocean.[5]

D'Almeida's fleet of 23 vessels included six destined for Sofala, but before the admiral hauled his anchor one of these vessels began to leak and sank to the bottom of the Tagus River. Nothing could be done to save it and the fleet left without the small Sofala group, all of which were detained until May when a replacement ship could be found.

If the start of d'Almeida's expedition had been less than glorious, the fate of the Sofala fleet under Pero d'Anhaya was to be no different. On the journey round the coast, one of the six captains fell overboard and drowned while harpooning fish from the bowsprit. During the rounding of the Cape of Good Hope, the small group of ships battled severe weather in snow and temperatures so low that the wine froze. Predictably, the fleet was separated.[6]

In September, d'Anhaya and two others of his small fleet arrived at Sofala and there waited for their companions. Two more shortly arrived, one with a tale that would have told the African people, had they known of it, all they needed about their new companions.

Reaching Delagoa Bay, the site of present-day Maputo, this party had seen a village ashore, from which the inhabitants fled at the sight of the Portuguese. Taking this as an opportunity for free booty, about 20 of the sailors landed and advanced on the village. The natives, now aware of Portuguese intent, returned to defend their property and did so with such vigour and success that only four or five Portuguese, and all of them injured, made it back to the boat alive. Among the dead was the captain, the only navigator. The crew would not have survived but for their good fortune in meeting with one of the strayed vessels, and with its help they arrived at Sofala.[7]

With his fleet at last united, Pero d'Anhaya cautiously advanced with three of his ships up the river, displaying a variety of trade goods and hoping to convince the locals of his intentions. Traders for hundreds of years, they needed little convincing and, initially, relations were good.

The Portuguese met with the blind and aged local sheik whose apparently sumptuous dwelling and lifestyle left them in little doubt as to his wealth and that of Sofala generally. They obtained permission to

erect a fort and by November 1505 had completed the task — but not before an unexpected price had been paid: more than 40 of their number died
of malaria.

As we have already seen in Chapter 7, the idea of trade was not new
to Africa; the Muslim traders had established an effective and appropriate
network by which it operated. The Portuguese intention was to destroy
this monopoly and replace it with their own. This, in the early days at
Sofala, they were effectively able to do. Early returns from Sofala were
excellent and prospects for the future were encouraging. But this was not
achieved without arousing the hostility of the Muslim traders.

They plotted against the Portuguese and gained the support of the sheik
and Mokondi, a local chief and vassal of Mwene Mutapa, whose support
was vital as he supplied the manpower. The conspirators had a spy within
their midst for the Portuguese were forewarned and were ready for the
attack by 1 000 men or more when it came.

With the superiority of firearms the defenders in their small fort easily
held the day, at great cost to the enemy who fell in large numbers. Sensing
final victory, the Portuguese sallied out in a counterattack, inflicting yet
more casualties on the native rebels. The captain, d'Anhaya, led his men
to the sheik's village. The sheik was beheaded and his head carried on
spearpoint in victory back to the fort.

The incident inspired the Muslims with a desire for revenge and the
attack on the fort was renewed, but eventually it lost purpose and both
sides readily accepted peace. Naturally, the victors dominated the question of who should succeed the murdered sheik, and so the first of many
Portuguese puppets acceded to a position of power.

I have dwelt at some length upon a brief moment in the history of the
Portuguese entry into and occupation of Mozambique. This is because
within this short time are demonstrated many of the themes that recur
frequently in the next 450 years; the Portuguese lack of resources, poor
organisation, greed, lawlessness and cruelty and, above all, lack of sen-
sitivity and inability to work within established systems.

Having revealed their true colours and their choice to rule by might, the
Portuguese earned Muslim animosity also. Denied a part in the gold trade
of Sofala, the Muslims withdrew from what appears to have been a small
and relatively unimportant part of the trading network, leaving the
Portuguese in command of empty coffers and a growing deficit.

With the passage of time, Portuguese knowledge of the region slowly
grew. They were aware of the Zambezi and of the so-called Moorish
trade along it and soon discovered that the Moors had simply shifted
the centre of trade from Sofala northwards. They suspected the gold
that they were being denied was passing through Arab hands to Kilwa
and beyond. Eventually, the time for action came and this action took
two forms.

They sent Antonio Fernandes on a journey of exploration into the hinterland. Fernandes was what was known as a degredado, a convicted criminal. Such people were given the opportunity to earn remission by acts in service of the state.

Little is known about this man who completed expeditions into the interior that in every way equalled those of many, more famous, who followed him, Livingstone included. We do not know his crime although it is said that he was granted his freedom from punishment and died at Sofala between 1522 and 1525.[8] There is a possibility that he had already proved his worth as an explorer and reconnaissance man at Kilwa, in east Africa. Here he had been left ashore for the purpose of gathering information, which may explain his later success for it gave him a chance to learn the African ways and to understand at least one African language.

Fernandes made three journeys between 1511 and 1514.[9] His brief was to establish contact with Mwene Mutapa, find out where the gold was mined and where it was going to. Judging from the reports of the *factor* at Sofala, Fernandes was successful in reaching Mwene Mutapa. His achievement was tremendous as each round trip would have been between 1 500 km and 2 000 km.

Sending Fernandes on reconnaissance was one step the Portuguese took. The other was to continue their efforts to gain by force the monopoly of the gold trade they now desperately needed. By 1511 they had discovered that the Muslim system was to encourage the flow of gold from the hinterland to established markets or 'fairs' inland, some of which were on the Zambezi. At these fairs, small quantities from individual sellers were purchased and collected and then moved in bulk either by boat down the river or overland to Angoche. This town was a long-established Arab stronghold on the coast north of the Zambezi and had been a centre of trade before the Portuguese arrival at Sofala. However, as a result of that event and Portuguese impact upon trade, Angoche experienced boom conditions and, at that time, is said to have had 12 000 inhabitants or more.[10]

Once again the Portuguese used force. In 1511 they attacked Angoche from the sea, burnt the town and sank some dhows. The military gains were minuscule. The political consequences were disastrous, for this act turned the hand of every coastal chief against them. The immediate consequence was that food supplies became very difficult to obtain. The long-term effect was twofold: they failed to make any significant impact on Muslim trade, and they guaranteed continued Muslim hostility and opposition.

With an unparalleled ability to put one foot after the other wrong, just a few years later, in 1523, the Portuguese made another attack on a Muslim stronghold. This time the target was the islands of Querimba. The same material destruction followed; in retrospect, looting seems to have been the prime purpose. One of the raiding party's boats, too heavily loaded with such ill-gotten gains, sank. The results of this raid were no different from the first. Nor were they any different after the Portuguese sacking of Mombasa in 1528.[11]

The Muslim traders' grip on the east coast and the gold mines of the interior was as elusive as the gold itself. The Muslims, unlike the Portuguese, were part of the people. They and their trade were a way of life. Perhaps it was a realisation of this that prompted the captain of the port at Sofala to make a momentous decision in 1531. If the Portuguese were in Mozambique for the gold, he reasoned, they would have to go inland and get it.

In the official written commands given by kings to captains, the religious aspect of Portuguese occupation never failed to be emphasised. The reality was an enormous gulf between the king's desire and the achievement of his officials. Or was it all lip service anyway?

The first serious attempt at real missionary enterprise in lands outside immediate Portuguese control did not take place until 1560 in Mozambique. When it did, it was more as a result of an individual's enterprise than an outcome of state policy. That it was not successful was due more to the personality of the individual than to any other factor.

The so-called martyrdom of the Jesuit priest Goncalo da Silveira is well documented and the principal facts quite widely known. Some of the detail is fascinating and much less well known.[12] It deserves a wider audience if only for the picture it paints of a man I do not hesitate to call a born martyr — looking for a place to happen.

Da Silveira was born of a noble family in Portugal in 1526, the tenth child. His mother died at his birth and his father soon after. An orphan, he was brought up by a much older sister. He attended university but did not stay there long, joining the Society of Jesus in 1543, nine years after it was formed, as one of the first Portuguese recruits. Clues to the personality of the man the Society had acquired lie in his alleged refusal to drink wine — at the age of seven — and his unblushing acknowledgement of the truth. There seems little doubt that da Silveira was brilliant and gifted. It is also plain that he was exceedingly stubborn.[13]

He served the Jesuits for 13 years in Portugal but this does not seem to have been a period that brought out the best in him. Finding their own human weakness the major obstacle in their service to God, many of those early Jesuits fought a battle with themselves that all but destroyed them. Goncalo was no exception. He rejected with contempt and without regard for the feelings of his family anything to do with his noble past. He deliberately placed himself in the most menial and debased positions and emerged from those years with a reputation for excellence marred only by his need to drive and punish himself (and those with him) without relief.

In 1556 Goncalo da Silveira was posted to India as 'Provincial', in charge of the Jesuit establishment there. He remained in India for three years and came to know intimately the viceroy, Francisco Barreto, who re-enters the story later.

Success was measured by number of converts and da Silveira's success was manifest. In his first year, 1 080 were recorded — more than expected, apparently. The following year the number rose to 1 916 and in da Silveira's last year, 3 233 were converted. Who can say how much more successful he might have been had not a call been received by the viceroy for a missionary in southern Mozambique. Da Silveira was instructed to answer the call and so he and two companions sailed for Africa in 1560.

Brother Andre da Costa was the first of da Silveira's companions. He was a member of the Society for only two years, and the hardships that he was about to face nearly killed him and he was soon sent from Africa. The second companion was made of sterner stuff. An ex-army officer, and ten years the senior, Father Andre Fernandes was probably the hardiest and most resilient of them all.

The small party landed at Mozambique Island in February 1560 and da Silveira wished to depart immediately. They were guests of his relative the governor, who offered his boat for the 800 km journey to Sofala. Predictably, da Silveira refused to take it, preferring instead a tiny open boat which was too small, offered no shelter and was only available in eight days' time.

The journey took them 27 days of incredible hardship. They ran out of food, caught no fish, were burnt and blistered by the sun and were cramped and wet for most of the time. Brother da Costa almost died of exhaustion. The governor's ship usually made the journey in ten days.

After a five-day pause at Sofala during which da Costa recovered, they set off again, in the same boat, for another 480 km and the village of Inhambane. On the journey it was da Silveira's turn to take ill and had they not made the passage swiftly and without incident he might well have died. At their destination a small group of Portuguese traders helped da Silveira survive but there was no question of his continuing immediately on his mission. He therefore despatched Fernandes to go the last 80 km to Gambe's kraal on foot and alone.

Da Silveira and da Costa arrived at the kraal 17 days later, three and a half months since they had sailed from India. Da Silveira had left the coast before he was fully recovered and he and da Costa were exhausted to the point where neither could walk when they arrived at Ontongue, where Gambe lived.

Da Silveira remained at Ontongue for seven weeks, during which time he fell victim to his own naivety, a disease that inspired fantastic dreams of Christian conquest and led directly to his death. Working among Gambe and his people, whose message it was that had summoned him from India in the first place, he and Fernandes became euphoric about the possibilities for converts.

The people believed in a supreme god and in a life after death in which man was punished or rewarded. Polygamy and Islam were recognised as obstacles but euphoria brushed them aside. The people were asking for baptism and women could not take their eyes off the picture of Our Lady (the first picture of its kind they had ever seen) and were queueing at the church to see it. It was a missionary's dream and inspired both priests to imagine Africa as an endless carpet of prostrate and suppliant converts waiting to be rolled up.

Da Silveira at once decided that, if all central and southern Africa was to be entered on God's scroll, the only efficient way to tackle so large a task was to start at the top. The top, to the Portuguese of the time, was the Mutapa, ruler of the Mwene Mutapa state. At once, da Silveira became anxious to leave Ontongue.[14]

More than 400 people were quickly baptised before, at the end of seven weeks, da Silveira returned to the coast and Mozambique Island, leaving da Costa and Fernandes to carry on the work. Da Costa, the frail reed, soon lagged, sickened and followed his master to the coast, leaving Fernandes alone for two years of purgatory on earth. Gambe's people, tired of Christian novelty and irked by its strictures, rapidly returned to their old ways, manifesting a cruel animosity towards Fernandes which would have killed him were he not recalled two years later, the mission a total failure.

Da Silveira left Mozambique Island in September 1560 and again sailed down the coast in a small boat, then up the Zambezi to Sena where he waited six weeks for permission to enter Mwene Mutapa territory. While waiting there he brought the mass and sacrament to the 10 or 15 Portuguese living at Sena and to some Indian Christians also there, at the same time baptising 400 slaves. At last, permission from the Mutapa came and da Silveira set off to the great African kingdom.

He travelled alone, but for a few African servants, and chose to do so on foot — a journey of some 800 km. He arrived at the Mutapa's town on 24 December 1560 and was met by a Portuguese who lived there, Antonio Caiado. Caiado, who spoke the local language, was used and trusted by all as an intermediary; because of him some details of da Silveira's last few months are known.

The Mutapa and the priests were probably mutually disappointed when they first met. Da Silveira expected the emperor-image and lifestyle of Portuguese propaganda. Instead he found an African culture he knew little about and a level of civilisation that he could only compare with that of his own, and find wanting. The Mutapa must have come to the same conclusions for he knew something of da Silveira's noble background, yet this man spurned every single traditional honour and gift due to such a person. Both men resolved to make the best of it, however, and concealed their disappointment beneath an overt welcome.

With the help, again, of a colourful and large picture of Our Lady, da Silveira captured the Mutapa's imagination. The picture soon changed hands as a gift and the gift led, within four weeks, to the baptism of both the Mutapa and his mother. A gift of 100 cows was made to the priest who ordered them killed and the meat dried and shared, earning the mission widespread popularity. As a result, nearly 300 of the Mutapa's most important subjects were begging for baptism. It all seemed so simple and so successful, da Silveira must have been elated beyond words.

There were, of course, people who opposed the conversion of the Mutapa and history has it that they engineered the priest's martyrdom. Islamic traders saw da Silveira's arrival as a thinly disguised bid for Portuguese hegemony and realised the need to act at once. The Mutapa was gullible and susceptible to their suggestions; it was easy to play on his fears.

His own position as Mutapa was vulnerable to the ambitions of a pretender, whom the Muslims claimed da Silveira had met on his journey to Mwene Mutapa. It was not difficult to suggest that the priest was a Portuguese spy, sent to reconnoitre the kingdom for future conquest. Nor were the Moors above appealing to witchcraft and magic, saying that da Silveira was a sorcerer who would bring drought, famine and war. Almost as quickly as the priest had achieved his conversion of the Mutapa did the Muslims achieve theirs, and by March 1561 da Silveira had sensed the changing atmosphere.

Antonio Caiado, who remained da Silveira's constant attendant, could not believe the priest's pronouncement that the Mutapa was about to kill him, for the Mutapa still seemed da Silveira's firm friend. Caiado confronted the Mutapa and, according to his later account, was told to remove any belongings he might have had in the priest's hut for da Silveira was about to be killed.

Caiado warned da Silveira of his danger and returned to the Mutapa to plead for the priest's life, the king allegedly relenting sufficiently to allow the priest to leave, but in the meantime, instructions were given for his death before dawn on Sunday 16 March.

There seems little doubt that if da Silveira had chosen to make a furtive escape he could have done so, but this was one of those fateful, star-crossed points in human existence to which a lifetime appears to have irrevocably led. For, surely, nothing on earth would have turned Goncalo da Silveira from where he clearly believed his destiny lay. All his training, his beliefs, his experiences, his obsessive religious convictions and his austere lifestyle focused on the immediate prospect of martyrdom — a prospect he willingly accepted.

He called about him the neighbouring Portuguese for a final mass, entrusting his possessions to them afterwards, keeping only a cassock, a surplice and a crucifix. Later, missionary zealot to the last, he baptised another 50 Christians and then took his leave of Antonio Caiado to whom his last recorded words were entrusted: 'It is certain that I am more ready to die than the Mohammedans are to kill me. I forgive the king who is young, and his mother because the Moors have deceived them.'[15]

That night, in the manner traditionally employed to despatch sorcerers, he was murdered. Dragged from his hut, he was thrown on his face and lifted by his hands and feet; a rope was passed round his neck. This was pulled from both sides until he was strangled. His body was dragged by the rope and thrown into the nearby river. Self-mortification persisted to the end: when his body was stripped, da Silveira was found to be wearing a shirt studded with iron points.

The Mutapa was thrown into confusion by the murderous deed he had ordered. He threatened first to execute the last 50 Christian converts and then rescinded the order in favour of another which demanded the deaths of the four leading Muslim activists. Two escaped that fate.

The mission to Mwene Mutapa was a notable failure and not for centuries would men of God tread the far interior as missionaries seeking converts to their faith. When they did arrive, they came not from the east but the south. One can speculate on the immediate religious consequences of da Silveira's martyrdom. His death loomed large in the eyes of the Portuguese then, as it does now on history's pages, but I wonder if that is not the result of social and religious conditioning and, as we shall see, political expediency. Apart from suffering its military consequences, the inhabitants of the interior seemed quite untouched by the inexplicable behaviour of this strange man and his unsurprising death.

The usually opportunistic Portuguese were slow to capitalise on the event of da Silveira's death; perhaps the state simply lacked interest. When the initiative to react was taken it came not from the government, but from an individual. It was Francisco Barreto, formerly viceroy of India, intimate of da Silveira, later general of the galleys of Portugal and the king's councillor, who offered his suggestions to the new monarch.

Barreto's idea was to mount an expedition against Mwene Mutapa with the aim of taking possession of the rich gold mines still believed to lie within its domain, and to make him, Barreto, commander of the king's forces.

The new king was susceptible to such thinking. Sebastiano had arrived on the throne in 1568 at the age of 15, a mere boy. He had had the benefits of a Jesuit education and was said to be a saint and a soldier. However, he was also described as a fanatic and a fatalist.[16] Eager, perhaps, for success and to prove his worth, he saw a chance for success where his grandparents, the previous king and queen, had failed.

The king gave his blessing to the expedition, the primary objective of which was said to be the promulgation of the gospel. Incidentals were the conquest of Africa, that its wealth might aid in meeting the expenses of the kingdom, and the revenge of Father Goncalo da Silveira's death.[17] A less readily acknowledged purpose might have been the personal aggrandisement of Francisco Barreto himself.

In March 1569, eight years exactly after da Silveira's death, Barreto, who was to avenge him, was formally appointed leader of the expedition. A reflection of its true nature might be found in the special book in which he was required to keep a record of all gold that came into his hands. It was to be evenly divided into 18 parts, nine of which went to the king, three to Barreto and six to the members of the expedition.[18]

The call for so Christian an expedition with such a capitalistic base had the desired effect and nobility flocked to arms and fought for places on board; many stowed away. There are differing estimates of those who travelled but it seems the figure may have exceeded 1 000 individuals, for there were 600 people on the flagship in a fleet of only three. In addition, so great was the lure of the expedition that many found their own way to Mozambique and joined independently there.

Departing in April 1569, the small fleet contained the most splendid company that had ever left Lisbon. As many as 200 people were drawn from Portuguese nobility and gentry who were delightfully described as experiencing 'the noise of gold drowning thoughts of danger'.[19]

Problems, as usual, quickly manifested themselves. Saluting the various churches with cannon fire as the ships moved down the river Tagus, one of the cannon burst, sweeping the deck with shrapnel and sending a fragment through Baretto's hat. It was an omen no one was sure how to interpret.

At sea, a day or two later, a mast broke and the ship had to turn back. A storm then separated the two remaining vessels. One, the flagship, wintered in Brazil and the other under Vasco Fernandes Homem was the only ship to arrive at Mozambique Island in August of that year. Homem, a reliable senior commander, eventually took over the expedition from Barreto.

Barreto arrived at Mozambique Island ten months later in May the following year.[20] Homem, reliable as ever, had not been idle. Men had been found and trained, food purchased, pilots and vessels acquired. Despite the absence of the third ship and the sickness and death that had dogged Homem and his crew, the company was more than powerful enough for the task ahead. It was important, argued Homem and the Jesuit contingent (who seemed to have a surprisingly powerful part to play) to move now, when the winds were favourable. But Barreto, less enthusiastic than before, had other ideas.

Procrastinating for five months, Barreto eventually sent off an expedition to the north, to Kilwa, Zanzibar, Malindi, Lamu and Pate. This foray took a year and a half and cost the lives of 100 men. Barreto dallied with the idea of going to the aid of the Portuguese in India but events compelled him at last to seriously set about the engagement of Mwene Mutapa.

There was immediately a dispute over the route to be followed. Experienced hands suggested going via Sofala. It had the shortest coastal crossing, the advantage of quicker access to the cooler, healthier highlands, passage through a known gold-producing area ruled by a man who was at war with Mwene Mutapa and who might, therefore, be a Portuguese ally. The Jesuits, however, wanted to go via the Zambezi, in the martyr's footsteps. Their view prevailed but at horrific cost, as we shall see.

On 4 November 1571 the expedition left Mozambique Island and arrived with 1 000 men of war at Sena, on the banks of the Zambezi, on 17 December. An envoy was sent to the Mutapa requesting that he return a delegation to negotiate with the Portuguese. In the meantime, the expedition remained idle at Sena and its members died like flies.

They knew nothing of tsetse flies or malaria and could not understand the incredible death rate: horses and men dropped daily. This was the height of the African summer and infection would have been at its very worst. Some explanation had to be found, however. After torture, this was obligingly provided by one of the local Muslims. As a result, a raid was carried out on their nearby village where many were killed and 17 'ringleaders' arrested and taken back to the Portuguese camp.

Here they were killed, at the rate of two a day and with an exhibition of macabre creativity, imagination and horrifying cruelty. For causing the death by magic of men and horses, some were impaled on sharp sticks, some torn apart by bent trees, others were used for target practice, chopped up with axes or fired from cannon. One claimed he was a Christian and was hanged, out of mercy. The king's coffers swelled by 15 000 meticals (units of currency) — his share of the loot.[21]

Possibly because they ran out of Moors to kill or perhaps because they had not heard from the Mutapa, or because they were dying too quickly, Barreto finally led his expedition out of Sena, in search of Mwene Mutapa and conquest. They departed on 19 July 1572, having spent eight months there.

The expedition included 650 arquebusiers and musketeers and more than 2 000 slaves with the baggage; 30 ox-wagons, ten horses, eight donkeys and five camels were part of the transport which was supported by a fleet of small boats that kept pace alongside, carrying food, powder and ammunition. The army crawled at 8 km a day along the pestilential and disease-ridden banks of the river which continued to take its toll in dead and sick.

After a month they came to the point where it was necessary to leave the river and turn inland. So many were sick and dying that groups were constantly left behind. At the Zambezi, for example, 130 members of the party remained by the river, together with a group to guard them. Shortly after this the expedition encountered the first opposition in a campaign that had now lasted three and a half years without a shot being fired.

Not more than 80 km from the Zambezi the way was barred by Batonga or some other subordinate tribe of Mwene Mutapa. They attacked the Portuguese who were able to drive them off but not before losing two dead and 25 wounded. Barreto's force occupied a village and rested for three days; more of the men fell ill and died. At the end of that time, the Batonga attacked again. They were said to number 16 000, of whom 4 000 fell before the combined fire of Portuguese musket and cannon. They sued for peace.

Barreto could not continue, however. His sick and wounded numbered 120 and every day two or three more died. The country was dry and barren and food and provisions were short. It was argued that if 16 000 had been able to wound 40 men then the 100 000 that the Mutapa was said to be able to put into the field would surely overcome them. The expedition retreated.

Barreto went on ahead to Sena and there found representatives from Mwene Mutapa waiting for him, with whom he entered into negotiations. As we saw in the last chapter the Portuguese wanted the Moors out of Mwene Mutapa, to help protect it from the threat of Islam and also to transfer to the Portuguese crown a number of gold mines. A large Portuguese delegation went back with the king's men to ensure that these demands were understood and met.

After the return of the remnants of his army under the command of Homem, at the end of October 1572, Barreto himself went to Mozambique. He left Homem in command of the base and some 400 men. It was May 1573 before he returned to find that 150 of those who had been left behind were dead — including most of the officers. Homem himself was seriously ill. Two weeks later Barreto died. Letters from the Portuguese king ordered Homem to take his place.

Homem took over at a most inauspicious time. He was without men, resources or money. Morale and enthusiasm could hardly have been at a lower ebb. The delegation from Mwene Mutapa had returned, bringing the Mutapa's agreement to the Portuguese terms, but now they could not take advantage of it without men or resources. The leader of the delegation had died, so too had its doctor. Of the 180 who returned to Sena, all were sick. A further retreat was the only sensible solution and so the tattered remains of Barreto's glorious expedition returned to the island of Mozambique, which they reached in December 1573, nearly five years after they had started out and twelve and a half years after the death they had still not avenged.

With great difficulty Homem built up another force, mainly by 'volunteering' men from passing ships. His army rose to 412 before 52 of them discovered what was in store and fled. By November 1574, Homem was at Sofala from where he followed the Buzi River westwards towards Zimbabwe and the land of Mwene Mutapa. Rain held him up, as did a running battle with a local chief, Quiteve.

Homem also had difficulties with his men trying continually to desert — especially when they were still alongside the Buzi and had canoes with them. To prevent this, Homem joined a long list of commanders who, literally, burnt their boats.

Eventually, Quiteve was subjected by force and Homem was able, at last, to ascend onto the Zimbabwe plateau. He was still a long way from Mwene Mutapa but he had reached, probably, the gold fields of Manica in eastern Zimbabwe. Here he stayed for nine days, examining more than 600 holes dug by the locals. From them the Portuguese obtained gold dust and nuggets. Homem had a Castilian mining expert with him who declared the mines richer than those of New Spain, although mills would be required to work them successfully.

It was a worthwhile discovery and did much to confirm Portuguese beliefs about the gold of the interior. In the meantime, however, Homem, high on the plateau with relatively few men, learned that the Mutapa was no longer in a mood to negotiate: he was on his way with a considerable army. It was time to leave and Homem returned to the coast.

The achievements of the Barreto expedition amounted to little. No direct contact was ever made with Mwene Mutapa and no shot was fired at its army. Africa remained far from being conquered, da Silveira's death went unavenged and I suspect that the Portuguese king's coffers did not do too well out of the expedition either. Thousands of lives, Portuguese and native, seem to have been horribly wasted.

Not that everything was entirely lost. Barreto's efforts had, for reasons that are hard to explain, sufficiently cowed the Mutapa into agreeing to peace on terms most favourable to the Portuguese. Although Barreto did not live to see the agreement signed in 1575, and although it did not survive for long, it was the beginning of ultimate Portuguese domination over Mwene Mutapa.

Homem at least reached the gold fields and confirmed their existence. He also brought a powerful chief, Quiteve, under Portuguese jurisdiction and confirmed the existence of a fabulous silver mine, which I have not yet mentioned and which is the subject of Chapter 16.

If there was ever any continuity of purpose and policy in developments in Mozambique and if the real intentions had been God, Gain and Glory, then at the end of the first century of occupation there was not much to count up on the credit side. Little wealth, few real converts to Christianity and certainly no glory were all there was.

15 Cannibals and Concubines

D ESPITE the comic book and penny thriller image, Africa has never been full of flesh-eating people, as we have been led to believe. Indeed, as a natural occurrence, cannibalism was very rare. This explains why reports of widespread cannibalism in 16th century Mozambique quickly caught my eye.

While I have some quite interesting detail of the phenomenon, I can find no really satisfactory explanation for the existence of cannibalism on the scale reported. The only explanation I can find dismisses too lightly an occurrence that is reported from the Zambezi to Mombasa and must, surely, have some truth in it. There is a need for more research on this question.

Among the Portuguese records of the late 16th century is a series of reports concerning a tribe of Africans whom the Portuguese called the Zimba and who were said to sustain themselves solely on human flesh. There is no information at all as to who these people were and a great deal of uncertainty as to where they came from. There are many contradictions in the story, but I suspect more than a little fire, for all the smoke there is about.

Zimba raiders are known from the Tete district from about 1570 and it is said that their first attacks upon the Portuguese date from this time. One authority has them arriving from the Great Lakes,[1] one of few brave enough to guess from where they might have come. Their major offensive against the Portuguese was in 1585. After that date, they appeared to move north, eating their way up the coast of Africa like so many locusts.

One account has 15 000 Zimba laying siege to Kilwa in the late 1580s. The siege was unsuccessful until betrayal gained them access to the city, which they sacked. More than 3 000 people were massacred, others were taken prisoner and gradually consumed as the hoard continued their northward migration, which eventually brought them to the gates of Mombasa.[2]

A Portuguese fleet arrived at the island of Mombasa in March 1589 from Goa, seeking a Turkish pirate by the name of Mirale Beque whose activities were threatening their hold over the east African coast. They found Mombasa in the hands of the very Turk and also discovered that it had been under siege for some time already from the same Zimba who had recently devastated Kilwa.

The Portuguese were able to destroy the Turkish ships anchored in the island's lee and their success brought them an immediate message of conciliation from the ruler of Mombasa. In response, the Portuguese demanded that all the Turks be handed over to them, and when this failed to happen, they sacked and looted the town.

Watching from the shore and seeing their work done for them, the Zimbas made a pact of non-interference with the Portuguese and, under its protection, entered Mombasa. Jesuit reports of the time say that the king and all the more important citizens were killed and eaten while others were imprisoned to suffer the same fate later.

A few months later, in mid-1589, the Zimba appeared at Malindi. The Portuguese captain of the town was in dire straits for he had only 30 men with whom to defend it and would have been overcome had not a local chief with 3 000 warriors attacked and driven off the Zimba.

According to this account, the Zimba defeat was a signal for all who had survived contact with them to turn against them and only their leader and 100 men are said to have returned to the Zambezi from whence they had come.[3]

The next instalment in this remarkable story takes place three years later near Sena on the Lower Zambezi. Here, in 1592, a chief from the north bank sought Portuguese assistance to re-instate him after he had been displaced by the Zimba.[4]

The captain of Sena, Andre de Santiago, was happy to oblige, taking two cannon from the fort with him. He found the enemy entrenched behind a double stockade and decided he needed reinforcements, which he sent for from Tete. A man called Chaves rounded up over 100 Portuguese and mulattoes and marched to Santiago's aid.

Hearing that they were coming, the Zimbas left their stockade at night to ambush the advancing force. At its head, the Portuguese were being carried in machilas (a shaded and comfortable seat, carried by four porters) and were quite unprotected. They were butchered and carried away for consumption while their porters fled.

Santiago's hoped-for help having been despatched so abruptly left him in something of a desperate situation and the next day, while the Zimbas inside their stockade celebrated their victory with feasting, he decided on the action he must take. As soon as darkness fell, he abandoned his siege and made his way back to the river and Sena beyond. Unfortunately, the Zimba caught up with the retreating Portuguese at the river bank and in the engagement that followed, slew them all. In the two engagements, a total of 130 Portuguese and mulattoes from Sena and Tete, including the two captains, were killed. It was a devastating blow for Portuguese prestige along the river.[5]

ABOVE LEFT
Chimvwinye, a young Batonga woman, grinds maize as people before her have done for thousands of years.

ABOVE RIGHT
Lake Kariba.

LEFT
Flowers at Kariba.

ABOVE
Crocodile farming is a flourishing business along the Zambezi's shores.

RIGHT
Nothing of the crop is wasted — even the heads are used.

VAMOS APRENDER PARA DOMINAR A CIENCIA E A TECNICA PARA MELHOR SERVIR O POVO
MOCAMBICANO

PRECEDING PAGE
Boromo mission, some 30 km upstream
from Tete, much as it was when built
at the end of the 19th century.

ABOVE
The neglected residence at Boromo
mission.

RIGHT
The church has been much
disrespected in recent times but there
is now hope for change.

For this reason the Captain of Mozambique, Pedro de Sousa, the man ostensibly in charge of the whole territory, felt compelled to react and so he gathered together an army of revenge. In 1593 he led a force out of Sena that consisted of 200 Portuguese and mulattoes of whom 80 were soldiers and, in addition, some 1 500 native conscripts. His objective was to attack and defeat the Zimba chief, Tondo.

He found the Zimba more firmly ensconced than ever. Their stockade was now surrounded by a ditch and was reinforced by a rampart of earth, which rendered his cannon less useful. By filling in the ditch, de Sousa was able to gain access to the wooden palisade but his men were kept away with boiling water poured from above; iron hooks were poked through convenient holes by the defenders which cruelly wounded his men or drew them to the wall where they were hacked to death.

De Sousa's attack failed. He tried to build wooden towers with which to dominate the stockade, but this was not successful for other problems arose. Rumour had it that another African chief was threatening Sena, so its residents who were with de Sousa insisted on returning home. He had no choice but to relent. He raised his siege and retreated. Once again, the Zimba saw their opportunity and attacked the rearguard, seizing the baggage and artillery while killing a number of de Sousa's force.[6]

Again the Portuguese were defeated, and although the Zimba later concluded peace, nothing could hide the fact that the crown had suffered major defeats in both 1592 and 1593. The only account I can find that attempts to explain Zimba cannibalism, that of Dr M.D.D. Newitt, relies heavily on this point.[7]

Newitt refers to a native people known as the Marave who are first reported in 1506 and who came from the west, eventually establishing themselves between the Luangwa and Shire rivers in the last quarter of the 16th century under a chief by the name of Rundo. A part of this group appears to have moved west across the Shire and come into conflict with the coastal Makua tribe in the hinterland of Angoche. It is this group, Newitt suggests, that went north to attack Kilwa, Mombasa and Malindi, beginning in 1587.

Newitt explains the two Portuguese offensives of 1592 and 1593 as moves made with the intention of checking the rising power of Chief Rundo, whose domain was immediately north of Portuguese settlements. The defeat that the government forces suffered, combined with the fear of the Marave that persisted for many years, may have given rise, he says, to the gruesome tales of cannibalism that were widespread at the time and later. It was the Portuguese who used the name Ma-zimba and it is interesting that that name is still used by a section of the Marave living north of Tete today.[8]

I thoroughly enjoy reading Newitt's work and think him a fine scholar but I suspect his explanation is only part of the truth. He suggests that the Zimba who remained in Mozambique were not cannibals but were only painted so by the brush of Portuguese propaganda. If the Marave were not of a cannibalistic disposition then why was a fragment of the same tribe so labelled in different parts of Africa as it worked its way up the coast? Why did the group travel north in the first place, and why is it, I wonder, that there are no reports of cannibalism either before or after this particular 25-year period at the end of the 16th century?

Cannibals were only part of the problem faced by the early Portuguese along the Lower Zambezi. As we already know, Portugal did not occupy Mozambique in the sense of it being a colony: the concept of colony did not exist then. Occupation was primarily motivated by commercial and trading potential for government benefit on the one hand, and strategic considerations — guarding the route to India — on the other. When circumstances demanded more high-sounding motives for foreign enterprises, extending and protecting Christianity seemed to be a catch-all phrase frequently employed.

In its commercial objective, the government was potentially in competition with the private sector and like similar governments in years to come, attempted to deal with this question by establishing a monopoly, thereby excluding competition. The most obvious step was not to encourage the development of a private sector, but this was almost impossible.

Hundreds of non-African people slipped without fanfare into the vastness of the interior: renegades, criminals, survivors of shipwrecks, people from all walks of life and fugitives from the forts and garrisons. Many found life within the confines of the royal monopoly too restrictive and chose instead the risks of going it alone. These were the people who, having chosen Africa, identified with it and became one with it. They married local women and raised families; they explored the country, learnt the languages, hunted and, by undercutting the royal *factors*, many made fortunes in trade. Even in the early days, it was said that such people numbered in the hundreds; in 1531 they outnumbered the official garrisons on the coast. From these people the new élite was drawn.[9]

Two non-African populations therefore existed side by side: one strictly Portuguese and 'official', the other strongly Portuguese but not enitrely so and certainly not official. The second group came to be called *sertanejos* (backwoodsmen) and some remarkable individuals emerged from among their number in the following centuries.

A curious characteristic of the *sertanejos* is their sudden appearance and disappearance in the pages of history. This is largely because only the officials recorded history, which was a record of what the government did or what it wanted people to know. Contributions from *sertanejos*, the 'shadow' European population, are mentioned only when convenient.

Thus one should not be surprised to find a Portuguese living at the court of Mwene Mutapa when the first missionary arrived. Other *sertanejos* of the earlier years whose names appear in Portuguese records include Goncalo da Arujo, said to have been the first to discover the famous silver mines (Chapter 16) and Sisnando Dias Bayao, who led the Portuguese forces in the attack on Khami (Chapter 13). The *sertanejos* were often men of considerable ability, stature and power in the land. They worked against the interests of the government as frequently as they did in its favour.

From their small beginnings in the 16th century and into the 17th, the *sertanejos* laid the groundplan of future non-African occupation of the Zambezi River. It was they who explored, they who sought and found the trade routes and contacts within the interior. I have no doubt that among these accomplished people there were brave men of talent who explored much more widely than we might suppose or know of today.

Much of the early exploration that took place along the Zambezi and Shire rivers was inspired by the thought of commercial gain, rather than discovery for discovery's sake. As such, information obtained having commercial value was guarded and kept secret rather than being published and made widely available.[10] This may well explain why apparently little of Mozambique had been explored before the wave of 19th century explorers laid bare the heart of the continent.

When the first of the Portuguese arrived at Sofala in 1505, the expedition's organisers had arranged for four women to be aboard. Given that there were also several hundred men on the expedition, it was obviously planned that these ladies should be pretty busy! Logistics aside, such a thoughtful gesture only served to highlight a perpetual problem of life in future Mozambique.[11]

Emigration of women to that country from Portugal was not popular until the 20th century, so the many potential benefits of Portuguese women's contribution were not felt. Advantageously, perhaps, a population of mixed blood was established from the very beginning.

Attempts at settlement were made but they were never very successful. One was planned for 1637 but abandoned in favour of needs in Brazil and India. Another, in 1680, saw the arrival of 78 men, women and children along the lower Zambezi River. Although their number doubled the existing Portuguese population their effect was quickly lost as they succumbed to malaria and other diseases.[12]

Reliable figures for the population of 'The Rivers', as the Zambezi and its delta were known, are few and where they exist, the categories are often confused. For example, it is said that in 1735 there were 437 Portuguese and Indians, including the half-breed families of both, while in 1835 there were 82 Portuguese and Indians and 280 miscellaneous 'foreigners'.[13]

The population was made up of a number of different groups. In addition to the indigenous Africans, there was a strong east African trading community, as well as people of Portuguese, Indian and Chinese descent.[14] Of these groups, which unquestionably formed the country's élite for nearly 300 years, those of Indian origin were universally unpopular.

The Indians were of two classes. The 'Banyan', who came from British India, were bankers and merchants and remained socially distant from the river folk. They married within their own circle, retained strong ties with India and sent their money back there, for which the Portuguese were quick to blame them for the economic stagnation of The Rivers. Perhaps resentful of their success and suspicious of their exclusiveness, people disliked them intensely and they had many enemies.

The second group of Indians were the Catholic Goans, known also as the Canarins. They dominated the administrative and military positions in the country and, despite being forbidden to do so, married local heiresses and soon formed a class of extremely wealthy and powerful landowners.

Between them, these two groups came to dominate many aspects of life in The Rivers. As elsewhere in Africa, they were resented and stood accused of setting high prices, establishing monopolistic controls and, through nepotism and favouritism, gaining complete control of commercial life.[15]

Ownership of the land played a crucially important role in the way the lower river was developed and in the events that befell it. In African societies, land is not generally owned by anyone — even the chief is only its custodian and thus responsible for its current deployment. Despite this, however, a few concessions were granted by chiefs in the 17th century to particular *sertanejos*, thereby setting a precedent.[16]

As increasing Portuguese pressure and interference brought Mwene Mutapa into a state of greater disorder, so, almost in direct ratio, did African chiefs seeking an alternative form of stability and order turn to *sertanejos* for protection. The price was tracts of land. Most of the great estates of following centuries can be traced to original grants by chiefs. What is less easy to determine is the manner in which these concessions had been made — they were not always granted willingly and peacefully.[17]

People of Portuguese extraction were slowly acquiring some form of right to the land and, from early in the 16th century, were settling on it. This process of settlement was not planned, organised or intended by the government in Mozambique but was a response to the needs of the *sertanejos*. Out of it, however, there developed a unique blend of Portuguese and African tradition that created the historically long-lived and fascinating institution called the *prazo*. In essence, a prazo was a large estate, but in time it came to mean much more than that.

While the land and the original right to occupy it formed the African contribution to the prazo, Portuguese tradition embellished the system and superimposed its own identity. Thus, from the early 17th century, the crown started to issue title to estates already occupied by *sertanejos* and, predictably, extracted a price for doing so. Bereft of resources and manpower yet needing to administer and control, the crown saw the opportunity of giving legal blessing to the *status quo*, thereby getting in return acceptance of certain administrative responsibilities.

To prazo owners were delegated judicial, administrative and fiscal duties by means of which the government hoped to achieve a rough and ready sort of administration as well as easing, if not ensuring, the flow of gold to the coast. A further objective of the crown in granting title was to maintain the fiction that it actually had the right to do so in the first place. Prazo owners, for their part, sought government sanction and recognition as defence against counterclaims to their own occupation. It was extraordinary that these simple and mutual benefits to owners and government alike were sufficient to maintain the system in haphazard operation for the next 300 years.[18]

In time, the prazos spread along the coast and up either side of the Zambezi to well beyond Tete. However, a number of those on the south side of the river upstream of Tete were not always occupied, because of the troubles associated with the collapse of Mwene Mutapa.

An intriguing aspect of the prazo system was the inclusion by the Portuguese of an unusual method of inheritance. The estate passed not from father to son, but from mother to daughter. In addition, it could only remain with a family for three generations.

This system originated in Goa where it had been devised as a method of rewarding women for their services to their husbands. Rather cleverly, the effect was to provide a dowry for the daughter; as such the system was seen as a means to attract husbands from the home country. It was hoped, therefore, that not only would the prazo system serve to enlarge. the European population in Mozambique, but it would also prevent the prazos from coalescing under the control of a few dominant families. In fact, it did neither.

Instead, very few men came to Mozambique from Portugal and the 'donas' tended to marry into strong, established families whose strength guaranteed protection of their dowry, even if it meant a husband who was not Portuguese.[19] In this way, some families became extremely powerful. In the 18th century the descendants of Sisnando Dias Bayao, for example, were among the most powerful and influential of the prazo landowners, occupying most of the huge triangle of land between Sena, Sofala and the mouth of the Zambezi. Other families became as powerful: the Nobre family controlled seven prazos, and the family cluster consisting of the Moura e Meneses-Moreira and Pereiras controlled between them as many as 15 prazos.[20]

Although the prazos were expected to maintain roads and forts, to provide men for defence and to fulfil all the duties of an administration, little of this was actually done. They tended to become 'mini-states' with increasing and despotic power accruing to the landlord. Like any state system that enjoys untrammelled authority, it eventually became corrupt. When the prazos were viewed by Lionel Decle in the 19th century, he described them as a striking piece of medievalism. He believed that the owners saw them simply as an opportunity for legalised slavery and for grinding money out of the native population.[21]

Originally, of course, they were not quite as bad as this and they served a useful purpose for a long period of time. They were in effect a substitute for African chieftainship and in many ways the prazo owner took over exactly this role. The inhabitants came to his aid in times of war, accepted his judgements in cases of dispute and paid the prazo owner tribute, just as they would an African chief. In some cases the owner even took over the ritual functions of a chief in regard to crops.[22]

Prazos maintained an economic existence through a system of tribute and trade. Few of them were farmed either commercially or on a big scale. Collection of tribute was the chief privilege of the prazo owner, and he expected it from all those who were not his servants or slaves and who made use of his land. Thus, on the bigger estates, there poured in a stream of ivory, honey, wax, salt, wood, grain, native cotton cloth, gold dust, oil, chickens and the like. These formed the basic items of trade and exchange to which were added gold and ivory from the hinterland and, as we shall see, slaves.

Closely identified with Africa and distant from metropolitan Portugal, being also a tiny minority with few infusions of fresh blood, the early Portuguese communities along the Zambezi River in Mozambique were destined to be absorbed by local cultures, as indeed they were. Many prazo owners simply 'went native', dressing in the African style, acquiring African names and becoming African in every way. Others successfully maintained more distance and attempted to build an identity of their own which was neither African nor Portuguese. The extent of this process of natural incorporation is indicated by the fact that, in the mid-19th century, only a few of the Zambezi settlers understood more than a smattering of Portuguese.[23]

As intimated earlier, the process of integration was greatly facilitated by the absence of Portuguese women which caused men of Portuguese descent to turn more and more to the local women. Prostitution in various guises was rife and concubinage was raised almost to the level of an institution.

By the mid-19th century it was the custom for European males to have as many as three or four native concubines, about whom was built up a most extraordinary morality. These women lived and were treated like servants, yet their half-caste children were fully acknowledged by the father. Even the church of the time appeared to condone the system, for the children were baptised.

The women played the most servile role imaginable, being apparently regarded as little more than machines for making mulattoes. Yet despite the absence of affection for them, the fathers were deeply attached to their children. There was no doubt that they would bear their father's name and be accepted by the church. Indeed, in the strange and topsy-turvy world invented to suit the special conditions of the time, to do otherwise would have been to bring shame and universal disapprobation on the scoundrel of a father.[24]

The dominant theme of life on the prazos was exploitation of natural resources: little was grown, nothing was manufactured. Inevitably, over-used resources would become more scarce and extraction more difficult. Such was the case with both ivory and gold along the Lower Zambezi. For this reason it is not surprising that the advantages of slavery were quickly seen, nor that it enjoyed such singular success.

Slaves had been a part of man's existence in Africa from time imme-morial, although, to be precise, that depends very much on how one defines slavery. Capturing people and selling them into bondage had pro-bably been taking place at a low level in Mozambique since ancient times, but it was not until the 1770s that organised slavery really got into its stride. It did so because of French activities in the Indian Ocean.

In the early 18th century, the French East India Company began its occupation of Mauritius, Reunion and Rodriquez, known collectively as the Mascarene Islands. Intensive plantations were established and the demand for slaves to work them rose rapidly. As early as 1721, slaves may have been leaving Mozambique at a rate of some 1 000 a year. One wit-ness, in 1752, noted that 1 100 slaves were exported, of whom 300 came from the Zambezi region.[25]

By the early 1800s the slave market reached its first peak when some 15 000 were carried away each year between 1820 and 1830.[26] Of these, most were going to Brazil but as many as 7 000 a year continued to be sent to the Mascarenes. Quelimane, at the mouth of the Zambezi, had probably become the most important single slave port in Africa at the time.[27]

As a result of British pressure, Lisbon had banned slave commerce north of the equator in 1815. By 1836 it had banned the trade itself and had signed an agreement that allowed the Royal Navy, in search of slaves, to board ships carrying the Portuguese flag. The profits in the black ivory trade were so high, however, that officialdom was soon completely corrupted and groups of slavers, African, Portuguese and Muslim alike, bought off government officials, thus allowing the trade to flourish. It was still significant in 1880.[28]

The prazo owners were, of course, among the vanguard of this new pro-fession. So energetic were they in their participation that many sold people from their own estates — which contributed towards the later downfall of some for, in effect, they were selling their military might.

An important element that helped sustain and prolong the peak of slavery was the Ngoni migrations that swept violently across Africa as a result of the Mfecane, described in Chapter 2. The raiding by one Ngoni group under chief Nqaba was reported by the coastal Portuguese in about 1830; Nqaba moved northwards creating mayhem and committing murder on his way across the Zambezi by about 1840. An immediate consequence was that the ancient fair at Manica in eastern Zimbabwe was closed by the Portuguese, since they could no longer defend such an isolated position.[29]

Barely four years later another group known as the Gaza Ngoni, under chief Manicusse, began raiding for tribute northwards to the Zambezi and into the towns of Sena and Shupanga, plus the delta. With no government protection the weaker prazo owners fled, leaving the remainder even more vulnerable.

The rate of absenteeism in the river prazos soared and three predatory groups immediately benefited. The Ngoni found more captives to swell their number and were able to purchase slaves from river dealers. The slavers themselves found plenty of pickings and the strong prazo owners grew immensely more powerful by absorbing the abandoned estates. This was to lead to an unparalleled concentration of their power, with significant results.

In the troubled times ahead the powerful prazos would be converted into armed fortresses, initially for their own protection. Some came, eventually, to defy the crown itself and had to be physically subjected by a government whose credibility survived into the 20th century by only the narrowest of margins.

The chaos and disorder caused by Ngoni raids was exacerbated by a prolonged drought and famine. To escape these two evils, many unfortunates crossed the river and fled east to the delta. Here, protected from Ngoni invasion by the Zambezi, they sought safety with more secure prazo owners and, by their presence, provided the means for the delta's development which dates from the early 1800s.

Because of Ngoni willingness to trade in slaves, there developed an aspect of slavery with important implications. For the first time, there was an internal African slave market that avoided the cruisers and diplomatic sanctions Britain had so laboriously deployed in an effort to bring the trade to a halt. Once established, the market flourished.[30]

Matabele Ngoni maintained good relations with the Portuguese who sold them slaves, especially female slaves taken from north of the Zambezi. The Kololo from Barotseland (Chapter 2) were also buyers, coming down the river as far as Zumbo and the Luangwa junction to trade.[31] Yao traders from Malawi made purchases and walked their unfortunate prizes to unpatrolled ports on the Swahili coast north of the Mozambique border, again avoiding British surveillance.[32] It was evidence of this hitherto unknown internal trade that David Livingstone came across and exposed for the first time to the world.

For just over 300 years, Mozambique continued in its own way, quietly and slowly, without the inquisitive interference of the outside world. Such a condition could not last, of course, and visitors from Europe, other than Portuguese, began to appear.

It is possible that anti-slavery interests may have been lying somewhere darkly behind the visit of HMS *Leven* to east Africa, but ostensibly she had been commissioned to make a survey of the coast. Taking advantage of the opportunity, the Horticultural Society of London engaged John Forbes to travel with her, so he became the first British botanical collector in Mozambique.[33]

HMS *Leven* enjoyed some remarkable adventures during the course of that survey, the least expected of which must have been the circumstances that required her captain, Commodore Owen, to occupy the fort and town of Mombasa for nearly 18 months. This was done to lend credibility to a ruse adopted by the natives there who had illegally raised an English flag to successfully delude an attacking Arab fleet.[34]

In 1823, before arriving in Mombasa, Owen had left at Quelimane a small party of five whose job it was to explore part of the Zambezi. Forbes was among them, of course, together with Lt Browne, Mr Kilpatrick and two servants. Tragically, all three Europeans died of malaria; the two faithful servants, less vulnerable to the disease, carried the journals and specimens back to HMS *Leven*.

An interesting aside to the expedition's reports is the extremely generous reception its members received from the river élite, in particular from a Dona Pascoa who lived in a large riverside house at Shupanga. A description of the house and its gardens, especially a grove of six very large fig trees, suggests that it might well be the same one in which Mrs Livingstone was to be laid to rest 39 years later. Dona Pascoa was described as a Creole lady who, although far above the others of her kind in the region, was still reckoned ignorant by her visitors.

The lifestyle of people such as Dona Pascoa is indicated by an account of a meal the trio enjoyed at her house. It 'was in every respect sumptuous, the table being covered with massive silver utensils, and wines and eatables of many descriptions cooked in a variety of ways.'[35]

Carlo Antonio Fornasini, an Italian, collected botanical specimens in and around Inhambane during 1839. The next recorded outside visitor on the Zambezi, however, was the celebrated Dr Wilhelm Carl Hartwig Peters who collected specimens of flora and fauna between 1843 and 1847.[36]

Without doubt, the visitor who made the most impact was David Livingstone. He and his Kololo porters arrived in Tete from Victoria Falls in 1856. Livingstone was far from being the first to cross the continent, but his presence and his achievements were to bring the focus of world attention onto the Lower Zambezi River in a way that was to leave it forever changed.

His porters remained in Tete awaiting Livingstone's return from England and the fulfilment of his promise to take them back to their own country beyond the falls. This happened, but not for four years. It is a small facet of the great Livingstone saga that has always intrigued me for somehow it does not ring quite true. In every account I have read, Livingstone is always credited with the most moral and humanitarian conduct towards his Kololo porters, for whom, it is said, he had the highest regard.

Fair enough, but I do have some questions: Having walked down the river, did they have to have Livingstone with them to walk back? Was it worth waiting four years before returning home? The fate of the Kololo while waiting for Livingstone also intrigues me.

There were 114 men who arrived in Tete with Livingstone in March 1856. In the following four years, 30 died of smallpox and another six were murdered following a quarrel with a local chief; 78 men remained. Although they greeted Livingstone with apparent relief and acclaim on his return to Tete, when the time came to walk back there was a curious lack of enthusiasm.

With difficulty a 'large party' of returning Kololo was mustered, but after a few days at least a quarter had deserted and others continued to do so. Eventually, of the number that had originally left Linyanti, only 25 returned there in 1860.[37] The remainder, perhaps as many as 50, may have been the origins of a curious and little-known anecdote associated with this story.

Some of the Kololo, armed with confidence, a knowledge of their political system, firearms and an understanding of warfare, established themselves as chiefs over the Nyanja people. Two of them, Kasisi and Molokwa, divided the Shire Valley between them and settled at least some other Kololo as sub-chiefs to help them supervise their new domain.[38]

It has been the fashion to denigrate Livingstone but it is not my intention to do that here. I am curious, however. Why did he go back to Victoria Falls with his Kololo when he apparently need not have done so? Is it possible that, with his defeat at Cahora Bassa so fresh in his mind and the uncertainty whether his Shire and Lake Nyassa discoveries would be enough to swing the balance of public opinion in his favour, he sought to remind people of his earlier achievements? Or was he just trying to escape from his troubles, back to the time when he was on his own, when he did not have the dreadful complications of other people and his only companions were simple porters with whom he related so well?

The Zambezi expedition was to become a low point in Livingstone's life (see Chapter 16), perhaps because it was the only one of his great expeditions where he had to lead men of his own kind and culture, a skill he simply did not have. There were a number of reasons for its lack of success. Livingstone had never seen the Cahora Bassa rapids and when he came down the river, it was unnaturally swollen by record floods. This gave him a false idea of the river and its size.

A number of other factors contributed to the failure. The boat selected, the *MaRobert,* did not meet the needs of the expedition and her successor, the *Pioneer,* was hardly an improvement. Much time, according to James Stewart, one of the expedition members, was wasted in poor planning and organisation, but perhaps the most important factor was the dissension among members. This, above all, was the area where strong leadership was required but was found lacking.[39]

Conditions along the Zambezi, especially in the lower reaches with its heat and humidity, are trying at the best of times. Add to this an expedition comprised of individuals of widely different backgrounds, personalities, interests and dispositions: artists to sailors, missionaries to geologists, homosexuals to explorers. Stir in a generous helping of hidden guilt, frustration, unreliable and inefficient equipment, top it off with non-existent leadership and a recipe for disaster surely is at hand. My heart goes out to Livingstone in sympathy: the wrong man caught with the wrong job. It is a pity that he did not know himself well enough to have avoided the pitfall of such an excursion. He would have achieved much more on his own.

Multiple disasters dogged the expedition for, during its course, he lost his wife Mary, who died at Shupanga. The immediate cause was malaria but there was much more to it than that. Scandalous accusations of Mary's having an illicit affair with James Stewart had followed them from Cape Town to Durban and to the mouth of the Zambezi itself.[40]

Dr John Kirk, a level-headed and responsible witness, believed this affair to be quite unfounded and attributable to noble, but foolish and thoughtless, behaviour on Stewart's part. For Stewart, an excessively ardent admirer of Livingstone and one quite prepared to ingratiate himself with the explorer by means of a good service to the explorer's wife, had discovered that Mary was an alcoholic. His immediate mission became the task of 'protecting' her.[41]

There is evidence from both Stewart and from Dr Kirk of Mary's drinking. Especially in the later stages of the condition, she drank far more than her allowance permitted and had to borrow to meet her needs. Loans came from Stewart, Kirk and the gossiping Rae, the engineer and man responsible for bringing the party, and much of the scandal, from Cape Town.

Alcohol was the only opiate available to a woman in those days and Mary may have started drinking as early as 1853 when Livingstone set off for Linyanti and, ultimately, the great African crossing. It is perhaps significant that Livingstone sadly recorded the absence of letters from his

wife among the many waiting for him at Luanda, at Linyanti on his way
back and at Quelimane at the journey's end. Why did Mary not write for
nearly four years?[42]

She had more than enough reason to have an alcohol problem. Livingstone was as hard on others as he was on himself. They had lost one child
at Kolobeng and Mary had given birth to another in an ox-wagon, after
trekking through the Kalahari and surviving considerable danger and
privation. She had good grounds to be perpetually worried about his
safety and though, as a missionary, she would have been the first to agree
that God's will must be obeyed, she could hardly have failed to notice how
frequently the wills of David Livingstone and God were in perfect
accord.[43]

Looking back on her death, Kirk's diary records that he thought Stewart
unwise in making Mary aware that others on the expedition knew of her
condition. Unwittingly, perhaps, Stewart had stripped away Mary's dignity and left her nothing to replace it with, certainly not the love, the companionship and the closeness of another that she probably craved and was
once too proud and duty-bound, and now felt too guilty, to ask for. At the
age of only 41 she died, a lonely woman.

Livingstone, distraught, saw his wife buried beneath a great baobab
that grew in the gardens of the house at Shupanga. In the grave beside
hers lay the body of Kilpatrick, the last survivor of the three Europeans
from Owen's 1823 expedition. By one of those strange and ironic twists
of fate, Kilpatrick had also died from malaria and the excesses of alcohol.[44]

The baobab fell in about 1890 but Mrs Livingstone's grave has survived,
outlasting that of Kilpatrick. Over the years people have tended the grave,
which remains much as it was in 1862 except for the addition of a tall
headstone with an inscription in Portuguese.[45]

Much further upstream was another large baobab. It grows on the south
bank about 5 km from Chiramba on the road to Tambara, itself at the foot
of Lupata Gorge. Like many of its kind, the great tree is hollow with a tent-
like opening at ground level.

In his diary, on 16 September 1858, Livingstone recorded his interest
in this tree, noting the convenient doorway, the bats roosting inside, the
diameter of the tree, the dimensions of the inner space and the fact that
baobabs bear bark on the inside as well as the outside surface. What he
did not record was that, inside the tree, he carefully carved a beautiful monogram of the initials D.L.

Discovered in 1958, 100 years after it was carved, the monogram is not
easily recognised. Although the carving is clear, the design is complex and
it needed a person with a special knowledge of Livingstone's signature to
see it for what it is. Such a man was Quentin Keynes who first brought
it to the world's attention.[46] Had Livingstone carved it on the outside of
the tree, it would long since have been grown over but, by being placed

inside, it has been preserved in almost pristine condition for 130 years. The tree was declared a national monument by the government of Mozambique in 1960. But of its present fate I can tell you nothing except to note that it was still intact in 1968.[47]

The lower reaches of the Zambezi are very little known. At the moment, because of civil unrest, it is out of the question to travel there. However, in the pages of literature there is much that tells of this area's fascination. After all, despite the bias involved, we do have some kind of written records that span 450 years. That alone, in Africa, is remarkable. There is much more to tell: of wars and forts, of strange mountains that stand alone in enormous plains, of remote trading posts, of goldsmiths and coal. All are part of the endless attraction of this hot and steamy coastal plain over which the Zambezi runs to the sea.

It is difficult to leave this part of the river without mentioning just one further place of interest. Some 25 km upstream of the provincial town of Tete is the village and one-time missionary base of Boromo.

Known for centuries as a place where alluvial gold could be found and a place therefore where the goldsmiths plied their trade, Boromo faded from prominence when the gold was finally exhausted. It came to life again when Portuguese missionaries decided to build a mission there.

Founded in 1890, the mission was originally sited at the river's edge where orchards and vegetable gardens were laid out on the rich alluvial soils. For comfort and coolness, however, permanent buildings of great magnificence were erected on the heights of a small nearby hill. On this glorious site, which commands magnificent views of the Zambezi, the extraordinary and beautiful church, which survives to this day, was built.

In many ways, Boromo is a symbol of hope for Mozambique. On independence, the missionaries left. The school and mission buildings, decorated with revolutionary graffiti, became a mouthpiece for the new order. A nearby shrine was desecrated and God was apparently banned or forgotten. But when I was at Boromo in 1988, Easter had just been officially celebrated for the first time in many years. The graffiti was still visible but was fading: nobody seemed interested in repainting it. There were freshly cut flowers in the shrine.

16   That Damned Gorge!

EVEN when the sun shines there is something sinister about the gorge at Cahora Bassa. It is not just the silence. It is the sheer, terrifying immensity of it. I have walked thousands of kilometres in southern Africa. I have climbed its mountains. I am at home in its wilderness and I have stood in silent awe at the vastness of its deserts, but nowhere has it reached out and touched me in quite the same way as at that gorge.

Of course, it is not the same now as it was in Livingstone's day. A tight curve of concrete has been fitted snugly across it and a great silver lake stretches back to the Luangwa River. Downstream it has not changed. There sections remain of the old gorge where it is possible to stare down onto the bare rocks that have surrendered to the sun and the water and to imagine what it must have been like.

Great slabs of grey drop almost vertically into the narrow riverbed which itself is a jumble of tumbled boulders. On the shoulders of grey above, a patchwork of rock and tree, defying gravity, stitches the mountainside together and holds it back from the abyss below. The river zigzags round the base of ridges that, scarred, plummet from the heights. Deep blue-black shadows throw themselves across the water as soon as the sun has passed.

It is a sight that David Livingstone did not see until it was too late.

Livingstone was euphoric after his successful crossing of the Luangwa (Chapter 3). From there it was an easy and well-known journey to Tete. The euphoria and the fact that the route was well known help to explain the curious and woefully significant blunder that Livingstone was about to make.

In England Livingstone had spoken of the Zambezi as God's highway and had allowed people to believe, as he himself apparently believed, that it was possible to take a boat up through the renowned rapids of Cahora Bassa into the heart of central Africa. Livingstone's statement led to the funding and organisation of the Zambezi expedition with which he came back to Africa. Of course, when the attempt was made to get a boat upstream through the rapids it was found to be quite impossible.

Could everybody have known about Cahora Bassa except Livingstone? Why did he, the trained scientist, the brilliant observer, miss something so obvious? I will venture to hazard a guess. The Portuguese had known of the rapids at Cahora Bassa for at least 300 years. The well-worn track that for centuries had led from Tete to the interior skirted them, for they rendered the river impassable. The cataracts appear on maps 100 years before

Livingstone arrived, and as he had maps of Angola when he walked west, is it not likely that he had maps of the east also?

Well downstream of the Luangwa, travellers crossed the Zambezi onto its south bank to follow the arc of the south-east bend the river makes, cutting out the section with Cahora Bassa. As Livingstone progressed down the river, he met a man from Tete who warned him of the need to make this crossing.[1]

No person, certainly not Livingstone, who did not know the country ahead would fail to question such an informant about the route, the obstacles and why the track left the river. In addition, he must have met villagers and other travellers along the way. Livingstone, of all people, would not have failed to ask questions and I simply cannot see that he failed to learn about the gorge and rapids at Cahora Bassa.

The most obvious thing for Livingstone to do as he approached the area of the rapids was not to ignore them but to go and investigate them. He did not. He allowed himself to be taken along the same, centuries-old path that everyone before him had taken, so he never saw the cataracts at Cahora Bassa. If the river was so important to him as a highway to the heart of Africa, why was he not immediately suspicious about the route abandoning it so dramatically? Surely he would have been sensitive to anything that threatened the role he had now assigned the river?

Livingstone says that it was not until he reached Tete that he was informed of a 'small' rapid in the river.[2] Had he learnt of it in time he would surely have investigated it, he says. There must be something wrong here. Who in Tete would have described Cahora Bassa as 'small'? Even if the Tete story were true, surely, if the river was as important to his plans as we are led to believe, his first concern would have been to enquire more about the 'small' rapid and then the story would have come out. In any case, was it really only at Tete that he first heard of the rapids? I find that difficult to accept.

There is one final and extraordinary piece of evidence to consider. Throughout his travels, Livingstone recorded the altitude of places visited by noting the boiling point of water. There are probably hundreds of such entries in his journals; it was a quite normal and simple routine to follow. He took measurements where he crossed to the Zambezi's south bank, above Cahora Bassa, and he took them again where he rejoined the river above Tete. When he worked out the difference he made a mistake in his calculations that amounted to 183 m! Consequently, he made the drop between those two points to be considerably less than it actually was, in this way inadvertently concealing the existence of the cataracts.[3]

Some biographers claim that because the drop suggested by his calculations was so small, Livingstone was not surprised by, nor did he question, descriptions of a 'small' rapid. But is it not possible that the reverse is true? That to admit such a discrepancy in height would be to admit to large, and possibly impassable, rapids — and to the end of a dream launched on the euphoria of Luangwa. I am not suggesting that Livingstone deliberately falsified the numbers, but I am suggesting a case of 'motivated error', the sort of thing that happens to us all when we very much want a particular outcome and try to force the answer we want from facts that would have it otherwise.

Sooner or later, of course, the day of reckoning had to come. On 14 May 1858 the Zambezi expedition stood at the mouth of the Zambezi. Despite every resistance from their inadequate vessel, the *MaRobert,* they painfully ascended the river to Tete, arriving on 8 September to the great joy of the surviving Kololo whom Livingstone had left there two years before. It was not yet time to go on, however, and Livingstone had to curb his impatience to see Cahora Bassa for a few more months.

He and the *MaRobert* returned to the coast and did not get back to Tete until 3 November. So impatient was he by this time that, despite the need to effect repairs to the boat, five days later they were on their way, and at midday on 9 November 1858 Livingstone reached the foot of Cahora Bassa Gorge. He was able to get the *MaRobert* only 3 km along it before further progress was impossible due to the current and the great boulders that filled the river.

The small group landed on the right bank and clambered ashore. As the roar of the river replaced the asthmatic wheezing of the *MaRobert,* the sheer walls of grey that marked the beginning of the gorge and hemmed in that chaotic pile of gigantic boulders which was the riverbed seemed to loom gloatingly above them. With that numbing sense of fearful foreboding that we have all experienced as we watch unwanted fate irrevocably advance, Livingstone was exposed to the appalling truth. Cahora Bassa was impassable.[4]

Predictably for a man who sought to conquer continents, men and hardship through the force of his own indomitable will, Livingstone refused to accept the evidence of his eyes. He spent two days exploring the gorge as far as he could before returning, frustrated and bad tempered but not yet beaten, to Tete on 13 November.

On the 23rd, he was back again. Early rains had already taken the river from its November annual low to half-flood level and he hoped this would improve the chances of navigability. For seven days the expedition battled its way 40 km upstream on foot, and found nothing to change the facts of the gorge's true and forbidding nature.[5]

At the end of that time, the men could go no further so they started back. However, hearing of a yet greater obstacle beyond, on 1 December Livingstone and Kirk continued upstream with four porters. The struggles these men endured were monumental, the hardest that Livingstone had ever undertaken, but they saw the waterfall called Morumbua, the most frightening cataract of all. Kirk knew then, beyond doubt, that it was hopeless. Livingstone chose to see things differently.

They were back in Tete on 6 December where Livingstone brooded for three weeks. As well he might. Everything he had planned, hoped for and convinced others about, including the British government, depended upon

LEFT
Kariba gold. A Kapenta catch spread in the sun to dry.

BELOW
Freshwater prawns (Macrobrachium rosenbergii) were imported to Kariba to found an industry that has never really flourished.

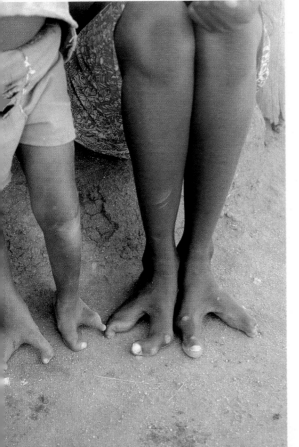

FAR LEFT
Nyaminyami, the river spirit of the Batonga people. This depiction, in the form of a walking stick, by the Shona woodcarver Rainos Tawonameso, has caught the imagination of the public and is eagerly sought by travellers to Kariba.

ABOVE LEFT
Thickly matted, water weeds flourish.

ABOVE RIGHT
A church in Tete.

LEFT
Vadoma — the so-called ostrich or 'two-toed' people.

ABOVE
*River-bank erosion is a constant threat
to trees and vegetation in the alluvial
flats of Zimbabwe's Zambezi Valley.*

RIGHT
*The potter's art thrives among the
people of the Zambezi.*

the navigability of the Zambezi and the necessity of boating through Cahora Bassa. How was he going to explain his discovery? He simply distorted the facts to make them fit what he considered to be God's plan for him, thereby misleading his government, supporters and friends.[6]

Writing to the Foreign Secretary on 17 December 1858, he said that in the opinion of *all* his staff 'a steamer of light drought of water, capable of going twelve or fourteen knots an hour, would pass up the rapids without difficulty when the river is in full flood';[7] on these grounds he asked for a replacement for the *MaRobert*. The *Pioneer* eventually arrived on the river but Livingstone never even took her to the cataracts!

On another occasion, perhaps as a result of wishful thinking, he underestimated by half the height above Tete of the cataract at Morumbua.[8]

In January Livingstone and Kirk left Tete to investigate the Shire River but not without having instructed Baines and his brother Charles to carry out a further reconnaissance of Cahora Bassa. Admittedly Charles, ever pliant to Livingstone's will, agreed that the gorge might be navigable but he had not, as Baines had, reached Morumbua, the uppermost cataract. Baines harboured no illusions as to the insuperable nature of Cahora Bassa. Blithely ignoring this in his journal, Livingstone had written that they had reported favourably on the possibility of passing and he told the Admiral Commanding at the Cape that Baines agreed a powerful steamboat could pass the top of the cataract.[9]

Livingstone had one more brush with Cahora Bassa. This was after his second visit to Victoria Falls. With his brother Charles and Dr John Kirk he had walked there with the Kololo and then, seeking a more speedy return, came down the river in dugout canoes.

Again they travelled in November, at the time of low water, and progressed without incident to Kariba Gorge, through which they passed with some difficulty. I am interested to note, having canoed the same stretch of river myself, that it is impossible to identify the rapids and obstructions that Livingstone met, perhaps because of Kariba dam. From the hydroelectric stations on both the north and south banks now, comes a high volume of water. The effect is to make the gorge an effortless and peaceful passage with no rapids or places of danger to speak of.

It would have been pleasing to Livingstone if he could have said the same of Cahora Bassa, which he reached on 12 November 1860, two years after he had first encountered it. Is was nothing like that at all. It was unmitigated hell.

They started with at least five dugouts. In crossing the river at the head of the gorge, one with its cargo was lost, snatched by the fast current, never to be seen again. A second was so leaky they abandoned it. Kirk and his crew managed to clear the first dangerous obstacle and saw Livingstone, behind them, in difficulty. Distracted momentarily, they were instantly in trouble themselves and their boat overturned; its cargo was also lost, including eight volumes of botanical notes and hundreds of Kirk's drawings.

Livingstone's boat survived and he rescued Kirk and his paddler. It was plain, however, they could not hope to continue. Abandoning the dugouts, they made their way painfully over the burning rocks and sand, arriving in Tete on 23 November. At last Livingstone seemed cured of his fantasy for he never mentioned the painful subject of Cahora Bassa again. Had he done so he might well have called it that damned gorge!

The lake that has taken the place of that fearsome gorge has the attraction of all great lakes in Africa — the fascination of open water — but it also has the attraction of a treasure house yet to be opened.

Cahora Bassa was never seen by its planners as just a dam. It was to be the key to a development scheme of unparalleled proportions. While generating revenue and earning foreign currency, it would lead to the construction of subsidiary dams, canals, perhaps a river navigation system and the irrigation of hundreds of thousands of hectares of agricultural land. Of course it depended upon South Africa, the only possible market in the early stages for such large quantities of electricity, but even she would have benefited since the power was intended to be the cheapest in the world.[10]

With a wall 160 m high, Cahora Bassa is 32 m deeper than Kariba. Although about the same length, the lake is roughly half Kariba's volume. Nevertheless, the head of water and nearly 20 years of improvements in the technology of electricity generation make it a far more powerful generating station. Although there is provision for a north bank power station, only the south bank at Cahora Bassa has been developed: there are five 415 MW (megawatt) generators capable of producing a maximum of 2 075 MW.[11]

Kariba, by comparison, began production with six 111 MW generators that have been upgraded to 125 MW each, giving a maximum of 750 MW on the south bank. On the north bank are four 150 MW generators. This gives Kariba a total of 1 350 MW,[12] substantially less than production at Cahora Bassa.

I do not pretend to understand the complexities of the political situation in southern Africa nor the special relationship that might exist between South Africa and Mozambique. Nor do I understand how the so-called rebel movement in Mozambique, MNR or Renamo, fits into the puzzle. I am clear on the fact that there is a war going on in Mozambique, that Cahora Bassa is highly vulnerable, and that the powerline carrying electricity 1 400 km to South Africa on 7 000 individual pylons is constantly being blown up with explosives. By which of the three sides, however, I am not sure.[13]

At the time of writing Mozambique and South Africa had signed an agreement that sounded of milk and honey and spoke of reopening the powerline, buying electricity and running the power plants at full capacity again. I earnestly wish it well but, having just returned from Cahora Bassa, having had bullets fired at my car and having seen the dead of yesterday's ambush left abandoned by the side of the road, I remain a little sceptical.

If the scheme does not work, it will be a pity. What I saw at Cahora Bassa underlined the tragedy of Africa: it has so much to give to itself if only the individual parts could learn to live together. At Cahora Bassa an astronomical sum was spent with the intention of generating huge quantities of cheap electricity. In 1988 it was producing 10 MW a day, the smallest amount possible, which served to light the towns of Songo, on the heights above the dam, and Tete, some 130 km away. Those two towns now share the most expensive power plant in the world!

The building of a dam the size of Cahora Bassa in so remote a locality created as many problems as it did at Kariba. The attractive town of Songo high in the misty hills above the gorge was built in virgin bush. What a welcome change it must have been to those coming out of the gorge in October and November from surface temperatures of 60 °C, when it was impossible to continue work.

Far fewer people than at Kariba had to be resettled as a result of flooding; even so, 24 000 needed new homes. It was difficult to get the men to see the advantage in the short term of working at the dam itself. So in the early days recruiting labour was extremely difficult. The reason for this is fascinating.

Mozambique has always exported huge quantities of labour to the gold mines in South Africa. In the mind of the local labourer, the experience of a contract in South Africa has gone far towards replacing the old initiation rites. Many Shangaans, for example, would not marry until they had completed at least one, if not two contracts. Of course, this was partly a function of economic necessity, but it had much to do with social pressure also. Like the coalface cutter in Wales or the man in South Africa who wields the rock drill or places the dynamite, pride in the responsibility and status of his job gives him a place in the social hierarchy.

At the beginning, Cahora Bassa was simply not seen as a challenge. Then came a ghastly accident in 1970. Seven African men were killed in a premature explosion. From this point onwards, the rate of recruiting quickly improved. Word went round that Cahora Bassa was a test of maturity and an experience worth recalling in old age. Recruiting problems became a thing of the past![14]

Everything about the project was big: its imaginative scope within the framework of a developing country, the size of the wall, the massive excavations required for the machinery and, of course, the machinery itself. For example, the single underground hall containing the five turbines was hewn from solid rock. It is large enough to take, side by side, two of London's St Paul's Cathedral![15]

Simply moving the necessary material into the area created logistical headaches of enormous magnitude. Some of the electrical equipment was the heaviest in the world; as a result roads, culverts and railways all had to be modified. Special lifting equipment was installed at the port of Beira and a bridge was built at Tete solely because of the transportation demands of Cahora Bassa. Named the Caetano bridge, this beautiful structure spans the Zambezi, bringing easy access to the north bank for the first time since the Portuguese occupied Tete 440 years before!

In addition to moving people to make way for the coming dam, consideration also had to be given to moving vegetation. As we saw in Chapter 8, attempts were made to clear huge areas of bush before the filling of Lake Kariba in order to facilitate the fishing industry that was expected to develop. The same arguments applied at Cahora Bassa but because of the experience gained at Kariba, the decision went the other way, and no bush clearing was undertaken.[16]

A noted expert on fish and fisheries, Dr P.B.N. Jackson, was involved in making this decision and some of his research findings make interesting reading.[17] The idea of bush clearing is that a bottom trawl can be used without the danger of snagging the net and destroying it. But Jackson noted that areas cleared in two large dams, Kariba and Kainji on the Niger River, were never used for the purpose for which they had been cleared.

Jackson's work on Lake Victoria showed that one trawl of about 16 m in length would, with a crew of eight men and during the course of a normal working day, catch about as many fish as would 125 canoes working with gill nets with a minimum of three men in each canoe. What this all adds up to is that trawling is most definitely more efficient than men with nets and high hopes. At the same time, however, where people engage in subsistence level fishing for a large number of people, one trawler puts 375 of them out of business.

Some evidence mentioned by Dr Jackson suggests that uncleared areas in large dams may actually have a beneficial effect on fish populations.[16] As we have seen in Chapter 9, considerable quantities of algal growth thrive on this substrate, providing a direct or indirect food source for fish.

There is a delightful word to which, if you have not already had the pleasure, I would enjoy introducing you. Apparently, fish are not unlike humans in preferring to be next to something big or solid — notice the way we choose a table near the wall in a restaurant — and this extraordinary behaviour in all animals is called thigmatropism! If nothing else, a forest of dead trees immersed in the water of a lake looks like it will produce an abundance of psychologically well-adjusted fish.[19]

Speaking of which, I must mention our friend the Kapenta from Lake Kariba. A pelagic fish — one that prefers open waters — it was introduced to maximise the use of the aquatic biosphere, there being none of the former riverine fish capable of adapting. Of course, there was great interest among the experts as to whether the lowly Kapenta would survive the long journey downriver from Kariba to Cahora Bassa. Majority opinion was against it until a discovery was made that somehow, incredibly, many of these small fish were getting *through the turbines* alive! Hundreds of thousands died in the filters and as they passed through the churning blades and pounding water — but thousands survived.

Apart from the turbines at Kariba, there were three factors that mitigated against the sardines successfully making the journey down 220 km of the Zambezi to Cahora Bassa: the water was too shallow; there was no plankton for them to eat; and there were too many predators to eat them. Happily, Kapenta do not read, so they did not know this, and there is a huge population in Cahora Bassa today — with nobody to exploit them commercially![20]

In Chapter 9 the problem of aquatic weeds was touched upon in relation to Kariba where *Salvinia molesta* was the principal culprit. The same *Salvinia* will be no less of a problem in Cahora Bassa, but the situation is much more complicated because, for the first time in the world, two prolific weeds are present. Besides *molesta* is the equally devastating *Eichornia crassipes*, more commonly known as the water hyacinth.[21]

Like *Salvinia*, the water hyacinth comes from South America. It was probably introduced accidentally into Africa because of its attractive blue flower. An extremely persistent plant, it propagates not only vegetatively but also by seeds. This makes it especially difficult to eradicate as there is no way of removing the seeds from the mud at the bottom of a dam.[22]

Because of its great fecundity and the dangerous threat it poses to aquatic systems in Africa, the water hyacinth has been the subject of considerable research. It turns out to be an extremely interesting plant, despite the serious problems with which it is associated.

For example, a surface covered with densely packed *Eichornia* will evaporate moisture at a rate three times faster than open water. Its growth rate is phenomenal: depending on such factors as water temperature, nutritional levels and sunlight, it can double its mass in anything between six and 27 days. When grown on sewerage effluent, figures of 800 kg dry mass have been recorded per hectare per day.

Less research has been applied to uses for this remarkable plant but some information is available. A small town in the southern USA uses *Eichornia*, which has already contaminated the local water systems, in the treatment of its sewerage. An area of only 3,6 ha was required for a town of 2 500 people. From this, every day, a staggering 20 to 30 tonnes (wet mass) of hyacinth was harvested and used for compost or stock feed. Consuming and converting the protein in raw sewerage, the plant exhibits phenomenal levels of productivity.

It turns out, also, that aquatic plants are especially good at concentrating heavy metals in their cell tissue. This means that metals such as cadmium, nickel and mercury are taken up by the plant and found in concentrations as much as 20 000 times higher than in the water itself. I understand work is in progress to establish whether these plants will scavenge gold and silver from mine washings![23]

I would have liked to tell you that the potential of this weed is being put to good use in Mozambique but I am afraid I cannot. Few people live on the shores of the lake today — because of the security situation — and organised life appears to have come to a standstill. I saw no weed on open stretches of water but, from a distance, saw considerable quantities in sheltered bays. I suspect that much the same has happened in Lake Cahora Bassa as took place in Kariba.

There are prophets of doom associated with every dam and Cahora Bassa is no exception. One I came across certainly seems to have an interesting point, however, and it might be worth repeating. Every dam has a limited life, if only because the incoming water has a silt load which is deposited in the still waters of the dam. Engineers can calculate the rate of filling and the space to be filled, and therefore the lifespan of the dam.

Lake Kariba is so vast that it is estimated to have a life of about 1 000 years. It has been said that the water flowing into Cahora Bassa will have had much of the silt removed by dams on the Kafue River, as well as by Kariba. 'And therefore', goes one report, 'Lake Cabora Bassa, though smaller in volume than Kariba, will have a life of the same order as Kariba'. This sounds encouraging and reassuring but one writer seriously suggests that a more realistic figure could be as little as only 35 years! He points out that the Luangwa River comprises 15% of Cahora Bassa's water, that it is undammed and its water has a high silt content.[24]

Visiting Cahora Bassa, I was attracted by an evident curiosity which, upon investigation, revealed what I think is a remarkable story. Compared to those at Kariba which are right at the top, the sluice gates at Cahora Bassa are very low in the wall. It may be that those at Cahora Bassa, in the bottom third as they are, serve to scour accumulating sediments once they build up beyond a certain level. The scouring effect is easy to imagine if you see one of the gates open. The water, under tremendous pressure, shoots out and is deflected upwards at about 45° so that it curves out, away from the wall, in a lace-veiled arch that seems to descend in slow motion into the river below. It is there, on the rocks below the waterline, that a fascinating phenomenon is revealed.

One gate is opened once a day for a limited number of hours. When it is closed, the river level below the wall drops, exposing an area of bright red-stained rocks. There are none at the foot of Kariba's wall. Thinking to be clever, I guessed this was a sign of a rich iron deposit somewhere upstream, but the correct explanation for this striking sight is a little more complicated and much more fascinating. Strangely, it has a lot to do with where the sluice gate is located in the wall: high up or low down!

The explanation is that iron, a very abundant material on earth, is commonly found suspended in water but very rarely dissolved in water. The difference is important. Sugar and coffee are solids that become dissolved in water, kaolin and milk of magnesia are substances suspended in water — if you leave them long enough, they will settle out. Iron suspended in water usually does not settle out because the particles involved are almost of molecular size, and other forces also keep them 'up' in the water. Nevertheless, the iron is usually suspended and not dissolved.

Iron does become dissolved, however, in rare circumstances, for example when there is no or very little oxygen in the water. This can happen in a dam when falling organic matter from above — dead fish, plants, plankton and the like — use up all the oxygen in the deeper levels as they rot. As a result, a deep deoxygenated zone can develop in which the iron formerly in suspension changes its form slightly and passes into solution. A feature of this process is that, once it has begun, relatively high concentrations of iron in the water can be achieved. Levels of 18 mg/l and 41 mg/l have been recorded.[25]

If, for any reason, oxygen is suddenly reintroduced into the water, the dissolved iron comes out of solution instantly and is precipitated at once, showing its characteristic bright red colour. At Cahora Bassa, the sluice gate that draws water from the deeper parts of the dam discharges water that is deoxygenated and full of dissolved iron. As the water shoots out in that great curve onto the rocks below, oxygen pours back into it while the iron is precipitated out, staining the rocks a vivid red. This is all a consequence of where the sluice gate is placed in the wall: the same thing does not occur at Kariba because the water discharged through floodgates there is highly oxygenated because it is drawn from the surface.

The result of all this is that I did not find the lode of iron ore that might have made me a wealthy man; but I am quite content with the fascinating tale instead. Besides, if one was interested in mineral wealth in the vicinity of Cahora Bassa, it is not iron one should be looking for, but silver. The early Portuguese were admittedly prone to exaggeration, but there is overwhelming evidence for their claim of extremely rich silver mines in the area of Cahora Bassa. Unfortunately, their location has been 'lost' for more than 300 years.

In Chapter 14 I wrote of Barreto's expedition to the lands of Mwene Mutapa. Barreto, you will recall, died at Sena and his place was taken by one of his lieutenants, Vasco Fernandes Homem. Homem took his forces to Sofala and from there explored the gold fields of Zimbabwe. Fearing an attack by the Mutapa he retired and returned to the Zambezi where he spent the summer, probably at Tete. His intention was to take possession of the silver mines promised to the Portuguese by the Mutapa the previous year.[26]

In 1576 Homem moved up the river to Pungue, at the mouth of Cahora Bassa Gorge. Here he left his boats and travelled a further 50 leagues to the lands where the silver mines were said to be. (Converting the distance depends on the type of league used: a Roman league measured 2,2 km; French 4,4 km and Spanish 6,7 km.) Here he met representatives from the Mutapa, who confirmed his promise of mines at both Boquisa and Chicova. However, the chief of Boquisa refused to reveal his mines, notwithstanding an order from the Mutapa, and Homem took him prisoner.

At this point it was necessary for Homem to proceed downriver, so he took with him four samples of silver and the native chief, but left behind some 200 of his own men. The natives first besieged and starved these men in their tiny fort, then flattered them with friendship. Later they slaughtered to a man a party to whom they had promised to show the mines. Driven by hunger, the remaining Portuguese sallied forth in a bid to escape but they too were annihilated.

So the first contact that the Portuguese authority had with the famed silver mines had been achieved only at a huge cost in blood. Was it worth it? Evidently so, for other attempts were to follow. This was hardly surprising for the samples that Homem had collected yielded 50% pure silver.[27]

This kind of yield is unheard of in Africa where no mines purely for silver exist. Silver always occurs as a by-product of the search for other minerals, including gold and copper. A mine yielding 50% silver would be an exceptionally rich one indeed.

Thirty years of conflict followed before a second serious attempt was made to formally take possession of Mwene Mutapa's mines. This was, unfortunately, left in the hands of Estevao Ataide, an avaricious 'gentleman' sent out from Mozambique in 1610.

It was both customary and politic for him, as a new and senior official, to make a payment to the Mutapa. This Ataide refused to do. Understandably, the Mutapa resented this attitude and refused to reveal the whereabouts of any mines until he had received his just payment. Ataide then threatened to take the mines by force but recalling previous experiences, stalled; so a stalemate ensued and lasted three years. At the end of that time, Ataide was relieved of his office, which allowed the principal character, Diogo Simoes Madeira, to move onto centre stage.[26]

In 1614 Madeira led troops to the Chicova region, where Homem's men had died 40 years previously. Here, it is said, he found silver and sent samples to Lisbon and Goa for assay. More was melted down and sent to Sena with which to purchase supplies. Madeira's first action was to build a stockade, which he called the Fort of San Miguel, and then to begin discussions with the local chief who was under instructions from the Mutapa, because of the treaty signed between the Portuguese and the Mutapa, to reveal the location of the silver mines. The chief refused.

The strong reluctance to reveal the mine's location is a persistent theme in the story but eventually, after several clearly 'salted' locations had been shown to them, the Portuguese were shown one they believed was real. From here, the natives said, they drew as much silver as they wanted and a large hole was seen to have been dug in the ground.

At this juncture, Madeira decided to make a report to Sena and to despatch for analysis the samples he had so far found. Thus he left the Chicova area, leaving 44 soldiers in command of San Miguel. These the Mutapa attacked and attempted to wipe out with a force several thousand strong. They were probably saved by Madeira's fortunate return. The Mutapa, realising his error, excused the misunderstanding, made peace and again sent an emissary whose job it was to show where the silver mines were. Once more the search for the principal mines continued.

During this interval the most valuable finds were made with the help of the new guide, Cherema. One 'fragment' of silver ore measured 1 kg, and another, from the same place, a little more. Both were found after digging deep into the earth. The largest fragment was found beneath the roots of a tree and was definitely considered not to have been placed there by human agency. Within a small area, some 270 kg were recovered, the poorest of which, when melted down, gave one part of silver to two of dross. Other pieces yielded half silver while some were almost pure.[29]

Madeira instructed a Dominican friar to take samples of this ore to Goa where it arrived in the latter half of 1615 and was found on assay to be more than half silver. Another man, Gaspar Bocarro, volunteered to take samples overland to Lisbon. We shall return to his story in a moment.

It is difficult to be certain exactly how much silver was removed from the Chicova area but an assessment made by a Portuguese Judge of Enquiry in about 1617 or 1618 claims that in the two years Madeira occupied the fort, at least 2 000 marks of silver were taken to Sena and Mozambique. A mark equalled 227 g, so we can say that Chicova yielded a minimum of 454 kg in that brief period.[30]

Clearly the potential was much higher, for Madeira and his men were not expert miners. In addition, it was said that there were many other mines in the vicinity but directions to them have not survived in the historical record. No one, apparently, investigated these other mines so their exact whereabouts and worth remain a mystery.[31]

The mines were legendary, even at that time, and it is said that so much silver reached Sena and Tete that there were few houses without silver vessels. You might recall from Chapter 15 that when Forbes, Browne and Kilpatrick were entertained by Dona Pascoa at Sena in 1823, they described the massive silver utensils on the table. Dona Pascoa was herself a scion of a long-established Zambezi family, so there is no reason why this could not have been some of the Chicova silver.

Highly prized, valuable, well known — all the more surprising then, that after the downfall of Madeira in 1616, which was brought about by political intrigue, the mines disappear from the pages of Mozambique's history and never reappear. Incredible as it may seem, they were 'lost'. Beyond a name for their general locality, nobody knows where they are.

There are passing and wistful references to them in the 18th and 19th centuries but no silver ever appears again. Judging from such directions as have survived, it seems that the silver is now under water or close to the south shore of Lake Cahora Bassa. A general book about Mozambique written in the 1960s says, 'There appears to be no trace of the famous and legendary silver mines of Chicova.'[32] I am at a loss to explain how this could have happened.

To return now to the story of Gaspar Bocarro: he was the son of a noble family, a close friend of Madeira's, and aware of the intrigue and political hostility directed against Madeira. This was the reason Bocarro offered to carry samples of ore and personal reports to the king of Portugal by pioneering a different route to the coast, bypassing the island of Mozambique. In doing so, Bocarro takes us away from silver and back to David Livingstone, to touch upon his so-called discovery of Lake Nyasa.

Accompanied by a dozen slaves, Bocarro detoured two days upstream to a village renowned for its copper products and acquired 1 000 bracelets to serve as currency during his journey. In just 53 days, Bocarro reached the east African coast opposite the island of Kilwa Kisiwani. On his journey, although he did not actually visit it, he had sight of modern Lake Malawi which, as Lake Nyasa, David Livingstone was to 'discover' 250 years later.[33] As it happened, Bocarro did not get his samples to the king for the way north was barred by war. Unable to get through, he returned to Mozambique and the Zambezi.

Bocarro's reporting of the lake must have reached the ears of cartographers for it clearly appears as L. Maravi in 1722 on *Carte d'Afrique* by de Lisle. In 1727 Jean Baptiste d'Anville produced his exceptional map which is considered to be the most accurate of any prior to the 19th century. 'Le lac du Maravi' is shown in greater detail than before.[34] There is no doubt therefore, whether Bocarro actually visited it or not, that Lake Malawi, Nyasa or Maravi was well known and appeared on maps nearly 150 years before Livingstone announced his discovery to the world.

Livingstone, frustrated at Cahora Bassa and probably anxious for some discovery of note to offset the failure of his expedition, turned downriver to explore the Shire in early 1859. It is unlikely that at this time he did not already know of the existence of Lake Nyasa. Ben Habib, the Arab trader he first met in Barotseland, told him of it.[35] I have already shown that it had been appearing on maps for well over 100 years. Finally, there is the case of the well-respected Senhor Candido Jose da Costa Cardoso who lived at Tete. Cardoso had himself been to 'Lake Maravi' in 1846.[36] In 1856, when Livingstone first arrived in Tete after his historic crossing of Africa, he stayed at the house of the commandant, Senhor Sicard, and there he met Cardoso.

Cardoso told Livingstone of his journey and drew a map for the Doctor in Livingstone's journal, which Livingstone himself annotated.[37] On his second visit to Tete, when he arrived with the Zambezi expedition, Livingstone avoided Cardoso as if that helpful man had some form of plague, although Dr John Kirk called on him at least twice.

In any event, Livingstone continued to avoid Cardoso, even after he had 'found' the lake for himself. He gave no credit for its discovery to the Portuguese, nor did he acknowledge in any way the help he had received. Rather, he accused Cardoso of having misled him and suggested that Cardoso had not been to the lake at all.[38]

This last was a totally unnecessary response, spiteful and hurtful, the more so because it appears to have been an attempt to discredit all others for the sole purpose that the measure of his own reports might be correspondingly elevated. This is sad, for the quality of Livingstone's reports, observations and discoveries was so great, compared to that of any contemporary, that he had no fear of competition and could easily afford to have been more generous and grateful.

The Livingstone whose achievements could be admired from afar was, it appears, a very different man from the one known by those close to him. The latter was a person who lacked generosity of spirit and could hardly have been a joy to know.

17 Men, Madmen and Maniacs

IT is popularly supposed that David Livingstone's success in so extensively penetrating the African continent led, as a natural consequence, to a heightening of European interest in Africa and an increase in the number of exploratory expeditions. No doubt, it did. Equally, without doubt, they would have happened anyway. There is a danger of allowing the achievements of Livingstone to dominate and this is not fair. Certainly he was an inspiration, but he was far from being the only significant explorer of southern and central Africa.

We have already touched on the remarkable achievements of that early Portuguese explorer and master of disguise, Pero da Covilha, who in the late 1490s hitch-hiked round the Indian Ocean, the Spice Islands, Arabia and the east African coast, passing the mouth of the Zambezi and visiting Sofala (Chapter 14). I have mentioned Antonio Fernandes, the *degradado* who made three journeys of exploration to modern Zimbabwe between 1511 and 1513. These were, for the times, incredible journeys of discovery.

I mentioned also that amazing young man, Karel or Carolus Trichardt, son of the Voortrekker Louis Trichardt. In 1838, with nothing more than some currency in his pocket and without the impediment of trains of porters or mountains of baggage, he explored the east African coast and Madagascar and visited the emperor of Ethiopia, all in the space of eight months.

The Portuguese, however, did not seem overly energetic when it came to exploring the huge tracts of Africa to which they had access from the 15th century onward, but that is not to say they did no exploring at all. It will be remembered that Sisnando Dias Bayao led an expedition from Mozambique right across Zimbabwe to the vicinity of Bulawayo in the mid-1600s — a considerable achievement. As I mentioned in Chapter 16, the *sertanejos* knew their country well, but kept information of commercial value to themselves. Indeed, it was two *sertanejos* who inspired one major Portuguese expedition at the heart of which lay hopes of considerable commercial gain.

Goncalo Caetano Pereira had come from Goa in about 1750 and had prospered as a trader and gold prospector. He and his son knew the interior well. In 1793 they met Bisa people from the kingdom of Kazembe.

These people had recently established their domination of the area south of Lake Mweru in what is now north-west Zambia, having moved from the Congo, and were anxious to establish trade links to the east.

It was fortuitous that when Pereira announced this news at Tete in 1798, the new governor, Lacerda, had just arrived. It also suited the political instructions Lacerda had received in Portugal, for in Lisbon he had been given orders to undertake a transcontinental journey.[1] Not only was there motive, but the guides in the form of the Pereiras and the ambassadors from Kazembe's court were immediately on hand.

An interesting sidelight is the Portuguese government's reasons for requesting this exploration. The Secretary of State in Lisbon was concerned that, with British annexation of the Cape of Good Hope in 1795, there may be a possibility of a wedge being driven between the two Portuguese possessions of Mozambique and Angola, on opposite sides of Africa. Lacerda's job was to prevent this by opening a route across the continent, directly linking the two states. The expedition, ill-starred as it was, did achieve considerable results and would certainly have achieved more but for the death of its leader.

Lacerda was an academic, a mathematician and a prickly individual, difficult to get on with. His lack of diplomacy together with his unrestrained contempt of the settler community did not endear him to them. An opportunist also, he took advantage of the death of his wife to marry into one of the most powerful Zambezi families and, in this way, obtained funding for the modest expedition he hastily threw together and with which he set out to cross Africa on 30 June 1798.[2]

Lacerda steadily sickened on the long journey up the Zambezi and towards the north-west, away from the river to the present Congo border. Two weeks after he arrived at Kazembe's kraal, he died. Kazembe received the Portuguese hospitably enough but would not allow them to cross to Angola. After staying there for seven months the members returned, ostensibly empty-handed, to Tete in 1799.

In fact, the expedition was not entirely a failure. It began a 40-year period of long-distance trade between Kazembe and Tete, marked the beginning of European penetration of the continent from the east and, as we saw in Chapter 3, inspired the first recorded return crossing of the continent in the next decade.[3]

While Lacerda's exploration took him away from the Zambezi River, that of Assumpcao e Mello and da Silva Teixeira, who started from their bases in Angola and travelled east, moved towards it. Assumpcao, a Brazilian immigrant to Angola, made several journeys to the region of the Zambezi's headwaters in the early 1790s before reaching northern Barotseland and its floodplains with Teixeira in 1795.[4]

We know from Chapter 3 that by early 1850 when Livingstone reached the southern regions of Barotseland other explorers had recently been there before him. Laszlo Magyar, the Hungarian who had adopted Angola as his new home, reached Linyanti years before Livingstone. Silva Porto from Bihe knew the river and the district well and was himself known by the people.

The point is that the central portion of Africa was a much busier place, from the point of view of non-Africans travelling through it, than we have been led to imagine by our limited Eurocentric perspective. Livingstone was not the start of exploration, merely the continuation of it.

Mention of Senhor Silva Porto brings to mind the extraordinary circumstances of his death. He had travelled widely throughout central Africa from 1849 for 40 years. He met and knew Livingstone, Arnot and Fisher and, without doubt, was one of the great characters of his part of the world.

In 1890 his village was attacked during a native uprising. He was 74 years old and had lived among the same people for nearly 60 of those years. To him, the attack was an insult he could not bear. Wrapping himself in a Portuguese flag, he proudly lay himself down on top of 13 kegs of gunpowder and blew himself right through the roof of his house, landing some distance away.

The trouble was, he did not die, but lingered through the night and into the following morning before finally succumbing to 'shock' with F.S. Arnot and Dr Walter Fisher (of Kalene Hill, see Chapter 1) in attendance.[5]

Another great character associated with the Zambezi was Thomas Baines. He had been a member of the Zambezi expedition until he was 'fired' by Livingstone, who alleged that Baines failed to look after the stores properly, as a result of which items were missing. The justice of the incident is highly questionable: it seems certain that if anything was missing, there was no malicious intent on Baines's part.

There are many who believe that the treatment by David Livingstone of Thomas Baines during the course of the Zambezi expedition was unnecessary, unwarranted and unacceptable and caused Baines great suffering and pain. But Baines was nothing if not resilient and he was back on the Zambezi surprisingly quickly.[6]

Baines had not yet been to Victoria Falls and knew the Zambezi only from its delta to the top of that terrifying gorge at Cahora Bassa which, with Livingstone, he had explored on foot. Clearly, despite the immense difficulties he had endured on the Lower Zambezi, Baines was excited, interested and ready for more. Back in Cape Town after his ignominious departure from the Zambezi expedition in November 1859, Baines quickly recovered from the stigma.

In the following year, Baines and James Chapman decided on a most ambitious expedition. Their idea was to complete a crossing of Africa by taking two boats down the Zambezi from a point some distance below Victoria Falls. Baines stayed in Cape Town to construct two copper boats in sections suitable for carrying in an ox-wagon.

Each boat consisted of six separate watertight compartments which, when joined, created a canoe-like vessel of about 7 m in length. The idea was that on open and easy stretches of the river, the two hulls would be attached to each other by a series of parallel supports. Covered with canvas, these supports would make a deck, thereby adding considerably to the comfort of the passengers. When rapids or other hazards, including Cahora Bassa, were approached, the hulls could be separated and either taken through or carried round the obstacle. Such a boat clearly was designed by a man who had seen only the lower stretches of the river!

The boats were to be transported by sea to Walvis Bay. From there the plan called for movement of the boats by ox-wagon across what is now Namibia and the Kalahari by way of Ghanzi and Lake Ngami, probably to Pandamatenga as the nearest point to the Zambezi where it was possible to take oxen.

After this incredible journey, the would-be explorers intended that porters would carry the boat sections the last 80 km or so to the river. There Baines and Chapman would assemble them and sail off, if not into the sunset, at least into the pages of history. It was much too much to hope that it would all work out, and it did not, but not for want of trying.

In fact, things did not go well at all; time was a great enemy. Chapman left Cape Town on 9 December 1860 and it took them until September 1862 to get only one boat to the Zambezi, where Baines had established the camp he called Logier Hill. Near the mouth of the Deka River, Logier Hill was on the south bank downstream of the point where the great Batoka Gorge abruptly comes to an end. They chose this point believing that from there on they would have no difficulty in negotiating the river.[7]

Before settling at their camp Baines and Chapman had taken three weeks to visit the Victoria Falls. It was then that Baines became the first artist at the falls: he began painting the many pictures for which he has become well known.

As mentioned, only one boat reached the Zambezi. The plan was that Baines would concentrate on assembling it, Chapman would hunt and keep the camp supplied with meat while the two other Europeans who were with them each had his own special duties to attend to. Unfortunately, malaria and other illnesses exhausted their medicines as well as the men themselves, they had difficulties in obtaining fresh food and they ran out of staple foods. Not surprisingly, friction between all members of the expedition except Baines and Chapman brought the attempt to a halt. It became plain that the two could not hope to succeed. Reluctantly, they gave up and turned back in March 1863.[8]

Eduard Mohr, a German explorer, discovered the abandoned site that Baines and Chapman had used. It was seven years later and the hut in which they had lived had partly collapsed. The rubbish of their stay still lingered on and the copper boat was where Baines had left it, unfinished.

For reasons I can only put down to grossly misplaced national pride, Mohr had the temerity to plant a German flag on the top of Logier Hill![9]

According to one report, the hill that Baines privately called Logier Hill was known in 1951 as 'Chapuman', and before that as 'Chamathama', both in reference to the time of Chapman's abode there. Regionally, however, the hill is known and has always been known as Dunu re ngoma. This means the hill of the drums for it was here, in small caves right at the summit, that Chief Hwange kept the sacred drums of his tribe; his village was located across the river.[10]

Others noted for their role as explorers of the Zambezi included Frederick Courteney Selous, one of the many who followed Livingstone in time. Essentially a hunter, he was an articulate man, kept extensive notes and wrote interesting accounts of his travels and adventures. His life spanned the turn of the century. It must have been strange for him to think back on his life: as a younger man the perils had been from wild animals and wilder natives, while as an older man he lived to see Europeans fighting each other and, indeed, was killed by a sniper's bullet in southern Tanzania while fighting for the British Empire against General von Lettow Vorbeck's troops.

Some of Selous's experiences in the Caprivi Strip have already been mentioned in Chapter 4, but he travelled widely and on a number of occasions was in the Zambezi Valley. His accounts are especially notable for the conditions of human suffering and decadence he discovered in the region between modern Chirundu and Kariba.

In 1877 Selous walked the Zambezi from Logier Hill to the Kafue River. He set off from Pandamatenga, following the traditional route down to Hwange's kraal on the River, just opposite where Baines and Chapman had abandoned their boat. Interestingly, he obtained guides from a Portuguese half-caste living on an island in the river in Gwembe Valley, much further up the Zambezi than people commonly suppose the Portuguese to have reached.

With the collapse of the administration there, lawlessness was now endemic on the lower river and spreading along it like a plague; Selous saw about him only conflict, starvation and cruelty. The Batonga people had fled their homes to avoid the depredations of slave-seeking Chikundas — themselves freed slaves, now operating for their own account in a trade they knew intimately.

Village after village was empty; the remains of pitiful crops, scorched by the sun and pillaged by wild animals, stood abandoned in the fields. Many huts had been burnt and the grain-bins emptied. Such men as they saw walked about in groups, fully armed. Women were few since they were especially sought after by the slavers. Occasionally Selous came across recently raided villages where the smell of burning and rotting flesh was strong on the air and the bodies of the dead, half-eaten by hyena, lay in the path at his feet.[11]

ABOVE
Rafting the wild white water of the Zambezi is an exhilarating and unforgettable experience.
(Courtesy of Shearwater, Zimbabwe)

LEFT
The presence of striking red algae on the rocks below the dam wall has to do with the height of the floodgates in the wall.

FOLLOWING PAGE
Increasingly, the waters of the Zambezi will be exploited for power and agriculture. We are at the dawn of a new and potentially destructive future for the river and its finely balanced ecosystems.

Downstream of Kariba Gorge he passed the one-time Portuguese settlement of Nhaucoe on the left bank at the junction with the Lusituo River. This, he learnt, had been abandoned about two years previously but until that time had been the home of up to 20 Portuguese traders. There is no indication in Selous's report of how long they had been there but it is significant that, at one stage at least, opportunities for trade in the valley had been good enough to support so large a population of Portuguese.

One of those traders remained on the island of Kasoko, a little downstream. For a short time Selous stayed there with Senhor Joaquim de Mendonca and experienced a valley trader's life at close quarters.

Also there were ten Batonga women, recently captured as slaves, all chained together. Each had an iron ring about her neck and was connected to the next by a length of chain. Some of the women had small babies on their backs. During his stay, Selous never saw these women separated from one another. In the day they were ferried by a large canoe to lands on the south bank in which they worked until evening. When they returned they were placed, still chained, inside a large building where they spent the night.

A man by the name of Manoel Diego visited Mendonca while Selous was there and proudly showed off the two slave girls he had just purchased: at 10 and 14 years respectively, they were young and had not been too expensive. One had cost 20 rupees and the other a musket which was valued at about £2.10.0.

To Selous's great delight, these young girls escaped, using their hands to paddle a dugout canoe in the darkness over to the north bank. Regrettably, they were recaptured, whereupon Selous discovered the significance of the blood-stained strips of hippo hide that hung on the wall by the slaves' shed.[12]

An idea of the extent to which the law had passed into the hands of individuals can be gained from Selous's meeting with Kanyemba. This man, an African with strong Portuguese 'overtones', virtually controlled the whole Zambezi Valley for his own benefit. He was able to muster a force of some 600 Chikundas, each with a firearm. These were the men who had completed the recent series of raids, the horrible aftermath of which Selous had witnessed on his way down the river.

Kanyemba also organised elephant hunts involving 200 to 300 armed Chikundas. It is hardly surprising that reports in later years speak of the absence of elephant from the Zambezi Valley. With such forces consistently hunting them, they must have been annihilated.[13]

The size of an explorer's expedition is a fascinating variable and seems related as much to the explorer's confidence and knowledge as to his pocket. One often wonders why it is that some men require so many porters and others seem to need none at all.

Livingstone, for example, took 27 porters with him to Luanda and 114 to Tete. Arabs and slave traders tended to have quite large groups with them since they relied on force to achieve their aims but hunters, men who knew the bush and were able to live off it easily, travelled in very small groups. Selous, for instance, typically was accompanied by not more than ten and often by just three or four men who were more servants than porters.

Without doubt, the man who travelled lightest of all and perhaps for that reason left the least impression despite his remarkable achievement, was a Mr F. Monks.

Monks was known in the colonies (for reasons I have been unable to determine) as Mr F. Foster, but as the brief account of his achievements in the Royal Geographic Society's proceedings appears under the name of Monks, so shall he be called here.[14]

Monks, apparently, had limited financial means but a great love of exploration. At an unspecified date, probably in the early 1880s, this extraordinary man decided to explore the Zambezi — on his own! With scarcely any money, he left the diamond fields in South Africa, on foot, driving a donkey before him.

He reached the Zambezi some 40 km downstream from the end of the Batoka Gorge. There this enterprising and courageous individual swapped his donkey for a canoe and continued his journey by water, still on his own! According to the Society, Monks kept a meticulous map giving minute topographical detail, especially of the numerous streams and tributaries of the Zambezi. This amazing map covered the entire distance from the confluence of the Gwaai River near the start of Monks's journey, right down to Tete.

What difficulties, if any, he experienced in getting his dugout through the gorge at Kariba, we shall never know. How, single-handed, he navigated the hazard of Cahora Bassa must remain a mystery, for his report, if he made one, does not appear in print. We do know, however, that eventually Monks appeared at Quelimane, still in his dugout and still alone.

Monks had successfully navigated over half the length of one of Africa's great rivers, plus he had made several excursions inland as well as ascending the Shire River towards Lake Malawi. It was an amazing achievement, made all the more so by the slender means on which it was managed and the fact that one individual overcame so many difficulties.

The manner of Monks's passing is not known. According to the last letter he wrote in 1887, it was his intention to take porters and some goods from Tete, to ascend the Luangwa and to establish a trading station near the shores of Lake Bangwelo in what is now north-west Zambia. He was never heard from again.

Boating down the river is one thing, but boating up it is quite another, especially if the expedition is to depend on something a bit more technologically advanced than a dugout canoe or a pair of good legs This, Major Gibbons and his six European companions discovered to their cost. The journey up the river was a particular kind of purgatory while the thousands of kilometres they walked seemed to give them little difficulty at all.[15]

The objectives of Major A. St H. Gibbons's great Zambezi expedition were to complete the mapping of Barotseland and to determine the geographical limits of Lewanika's territory, whose western border was in dispute at the time. In addition, Gibbons wanted to study the resources and industrial prospects of Barotseland, to find the Zambezi's source, to define the Congo-Zambezi watershed and to gather for Rhodes such information as might assist him in finding a route for his proposed transcontinental railway. Another objective of the expedition was to resume the testing of Livingstone's belief that the Zambezi was navigable. For this reason the plan was to travel by boat up the river. Originally the intention had been to travel as far as Barotseland, portering the boats around Victoria Falls. But this did not happen, as we shall see. A final objective, which Gibbons stated was quite subsidiary to the primary aims, was to return to England, on foot, *by way of the Great Lakes and the Nile!*

The participants, of whom there were seven in all, were mostly serving military men who had been given a year's leave of absence. Gibbons himself was 50 years of age. He had with him a medical man who, at 65, found the Zambezi Valley a very trying experience. One member joined when the expedition was at Tete. This was Theodor Muller, who had heard about the expedition in Salisbury and had decided to offer his services. He acquired half-a-dozen donkeys, rode to the Zambezi below Tete and simply waited for the party to come by.

Gibbons himself found Muller's approach refreshing. The expedition was moving up the river when a canoe came out at them from the bank. Muller was aboard. He introduced himself, said he was not a scientist, knew nothing about surveying but had no doubt he could make himself useful. Gibbons replied that the boats were already overloaded and that they had no need of an extra man. In his account of the journey, Gibbons went on to muse: 'it was quite refreshing to receive an application from a man who did not describe himself as capable of doing anything and everything and gifted with an excessive omniscience usually denied mortal man. Probably ninety per cent of the numerous applicants for employment which reached me from home and abroad were thus supernaturally endowed.'[16] Muller got the job!

Raising funds for the expedition was difficult. In the end, five of the members each put in £500 to which Military Intelligence added a little and the Royal Geographical Society supplied free instruments, as well as a course of instruction on how to use them.

There are really two parts to this extraordinary expedition, which achieved incredible successes and in terms of the total distances covered, surely exceeded anything before or since. The waterborne section of the journey began in London in May 1898. By July they were in Chinde, the tiny British enclave at the mouth of the Zambezi. Then, thanks to a stern-wheeler of the Mississippi type, one of several operating on the Lower Zambezi at this time, they were hauled upriver to Tete by 9 August.[17]

To achieve the expedition's objective, three boats were built, two launches and a barge. All were made of aluminium, each had a width of just under 2 m and each was made in portable sections, those of the launches being interchangeable so that it was possible to combine two 8 m boats into one of 16 m. The launches carried a mast and sails as well as a boiler with a small three-horsepower engine. The intention was that the boats should be of shallow draught, offer the least resistance to the water and respond quickly to the helm.

There were no illusions about the navigability of Cahora Bassa. The arrangement was that the Centipede, the stern-wheeler that had towed them from Chinde, would take them as far up the river from Tete as it could. They would then manage on their own, using porters to bypass the gorge. The Centipede managed only three days beyond Tete and left them on 12 August 1898. The expedition travelled one day beyond that point before reaching the foot of the great gorge. Here their travails began.

It is one thing to sit in an English sitting-room or a regimental pub designing pull-apart boats and convenient loads for porters. It is quite another to turn the theory into practice. At the foot of the rapids everything had to be taken to pieces, sorted and packed. There were too few porters and they were not used to such strange and awkward loads. What I call a 'barstool cart' had been brought along, the idea (invented at the bar) being that it would be a convenient way of moving the boilers and other bulky items. With two boilers, tool boxes and one or two other items, it was so heavy that it could not be moved. It was soon abandoned.

It took five weeks to dissemble, transport overland and reassemble the two launches and the barge as well as getting all the equipment from one end of Cahora Bassa to the other. Then they started off on the first serious waterborne section of the expedition and managed no more than a killing 10 km in five days.[18]

The engines were not powerful enough, steering something so long was difficult, the current was too strong and the river too shallow, sandbanks littered the route and the men spent more time in the water than out of it, hauling the stranded vessels behind them.

Having established that a launch lashed to either side of the barge did not work, they tried making one launch out of two, with an engine at either end. This scheme also failed and they were left to struggle on as best they could. The longer vessel, which they named the Constance, went on ahead. The second launch, now much reduced in size, and the barge brought up the rear.

They fought every metre of the way to the middle section of the Zambezi and there found that what they had passed was tame compared with what was to come. After reaching Zumbo and the confluence with the Luangwa they found themselves in the oven of the Zambezi Valley at the hottest time of the year — also the time when the water level was nearly at its lowest. The details of their fight through Mupata Gorge and Kariba Gorge must be read to be believed but even that paled beside their struggle through the Gwembe Valley.

The water was then so low that the boats seemed to do little more than get stuck in one set of rapids after another. In Kariba Gorge they abandoned one of the boilers which was discovered some 40 years later, whereupon it was taken as a valued historical treasure to Salisbury, delivered in error to the wrong premises and disappeared from the face of the earth!

The expedition bounced, battered and battled its way as far as it possibly could and, in doing so, set records of endurance and perseverence that cannot but be admired. Ultimately, however, they had to stop and somewhere in the modern Devil's Gorge, which now marks the upstream limit of Lake Kariba, Gibbons called it a day.

His boats had become separated and he decided that he, Stevenson-Hamilton and Captain Quicke should continue on foot with the second part of the expedition while the others returned to the boats behind and from then on to base. Dr Smith, a man called Weller and four Africans on the launch turned back. They reached the mouth of the Kafue River in nine days, a distance they had taken 50 to cover on the way upstream.

The river section of the expedition had been completed with honour. Under the most perfect of conditions they would not have travelled very much further, for Devil's Gorge where they stopped is less than 40 km from the mouth of the Batoka Gorge, beyond which they would not have been able to go because of the difficulty of getting out of the gorge itself.

With only three men and still half of the expedition's work to do, Gibbons attacked the problem in a down-to-earth manner. There was no time to think of recuperation from their incredible journey, no time to rest. Together, they climbed out of the unhealthy river valley onto the Batonga plateau. Here they split up, each with a different task to do and a different area to reconnoitre. It was December 1898, seven months from when they started and only five more were left to go.

Gibbons reached Kazungula on 9 January 1899 with the other two following him via different routes. They met again at Sesheke on 28 February. Here local exploration and writing up their notes took some time; then on 21 March they separated again. Quicke went east, Stevenson-Hamilton south and Gibbons west to the border area of Lewanika's kingdom. They agreed to meet again in three months' time in Lealui, the capital of Lewanika, the Barotse king.

Let us pause here to consider the incredible feats that were apparently so casually being achieved. Even today, with maps and aerial photographs and all the development that has taken place in nearly 90 years, such a journey would be remarkable. To undertake to meet 'in three months' time' at such and such a place, when none of the individuals had been there nor really knew where they were, is quite amazing.

As one might expect of these men who had walked for six months in unmapped and unexplored parts of central Africa, mostly on their own or with a few porters, they arrived at Lealui within about 35 days of one another!

At Lealui, a year and four months after they had started, Gibbons was handed a newspaper (yes, a newspaper, the British administration had been in the driver's seat for two years by this time!) in which he read a report about the expedition. Totally erroneous, it claimed that Gibbons had quarrelled with his companions who had left him, that the expedition had broken up and that it had failed dismally! The true situation was quite the opposite: they had succeeded magnificently.

At this point, with the objectives of the expedition mostly achieved, two of the members returned home by the most convenient means. Gibbons, however, had clearly got the bit between his teeth. He was all for rushing off to Luanda and the Atlantic coast. It took the Resident Commissioner, Coryndon, to persuade him otherwise. Instead, Gibbons followed the original plan and, alone, walked north from Lealui.

He next appeared one year later, in Khartoum, having walked the whole way!

It is worth pausing for a moment longer to recount the fate of some of the individuals on this expedition. From Khartoum, Gibbons rejoined his regiment in South Africa and was pitched into the Boer War, which he fought through, only to be killed in the battle of the Somme in August 1916. Muller, who was following the expedition upriver in the barge, was severely stricken with dysentery and died at Tete. Captain Quicke was killed in the Boer War and Lt Boyd-Alexander, the ornithological expert, was eventually hacked to death in 1910 on a bird-collecting trip in the French Cameroons. His half-caste Portuguese servant from Cape Verde, who had also accompanied him up the Zambezi, remained alive to bring the news of the murder to the outside world.

Stevenson-Hamilton, whose diary provides fascinating insights into the achievements of the expedition and the interaction of the individuals as it progressed, survived rather longer than the others. Interestingly Stevenson-Hamilton, the expedition's hunter, became one of South Africa's earliest and most celebrated conservators. He was appointed the warden of Sabie Game Reserve in the eastern Transvaal, a game reserve that eventually grew into the Kruger National Park under his care.

Stevenson-Hamilton's life of wandering did not stop, however. In 1908 he was cartographer with an expedition that walked from the island of Ibo on Mozambique's coast to Lake Malawi. In 1909 he travelled on foot through Kenya, Uganda and the Upper Nile to Khartoum, Cairo and

England. Later he led zoological excursions into the Kalahari and Portuguese East Africa.

I am irresistibly drawn by the excitement, the challenge, the adventure and the achievement of Gibbons and his companions. Stevenson-Hamilton is the one I can most easily identify with, not only because I have read his journal but because he had the excellent good sense to take his dog with him on the expedition! I too have a dog who travels with me everywhere, a Jack Russell named Gypsey, not a Great Dane as Stevenson-Hamilton had. Gypsey has canoed and kyaked parts of the same river and, like any Jack Russell worth her salt, of course, she had the good sense to travel downstream, not up!

The amazing achievement of F. Monks, described a little while ago, did not long stand alone. After Gibbons had fought his way upriver, it was time for another to go down the river. An individual very much in the Monks mould followed soon in his footsteps, or should I say in his wake?

The man was Harold Henry Abraham de Laessoe. In 1903 Laessoe travelled by boat all the way from the Gwaai-Zambezi confluence to Chinde at the sea, including the only known passage through Cahora Bassa Gorge. Travelling with one unnamed European companion and ten Africans, he completed the journey in less than two months, from 9 August to 7 October.[19]

Anxious to contribute to the growing fund of scientific data relating to the river, he carried with him and recorded readings with barometers, a theodolite, prismatic compasses and thermometers. He had two boats: one of 6,5 m, made of steel and so constructed that it could be taken to pieces and carried; the other was a smaller, wooden boat, designed to withstand rough passages.

By the standards of what we have read, Laessoe's journey down the Zambezi was uneventful, except at two points. At Kariba Gorge he had arranged for porters to be waiting to portage him around the only rapid. He said that in retrospect, after his experiences further down the river, he would never have hesitated to take his boats through.

The other eventful place, of course, was Cahora Bassa. The Portguese with whom he came in contact on the way down did all they could to dissuade him from attempting the gorge. They pointed to the fact that no one had ever got through by water, that the rapids were impassable and that it was almost impossible to walk the banks. At Caxomba, the traditional upstream point for leaving the river and following the overland route to Tete, porters were arranged while Laessoe tried to discover as much as he could about the obstacle ahead.

In any event he decided to make the attempt and sent as much luggage as possible overland to Tete. He also resolved to leave the largest boat at the first serious rapids and to have his native crew follow the boats down the banks in the gorge, helping the remaining smaller boat only when absolutely necessary.

The plan worked out very much along those lines. They ran the first few, smaller rapids and discovered the terrifying power of the river. They also discovered the technique of driving the boat onto the rocks as one desperate way of stopping it! Laessoe described the walls of the gorge as rising sheer for 25 m in places, and the channel sometimes being less than 100 m wide. He told of the water thundering down in a wild zigzag pattern as it raced between the rocks, swirling in mad whirlpools that sucked the boat under.

They tried holding the boat with ropes and following it on foot from the shore. They could not, however, exercise control of it and at the end of its tether, the boat bounced from rock to rock, risking serious damage. The only solution Laessoe found was to get in with two others and trust to luck! Their only protection against a waterfall or major rapid was the deafening sound it made. This was a cue to hurriedly beach the boat and move forward on foot to investigate.

Nyakataku was the rapid at which Livingstone had fared so badly that he abandoned the attempt to boat the gorge. Here Laessoe roped his boat through. For three more days he and his companions negotiated numerous rapids, either boating through some or carrying the vessel overland around them. After this section, in his words, they entered the gorge proper.

Here 1 300 m mountains rose on either side and great boulders that had fallen from them, some the size of two-storied buildings, littered the riverbed. During the day the rocks became so hot that hands, legs and feet blistered from touching them. The few porters absconded with the luggage and had to be caught and persuaded to continue. Progress was painfully slow.

Laessoe calls Morumbua a cataract and describes it as a clear 5 m fall of water. Around this he carried his boat. In the mountainous section alone, which took him five days, Laessoe encountered ten cataracts and 30 rapids. Beyond the mountains the gorge opens out, but the rapids continue. In all, it took Laessoe ten days from one end to the other; over the whole distance he passed 13 cataracts and 64 rapids, the last of which is some 70 km from Tete.[20]

Of all the explorers mentioned, the following is the one who most deserves the third word in the chapter title. Strictly speaking it is not wholly a Zambezi story, but since it indisputably has its origins on the river I feel entitled at least to make a passing reference to Paul Graetz and his glass eyes![21]

Graetz was a German of an adventurous disposition. Between 1907 and 1909 he had driven a car from the east to the west coast of Africa, travelling from Dar es Salaam to Swakopmund, taking 21 months to complete 9 000 km along much of which there was no road at all!

This was the man who now looked for some new adventure and who therefore decided that it would be worthwhile to take a motor-boat *across Africa!* Since, somewhat inconveniently, the rivers did not obligingly run exactly where Graetz might have required them, he devised a mechanism whereby he could attach two automobile wheels to the sides of his boat, thus facilitating its passage overland.

Sarotti was 10 m long, less than 2 m wide with double sides of oak protected by a thin sheet of aluminium, and sported a single-cylinder petrol engine that gave a speed of about 14 km/h. Trials showed that *Sarotti's* engine was not powerful enough to travel fully laden against the Zambezi's current. Graetz therefore had the boat carried on a stern-wheeler to the Nyasaland railhead at Port Herald, up the Shire River, then by rail to Blantyre from which point he pushed it overland to the upper Shire River and by that means to Lake Nyasa.

Travelling up Nyasa was easy of course but he then faced a 250 km stretch over mountains before he reached his next river, the Chambesi. His adventures from that point onwards are wonderful reading but not really part of our story. Graetz was gored by a buffalo but luckily escaped with his life. On another occasion he had trouble with the natives and brought out his bag of glass eyes, which he thought might be useful in an emergency! The magical effect of the glass eyes ensured that Graetz had no further trouble from Africans he met.

He did not complete his journey as he had hoped. Dreadful difficulties were his lot and eventually his boat was destroyed in a waterfall on a river leading to the Congo. Persistent however, Graetz, knowing that he had passed the worst, returned a year later to complete the journey in the same manner but from the opposite direction, linking up with his original course. His crossing of Africa was complete!

The most unlikely explorer of Africa I have come across is described in a story that dates from 1908. In that year a man called Creswell, a dangerous criminal, was arrested by the British South Africa Police in Southern Rhodesia. While being transferred by train from prison in Bulawayo to Salisbury, he escaped. At the time he was in leg-irons as well as handcuffs. While his escort slept, Creswell was able to get hold of the keys to the leg-irons but not the handcuffs. Despite an intensive search, Creswell seemed to have vanished off the face of the earth.

Eventually, however, Creswell was rearrested — in London! It seems that from Sherwood in Rhodesia, penniless, with nothing but that which he stood up in and wearing handcuffs, he had made his way on foot right across Africa. The handcuffs were soon removed with the help of some natives, and he slowly worked his way to the west coast. At Boma, a port in the Congo, he took passage as a deck-hand to England. There, one night at Mile End Road Police Station, the duty sergeant saw a man stagger in. It was Creswell, riddled with malaria and broke. He had come to give himself up.

Creswell was sent back to Rhodesia and Bulawayo to stand trial. At the railway station, however, he was so sick that he was taken straight to hospital. Two days later he was dead.[22]

The lure of adventure has drawn many kinds of men to the Zambezi River. Missionaries, mathematicians, diamond diggers, doctors, and many others. Launched upon it have been expeditions with a great variety of objectives and the explorers themselves have been even more diverse. It is among the explorers, however, that the greatest interest lies. What rewards make a man risk his life to explore a river? All the obvious answers come to mind — the challenge, adventure, excitement, fame and fortune. I wonder if all the answers is there. Perhaps, in addition, you do have to be just a little bit mad!

18   At the River's End

AFTER a journey of thousands of kilometres, from the misted plateaux on the spine of Africa, over the ancient planed surfaces of the inner continent, down spectacular steps, through deep valleys and narrow gorges, out onto the coastal plain, the Zambezi, at last, slides silently into the sea, its epic over.

The end is indecisive for the river does not enter the sea as one, but as many. It divides and its divisions divide again into a maze of distributaries, large and small, so that the characters of sea and river are sometimes hard to separate. With tides reaching 40 km or 50 km inland, it is difficult to discern where sea begins and river ends.

Channels change and shorelines move so that where one is today, the other may be tomorrow. Untold millions of tonnes of silt and mud have been dumped by the river at the joining with the sea and both seem bent on waging, backward and forth, a battle for possession. Through millennia of abandoned sediments the river snakes its way, possessively, while the sea claws endlessly at the shore, mote by mote, grain by grain, shifting it ceaselessly away.

The delta of the Zambezi is ancient: the river has been flowing into the sea in this region for millions of years (Chapter 1). Hardly surprising, then, that the delta should be of such enormous size. Shaped like a huge triangle, with a sea frontage of 120 km stretching from Quelimane in the north to the Melambe mouth in the south and a distance inland of more than 100 km, the entire area covers about 8 000 km².[1]

This great alluvial fan, across which the Zambezi flows, is entirely flat and comprises a remarkable mix of vegetation types which, controlled by soil type, water table and salinity, reflect the gradual approach to the Indian Ocean.

As the Zambezi approaches the sea, the woodlands of Mozambique's vast coastal plain, which have followed the river faithfully, seem suddenly to halt as if a line, invisible to us, were drawn through the sandy soil at their feet. A few trees, perhaps more reckless or daring than the others, set out to conquer the vast grassy plain by tiptoeing onto it from one giant termite mound to another. But these hardy types quickly lose confidence, diminish in size with growing distance from the tree line and soon disappear altogether. The great grasslands of the delta have begun.

Threading through the grasslands in distinct belts, where the soils are suitable, are stands of Borassus palms. Giants of their family, they dominate the skyline like guardians of the lesser palms that cluster in their slender shadow. Vegetable ivory and the graceful *reclinata* are found here also but soon soil conditions change and the palms are seen no more. Once again the grass holds away.

As the shore is approached more closely, the water table rises and the grass is frequently inundated. Immense flooded fields reflect the blue and white of sky and cloud and, through the image, trails of trees languidly follow slow-moving streams. The delta turns into a patchwork mantle of matching greens, securely stitched in crazy patterns with a double line of dark green riverine trees.

At last the ocean is reached and here the grass gives way to mud, salt and the mangrove army that vigorously defends the shore. A solid phalanx of green, the mangroves hold back the sand and soil of Africa in twice daily battles with the waves.

The northern side of the triangle is where most of the people live. Behind the shelter of the coastal dunes, perched along the crest of others inland, away from the endless flooding, they make a living from cassava which thrives on the slopes and fertile dune valleys. They also enjoy the bounty of coconuts which grow wild, and some work in the well-ordered plantations.

John Barnes[2] was employed for three months in this area in 1974 and came away glad of the experience but not enthusiastic about returning. Temperatures are high, averaging 34 °C to 36 °C in the hot months and reaching a staggering maximum of 45 °C. Humidity, at 80%, is also high and in combination with the temperature makes life almost impossible.[3]

In the relatively small inhabited area, conditions are overcrowded. Malaria and syphilis are common and the region is generally unhealthy. Jiggers, those beastly creatures that burrow into the skin of one's feet, laying eggs there that cause them to swell painfully, are so numerous that John spent three months in wellingtons as the only way of avoiding them.[4]

Living at subsistence level, many of the people depend on fishing, using the delta and venturing out to sea. On this coast one sees the stitched bark boats, remarkable vessels made exactly as their name suggests. The bark is stripped from the boles of great trees, but not necessarily in one piece. A boat I saw was made up of some nine sections, all sewn with thread made from the husks of coconuts. The vessel is shaped rather like a canoe, is lightweight, sturdy and carries two people as well as a small sail. Generally, it is used within reefs, sheltered areas and lagoons of the coast.

The outrigger canoe which is said to provide evidence of links between Indonesia and the eastern coast of Africa (see Chapter 7) is also found on this coast, not at the delta itself, but much further north beyond Mozambique Island. Having found much favour in the north, why the idea has not travelled further south is a mystery.[5]

It is to the north of the delta, also, that the better soils are found. Here is the black, deep alluvium of the great sugar estates which themselves may have grown out of the successful farms of early Portuguese agriculturists. Daniel Rankin, former Acting Consul at Mozambique, wrote of his experiences and observations in the delta in 1890.[6] He praised the estate of Sumbo on the Chinde River (see later in this chapter), owned and run by Senhor Caesar d'Andrade, and was excited by the variety and quality of the fruit, vegetables and cereals that were grown there. Rankin visualised an agricultural empire reaching from horizon to horizon but, as in other things, he was perhaps a little too enthusiastic.

Sena Sugar, one of three sugar-producing corporations in Mozambique, owns vast estates with refineries on either side of the Zambezi at the head of the delta. To combat annual flooding, they have installed an extensive system of dykes, barriers and canals that has completely tamed this portion of the delta.

Established in 1893, Sena Sugar once employed 8 000 Africans and 500 Europeans and contributed significantly to the country's foreign earnings. Now, however, like the rest of the country, the estates seem to have fallen victim to the tragic conflict. Mozambique once produced 360 000 tonnes of sugar a year; a recent annual figure was 18 000 tonnes.

Although they did not introduce them, the sugar estates provided the economic activity that helped support a fleet of stern-wheelers, paddle ships of the old Mississippi type. Originally put on the river in 1878 by the Livingstonia Central Africa Company, their task was to ferry goods from Chinde in the delta up the Zambezi and the Shire River to Chiromo in what is now Malawi. With names like *Bruce, Scott* and *Sir Harry Johnston,* the Scottish connection was not hard to discern.[7]

Fifteen years later, in 1893, the Central African Lakes Company took over the assets of the previous owners, including the original steamers, and shortly added more. Soon a sizeable fleet was operating. Some of the vessels were quite large, more than 30 m in length in one case, and capable of moving up to 70 tonnes. Often, the paddle steamers travelled with barges lashed to either side.

As the years passed, more ships, with less Celtic names, were added: in the early 1900s *Cobra, Centipede, Scorpion, Hydra* and *Mosquito* joined the ranks.

Slowly, railways were creeping across the vast interior of Africa, bringing with them more efficient handling of freight. In 1922, a line reached the south bank of the Zambezi from Beira and its arrival, together with the promise of a bridge across the river at Sena, sealed the fate of these romantic steamers. As if they had already been written off, ten of these ships were destroyed at Chinde when a tornado or hurricane struck in 1922.

Despite the dual threat, some of the vessels continued in service, many with the sugar estates. In 1970, for example, Sena Estates still owned and ran nine of them.[8] The *Hydra,* built in about 1903, was still working in 1962 when it was sold to Portuguese owners and probably went on working for many years after that. Despite the lack of success Livingstone had in the choice of a suitable vessel for the river, the old paddle-steamers showed that the right kind of boat did exist and proved their point with almost a century of service.[9]

What was once known as the Marromeu Buffalo Reserve holds the remaining herds of wildlife in the Zambezi's delta. Marromeu is unusual among protected areas for game: it must be one of the few in Africa where large numbers of many different varieties of game find sanctuary in a freshwater wetland beside the sea. This uncommon combination gives rise to some unusual sights.

Where else in Africa, for example, would one see 1 000 buffalo churning the sands of unblemished beaches and watching with bovine curiosity the ceaseless sweeping of the waves? Where have you seen a reedbuck bounding through the receding foam? Where could you see a troop of baboons methodically working their way across the sand, their nimble fingers snatching at the racing crabs, nothing left behind them but innumerable discarded claws and the occasional half-chewed shell? [10]

Because of conservation in this area game, once hunted to virtual extinction, has slowly been returning. Numbers of hippo and elephant have both increased, the former to such a point that they are now common. This must be the only place in Africa where hippos bathe regularly in the sea and are often seen as much as 2 km off shore! [11]

Crocodiles have not been recorded in the sea off the mouth of the Zambezi but this has been noted from elsewhere. On several occasions, for instance, crocodiles have been encountered in the sea off St Lucia in Natal and a fight between a shark and a crocodile has been witnessed. After a particularly severe flood in 1917, one crocodile was seen 10 km out to sea, a fact noted down in the ship's log by the master at the time.[12]

Fish eagles are as common in the delta as they are elsewhere along the Zambezi and undoubtedly have to modify their diet in the saline estuary, for some of the food they commonly eat is not found there. Reports from elsewhere along the coast describe the birds catching and eating young waterfowl, stranded fish, mullet and carrion. There is also a delightful account of a young fish eagle wrestling with the complexities of an octopus. Eight wriggling tentacles are more than a talon-full, it seems, and the bird struggled to fly in the face of the octopus's violent objections and attempts to interfere with the eagle's wings. Both plummeted towards the sea as the eagle tried to stab the life from its uncooperative meal, recovering at the last possible moment and gaining height before beginning the stabbing match again. Eventually the eagle won and was seen flying on an even keel with its vanquished prey hanging limply from it.[13]

Two little-known curiosities of the coast in this region are its turtles and dugongs. The former are of particular interest for several reasons.

There are five species of marine turtle found along the south-east African coast. One of them, the leatherback, does not occur as far north as the Zambezi but all others are present and abundant, although threatened by domestic hunting.[14] Overexploitation of a marine resource at times when other food may be scarce is easy to understand, tragic though it may be. However, turtle populations have proved themselves to be enormously resilient.

For example, on the island of Aldabra in the Comoros, no management of turtle harvesting was initially undertaken. The result was that more and more animals were killed annually, with a peak in 1912 of 9 000 turtles being slaughtered on this one very small island. Controls followed, but only after the population of turtles had been decimated. Eventually the turtle population recovered, but never to its former levels; today less than 1 000 females nest there.[15]

The experience in Madagascar also shows that turtles respond to protection. The wholesale slaughter of nesting turtles was stopped by the French authorities in 1923 and now the island is probably the main source for restocking the entire region. The same results followed the protection, from 1963, of turtle nesting sites on the Maputaland (Tongaland) beaches in northern Natal. Since then, yearly totals of nesting females visiting the beach have shown a continued increase.[16]

Turtles are of interest for other reasons also. It is widely known today that the future sex of a crocodile embryo is determined by the temperature at which the egg is incubated. It is possible today, for example, to take a clutch of crocodile eggs and to incubate them at such a temperature that all the young turn out to be males or all females, depending on your choice! What is not as well known is that the sex/temperature link was not discovered in crocodile research.

As early as 1929 and 1930 scientists had shown that temperature during the development of tadpoles determines sex differentiation under certain circumstances. Building on this idea, other researchers found the same to be true of fish and of lizards. Pursuing the idea further, a Dr C.L. Yntema, in America, began an in-depth study of the phenomenon using the turtle as his subject. He hatched eggs of the common snapping turtle and discovered that all those incubated at 20 °C and 30 °C developed into females while 100% of those reared at 24 °C became males.[17]

Having established conclusively that the level of temperature played an important part in determining sex, Yntema went on to prove that the timing of the temperature during the period of incubation was even more important.[18] In the last decade, this work has been transferred to researchers working on crocodiles and has proved to be of great importantce for commercial crocodile farms.

One cannot but admire the ingenuity of crocodiles and turtles. Both lay eggs in an inverted cone-shaped hole scooped out of the sand in which the eggs are placed in layers, one on top of the other. It makes perfectly good sense, when one thinks about it, that those at the top of the pile, being nearer the warmth of the surface, will be at a higher temperature than those at the lowest part of the nest. How clever to let the natural gradation of temperature control the distribution of sexes among the clutch.

A second, less well-known inhabitant of the coast and the Zambezi delta is the dugong. This extraordinary creature, a marine mammal, belongs to the order Sirenia. It is always a pleasure to find that those responsible for the dull job of scientifically naming animals, have a sense of humour. Sirenia is a reference to those svelte and alluring young maidens, the Sirens, whose song was intended to lead both Odysseus and the Argonauts to an unpleasant fate.

Sirenia, which occur worldwide, are undoubtedly responsible for the mermaid myth and may even underlie the Siren story itself, for in some versions the Sirens develop fish's tails. As mammals, dugongs suckle their young and have two mammary glands between the front flippers for this purpose.

I have to admit that I would put up with a great deal before swapping a female of my own species for one with a mass of more than 180 kg, a length of between 2,5 and 3,2 m, a thick hide which is brown to grey in colour and a mouth surrounded by extremely thick bristles.[19] After all, what could I buy her for Christmas? I suppose, however, that the vaguely female form might be sufficient to jolt the loins of a lusty sailor, far from home, allowing his imagination to do the rest.

It is said that dugongs generally do not tolerate fresh water and are therefore unlikely to be found in the great estuaries of the coast. Several reports contradict this, however, and dugongs have been recorded in the Maputo River, the Incomati and the Luabo, one of the major distributaries of the Zambezi mouth.[20]

Dugongs are found along the entire length of the Mozambique coast but are concentrated in areas such as Maputo Bay, the Bazaruto archipelago, Antonio Enes and northwards from Mozambique Island where seaweed is abundant. As vegetarians, dugongs eat seaweed; as omnivores, humans are quite happy to eat the dugong — and therein lies a problem for the dugong.[21]

A survey in 1971 concluded that while the range of the dugong had remained unaltered since previous surveys, the populations did appear to be declining — mainly because of man's predation. The area of most concentrated hunting is somewhat north of the Zambezi, in the region of Antonio Enes. Here, as many as six dugongs a month are caught and sold in the local market.[22]

Despite the deliberate hunting in Antonio Enes, an aerial search there at a time when conditions for observation were not good revealed 27 of the creatures in just two flights.[23] The implication is that more may have been present. One would hope that this is the case for the market demand would otherwise surely eliminate the species very quickly.

The fishermen off the African coast catch dugongs with large-mesh nets that allow the juveniles through. Some Aborigines in Australia use power-boats with outboard engines. With these, they chase and harpoon the dugong and, with amazingly little effort, kill it by drowning. The ease with which these creatures are despatched prompted one researcher to apply lessons in capture stress, learnt on land, to these marine mammals. Sure enough, his investigations showed that, just like terrestrial mammals, dugongs are susceptible to the stress of capture. The cause is partly ruptured muscle fibres and partly anaerobic metabolism, which leads to a build-up in levels of lactic acid and a marked drop in blood pH. Capture stress is measured by the level of serum potassium in the blood. It seems that, once the process has started, its effects are rapid. An instance is given where a dugong, captured in a net, collapsed and died before it could be cut free, even though it was able to breathe freely.[24] The reader might recall the examples of shock and capture stress given in Chapter 8.

The Zambezi Wildlife Utilisation Area, declared in 1981, extends over 20 000 km². It incorporates Marromeu on the south bank of the Zambezi in the delta, as well as much of the surrounding area, and has two impor-tant functions: to conserve the wildlife asset within its boundaries and to exploit it through cropping and other means to benefit the people in the region.

A 1982 estimate was that the protected region contained about 45 000 buffalo, 1 000 elephant, 40 000 waterbuck, 5 000 hippo and 3 500 sable antelope. Other animals included nyala, impala, kudu, black rhino, leopard and lion. The vast protected area includes a corridor that links it with the once famous Gorongosa National Park.

Since about 1938 organised, licensed professional hunting had been permitted in the delta but it was poorly controlled and there seems little doubt that the resource was badly abused. In the years 1950 to 1960, for example, between 7 000 and 12 000 buffalo were killed, and in the first five years of that period, about 4 000 crocodile. Professional meat hunting was also allowed and poaching, at various times, took place at very high levels. Eventually, in 1974, all kinds of hunting were banned but poaching then got completely out of control.

Between 1976 and 1980 it was decided by the government of Mozam-bique that controlled cropping should be permitted in order to utilise the food resource which was otherwise being wasted. The scheme had some rewards, for poaching was immediately reduced and the local people re-ceived some benefit from the herds of game in the area.

This success led to the declaration of the Wildlife Utilisation Area. Having created greater involvement of the local people and more systematic control both of organised hunting and of poaching, the scheme appears to have become a great success.

According to the man behind its inception and organisation, José Tello, 'now, all organised and commercial poaching has been stopped [a result not yet achieved in many other wildlife areas, including some national parks and game reserves]. Much of the seasonal poaching and fishing by rural people invading the floodplains, mostly in the dry season, has also been stopped.'[25]

Tello gives figures for the meat 'harvested' from the area between 1976 and 1982. No annual figures are included but, in those six years, among the 14 386 animals culled were 13 087 buffalo, 1 192 waterbuck and 6 elephant. He says that the total production, which includes fresh carcasses, dry meat, biltong, internal organs and stomachs, amounted to the equivalent of 16 000 cattle carcasses. A sustainable yield of 2 500 'free' beef cattle every year is an outstanding achievement.

Since 1981 hunting safaris have been started in the area again, with overseas clients paying high fees, and are also reported as a great success. At the same time other activities, newly being undertaken, include limited agriculture (to feed the workers), the rearing of poultry, exploitation of fish and the establishment of a small crocodile farm.

Other indicators of success are taken to include the return of elephant and the increasing use by them of all habitats within the protected area. At the same time, despite continued culling, the number of buffalo and waterbuck has not been reduced. The first appearance of impala, as well as the increase in monkey, hippo, crocodile and leopard populations all tend to confirm the optimism.[26]

An interesting approach to the better control of poaching has been to employ some of the more infamous poachers within the staff of the region's administration. Now they are skinners, hunters or game guards.

It is seven years since José Tello wrote his paper and I have not been able to find out what has happened since. The war in Mozambique appears to have intensified and spread in that time and there are long stretches of the Zambezi where people do not, cannot, go at all, for fear of warring factions. In many of the rural areas all forms of administration have completely collapsed and the importance of wildlife as a future resource will have shrunk to nothing against the immediate need to fill hungry stomachs.

If one were able to view the delta from a helicopter one would see that it is not entirely flat and that, traced across its surface in numerous localities, are low, raised ridges which are the relic beaches of forgotten shorelines.

The delta is ancient and consequently rather like a geological history book. For in its deep layers of sediments are indelibly recorded the Zambezi's wanderings and the ebb and flow of the sea as it, responding to northern ice ages, rose or fell, engulfing or stranding the African coast.

Sea levels have varied enormously. About 13 000 years ago, the sea was 50 m lower than at present; since then, it rose rapidly, with many minor fluctuations, to near modern levels about 6 000 years ago.[27] Generally speaking, it has remained there but recent trends show the sea level again to be rising slowly. Changes in the volume of the sea are directly linked to the amount of water that is locked up in the world's ice caps.

This is an important factor in considering the fate and future of a stretch of coast but it is sometimes difficult to separate the effect of a rising sea when, at the same time, an entire region might be sinking, because of iso-static loading. Rivers like the Zambezi carry unimaginable quantities of silt to the sea, so great in fact that the total mass, collected over centuries, may be enough to depress the earth's surface in that particular area.

The ancient beaches, which reflect the constantly changing level of the sea, are most common nearer the shore but some are to be found as much as 30 km from the coast.[28] This underlines the relative flatness of the region and highlights a point of interest about the coast itself. Perhaps because of the sediment deposits made upon it, the continental shelf is extremely wide, extending to the east for 140 km. The effect of such a great expanse of shallow shelf is to give Beira and the Zambezi mouth, at 6,4 m, the highest tidal range anywhere on the African coast.[29]

Given the great quantity of sand about the river mouth it is not sur-prising that a delta should have developed. Nor is it surprising that the delta is dynamic, constantly changing, or that, over centuries perhaps, dis-tributaries appear and disappear, channels open and close.

This fact has been a great plague to mariners. Perhaps not to those of earlier centuries, for their trade and travel was moulded to the form of a small, light boat. These travelled great distances but hugged the shore, relying on speed to run for safety and a shallow draft to take them over the innumerable sand bars of the river. Perhaps David Livingstone was the first to bring the wrong type of boat to the Zambezi. The *Pearl*, the ex-pedition's main vessel and the one they hoped would take them to Tete, reached only 65 km from the sea, leaving the asthmatic *MaRobert* to do the remainder, painfully wheezing and resting upon each sand bar on the way!

It also took the Zambezi expedition some time just to enter the river they had come to explore because they could not find the way in. Days were spent steaming up promising leads that eventually closed in upon them or opened out onto the great floodplains, preventing further progress and forcing them to turn back. Finally, entry into the main river was made by means of a route up a channel, the Kongone, unknown even to the Portuguese![30]

There was a route into the Zambezi proper that bypassed the delta completely. This led from Quelimane in the north, almost due east until it struck the Zambezi near Mopeia or Mazaro, about 120 km inland. The disadvantage was that the channel dried up or was blocked before it reached the main river and a portage was required over the last 20 km or 30 km.

It seems certain that the Kwa Kwa, Qwa Qwa or Mutu Channel, as it is variously called, was once the course of the Zambezi itself which flowed then into the sea at Quelimane. Long ago the channel closed but was, and is, still used, despite the portage involved. Because of this, Quelimane, which offered a deep and sheltered estuary although a risky access to the sea, was established as a port and may well be numbered among the oldest ports on the coast, for Arab traders were using it long before the Portuguese.

Livingstone had been made H.M. Honorary Consul at Quelimane and the tiny town was the centre to which passengers and mail for the Zambezi expedition were directed. It was also where Livingstone went, at the end of the expedition, in order to return to England. Ships of the British Navy, ever on the lookout for Livingstone, had been instructed to call in at Quelimane when passing. One ship, the *Dart,* did so and sent a boat ashore. Tragically, it had trouble in crossing the bar and overturned. All eight men in it, including the captain and two officers, were drowned, a fact that caused Livingstone bitter sorrow[31] and graphically illustrated the difficulty of using the river as a route into the interior.

Unknown, unmapped and unsuitable for navigation. Thus might the mouth of the Zambezi have been described a little over 100 years ago. However, change was afoot. With the rapid development of Nyasaland, some improved means of access to the Zambezi became essential and, in 1890, a Daniel J. Rankin, formerly Acting Consul at Mozambique, reported to the world at large, and the Royal Geographic Society in particular, that he had solved the problems of entering the Zambezi and of getting supplies to Nyasaland.

Rankin reported at some length on his investigations and described his discovery of a channel, the Chinde River, that led from the sea to the main Zambezi, bypassing the central part of the delta with its complicated maze of waterways.

The British government had declared a protectorate over British Central Africa on 14 May 1891 and had appointed Harry Johnston as the first commissioner. On his way to take up his appointment, and undoubtedly because of Rankin's work, Johnston 'acquired' squatter rights and a section of river frontage on the Chinde, a river region hitherto quite uninhabited.

Later this settlement was ratified by the Portuguese and 10 hectares with 400 m of river front were formally leased to the British in an agreement that dates from 1 January 1892. This was the beginning of the settlement of Chinde.[32]

In its time, Chinde became quite infamous. Unattractive, unhealthy, sitting on a tiny spit of sand in a mangrove swamp, which the sea threatened to sweep away at any moment, and located in what seemed the most malo-dorous, malarious part of Africa possible. Yet, for all its disadvantages, Chinde was at least memorable and not without a certain charm of its own.

The settlement grew and, unwillingly, the Portuguese added more ground to the lease. Chinde certainly flourished as a transport settlement and, in 1896, was able to boast 21 British and 31 Protected Person Residents!

By 1910 there were two double-storey houses (admittedly in wood and corrugated iron) and there was also a not entirely smooth tennis court. This splendid addition to the sporting amenities of the centre was innovative and many decades ahead of its time in two respects at least. Firstly, to reduce the glare from its cement surface, the Senior Naval Officer had coated it with olive-green paint. Secondly, perhaps to add interest, the Assistant Agent had ventured his considerable artistic talents in a riotous display of beautifully painted flowers, neatly arranged in and occupying most of the four corners of the court.

It is reported that many players, dancing lightly from buttercup to marigold, sunflower to rose, violet to iris, found the experience unnerving, bizarre and somewhat offputting. The court was not appreciated as much as the artist might have liked.[33]

Tennis, however, was not the proper business of Chinde. The settlement's purpose was to facilitate the handling of goods to and from the burgeoning Protectorate of Nyasaland. And burgeoning it was. In 1904, for example, one German, two Portuguese and 19 British steamers called at Chinde. They delivered 4 544 tonnes of freight and 3 882 passengers. All of this was transferred to the coast by lighters (for the larger steamers anchored 30 km off-shore) who lifted the cargo and passengers from boat to barge by basket.

The transfer of all this activity by smaller boat up the Zambezi and the Shire to Nyasaland took place under the protective presence of two British Navy gunboats. One was the Herald. The other was called the Mostqito![34]

The future life of Chinde was limited, however, and it is curious to see how a succession of events brought it to an end. Erosion of the bank was a constant problem and the settlement, therefore, was continually 'on the move'. By 1922, the original grant of land had been entirely eroded away.

Chinde's role as a transit camp was about to be successfully challenged by the railways which reached the south bank of the Zambezi, near Sena, in 1922. As if these difficulties were not enough, nature delivered the final blow in the form of a violent cyclone which struck on 24 February 1922.[35]

In that disastrous storm, 55 people were drowned, buildings were deroofed, damaged or completely knocked down. There were 12 stern-wheelers in the harbour of which only two survived the catastrophe. The rest were driven aground — some into the streets of the town — badly damaged or sunk.[36]

It simply was not worth rebuilding Chinde. With the opening of the rail-way, its *raison d'être* had gone and in 1923, the British Concession was abandoned. The Protectorate Annual Report for the year tersely com-mented, 'British interests in the port of Chinde . . . have ceased to exist.'[37]

The future of the delta, as the ecosystem that it now is, is uncertain because the natural systems that maintain it have been interfered with by man. Dams at Kariba and Cahora Bassa have reduced the quantity of silt reaching the area and have radically altered the flood regime. Three imme-diate consequences of this are already evident.

Regulation of the river flow has stopped or reduced the flooding. As a result, grazing is no longer protected and destruction of the grass cover is taking place. The highly nutritious grasses, which support a large buffalo population and are heavily grazed upon by them, were previously rested for part of the year under floodwater. The decrease in the intensity of deep flooding and consequent reduction in the deposit of alluvia will, in the long term, adversely affect the fertility of the area. Less waterlogged than for-merly, the floodplains are being encroached upon by woody species.[38]

Change is synonymous with the Zambezi and to see it in perspective we can first review changes that have taken place to date before finally con-sidering what the future may hold for this fascinating river.

The natural role of the Zambezi has not altered since the time when hominids came to its shores. It includes the provision of water for people, their animals and their crops, a means as well as a route for transportation and, through the fish and plants that are found within it, a source of protein.

Modern man has superimposed much that is new on this archaic role. Two major hydroelectric schemes have dramatically, and some would say drastically, altered the quantity of sediments carried by the river and also the nature of its annual flow. Two areas are threatened by these changes: Mana Pools, part of a World Heritage Site in the Zambezi Valley, and the delta at the coast.

Already the river is being utilised in ways undreamed of 100 years ago. Paul Connolly, a friend of mine, literally opened the whole of Zimbabwe's Zambezi to my personal acquaintance through his generous loan of canoes and rafts. Paul's organisation offers three distinctive and memorable ways of enjoying the river: kyaking the white water above Victoria Falls, rafting the rapids below it and canoeing more than 300 km from Kariba to Kanyemba. Many others have emulated him with similar services.

The dams themselves have generated a range of new and different ways in which the Zambezi is used. These include competitive team fishing, underwater, leisure and commercial fishing, game viewing, sailing and power boating, all part of a rapidly growing tourist industry. A sight-seeing, commercial float plane service is being considered and hot air bal-looning will be available.

Good evidence of some future trends is found on the north bank, in Zambia, downstream of Chirundu. Here, on the farm Zambezia, in one of the most beautiful settings on the river, the owner, Farlie Winson, says he has spent much of his personal fortune developing a waterpump driven by the four-knot current in the river. A design has been finalised and can pump 22 000 ℓ/h a distance of 8 km with a lift of 13 m.[39]

Farlie claims that there are 340 000 arable hectares on the north bank of the Zambezi and the west side of the Luangwa, outside the game reserve. These, he said, are not being used by subsistence farmers because they lack the water. His pump will deliver that to them at a low recurrent cost and it is his belief that this will enable them to produce two crops a year, with colossal economic impact for the region as a whole.

The electricity needs of Zambia, Zimbabwe and Mozambique have been satisfied for the immediate future but, sooner or later, more will be required. There is a powerful coal lobby in Zimbabwe, which has huge reserves of this resource; for as long as the lobby remains powerful, coal-fired stations will meet the country's needs. Despite this, eventually, another dam will be built. Almost certainly, it will be in Batoka Gorge. The damming of Mupata Gorge still remains a possibility for by building a slightly lower wall, a useful dam can be created without flooding Mana Pools.

I believe three factors will underlie future utilisation of the Zambezi. One is the growth of the SADCC (Southern African Development Co-ordination Conference) which incorporates nine southern and central African territories in a co-operative effort to improve their self-sufficiency, productivity and standards of living. If this effort succeeds, enormous growth will be generated.

Ultimately, there will be peace in Mozambique. This second factor will also lead to rapid economic growth. Thus two of the issues that I see affecting the future of the Zambezi involve the consequences of rapid growth — more power, increased consumption of water, greater use of the fishing and recreational resources and, also important, more pollution in the form of industrial and agricultural waste.

The third and final factor involves South Africa and Botswana. South Africa, industrial giant of the subcontinent, has reached, in terms of its water supply, the limits of growth and, already, in periods of drought, its water consumption has exceeded supply so that consumption has had to be modified. There are short-term solutions to this problem which are currently being pursued, but they only briefly postpone the grim reality.

Botswana, an infinitesimally small economy compared to South Africa, has just over a million residents and water supplies in that arid, drought-ridden country have already reached a critical stage in several areas. By the end of the millennium both South Africa and Botswana will be drawing water from the Zambezi, as the only viable supply big enough to meet their combined needs. The Okavango River is an alternative but it will be more costly and environmentally more risky.

The needs of humans will not be denied, the water of the Zambezi will be consumed in their cities and on their farms and the river will be used again to generate more power. The strategy for the future must strike a balance between the needs of man and his environment. Encouraging signs that this might be possible are to be found in the SADCC's Zacplan. The Zambezi Action Plan is an historic agreement between nations who share an interest in a common river system to work together for its sound environmental management. I would like to wish them wisdom and understanding, patience and tact. The job that lies ahead of them, with its myriad of conflicting demands, is not easy.

Savage, wild, gentle, beautiful, frightening and endlessly interesting; the Zambezi is all of these things. It has dominated three years of my life and I have come to stand in awe of it and to be absorbed by it. I know that we must use it and all I ask is that, in doing so, we act not only for ourselves but for future generations.

References

CHAPTER 1: THE GREAT AFRICAN DIVIDE

1. Verboom, W.C. & Brunt, M.A. 1970. *An Ecological Survey of Western Province, Zambia, with Special Reference to the Fodder Resources. Vol. 1, The Environment. Land Resource Study No. 8,* Directorate of Overseas Surveys, England, p. 38.
2. Broderick, T.J. 1976. *Explanation of the Geological Map of the Country East of Kariba.* Rhodesia Geological Survey, Short Report No. 43, Government of Zimbabwe, Harare.
3. Zimbabwe Govt. 1985. *Provisional Geological Map of Zimbabwe.* Zimbabwe Geological Survey, Government of Zimbabwe, Harare.
4. Vail, J.R. 1968. 'The Southern Extension of the East African Rift System and Related Igneous Activity', in *Geologische Rundschau,* Vol. 57, p. 605.
5. ibid. p. 610.
6. Dixey, F. 1928. 'The Lupata Gorge on the Lower Zambezi', in *Geographical Journal,* Vol. 72, December, p. 452.
7. Lister, L.A. 1988. Personal communication.
8. Bell-Cross, G. 1982. 'The Biogeography of the River Zambezi Fish Fauna', Unpublished M.Sc. thesis, Dept. of Zoolology, University of Natal, Pietermaritzburg.
9. Thomas D.S.G. & Shaw, P.A. 1988. 'Late Cainozoic Drainage Evolution in the Zambezi Basin: Geomorphological Evidence from the Kalahari Rim', in *Journal of African Earth Sciences,* in press.
10. Bond, G. 1975. 'The Geology and Formation of the Victoria Falls', in *Mosi-oa-Tunya: A Handbook to the Victoria Falls Region,* Ed. Phillipson, D.W., Longman, London, p. 24.
11. Lister, L.A. 1979. 'The Geomorphic Evolution of Zimbabwe Rhodesia', in *Transactions of the Geological Society of South Africa,* Vol. 82, p. 369.
12. Cooke, J.H. 1979. 'The Origin of Makgadikgadi Pans', in *Botswana Notes and Records,* Vol. 11, pp. 37-42.
13. Mallick, D.I.J., Habgood, F. & Skinner, A.C. 1981. 'Geological Interpretation of Landsat Imagery and Air Photography of Botswana', in *Overseas Geological and Mineral Resources,* No. 56, pp. 1-35.
14. Shaw, P.A. 1987. Personal communication.
15. Lister, L.A. 1979. op. cit.
16. Lamplugh, G.W. 1905. 'Report on an Investigation of the Batoka Gorge and Adjacent Portions of the Zambesi Valley', in *Report of the British Association for the Advancement of Science.* p. 298.
17. Cox, K.G. 1970. 'Tectonics and Vulcanism of the Karroo Period and their Bearing on the Postulated Fragmentation of Gondwanaland', in *African Magnetism and Tectonics,* Eds Clifford, T.N. and Gass, I.G., Oliver & Boyd, London, p. 211.
18. Bond, G. 1975. op. cit. p. 20.
19. Dingle, R.V., Siesser, W.G. & Newton, A.R. 1983. *Mesozoic and Tertiary Geology of Southern Africa,* A.A. Balkema, Rotterdam, p. 7.
20. Cox, K.G. 1970. op. cit.
21. Irwin, P., Ackhurst, J. & Irwin, D. 1980. *A Field Guide to the Natal Drakensberg,* Wildlife Society of Southern Africa, Durban, p. 66.
22. Willock, C. 1974. *Africa's Rift Valley,* Time-Life Books, Amsterdam, pp. 17-26.
23. Stagman, J.G. 1978. *An Outline of the Geology of Rhodesia,* Rhodesia Geological Survey Bulletin No. 80, Reprinted edition, 1981, Government of Zimbabwe, Harare, p. 5.

24. Wellington, J.H. 1955. *Southern Africa: A Geological Study, Vol. 1, Physical Geography*, Cambridge University Press, Cambridge, p. 401.

25. Tavener-Smith, R. 1958. 'The Development of the Mid-Zambezi Valley in Northern Rhodesia since Early Karroo Times', in *The Geological Magazine*, Vol. 95, No. 2, March-April, p. 105-18.

26. Bond, G. 1967. 'A Review of Karroo Sedimentation and Lithology in Southern Rhodesia', Paper presented at First Symposium in Gondwana Stratigraphy, International Union of Geological Sciences, pp. 173-95.

27. _____ 1974. 'The Stratigraphic Distribution of Plant and Animal Macro-Fossils in the Karoo System of the Mid-Zambezi Region', *Arnoldia*, Vol. 7, No. 3, 2 August, p. 5.

28. Lister, L.A. 1979. op. cit. p. 363-70.

29. Bond, G. 1973. *The Palaeontology of Rhodesia*, Rhodesia Geological Survey Bulletin No. 70, Government of Zimbabwe, Harare.

30. _____ 1974. op. cit.

31. _____ 1972. 'Fossil Vertebrate Studies in Rhodesia: A New Dinosaur (Reptilia: Saurischia) from Near the Trias-Jurassic Boundary', *Arnoldia*, Vol. 5, No. 30, 31 July, p. 1.

32. Bingham, M.G. 1980. 'The Vegetation of Mwinilunga District', in *Zambia Geographical Association, Regional Handbook*, No. 8., Ed. Johnson, D.S., p. 31.

33. Letcher, O. 1913. *The Bonds of Africa*, John Long, London, p. 26.

34. Milligan, E., Nightingale, C.R. & Hess, L.R. 1975. *A Brief History of Sakeji School*, Published by Sakeji School, Box 20, Ikelenge, Via Kitwe, Zambia.

35. Fisher, W.S. & Hoyte, J. 1987. *Ndotolu*, Revised edition, Lunda-Ndembu Publications, Ikelenge Zambia, p. 92 (Formerly: *Africa Looks Ahead*, Pickering and Inglis, London, 1948).

36. ibid. p. 118.

37. ibid. p. 105-6.

38. Barnett, G.G. 1988. Personal communication.

CHAPTER 2: A RIVER KINGDOM

1. Verboom, W.C. 1974. 'The Barotse Loose Sands of Western Province, Zambia', in *Zambia Geographical Association Magazine*, No. 27, July, p. 15.

2. Verboom, W.C. & Brunt, M.A. 1970. *An Ecological Survey of Western Province, Zambia, with Special Reference to the Fodder Resources, Vol. 1, The Environment*, Land Resource Study No. 8, Directorate of Overseas Surveys, England, p. 49.

3. Muuka, L.S. 1966. 'The Colonization of Barotseland in the 17th Century', in *The Zambesian Past: Studies in Central African History*, Eds Stokes, E. & Brown, R., Manchester University Press, p. 248.

4. Caplan, G.L. 1970. *The Elites of Barotseland 1878-1969*, C. Hurst & Co., London. p. 1.

5. Jalla, A.D. 1921. *History, Traditions and Legends of the Barotse Nation*, Revised 2nd edition, Paris Evangelical Mission, Lialui, Barotseland, Zambia, p. 4.

6. Needham, D.E. 1980. *Iron Age to Independence; A History of Central Africa*, Longman, London, pp. 32-4.

7. Edgecombe, R. 1987. 'The Mefecane or Difaquane', in *An Illustrated History of South Africa*, Eds Cameron T. & Spies, S.B., Jonathan Ball, Johannesburg, p. 115.

8. ibid. pp. 115-26.

9. Smith, E.W. 1956. 'Sebetwane and the Makololo', in *African Studies*, Vol. 15, No. 2, p. 4.

10. Tlou, T. & Campbell, A.C. 1984. *History of Botswana*, Macmillan Botswana, p. 106.

11. Tabler, E.C. 1955. *The Far Interior*, A.A. Balkema, Cape Town, p. 187.

12. Marshall Hole, H. 1967. *The Making of Rhodesia*, Frank Cass & Co., London, p. 205.

13. Tabler, E.C. 1955. op. cit. p. 196.

14. Gibbons, St. H. 1897. 'Barotseland and the Tribes of the Upper Zambezi', in *Proceedings of the Royal Colonial Institute*, Vol. 29, p. 263.

15. Tabler, E.C. 1963. *Trade and Travel in Early Barotseland*, Chatto and Windus, London, p. 8.

16. Mainga, M. 1973. *Bulozi under the Luyana Kings*, Longman, London, p. 128.

17. Tabler, E.C. 1963. op. cit. p. 5.

18. Gann, L.H. 1969. *A History of Northern Rhodesia*, Humanities Press, New York, p. 41.

19. Tabler, E.C. 1963. op. cit. pp. 6-7.

20. ibid.
21. ibid. p. 4.
22. Gann, L.H. 1969. op. cit. p. 47.
23. Mackintosh, C.W. 1950. 'Some Pioneer Missions of Northern Rhodesia and Nyasaland', in *The Occasional Papers of the Rhodes-Livingstone Museum*, Nos 1-16 (in one volume), p. 257.
24. ibid. p. 263.
25. Marshall Hole, H. 1967. op. cit. pp. 214-15.
26. ibid.
27. Needham, D.E. 1980. op. cit. p. 103.
28. Mackintosh, C.W. 1950. op. cit. p. 263.
29. Marshall Hole, H. 1967. op. cit. pp. 212-21.
30. ibid.
31. ibid.
32. Needham, D.E. 1980. op. cit. p. 103.
33. Caplan, G.L. 1970. op. cit. p. 55.
34. Needham, D.E. 1980. op. cit. p. 104.
35. ibid. p. 106.
36. Harding, C. 1904. *In Remotest Barotseland*, Hurst and Blackett, London, p. 114.
37. Mubita, R. Personal communication.
38. Cunningham, W. Personal communication.

CHAPTER 3: IN THE NAME OF THE FATHER

1. Listowel, J. 1974. *The Other Livingstone*, David Philip, Cape Town, pp. 228-9.
2. ibid. p. 38.
3. Ransford, O. 1977. 'David Livingstone, A Reassessment with Particular Reference to his Psyche', Unpublished Ph.D. thesis, University of Rhodesia, p. 95.
4. Listowel, J. 1974. op. cit. p. 45.
5. ibid. pp. 49-50.
6. Seaver, G. 1957. *David Livingstone: His Life and Letters*, Harper & Brothers, New York, p. 140.
7. ibid. pp. 137 & 141.
8. Ransford, O. 1977. op. cit. p. 116.
9. ibid. p. 140.
10. Brelsford, W.V. 1965. *Generation of Men: The European Pioneers of Northern Rhodesia*, Stuart Manning, Salisbury, Rhodesia, p. 5.
11. Listowel, J. 1974. op. cit. p. 123.
12. Livingstone, D. 1960. *Livingstone's Private Journals*, Ed. Schapera, I., Chatto & Windus, London, pp. 176-9.
13. ibid. p. 207.
14. ibid.
15. Listowel, J. 1974. op. cit. p. 126.
16. Livingstone, D. 1960. op. cit. p. 229.
17. Gann, L.H. 1964. *A History of Northern Rhodesia: Early Days to 1953*, Chatto and Windus, London, p. 25.
18. Listowel, J. 1974. op. cit. p. 130.
19. Seaver, G. 1957. op. cit. p. 180.
20. Ransford, O. 1977. op. cit. p. 140.
21. ibid. p. 190.
22. ibid. p. 193.
23. Mackenzie, J. Rev. 1883. *Day-Dawn in Dark Places*, Cassell & Company, London.
24. Smith, E.W. 1957. *Great Lion of Bechuanaland*, London Missionary Society, London, pp. 60-80.
25. ibid. p. 88.
26. ibid. p. 104.
27. ibid. pp. 411-23.
28. Seaver, G. 1957. op. cit. p. 176.
29. Smith, E.W. 1957. op. cit. p. 416.

30. Watt, N.J.V. 1951. 'A Lonely Grave', in *The Northern Rhodesia Journal*, Vol. 1, No. 3, p. 80.
31. Gelfand, M. (Ed.) 1968. *Gubulawayo and Beyond*, Geoffrey Chapman, London, pp. 342-3.
32. ibid. pp. 18-19.
33. Rea, W.F. 1968. *George Westbeech and the Barotseland Missionaries 1878-1888*, The Central Africa Historical Association, Salisbury, p. 7.
34. Arnot, F.S. 1889. *Garenganze*, James E. Hawkins, London, p. 80.
35. Rea, W.F. 1968. op. cit. p. 11.
36. Gelfand, M. 1968. op. cit. p. 407.
37. Rea, W.F. 1968. op. cit. p. 19.

CHAPTER 4: COUNT CAPRIVI'S FOLLY

1. Trollope, L.F.W. 1956. 'The Eastern Caprivi Zipfel', in *Northern Rhodesia Journal*, Vol. 3, No. 2, p. 112.
2. Selous, F.C. 1970. *A Hunter's Wanderings in Africa*, Books of Rhodesia, Bulawayo (Reprint of Richard Bently & Sons, London, 1881), pp. 395-401.
3. Miller, Charles 1987. *The Lunatic Express*, Westlands Sundries, Nairobi, Kenya, p. 180.
4. ibid. pp. 190-99
5. Hallet, R. 1975. *Africa Since 1875*, Vol. 2, Heinemann Educational Books, London, p. 433.
6. Hertslet, Sir E. 1894. *The Map of Africa by Treaty*, HM Stationery Office, London, p. 323.
7. ibid. p. 646.
8. Robinson, R. & Gallagher, J. with Denny, A. 1974. *Africa and the Victorians*, Macmillan, London, p. 294.
9. British Government 1890. *British and Foreign State Papers*, HM Printer Stationery Office, London, p. 39.
10. Brelsford, W.V. 1965. *Generation of Men: The European Pioneers of Northern Rhodesia*, Stuart Manning, Salisbury, Rhodesia, pp. 106-9.
11. Trollope, L.F.W. 1940. 'Report on the Administration of the Eastern Caprivi Zipfel to Secretary of Native Affairs', (Unpublished), Pretoria (Copy held at the office of the Administrator, Katima Mulilo), p. 9.
12. ibid.
13. ibid. p. 8.
14. ibid.
15. Stevens 1953. 'With No. 1 Mobile Troop to Schuckmansburg', in *Blue and Old Gold*, Howard Timmins, Cape Town, pp. 83-5.
16. Thomas, F.M. & Billing, M.G. 1965. 'Mwandi: Old Sesheke', in *Northern Rhodesia Journal*, Vol. 6., pp. 54-5.
17. Brelsford, W.V. 1965. op. cit. p. 99.
18. Anonymous 1931. 'The Lighter Side of War', in *The Outpost*, Vol. 8, No. 10, April, p. 11.
19. Colenbrander, A.B. Personal communication.
20. Trollope, L.F.W. 1940. op. cit. p. 1.

CHAPTER 5: WHERE ANGELS GAZE

1. Govt. of Zambia 1986. Information board at the carpark on the Zambian side of Victoria Falls.
2. Clark, J.D. 1964. 'Introduction', *The Victoria Falls: A Handbook to the Victoria Falls, the Batoka Gorge and Part of the Upper Zambezi*, Ed. Fagan, B.M., 2nd edition, Commission for the Preservation of National and Historical Monuments and Relics, Livingstone, Zambia, pp. 18-20.
3. Phillipson, D.W. (Ed.) 1975. *Mosi-Oa-Tunya: A Handbook to the Victoria Falls Region*, Longman, Rhodesia, p. 7.
4. Chaplin, J.H. & Clark, J.D. 1957. 'Day of Month of Discovery of Victoria Falls', in *The Northern Rhodesia Journal*, Vol. 3, No. 3. pp. 279-81.
5. Wallis, J.P.R. 1982. *Thomas Baines of King's Lynn, Explorer and Artist, 1820-1875*, Facsimile reprint, Books of Zimbabwe, Bulawayo, Footnote 1, p. 207.
6. Punt, W. 1974. 'Trichardt, Carolus Johannes', in *Standard Encyclopaedia of Southern Africa*, Ed. Potgieter, D.J., Nasou, Cape Town, pp. 628-9.

7. Norwich, O.I. 1988. *Maps of Africa*, A.D. Donker, Johannesburg.

8. Clay, G. 1959. 'The Discovery of the Victoria Falls', in *The Northern Rhodesia Journal*, Vol. 4, No. 1, p. 20.

9. Baldwin, W.C. 1967. *African Hunting and Adventure*, Facsimile reprint, C. Struik, Cape Town, p. 380.

10. Williams, R. 1913. *How I Became Governor*, John Murray, London, p. 102.

11. Clay, G. 1964. *The Victoria Falls: A Handbook to the Victoria Falls, the Batoka Gorge and Part of the Upper Zambezi*, Ed. Fagan, B.M., 2nd edition, Commission for the Preservation of National and Historical Monuments and Relics, Livingstone, Zambia, pp. 40-41.

12. Baxter, T.W. 1952. *The Victoria Falls: A Handbook to the Victoria Falls, the Batoka Gorge and Part of the Upper Zambezi*, Ed. Clark, J.D., Commission for the Preservation of National and Historical Monuments and Relics, Livingstone, Zambia, pp. 25-6.

13. Baldwin, W.C. 1967. op. cit. p. 380.

14. Baines, T. 1973. *Explorations in South-West Africa*, Facsimile reprint, Pioneer Head, Salisbury, Rhodesia, p. 520.

15. Clay, G. 1964. op. cit. p. 29.

16. Coupland, R. 1928. *Kirk on the Zambesi*, Clarendon Press, Oxford, p. 175.

17. Baxter, T.W. 1952. op. cit. pp. 25-6.

18. Khama, Lady R. 1987. Personal communication.

19. Dixon, I. 1988. Personal communication.

20. Lamplugh, G.W. 1908. 'The Gorge and Basin of the Zambezi Below the Victoria Falls, Rhodesia', in *The Geographical Journal*, Vol. 31, No. 2, February, p. 139.

21. Stagman, J.G. 1978. *An Outline of the Geology of Rhodesia*, Rhodesia Geological Survey Bulletin No. 80, Reprinted 1981, Government of Zimbabwe, p. 97.

22. Clark, J.D. 1975. *Mosi-Oa-Tunya: A Handbook to the Victoria Falls Region*, Ed. Phillipson, D.W., Longman, Rhodesia, p. 30.

23. Bond, G. 1975. op. cit. p. 27.

24. Clark, J.D. 1975. op. cit.

25. Sillitoe, P. 1955. *Cloak Without a Dagger*, Cassell and Co., London, p. 13.

26. Tabler, E.C. 1955. *The Far Interior*, A.A. Balkema, Cape Town, p. 143.

27. Cooke, C.K. 1975. 'The Zeederberg Coach', in *Rhodesiana*, No. 32, March, pp. 43-7.

28. White, P. 1974. 'Origins of Postal Communications in Central Africa', in *Rhodesiana*, No. 31, September, p. 32.

29. Murray, F.C. 1965. 'Zeederberg in Northern Rhodesia', in *Zambia (Northern Rhodesia) Journal*, Vol. 6, p. 226.

30. Williams, G.D.B. 1961. 'Some Early Mail Runner Services', in *The Northern Rhodesia Journal*, Vol. 4, No. 5, pp. 601-4.

31. Dann, H.C. 1981. *The Romance of the Posts of Rhodesia*, and *The Cancellations of Rhodesia and Nyasaland*, Facsimile reprint of the 1940 and 1950 editions, respectively, Books of Zimbabwe, Bulawayo, Zimbabwe.

32. ibid.

33. ibid. p. 22.

34. Moore, J.W.H. 1965. *A Dam on the Zambezi*, Occasional Paper No. 1, National Archives of Zimbabwe, Government Printer, Harare, Zimbabwe, p. 43.

35. Morrison, E.R. 1985. 'Geological Society of Zimbabwe Coal Workshop: Inaugural Address', in *Chamber of Mines Journal*, May, p. 19.

36. Hobson, D. 1959. 'The recollections of Piet Erasmus', in *The Northern Rhodesia Journal*, Vol. 4, No. 2, p. 161.

37. Sillitoe, P. 1955. op. cit. p. 14.

38. Smith, R.C. 1963. *Rhodesia, A Postal History*, R.C. Smith, Harare, Zimbabwe, p. 105.

39. Varian, H.F. 1973. *Some African Milestones*, Facsimile reproduction of 1953 edition, Books of Rhodesia, Bulawayo, Zimbabwe, pp. 104-5.

40. ibid.

41. Hobson, G.A. 1905. 'The Victoria Falls Bridge', in *The African World*, Vol. 3, 8 December, p. 107.

42. Brelsford, W.V. 1965. *Generation of Men: The European Pioneers of Northern Rhodesia*, Stuart Manning, Salisbury, Rhodesia, p. 103.

43. Baxter, T.W. 1952. op. cit. p. 42.
44. Brelsford, W.V. 1965. op. cit. p. 50.

CHAPTER 6: STONE AND IRON

1. Barghoorn, E.S. 1979. 'The Oldest Fossils', in *Life, Origin and Evolution*, W.H. Freeman & Co., California, p. 67.
2. Inskeep, R.R. 1978. *The Peopling of Southern Africa*, David Philip, Cape Town, p. 40.
3. Campbell, A.C. 1988. Personal communication.
4. Desmond Clark, J. 1975. 'Stone Age Man at the Victoria Falls', in *Mosi-Oa-Tunya: A Handbook to the Victoria Falls Region*, Ed. Phillipson, D.W., Longman, Rhodesia, pp. 32-3.
5. ibid. p. 35.
6. Campbell, A.C. 1988. Personal communication.
7. Bisson, M. 1980. 'Pre-Historic Archaeology of North-Western Province, Zambia', in *A Handbook to the North-Western Province*, Ed. Johnson, D.S., Handbook Series No. 8, Zambia Geographical Association, Lusaka, August, pp. 53-66.
8. Campbell, A.C. 1988. Personal communication.
9. Phillipson, D.W. 1972. *National Monuments of Zambia, an Illustrated Guide*, National Monuments Commission, Lusaka, Government of Zambia, p. 11.
10. Desmond Clark, J. 1975. op. cit. pp. 42-3.
11. Derricourt, R.M. 1976. 'Chronology of Zambian Pre-History', in *Transafrican Journal of History*, Eds Ogot, B.A. & Kipkorir, B.E., Vol. 5, No. 1, p. 3.
12. Desmond Clark, J. 1970. *The Prehistory of Africa*, Thames and Hudson, London, p. 145.
13. Drysdall, A.R. & Utting, J. No date. 'Zambia's Fossil Heritage', in *Black Lechwe*, Vol. 11, No. 4, no page numbers.
14. New Scientist 1988. 'Neanderthals had Sharp Manners', in *New Scientist*, Vol. 117, No. 1601, 25 February, p. 34.
15. Phaup, A.E. 1932. 'The Patina of the Stone Implements Found Near the Victoria Falls', in *Proceedings of the Rhodesia Scientific Association*, Vol. 31, pp. 40-43.
16. Dorn, R.I. et al. 1986. 'Cation-ratio and Accelerator Radiocarbon Dating of Rock Varnish on Mojave Artifacts and Landforms', in *Science*, Vol. 231, 21 February, pp. 830-33.
17. ibid.
18. ibid.
19. Whitley, D.S. & Dorn, R.I. 1987. 'Rock Art Chronology in Eastern California', in *World Archaeology*, Vol. 19, No. 2., pp. 150-64.
20. Toth, N. 1985. 'Archaeological Evidence for Preferential Right-Handedness in the Lower and Middle Pleistocene, and its Possible Implications', in *Journal of Human Evolution*, Vol. 14, pp. 607-14.
21. Anderson, I. 1987. 'How Human Ancestors Put on a Spurt', in *New Scientist*, No. 1561, 21 May, p. 27.
22. Cann, R.L. 1987. 'In Search of Eve', in *The Sciences*, September/October, pp. 30-37.
23. ibid.
24. Bond, G. 1983. 'The Stone Age in the Middle Zambezi Valley', in *Zimbabwean Prehistory*. No. 19, December, pp. 2-6.
25. _____ 1948. 'Rhodesian Stone Age Man and his Raw Materials', in *South African Archaeological Bulletin*, Vol. III, No. 11, September, pp. 55-60.
26. Campbell, A.C. 1988. Personal communication.
27. ibid.
28. Phillipson, D.W. 1975. *The Iron Age in Zambia*, The Historical Association of Zambia, HAZ No. 5., p. 6.
29. _____ 1981. 'The Beginnings of the Iron Age in Southern Africa', in *General History of Africa*. Vol. II, Ed. Mokhtar, G., Heinemann, California, p. 674.
30. Campbell, A.C. 1988. Personal communication.
31. Phillipson, D.W. 1987. Personal communication.
32. ibid.
33. ibid.
34. Campbell, A.C. 1988. Personal communication.

35. Huffman, T.N. In press. 'Ceramics, Settlements and Late Iron Age Migrations', Paper read at SA3 conference, Southern Africa Association of Archaeologists, April 1988, pp. 1-8.

36. Phillipson, D.W. 1976. 'The Early Iron Age in Eastern and Southern Africa: A Critical Reappraisal', in *Azania*, Vol. XI, pp. 2-19.

37. Huffman, T.N. In press. op. cit.

38. Denbow, J. 1988. Personal communication.

39. Huffman, T.N. In press. op. cit.

40. Campbell, A.C. 1988. Personal communication.

41. Huffman, T.N. In press. op. cit.

42. McCosh, F.W.J. 1979. 'Traditional Iron-Working in Central Africa with Some Reference to the Ritualistic and Scientific Aspects of the Industry', in *Zambezia*, Vol. 7, No. ii, pp. 156-66.

43. ibid.

44. Campbell, A.C. 1988. Personal communication.

45. Vogel, J.O. 1971. *Kamangoza: An Introduction to the Iron Age Cultures of the Victoria Falls Region*, Zambia Museum papers, No. 2, National Museums of Zambia, p. 7.

46. Phillipson, D.W. 1975. op. cit. p. 5.

47. Campbell, A.C. 1988. Personal communication.

48. ibid.

49. Phillipson, D.W. 1987. Personal communication.

50. Denbow, J.R. 1980. 'The Toutswe Tradition: A Study in Socio-Economic Change' in *Settlement in Botswana*, Heinemann and the Botswana Society, Gaborone, Botswana, pp. 73-86.

51. _____ 1981. 'Broadhurst – A 14th Century AD Expression of the Early Iron Age in South-Eastern Botswana', in *The South African Archaeological Bulletin*, Vol. 36, No. 134, December, pp. 66-74.

52. Fagan, B.M. 1965. *Southern Africa During the Iron Age*, Thames and Hudson, London, pp. 146-50.

53. ibid.

54. Needham, D.E. 1974. *Iron Age to Independence: A History of Central Africa* (Reprinted 1980), Longman, London, p. 63.

55. Meeus, J. 1987. Personal communication (Computer-generated eclipse information for Africa).

56. Posselt, F. 1929. 'The Watawara and the Batonga', in *Nada*, No. 7, p. 93.

57. Ransford, O. 1966. *Livingstone's Lake*, John Murray, London, p. 60.

CHAPTER 7: BEADS, BANGLES AND BARTER

1. Saddington, D.B. 1983. 'The Exploration of Africa in Roman Times', in *Zimbabwean Prehistory*, No. 19, December, p. 7.

2. Quiggin, A.H. 1949. 'Trade Routes, Trade and Currency in East Africa', in *The Occasional Papers of the Rhodes-Livingstone Museum*, Institute of African Studies, University of Zambia, Vols. 1-16, No. 5, p. 147.

3. Axleson, E. 1940. *South-East Africa 1488-1530*, Longman, Green & Co., London, p. 1.

4. ibid. pp. 4-6.

5. Quiggin, A.H. 1949. op. cit.

6. Axleson, E. 1940. op. cit. p. 10.

7. Verin, P. 1976. 'The African Element in Madagascar', in *Azania*, Vol. XI, pp. 137-8.

8. Campbell, G. 1987. Personal communication.

9. Davidson, B. 1967. *The African Past*, Longman, London, p. 104.

10. _____ 1959. *The Lost Cities of Africa*, Little, Brown and Co., Boston, p. 186.

11. Fripp, C.E. 1941. 'Chinese Mediaeval Trade with Africa', in *Nada*, No. 18, p. 18.

12. Hromnik, C.A. 1981. *Indo-Africa*, Juta & Co., Cape Town.

13. Vogel, J. 1971. 'Kumadzulo', *Zambia Museum Papers*, No. 3, Livingstone, Zambia, pp. 7-114.

14. Fagan, B. 1966. 'The Iron Age of Zambia', in *Current Anthropology*, Vol. 7, No. 4, October, pp. 458-9.

15. Grey, R. & Birmingham, D. 1970. *Pre-Colonial African Trade*, Oxford University Press, London, p. 5.

16. Sinclair, P. 1982. 'Chibuene – An Early Trading Site in Southern Mozambique', in *Paideuma*, No. 28, pp. 149-64.

17. Axleson, E. 1940. op. cit. p. 9.
18. Summers, R. 1969. *Ancient Mining in Rhodesia*, Museum Memoir No. 3, National Museums of Rhodesia, Salisbury, p. 206.
19. Axleson, E. 1940. op. cit. p. 9.
20. Phillipson, D.W. 1977. *The Later Prehistory of Eastern and Southern Africa*, Heinemann, London, pp. 193-4.
21. Fagan, B.M., Phillipson, D.W. & Daniels, S.G.H. 1969. *Iron Age Cultures in Zambia*. Vol. 2, Chatto and Windus, London, p. 138.
22. Phillipson, D.W. 1977. op. cit.
23. Huffman, T.N. 1971. 'Cloth from the Iron Age in Rhodesia', in *Arnoldia*, Vol. 5, No. 14, 29 December, pp. 1-19.
24. Tylden, G. 1953. 'The Gun Trade in Central and Southern Africa', in *Northern Rhodesia Journal*, Vol. 2, No. 1, pp. 43-4.
25. Davidson, B. 1967. op. cit. p. 110.
26. Elkiss, T.H. 1981. *The Quest for an African Eldorado: Sofala, Southern Zambezia and the Portuguese, 1500-1865*, Crossroads Press, Mass, p. 4.
27. Summers, R. 1969. op. cit. p. 218.
28. ibid. p. 195.
29. Sicard, H.V. 1963. 'The Ancient Sabi-Zimbabwe Trade Route', in *Nada*, No. 40, p. 7.
30. Quiggin, A.H. 1949. op. cit. pp. 163-4.
31. ibid.
32. Summers, R. 1969. op. cit. p. 196.
33. Strandes, J. 1971. *The Portuguese Period in East Africa*, East African Literature Bureau, Nairobi, p. 30.
34. Hepburn, E.T. 1973. 'European Pre-Pioneers, 1500-1890', in *Rhodesiana*, No. 29, Lecture No. 5, December, p. 38.
35. Stewart, J. 1952. *The Zambezi Journal of James Stewart*, Ed. Wallis, J.P.R., Chatto and Windus, London, p. 150.
36. Thomas, T.M. 1970. *Eleven Years in Central South Africa*, Facsimile reproduction of 1873 edition, Books of Rhodesia, Bulawayo, pp. 380-81.
37. Campbell, A.C. 1988. Personal communication.

CHAPTER 8: KARIBA

1. Van Jaarsveldt, K. 1987. Personal communication.
2. Critchley, R.A. 1959. 'Operation Noah', in *Oryx*, p. 105.
3. Child, G. 1968. 'Behaviour of Large Mammals during the Formation of Lake Kariba', *Kariba Studies*, National Museums of Rhodesia, Bulawayo, p. 10.
4. ibid. p. 6.
5. Deere, A.G. 1971. 'Kariba', Unpublished report, District Officer to D.C., Kariba, August, p. 17.
6. Child, G.F.T. & Riney, T. 1987. 'Tsetse Control Hunting', in *Zambezia*, Vol. 14, No. 1, p. 23.
7. Simpkins, A. Personal communication.
8. Kenmuir, D. 1983. *Fishes of Kariba*, Wilderness Publication, Harare, Zimbabwe, p. 3.
9. Sleigh, R.W. 1969. 'How Kariba Dented the Earth', in *The Rhodesia Science News*, Vol. 3, No. 5, p. 129.
10. Sleigh, R.W., Worrall, C.C. & Shaw, G.H.L. 1969. *Crustal Deformation Resulting from the Imposition of a Large Mass of Water*, Report to Department of Surveyor General, Salisbury, Rhodesia, National Archives, Harare, Zimbabwe, pp. 7-8.
11. Sleigh, R.W. 1969. op. cit. p. 131.
12. _____ 1976. 'Further Investigation of Crustal Deformation at Kariba', in *The Rhodesia Science News*, Vol. 10, No. 1, January.
13. _____ 1969. op. cit.
14. Thomson, E. Personal communication.
15. Erasmus, P. 1959. 'The Recollections of Piet Erasmus', in *Northern Rhodesia Journal*. Vol. 4, No. 2, p. 160.
16. Archer, C.B. 1969. 'Ten years of Kariba Earthquakes', in *The Rhodesia Science News*, Vol. 3, No. 5, p. 132.

17. Gough, D.I. & Gough, W.I. 1970. 'Load Induced Earthquakes at Lake Kariba', in *The Geophysical Journal of the Royal Astronomical Society*, Vol. 21, p. 79.

18. Govt Zimbabwe 1981. *A Supplementary Catalogue of Earthquakes in the Lake Kariba Area, 1978-1980*, Dept of Meteorological Services, Bulawayo.

19. Archer, C.B. op. cit. p. 132.

20. Gough, D.I. & Gough, W.I. op. cit. p. 79.

21. Santa Clara, J. Personal communication.

22. Gough, D.I. & Gough, W.I. op. cit. p. 99.

23. Author unknown 1969. 'A Catalogue of Earthquakes in the Lake Kariba Area: 1959 to 1968', Typed report (details unknown), National Archives of Zimbabwe.

24. Hattle, J.B. 1970. 'The Effect on Climate of Inland Lakes', in *The Rhodesia Science News*, Vol. 4, No. 6, June, p. 207-8.

25. Hutchinson, P. 1975. 'Increase in Rainfall Due to Lake Kariba', *Handbook to the Southern Province, Zambia Geographical Association Handbook*, Series No. 4., Eds Elgie, I.D. & Johnson, D.S., Lusaka, August, p. 53.

26. Hutchinson, P., Mtada, O.S., Phiri, J.K. & Radebe, B. 1975. 'The Climate of the Mazabuka Area', *Handbook to the Southern Province, Zambia Geographical Association Handbook*, Series No. 4, Eds Elgie, I.D. & Johnson, D.S., Lusaka, August, p. 44.

27. Ward, P.R.B. 1979. 'Seiches, Tides and Wind Set-Up on Lake Kariba', in *Limnology and Oceanography*, Vol. 24, No. 1, p. 154.

28. Ruttner, F. 1953. *Fundamentals of Limnology*, University of Toronto Press, Toronto, p. 43.

29. Ward, P.R.B. op. cit. p. 154.

30. Beadle, L.C. 1974. *The Inland Waters of Tropical Africa*, Longman, London, pp. 60-61.

31. Ward, P.R.B. op. cit. p. 154.

32. Balon, E.K. & Coche, A.G. 1974. *Lake Kariba, a Man-Made Tropical Ecosystem in Central Africa*, W. Junk, The Hague, p. 43.

33. Van der Lingen, M.I. 1973. 'Lake Kariba: Early History and South Shore', in *Geophysical Monograph Series*, Vol. 17. *Man-Made Lakes: Their Problems and Environmental Effects*, Eds Ackermann, W.C., White, G.F. & Worthington, E.B., Washington, p. 140.

34. Child, G. 1968. op. cit. p. 32.

35. Van der Lingen, M.I. 1973. op. cit.

36. Jackson, P.B.N. 1974. 'Development of a Fisheries Industry at Cabora Bassa', Unpublished report for Loxton, Hunting & Association, Johannesburg, p. 20.

37. McLachlan, A.J. 1970. 'Submerged Trees as a Substrate for Benthic Fauna in the Recently Created Lake Kariba (Central Africa)', in *Journal of Applied Ecology*, Vol. 7, August, p. 253-66.

38. Clements, F. 1959. *The Struggle with the River God*, Methuen & Co., London, pp. 54-5.

39. Hall, G. Personal communication.

40. Thomson, E. Personal communication.

41. Essex Capell, A. 1944. 'Tales of the Makorrie-Korrie', in *Nada*, Vol. 21, p. 39.

42. Deare, A.G. 1976. 'Kariba', in *Nada*, Vol. 2, No. 3, p. 271.

43. Federal Power Board 1960. 'Kariba, Opening by Her Majesty Queen Elizabeth, the Queen Mother, Tuesday 17th May, 1960', Federal Power Board, Salisbury, Rhodesia.

44. ibid.

45. Santa Clara, J.M.A. 1985. 'The Hydropower Resources of Zimbabwe', in *Water Power and Dam Construction*, Vol. 37, No. 9, September, p. 20.

46. Allison, G.F. 1970. 'The Hydrocological Management of Kariba', in *The Rhodesia Science News*, Vol. 4, No. 2, February, p. 49.

47. Federal Meteorological Department 1958. *The Zambezi Flood: February-March 1958: Analysis of Rainfall*, Federal Meteorological Department, Salisbury, Rhodesia, National Archives of Zimbabwe, p. 1.

48. ibid.

49. Tawonameso, R. Personal communication.

50. Allison, G.F. 1969. 'Operation Bulkhead; The Repair of an Underwater Intake at Kariba', in *Rhodesian Engineer*, Vol. 7, No. 4, pp. 831-8.

CHAPTER 9: MATTERS AQUATIC

1. Marshall, B.E., Junor, F.J.R. & Langerman, J.D. 1982 'Fisheries and Fish Production on the Zimbabwean Side of Lake Kariba', *Kariba Studies Paper No. 10*, National Museums and Monuments of Zimbabwe, Harare, Zimbabwe, p. 224.
2. Marshall, B.E. 1982. 'The Influence of River Flow on Pelagic Sardine Catches in Lake Kariba', in *Journal of Fish Biology*, Vol. 20, p. 466.
3. ibid.
4. Balon, E.K. & Coche, A.G. 1974. *Lake Kariba, a Man-Made Tropical Ecosystem in Central Africa*, W. Junk, The Hague, p. 228.
5. McLachlan, S.M. 1971. 'The Rate of Nutrient Release from Grass and Dung Following Immersion in Lake Water', in *Hydrobiologia*, Vol. 37, Nos 3-4, pp. 521-30.
6. Mitchell, S.A. 1976. 'The Marginal Fish Fauna of Lake Kariba', *Kariba Studies*, Paper No. 8, National Museums and Monuments of Rhodesia, p. 128.
7. Marshall, B.E. & Junor, F.J.R. 1983. 'The Decline of *Salvinia molesta* on Lake Kariba', in *Hydrobiologia*, Vol. 83.
8. Botanical Research 1980. *Kariba Weed*, W.8, Botanical Research Institute, Pretoria, South Africa.
9. Procter, D.L.C. 1983. 'Biological Control of the Aquatic Weed *Salvinia molesta* in Botswana', in *Botswana Notes and Records*, Vol. 15, p. 99.
10. Mitchell, D.S. & Rose, D.J.W. 1979. 'Factors Affecting Fluctuations in Extent of *Salvinia molesta* on Lake Kariba', in *Pans*, Vol. 25 (2), p. 173.
11. Proctor, D.L.C. op. cit.
12. McLachlan, S.M. 1971. op. cit.
13. Bowmaker, A.P. 1973. 'Hydrophyte Dynamics in Mwenda Bay Lake Kariba', *Kariba Studies*. Paper No. 3, National Museums and Monuments of Rhodesia, p. 49.
14. McLachlan, S.M. 1971. op. cit.
15. Boughey, A.S. 1962. 'Africa's Strangled Waterways', in *Geographical Journal*, Vol. 35, November, p. 410.
16. Mitchell, D.S. & Rose, D.J.W. 1979. op. cit. p. 176.
17. Marshall, B.E. & Junor, F.J.R. 1983. op. cit. p. 480.
18. ibid.
19. Kenmuir, D. 1983. *Fishes of Kariba*, Wilderness Publications, Harare, Zimbabwe, p. 9.
20. Bell-Cross, G. & Bell-Cross, B. 1971. 'Introductions into Lake Kariba', in *Fisheries Research Bulletin*, Vol. 5, Zambia, p. 208.
21. ibid.
22. Marshall, B.E. & Langerman, J.D. 1979. 'The Tanganyika Sardine in Lake Kariba', in *The Rhodesia Science News*, Vol. 13, No. 4, April.
23. Langerman, J.D. 1979. *The Rhodesia Science News*, Vol. 13, No. 4, April, p. 106.
24. Begg, G.W. 1976. 'The Relationship between the Diurnal Movements of Some of the Zooplankton and the Sardine *Limnothrissa miodon* in Lake Kariba, Rhodesia', in *Limnology and Oceanography*, Vol. 21, No. 4, July, p. 529.
25. Langerman, J.D. 1979. op. cit.
26. Marshall, B.E. 1982. 'Fish Production Potential of Lake Kariba', in *Zimbabwe Agricultural Journal*, Vol. 79, No. 5, pp. 173-7.
27. _____ 1988. Personal communication.
28. Minshull, J. 1984. *Angling and Spearfishing Records – Zimbabwe Freshwater Fishes*, Information Circular No. 8, National Museums and Monuments of Zimbabwe, December.
29. Marshall, B.E., Junor, F.J.R. & Langerman, J.D. 1982. op. cit. p. 230.
30. Marshall, B.E. 1982. op. cit. p. 176.
31. Jubb, R.A. 1961. 'The Freshwater Eels (*Anguilla* spp.) of Southern Africa. An Introduction to their Identification and Biology', *Annals of the Cape Province Museum*, No. 1, p. 34.
32. Bond, C.E. 1979. *Biology of Fishes*, Saunders College Publishing, Philadelphia, USA, p. 283.
33. Pienaar, U. de V. 1978. *The Freshwater Fishes of the Kruger National Park*, Trustees of the National Parks Board, Pretoria, South Africa, p. 25.
34. Jubb, R.A. 1961. op. cit.
35. _____ 1963. 'Some Interesting Freshwater Eel Records', in *Piscator*, No. 57, pp. 13-14.

36. Bond, C.E. 1979. op. cit. p. 360.
37. MacGregor, E. Personal communication.
38. Balon, E.K. 1975. 'The Eels of Lake Kariba: Distribution, Taxonomic Status, Age, Growth and Density', in *Journal of Fish Biology*, Vol. 7, p. 805.
39. ibid. p. 813.
40. Marshall, B.E. Personal communication.
41. Bell-Cross, G. 1976. *The Fishes of Rhodesia*, National Museums and Monuments of Rhodesia, Salisbury, p. 84.
42. Minshull, J. Personal communication.
43. Kenmuir, D. 1983. op. cit. p. 43.
44. Jackson, P.B.N. 1986. 'Fish of the Zambezi System' in *The Ecology of River Systems*, Eds Davies, B.R. & Walker, K.F., W., Junk, The Hague, Netherlands, p. 269.
45. Davies, D.H. 1964. *About Sharks and Shark Attack*, Brown, Davis and Platt, Durban, South Africa, p. 59.
46. Kenmuir, D. 1980. 'The Mussel Resources of Lake Kariba', *Transactions of the Zimbabwe Scientific Association*, Vol. 60, No. 2, p. 8.
47. Begg, G.W. & Junor, F.J.R. 1971. 'Some Notes on a Sponge, a Jellyfish and a Shrimp from Lake Kariba' in *Piscator*, No. 81, p. 17.
48. Mills, M.L. 1973. 'The "Explosive" Occurrence of the Freshwater Medusa, *Limnocnida tanganyicae gunther*, in Lake Kariba during 1972', pp. 1-8.
49. Begg, G.W. & Junor, F.J.R. 1971. op. cit. pp. 17-18.
50. ibid. pp. 18-19.
51. Marshall, B.E. Personal communication.
52. Langerman, J.D. Personal communication.
53. Kenmuir, D. 1983. op. cit. p. 87.
54. Bond, C.E. 1979. op. cit. p. 337.
55. Vines, G. 1982. 'The Stimulating World of the Electric Fish', in *New Scientist*, 10 June, p. 705.
56. Kenmuir, D. 1983. op. cit. p. 47.
57. Keynes, R.D. 1957. *The Physiology of Fishes*, Ed. Brown, M.E., Academic Press, New York, p. 340.

CHAPTER 10: GNAT CHAT

1. Clark, V. de V. 1982. 'Parasites of Popular Interest: II, The Malaria Parasites', in *The Zimbabwe Science News*, Vol. 16, No. 9, September, p. 216.
2. ibid.
3. ibid.
4. Gillett, J.D. 1972. *Common African Mosquitos and their Medical Importance*, William Heinemann Medical Books, London, p. 1.
5. Jenkins, T. & Ramsay, M. 1986. 'Malaria Protective Alleles in Southern Africa: Relict Alleles of No Health Significance?' in *Genetic Variation and its Maintenance*, Eds Roberts, D.F. & De Stafano, G.F., Cambridge University Press, Cambridge, p. 135.
6. Author unknown 1988. 'Malaria, a Review', in *The South African Connexion*, Vol. 3, First Quarter, pp. 57-60.
7. ibid.
8. Penfold, G. 1988. Personal communication.
9. Gear, J.H.S. 1974. 'The Occurrence and Diagnosis of Malaria', in *The South African Medical Journal*, 25 May, p. 1079.
10. Jenkins, T. & Ramsay, M. 1986. op. cit. p. 136.
11. Author unknown 1987. 'Sickle-Cell Alert', *Time Magazine*, 5 October, p. 46.
12. Penfold, G. 1988. Personal communication.
13. Serjeant, G.R. 1985. *Sickle Cell Disease*, Oxford University Press, Oxford, p. 19.
14. Beet, E.A. 1946. 'Sickle Cell Disease in the Balovale District of Northern Rhodesia', in *The East African Medical Journal*, March, pp. 75-86.
15. Thompson, D. & Dunbar, R. 1988. 'Sex for Dragons and Damsels', in *New Scientist*, Vol. 117, No. 1601, 25 February, pp. 45-8.

16. Pinhey, E. 1961. 'Dragonflies (Odonata) of Central Africa', in *The Occasional Papers of the Rhodes-Livingstone Museum*, Nos 1-16 (in one volume), Paper 14, p. 544.

17. Skaife, S.H. 1979. *African Insect Life*, Country Life Books, London, pp. 108-9.

18. Jooste, R. 1987. Personal communication.

19. ibid.

20. Cabaret, J. 1984. 'Sheep and Goats: Epidemiology of Protostrongylid Lungworm Infections', in *International Sheep and Goat Research*, Vol. 2, No. 2, p. 142.

21. Zumpt, F. 1965. *Myiasis in Man and Animals in the Old World*. Butterworth, London, pp. 70-73.

22. ibid. p. xi.

23. ibid. p. 101.

24. Clark, V. de V. 1987. Personal communication.

25. Zumpt. F. 1965. op. cit. p. 181.

26. Norval, R.I.A. 1983. 'The Ticks of Zimbabwe: VII, The Genus *Amblyomma*', in *Zimbabwe Veterinary Journal*, Vol. 14, No. 1/4, pp. 3-18.

27. ibid.

28. _____ 1987. Personal communication.

29. ibid.

30. Author unknown 1988. 'Cattle Vaccine Turns the Tables on Ticks', in *New Scientist*, Vol. 119, No. 1626, 18 August, p. 34.

31. Smithers, R.H.N. 1986. *Land Mammals of Southern Africa*, Macmillan South Africa, Johannesburg, p. 173.

32. Colborne, J., Norval, R.I.A. & Spickett, A.M. 1981. 'Ecological Studies on *Ixodes (Afrixodes) matopi* Spickett, Keirans, Norval & Clifford, 1980 (Acarina: Ixodidae)', in *Onderstepoort Journal of Veterinary Research*, Vol. 48, pp. 31-5.

33. ibid.

34. Child, G.F.T. & Riney, T. 1987. 'Tsetse Control Hunting', in *Zambezia*, Vol. xiv, No. i.

35. Vale, G.A. & Cumming, D.H.M. 1976. 'The Effects of Selective Elimination of Hosts on a Population of Tsetse Flies (*Glossina morsitans morsitans* Westwood (Diptera, Glossinidae))', in *Bulletin of Entomological Research*, Vol. 66, p. 713.

36. Wilson, V.J. 1972. 'Observations on the Effect of Dieldrin on Wildlife during Tsetse Fly *Glossina morsitans* Control Operations in Eastern Zambia', in *Arnoldia*, Vol. 5, No. 34, 31 August, pp. 1-12.

37. ibid.

38. Dean, G.J.W., Dame, D.A. & Birkenmeyer, D.R. 1969. 'Field Cage Evaluation of the Competitiveness of Male *Glossina morsitans orientalis* Vanderplank Sterilised with Tepa or Gamma Irradiation', in *Bulletin of Entomological Research*, Vol. 59, pp. 339-44.

39. Vale, G.A., Bursell, E. & Hargrove, J.W. 1985. 'Catching Out the Tsetse Fly', in *Parasitology Today*, Vol. 1, No. 4., October, pp. 1-5.

40. Allsopp, R. & Hursey, B.S. 1986. *Integrated Chemical Control of Tsetse Flies* (Glossina spp.) *in Western Zimbabwe, 1984-1985*, Tsetse and Trypanosomiasis Control Branch, Department of Veterinary Services, Government of Zimbabwe, Harare, pp. 1-39.

41. Allsopp, R. 1987. Personal communication.

42. Phelps, R.J. 1987. Personal communication.

43. Vale, G.A., Hargrove, J.W., Cockbill, G.F. & Phelps, R.J. 1986. 'Field Trials of Baits to Control Populations of *Glossina morsitans morsitans* Westwood and *G. pallidipes* Austen (Diptera: Glossinidae)', in *Bulletin of Entomological Research*, Vol. 76, pp. 179-93.

44. Allsopp, R., Hall, D. & Jones, T. 1985. 'Fatal Attraction for the Tsetse Fly', in *New Scientist*, No. 1481, 7 November, pp. 40-43.

45. Allsopp, R. 1984. 'Control of Tsetse Flies (Diptera: Glossinidae) Using Insecticides: A Review and Future Prospects', in *Bulletin of Entomological Research*, Vol. 74, pp. 1-23.

46. Redfern, M. 1988. 'Sugar Pills for Tsetse Flies', in *New Scientist*, Vol. 117, No. 1594, 7 January, p. 41.

47. Author unknown 1867. 'Antidote to the Tsetse', in *The Field*, Vol. 30, 28 September, p. 253.

CHAPTER 11: A BIRD IN THE BUSH

1. Wickens, G.E. 1982. 'The Baobab — Africa's Upside-Down Tree', in *Kew Bulletin*, Vol. 37 (2), p. 181.
2. ibid. p. 190.
3. Guy, G.L. 1970. '*Adansonia digitata* and its Rate of Growth in Relation to Rainfall in South-Central Africa', in *Rhodesia Scientific Association*, Vol. 54, Part 2, November, p. 70.
4. Swart, E.R. 1963. 'Age of the Baobab Tree', in *Nature*, Vol. 198, No. 4881, p. 708.
5. Mogg, A.O.D. 1950. 'The Baobab', in *Trees in South Africa*, Vol. 1, Part 4, p. 14.
6. Von Breitenbach, F. 1985. *Journal of Dendrochronology*, Vol. 5, No. 3/4, p. 68.
7. Guy, P.R. 1982. 'Baobabs and Elephants', in *African Journal of Ecology*, Vol. 20, p. 215.
8. Davison, G. 1982. 'Is This the Beginning of the End?' in *The Zimbabwe Science News*, Vol. 16, No. 1, January, p. 21.
9. Swanepoel, C.M. & Swanepoel, S.M. 1986. 'Baobab Damage by Elephant in the Middle Zambezi Valley, Zimbabwe', in *African Journal of Ecology*, Vol. 24, pp. 129-32.
10. Van Hoven, W. 1984. 'Trees' Secret Warning System', in *Custos*, Vol. 13, No. 5, pp. 11-16.
11. _____ Personal communication.
12. Damstra, K. St J. Personal communication.
13. Fenton, B. Personal communication.
14. Damstra, K. St J. Personal communication.
15. Weaving, A. 1977. *Insects: A Review of Insect Life in Rhodesia*, Regal Publishers, Harare, Zimbabwe, pp. 20 & 41.
16. Palgrave, K.C. 1981. *Trees of Southern Africa*, 2nd impression, C. Struik, Cape Town, pp. 833-4.
17. Campbell, A.C. Personal communication.
18. Van Eyssen, D. Personal communication.
19. Harris, D. Personal communication.
20. Palgrave, K.C. 1981. op. cit.
21. Damstra, K. St J. Personal communication.
22. Hobson, R.H. 1960. 'Rubber: A Footnote to Northern Rhodesian History', in *The Occasional Papers of the Rhodes-Livingstone Museum*, Nos 1-16 (in one volume), Institute of African Studies, University of Zambia, pp. 491-3.
23. Palgrave, K.C. 1981. op. cit. p. 65.
24. Harris, D. Personal communication.
25. Corner, E.J.H. 1966. *The Natural History of Palms*, Weidenfeld and Nicholson, London
26. ibid.
27. Ritchken, J. 1970. 'Palms of Rhodesia; Part 4, The Borassus Palm', in *The Rhodesia Science News*, Vol. 4, No. 2, February, p. 64.
28. Damstra, K. St J. 1984. 'Notes on the Zimbabwean Tree Families', in *The Zimbabwe Science News*, Vol. 18, Nos 9/10, October, p. 120.
29. Sabiiti, E.N. & Wein, R.W. 1988. *Journal of Ecology*, Vol. 75, p. 937.
30. Harlan, J.R. 1982. 'The Origins of Indigenous African Agriculture, in *The Cambridge History of Africa*, Ed. Clark, J.D., Vol. 1, Cambridge University Press, Cambridge, p. 649.
31. Laufer, B. 1930. 'The Introduction of Tobacco into Africa', in *Tobacco and its Uses in Africa*, Field Museum of Natural History, Chicago, Leaflet No. 29, p. 5.
32. Harlan, J.R. 1982. op. cit.
33. Wild, H. 1972. *A Rhodesian Botanical Dictionary of African and English Plant Names*, Revised and enlarged by Biegel, H.M. & Mavi, S., National Herbarium, Ministry of Agriculture, Government of Zimbabwe, Harare.
34. Mock, D.W. & Mock, K.C. 1980. 'Feeding Behaviour and Ecology of the Goliath Heron', in *The Auk*, Vol. 97, July, pp. 433-48.
35. ibid.
36. ibid.
37. Billing, K.J. & Phelps, R.J. 1972. 'Records of Chlorinated Hydrocarbon Pesticide Levels from Animals in Rhodesia', in *Rhodesia Scientific Association, Proceedings and Transactions*, Vol. 55, Part 1, August, pp. 6-9.

38. Whitwell, A.C., Phelps, R.J. & Thomson, W.R. 1974. 'Further Records of Chlorinated Hydrocarbon Pesticide Residues in Rhodesia', in *Arnoldia*, Vol. 6, No. 37, 14 June, pp. 1-8.
39. Taylor, R.D. & Fynn, K.J. 1978. 'Fish Eagles on Lake Kariba', in *The Rhodesia Science News*. Vol. 12, No. 2, February, pp. 52-3.
40. Hustler, K. Personal communication.
41. Barnes, J. 1988. Personal communication.
42. Lorber, P. 1985. 'What Makes a Hamerkop's Nest?' in *The Honeyguide*, Vol. 31, No. 1, March, p. 49.

CHAPTER 12: THE ZAMBEZI MENAGERIE

1. Tatham, G. 1987. Personal communication.
2. Pile, J.A. 1988. Personal communication.
3. Attwell, R.I.G. 1970. 'Some Effects of Lake Kariba on the Ecology of a Floodplain of the Mid-Zambezi Valley of Rhodesia', in *Biological Conservation*, Vol. 2, No. 3, April, pp. 189-96.
4. Du Toit, R.F. 1982. *A Preliminary Assessment of the Environmental Implications of the Proposed Mupata and Batoka Hydro-Electric Schemes (Zambezi River, Zimbabwe)*, Natural Resources Board, Ministry of Natural Resources and Tourism, Government of Zimbabwe, p. 78.
5. Begg, G.W. 1973. 'The Biological Consequences of Discharge Above and Below Kariba Dam', in *Commission Internationale des Grandes Barrages*, Onzieme Congres des Grand Barrages, Madrid, Q.40R.29, p. 428.
6. Guy, P.R. 1981. 'River Bank Erosion in the Mid-Zambezi Valley, Downstream of Lake Kariba', in *Biological Conservation*, No. 19, February, pp. 199-212.
7. Nugent, C. 1983. 'Channel Changes of the Middle Zambezi', in *The Zimbabwe Science News*. Vol. 17, Nos 7/8, July/August, pp. 127-9.
8. Kerr, M.A. & Fraser, J.A. 1975. 'Distribution of Elephant in a Part of the Zambezi Valley, Rhodesia', in *Arnoldia*, Vol. 7, No. 21, 1 July, p. 2.
9. Pitman, D. 1985. *The Mighty Zambezi*, Modus Publications, Harare, Zimbabwe, p. 43.
10. Du Toit, R.F. 1983. 'Hydrological Changes in the Middle-Zambezi System', in *The Zimbabwe Science News*, Vol. 17, No. 78, July/August, p. 123.
11. Attwell, R.I.G. 1970. op. cit. p. 194.
12. Begg, G.W. 1973. op. cit. p. 427.
13. Ferrar, A.A. 1981. Editorial in *The Zimbabwe Science News*, Vol. 15, No. 5, p. 111.
14. Du Toit, R.F. 1983. op. cit. p. 124.
15. Swanepoel, C. 1988. 'The Wildlife of the Mana Pools Region', in *The Zimbabwe Science News*. Vol. 22, Nos 1/2, January/February, p. 25.
16. Taylor, R.D. 1988. 'The Indigenous Resources of the Zambezi Valley: An Overview', in *The Zimbabwe Science News*, Vol. 17, No. 78, July/August, pp. 5-7.
17. ibid.
18. Zimbabwe Govt 1987. *The National Conservation Strategy*, Ministry of Natural Resources and Tourism, Government of Zimbabwe, Harare, p. 11.
19. *The Herald* 1987. Newspaper report, Harare, Zimbabwe, Friday, 29 May.
20. Harland, D. 1988. 'The Ivory Chase Moves On', in *New Scientist*, Vol. 117, No. 1594, p. 30.
21. ibid.
22. Achiron, M. & Wilkinson, R. 1986. 'The Last Safari', in *Newsweek*, 11 August, p. 24.
23. Caughley, G. & Goddard, J. 1975. 'Abundance and Distribution of Elephants in Luangwa Valley, Zambia', in *East African Wildlife Journal*, Vol. 13, p. 39.
24. Faddy, M.J. 1983. 'Warriors of Luangwa', in *Mzuri Drumbeat*, Vol. 4, No. 12, p. 13.
25. Parker, I.S.C. & Martin, E.B. 1982. 'How Many Elephants Are Killed for the Ivory Trade?', in *Oryx*, Vol. 16, No. 3, February, p. 238.
26. Hall, G. 1988. Personal communication.
27. Poole, J.H. & Moss, C.J. 1981, 'Must̶ in the African Elephant, *Loxodonta africana*'. in *Nature*. Vol. 292, 27 August, pp. 830-31.
28. *New Scientist* 1987. Report, No. 1561, 21 May, p. 33.
29. MacGregor, E. 1986. Personal communication.

30. Ng'uni, F.P. 1957. 'Copies of Reports by African Game Wardens', in *The Black Lechwe*, Vol. 1, No. 2, July, pp. 23-4.
31. The Editor 1963. 'Giants Kill Each Other', in *Black Lechwe*, Vol. 3, No. 4, February, p. 44.
32. The Editor 1962. 'The Strength of a Hippo Bull', in *Fauna and Flora*, Transvaal, No. 13, p. 52.
33. Luck, C.P. & Wright, P.G. 1964. 'Aspects of the Anatomy and Physiology of the Skin of the Hippopotamus *(H. amphibius)*', in *Quarterly Journal of Experimental Physiology and Cognate Medical Sciences*, Vol. 49, No. 1, pp. 2-3.
34. ibid. pp. 4-5.
35. Fenton, M.B., Cumming, D.H.M., Hutton, J.M. & Swanepoel, C.M. In Press. 'Foraging Strategies and Habitat Use by *Nycteris grandis* (Chiroptera: Nycteridae) in Zimbabwe'.
36. Childs, S.B. & Buchler, E.R. 1981. 'Perception of Simulated Stars by *Eptesicus fuscus* (Vespertilionidae): A Potential Navigational System', in *Animal Behaviour*, Vol. 29, pp. 1028-35.
37. Tomasi, T.E. 1979. 'Echolocation by the Short-Tailed Shrew *Blarina revicauda*', in *Journal of Mammology*, Vol. 60, No. 4, November, pp. 751-9.
38. Kaltwasser, M.T. & Schnitzler, H.U. 1981. *Zeitschrift fur Saugetierkunde*, Vol. 46, No. 6, pp. 337-400.
39. Smithers, R.H.N. 1975. *Guide to the Rats and Mice of Rhodesia*, Trustees of the National Monuments and Museums of Zimbabwe, Harare, pp. 10, 14-15.
40. _____ 1984. Personal communication.
41. Wilson, V.J. 1970. 'Notes on the Breeding and Feeding Habits of a Pair of Barn Owls, *Tyto alba* (Scopoli), in Rhodesia', in *Arnoldia*, National Museums of Rhodesia, Bulawayo, pp. 1-8.
42. Broadley, D.G. 1986. Personal communication.
43. Broadley, D.G. & Cock, E.V. 1982. *Snakes of Zimbabwe*, 2nd impression, Longman, Zimbabwe, pp. 80-81.
44. Broadley, D.G. 1986. Personal communication.
45. Honegger, R.E. 1974. 'The Reptile Trade', in *International Zoo Yearbook*, Ed. Duplaix-Hall, N., Zoological Society of London, pp. 47-52.
46. Broadley, D.G. 1984. 'The Nkhasi or Zambezi Soft-Shelled Turtle', in *The Hartebeest* (Magazine of the Lowveld Natural History Society), Zimbabwe, No. 15, pp. 8-11.
47. Ng'uni, F.P. 1957. op. cit. p. 23.

CHAPTER 13: GREAT ZAMBEZI MYTHS

1. Dickinson, R.W. 1971. 'Antonia Fernandes — A Reassessment', in *Rhodesiana*, No. 25, December, p. 47.
2. Huffman, T.N. 1982. 'Archaeology and Ethnohistory of the African Iron Age', in *Annual Review of Anthropology*, No. 11, p. 143.
3. _____ 1984. 'Expressive Space in the Zimbabwe Culture', in *Man, New Series*, No. 19, p. 593.
4. _____ 1986. 'Iron Age Settlement Patterns and the Origins of Class Distinction in Southern Africa', in *Advances in World Archaeology*, Vol. 5, p. 323.
5. Beach, D.N. 1980. *The Shona and Zimbabwe 900-1850*, Mambo Press, Gweru, Zimbabwe, pp. 50-51.
6. Huffman, T.N. 1988. Personal communication.
7. Beach, D.N. 1980. op. cit. p. 51.
8. Huffman, T.N. 1988. Personal communication.
9. Ransford, O.N. 1973. 'Europeans, Nineteenth Century Onwards; British, Dutch, Portuguese', in *Rhodesiana*, No. 29, December, p. 46.
10. Beach, D.N. 1980. op. cit. p. 114.
11. Douglas, R.G.S. 1986. 'Two Early Portuguese in the Mutapa State', in *Heritage of Zimbabwe*, No. 6, p. 43.
12. Fuller, C.E. 1959. 'Ethnohistory in the Study of Culture Change in South-East Africa', in *Continuity and Change in African Cultures*, Eds Bascom, W.R. & Herskovits, M.J., University of Chicago Press, Chicago, p. 114.
13. Axleson, E. 1973. *Portuguese in South-East Africa; 1488-1600*, C. Struik, Cape Town, pp. 48-9.
14. ibid.

15. Huffman, T.N. 1988. Personal communication.
16. Abraham, D.P. 1959. 'The Monomotapa Dynasty', in *Nada*, No. 36, p. 73.
17. Newitt, M.D.D. 1973. *Portuguese Settlement on the'Zambezi*, Longman, London, pp. 53-4.
18. Huffman, T.N. 1988. Personal communication.
19. Summers, R. 1971. *Ancient Ruins and Vanished Civilizations of Southern Afrca*, T.V. Bulpin, Cape Town, p. 20.
20. Beach, D.N. 1980. op. cit. p. 138.
21. Mudenge, S.I. 1974. 'The Role of Foreign Trade in the Rozvi Empire: A Reappraisal', in *Journal of African History*, Vol. 15, No. 3, p. 373.
22. Huffman, T.N. 1988. Personal communication.
23. Henriksen, T.H. 1978. *Mozambique: A History*, Rex Collings, London, with David Philip, Cape Town, p. 39.
24. ibid.
25. Randles, W.G.L. 1979. *The Empire of Monomotapa: from the Fifteenth to the Nineteenth Century*, Translated by Roberts, R.S., Mambo Press, Zimbabwe, p. 32.
26. Henriksen, T.H. 1978. op. cit.
27. Douglas, R.G.S. 1986. op. cit. p. 43.
28. Henriksen, T.H. 1978. op. cit. pp. 40-43.
29. ibid. p. 44.
30. Mudenge, S.I. 1974. op. cit. pp. 373-91.
31. Randles, W.G.L. 1979. op. cit. p. 37.
32. ibid.
33. Newitt, M.D.D. 1973. op. cit. p. 71.
34. Vlahakis, D. 1987. Personal communication.
35. Chundu, Chief 1987. Personal communication.
36. Huffman, T.N. 1986. op. cit. p. 301.
37. Du Toit, R.F. 1982. *A Preliminary Assessment of the Environmental Implications of the Proposed Mupata and Batoka Hydro-Electric Schemes (Zambezi River, Zimbabwe)*, Natural Resources Board, Ministry of Natural Resources and Tourism, Government of Zimbabwe, Harare, p. 131.
38. Brelsford, V. 1935. 'The Bemba Tridents', in *Nada*, Vol. 13, p. 19.
39. Mack, B.J. 1987. Personal communication.
40. Phillipson, D.W. 1987. Personal communication.
41. Beach, D.N. 1980. op. cit. p. 74.
42. Fagan, B.M. 1961. 'A Collection of Nineteenth Century Soli Ironwork from the Lusaka Area of Northern Rhodesia', in *The Journal of the Royal Anthropological Institute of Great Britain and Ireland*, Vol. 19, Parts I and II, Jan.-Dec., pp. 228-50.
43. Jijide, J. 1986. Personal communication.
44. Du Toit, R.F. 1982. op. cit. pp. 131 & 135.
45. Viljoen, D., Farrell, H.McD., Brossy, J.J., McArthur, M., Maheswaran, M. & Beighton, P. 1985. 'Ectrodactyly in Central Africa', in *South African Medical Journal*, Vol. 68, p. 658.
46. Du Toit, R.F. 1982. op. cit. pp. 131 & 135.
47. Jijide, J. 1986. Personal communication.
48. Gelfand, M., Roberts, C.J. & Roberts, R.S. 1974. 'A Two-Toed Man from the Doma People of the Zambezi Valley', in *Rhodesian History*, Vol. 5, p. 94.
49. Nyakutepa, K. 1986. Personal communication, Kanyemba.
50. *The Herald* 1981. Newspaper report, 9 October, Harare, Zimbabwe.
51. Viljoen, D. et al. 1985. op. cit. p. 658.
52. Barritt, D. 1979. 'The Incredible Ostrich People', in *Scope Magazine*, 6 July, p. 78.
53. Viljoen, D. et al. 1985. op. cit. p. 656.
54. Farrell, H.B. McD. 1984. 'The Two-Toed Wadoma — Familial Ectrodactyly in Zimbabwe', in *South African Medical Journal*, Vol. 65, March, p. 531.
55. Viljoen, D.L. & Beighton, P. 1984. 'The Split-Hand and Split-Foot Anomaly in a Central African Negro Population', in *American Journal of Medical Genetics*, Vol. 19, p. 547.
56. ibid. p. 552.

CHAPTER 14: WOOLLEN HATS AND BRASS POTTIES

1. Dickinson, R.W. 1968. 'Sofala — Gateway to the Gold of Monomotapa', in *Rhodesiana*, No. 19, December, p. 44.
2. ibid.
3. Axleson, E. 1973. *Congo to Cape*, Faber and Faber, London pp. 183-7.
4. ibid.
5. Dickinson, R.W. 1968. op. cit.
6. Axleson, E. 1940. *South-East Africa 1488-1530*, Longman, Green & Co., London, p. 80.
7. ibid.
8. Newitt, M.D.D. 1973. *Portuguese Settlement on the Zambezi*, Longman, London, p. 35.
9. Dickinson, R.W. 1971. 'Antonio Fernandes — A Reassessment', in *Rhodesiana*, No. 25, December, pp. 46-7.
10. Newitt, M.D.D. 1973. op. cit. p. 34.
11. ibid.
12. Rea, W.F. 1961. 'Rhodesia's First Martyr', in *Rhodesiana*, No. 6, pp. 1-40.
13. ibid.
14. ibid.
15. Theal, G.R. 1898. *Records of South-East Africa*, Vol. II, Government of the Cape Colony, p. 103.
16. Young, G. 1917. *Portugal*, Oxford University Press, Oxford, p. 137.
17. ibid.
18. Axleson, E. 1973, *Portuguese in South-East Africa; 1488-1600*, C. Struik, Cape Town, pp. 152-64.
19. Quiggin, A.H. 1949. 'Trade Routes, Trade and Currency in East Africa', in *The Occasional Papers of the Rhodes-Livingstone Museum* (in one volume), Reprinted by the Institute of African Studies, University of Zambia, No. 5, p. 149.
20. Monclaro, S.J. 1899. 'Account of the Journey Made by the Fathers of the Company of Jesus with Francisco Barreto in the Conquest of Monomotapa in the Year 1569', in *Records of South-Eastern Africa*, Ed. Theal, G.M., Vol. III, 1899, Facsimile reprint, C. Struik, Cape Town, 1964, pp. 202-495.
21. Axleson, E. 1973. op. cit.

CHAPTER 15: CANNIBALS AND CONCUBINES

1. Fagan, B.M. 1965. *Southern Africa During the Iron Age*, Thames and Hudson, London, p. 142.
2. Strandes, J. 1961. *The Portuguese Period in East Africa*, Reprinted 1971, East African Literature Bureau, Nairobi, pp. 134-43.
3. ibid.
4. Axleson, E. 1973. *Portuguese in South-East Africa 1488-1600*, C. Struik, Cape Town, pp. 176-7.
5. ibid.
6. ibid.
7. Newitt, M.D.D. 1973. *Portuguese Settlement on the Zambezi*, Longman, London, p. 28.
8. ibid.
9. ibid. pp. 36-8.
10. Ransford, O.N. 1966. *Livingstone's Lake*, John Murray, London, p. 45.
11. Axleson, E. 1973. op. cit. p. 47.
12. Henriksen, T.H. 1978. *Mozambique: A History*, Rex Collings, London, with David Philip, Cape Town, p. 43.
13. Newitt, M.D.D. 1968. 'The Portuguese on the Zambesi from the Seventeenth to the Nineteenth Centuries', in *Race*, p. 479.
14. _____ 1973. 'The Portuguese Muzungos and the Zambesi Wars', University of London Institute of Commonwealth Studies, Collected Seminar Papers, No.17: *The Societies of Southern Africa in the 19th and 20th Centuries*, Vol. 4, p. 19.
15. Henriksen, T.H. 1978. op. cit. p. 69
16. Newitt, M.D.D. 1973. op. cit. pp. 54-9
17. ibid.

18. Henriksen, T.H. 1978. op. cit. p. 56
19. ibid. p. 57
20. Newitt, M.D.D. 1968. op. cit. p. 480
21. Decle, L. 1898. *Three Years in Savage Africa*, Methuen and Co., London, pp. 241-3.
22. Henriksen, T.H. 1978. op. cit. p. 59.
23. ibid.
24. Decle, L. 1898. op. cit. pp. 250-51.
25. Newitt, M.D.D. 1973. op. cit. p. 220.
26. Henriksen, T.H. 1978. op. cit. p. 65.
27. Newitt, M.D.D. 1973. op. cit. p. 221.
28. ibid. p. 222.
29. ibid. pp. 223-6.
30. ibid.
31. ibid.
32. Henriksen, T.H. 1978. op. cit. p. 65.
33. Excell, A.W. 1960. 'History of Botanical Collecting', in *Flora Zambesiaca*, Vol. One, Part One, Eds Exell, A.W. & Wild, H., Crown Agents for Overseas Governments and Administration, London, p. 24.
34. Strandes, J. 1961. op. cit. p. 193.
35. Owen, W.F.W. 1832. 'An Expedition up the Zambezi to Senna', in *Journal of the Royal Geographical Society*, Vol. II, p. 136-52.
36. Henriksen, T.H. 1978. op. cit. p. 65.
37. Seaver, G. 1957. *David Livingstone: His Life and Letters*, Harper and Brothers, New York, pp. 364-5.
38. Needham, D.E. 1974. *Iron Age to Independence, A History of Central Africa*, Reprinted 1980, Longman, London, p. 62.
39. Stewart, J. 1952. *The Zambesi Journal of James Stewart, 1862-1863*, Ed. Wallis, J.P.R., Chatto and Windus, London, pp. 262-3.
40. Author unknown. No date. 'Mary Moffat Livingstone', From an unsigned typescript, National Museum and Art Gallery, Gaborone, Botswana, Ref. P 920 Liv., pp. 14-21.
41. ibid.
42. Huxley, E. 1974. *Livingstone*, Weidenfeld and Nicholson, London, pp. 72, 81 & 90.
43. Author unknown 'Mary Moffat Livingstone', op. cit.
44. Owen, F.W.F. 1832. op. cit. p. 152.
45. Edwards, S.J. 1974. *Zambezi Odyssey*, T.V. Bulpin, Cape Town, p. 212.
46. Keynes, Q. 1973. 'Dr Livingstone's Monogram, I Presume?', in *Livingstone: 1873-1973*. Ed. Lloyd, B.W., Struik, Cape Town, pp. 53-62.
47. Author unknown 1969. 'Njuzi and the River People', in *Outpost*, Magazine of the BSA Police, Rhodesia, Vol. 47, June, p. 16.

CHAPTER 16: THAT DAMNED GORGE!

1. Seaver, G. 1957. *David Livingstone: His Life and Letters*, Harper and Brothers, New York, p. 258.
2. ibid. p. 260.
3. ibid.
4. ibid. pp. 332-3.
5. Ransford, O. 1977. 'David Livingstone, A Reassessment with Particular Reference to his Psyche', Unpublished Ph.D. thesis, University of Zimbabwe, p. 262.
6. ibid. p. 263.
7. ibid.
8. ibid.
9. ibid.
10. Williams, E.L. 1974. 'African Giant', in *Optima*, Vol. 24, No. 3, p. 100.
11. De Begonha, F.B. & Du Cunha, H.C. 1985. 'Cahora Bassa and SADCC', in *Cahora Bassa Hydroelectricity Scheme*, Publicity Brochure, Songo, Mozambique, p. 60.
12. Wentworth, P. 1988. Chief Electrical Engineer, Kariba, Zimbabwe, Personal communication.

13. Author unknown 1971. 'A Look at Some of the Implications of the Cabora Bassa Dam Project', in *Journal of the South African Federation of Engineering Students*, Vol. 1, No. 9, p. 29.
14. Middlemas, K. 1975. *Cahora Bassa*, Weidenfeld and Nicholson, London, p. 102.
15. ibid. p. 97.
16. Davies, B.R., Hall, A. & Jackson, P.B.N. 1975. 'Some Ecological Aspects of Cabora Bassa Dam', in *Biological Conservation*, Vol. 8, p. 196.
17. Jackson, P.B.N. 1974. 'The Development of a Fisheries Industry at Cahora Bassa', Company report, Loxton, Hunting & Associates, Johannesburg, South Africa, pp. 18-19.
18. Bowmaker, A.P. 1970. 'A Prospect of Lake Kariba', in *Optima*, Vol. 20, p. 68.
19. Jackson, P.B.N. 1974. op. cit. p. 19.
20. Kenmuir, D.H.S. 1975. 'Sardines in Cabora Bassa Lake?' in *New Scientist*, Vol. 65, No. 936, 13 February, p. 379.
21. Jackson, P.B.N. 1974. 'The Potential Aquatic Weed Problem at Cabora Bassa', Company report, Loxton, Hunting & Associates, Johannesburg, South Africa, p. 2.
22. Jarvis, M.J.F., Van der Lingen, M.I. & Thornton, J.A. 1981. 'Water Hyacinth', in *The Zimbabwe Science News*, Vol. 15, No. 4, April, p. 97.
23. Fair, P. 1982. 'Aquatic Weeds — A Curse or an Asset for Zimbabwe', in *The Zimbabwe Science News*, Vol. 16, No. 10, October. pp. 233-6.
24. Bolton, P. 1978. 'The Control of Water Resources in the Zambezi Basin and its Implications for Moçambique', in *Moçambique*, Proceedings of a seminar held in and published by the Centre of African Studies, University of Edinburgh, p. 152.
25. Rutter, F. 1953, *Fundamentals of Limnology*, University of Toronto Press, Canada, p. 74.
26. Axleson, E. 1973. *Portuguese in South-East Africa 1488-1600*, Struik, Cape Town, p. 161.
27. ibid. p. 163.
28. _____ 1969. *Portuguese in South-East Africa: 1600-1700*, Witwatersrand University Press, Johannesburg, pp. 34-9.
29. ibid. p. 46.
30. ibid. p. 54.
31. ibid. p. 46.
32. Spence, C.F. 1963. *Moçambique*, Howard Timmins, Cape Town, p.69.
33. Axleson, E. 1969. op. cit. p. 47.
34. Lane-Pool, E.H. 1950. 'The Discovery of Africa', in *The Occasional Papers of the Rhodes-Livingstone Museum*, Nos 1-16 (in one volume), Paper No. 7, Institute of African Studies, University of Zambia, p. 241.
35. Listowel, J. 1974. *The Other Livingstone*, David Philip, Cape Town, and Julian Friedmann, London, p. 158.
36. Ransford, O. 1977. op. cit. p. 294
37. Listowel, J. 1974. op. cit. p. 158.
38. ibid. p. 166.

CHAPTER 17: MEN, MADMEN AND MANIACS

1. Newitt, M.D.D. 1973. *Portuguese Settlement on the Zambezi*, Longman, London, pp. 84-5.
2. ibid. pp. 85-6.
3. Fagan, B.M. 1965. *Southern Africa During the Iron Age*, Thames and Hudson, London, p. 151.
4. Brelsford, W.V. 1965. *Generation of Men: The European Pioneers of Northern Rhodesia*, Stuart Manning, Salisbury, Rhodesia, p. 4.
5. ibid. p. 6.
6. Livingstone, D. 1956. *The Zambezi Expedition of David Livingstone*, Vol. One, Journals, Ed. Wallis, J.P.R., Chatto and Windus, London, pp. 115-34.
7. Tabler, E.C. 1966. *Pioneers of Rhodesia*, C. Struik, Cape Town, pp. 7-8.
8. Chapman, J. 1971. *Travels in the Interior of South Africa*, Part 2, Ed. Tabler, E.C., A.A. Balkema, Cape Town, p. ix.
9. Mohr, E. 1973. *To the Victoria Falls of the Zambesi*, Rhodesia Reprint Library, Facsimile reproduction of the English edition of 1876, Books of Rhodesia, Bulawayo, pp. 311-15.
10. Howman, R. 1951. Correspondence from Native Commissioner, Wankie, to G.M. Wankie Colliary, dated 23 April.

11. Selous, F.C. 1881. *A Hunter's Wanderings in Africa*, Richard Bently and Sons, London (Facsimile reprint, Books of Rhodesia, Bulawayo, 1970), pp. 291-9.
12. ibid.
13. ibid.
14. Knight-Bruce, G.W. 1889. 'Mr F. Monks' Adventurous Journeys in the Interior of South-Eastern Africa', in *Proceedings of the Royal Geographical Society, Geographical Notes*, Vol. 11, No. 10, p. 608.
15. Stevenson-Hamilton, J. 1953. *The Barotseland Journal of James Stevenson-Hamilton: 1898-1899*, Ed. Wallis, J.P.R., Chatto and Windus, London, pp. xxi-xxxi.
16. Gibbons, A. St H. 1904. *Africa from South to North Through Barotseland*, John Lane, The Bodley Head, London, p. 19.
17. Stevenson-Hamilton, J. 1953. op. cit.
18. ibid.
19. Randles, B.M. 1971. 'H.H.A. de Laessoe', in *Rhodesiana*, Vol. 4, No. 25, December, pp. 35-44.
20. De Laessoe, H. 1908. 'The Zambesi River (Victoria Falls-Chinde): A Boat Journey of Exploration, 1903', in *Proceedings of the Rhodesia Scientific Association*, Vol. 8, Part 1, pp. 19-50.
21. Baxter, T.W. 1965. 'Paul Graetz's Journey Across Africa by Motor-Boat', in *Zambia (Northern Rhodesia) Journal*, Vol. 6, pp. 259-65.
22. Turner, J.N. 1953. 'Coincidence or Plot?' in *Blue and Old Gold*, Howard Timmins, Cape Town, pp. 76-7.

CHAPTER 18: AT THE RIVER'S END

1. Tinley, K.L. 1975. 'Marromeu', in *African Wildlife*, Vol. 29, No. 2, p. 23.
2. Barnes, J. 1987. Personal communication.
3. Loxton, Venn & Co. 1975. 'Report on the Ecology of Block 10: Agricultural Resources and Land Use Planning, Zambezi Valley, Mozambique', for the Gabinete do Plano do Zambeze, Loxton Venn, Johannesburg, p. 11.
4. Barnes, J. 1987. Personal communication.
5. Tinley, K.L. 1971. 'Determinants of Coastal Conservation: Dynamics and Diversity of the Environment as Exemplified by the Moçambique Coast', in *Proceedings, Symposium on Nature Conservation as a Form of Land Use*, Gorongosa National Park, Mozambique, 13-17 September, p. 139.
6. Rankin, D.J. 1892. 'The Discovery of the Chinde Entrance to the Zambesi River', in *Fortnightly Review*, Vol. 52, p. 826.
7. Fairfax-Francklin, J.W. 1968. 'Paddlers Among the Pythons', in *Ships Monthly*, Vol. 3, No. 6, pp. 204-8.
8. Author unknown 1969. 'Njuzi and the River People, Part 8', in *Outpost*, Vol. 47, No. 8, August, p. 48.
9. Fairfax-Francklin, J.W. 1968. op. cit.
10. Tinley, K.L. 1975. op. cit.
11. Tello, J.L. 1986. 'Wildlife Cropping in the Zambezi Delta, Moçambique', in *Proceedings of Working Party on Wildlife Management and National Parks of the African Forestry Commission, Arusha, Tanzania, September 1983*, United Nations Food and Agricultural Organization, Rome, p. 15.
12. Cott, H.B. *The Nile Crocodile in Uganda and Northern Rhodesia*, p. 231.
13. Junor, F.J.R. 1968. 'The African Fish Eagle', in *Piscator*, No. 72, p. 26.
14. Tinley, K.L. 1971. op. cit. p. 136.
15. Hughes, G.R. 1971. 'Sea Turtles — A Case Study for Marine Conservation in South-East Africa', in *Proceedings, Symposium on Nature Conservation as a Form of Land Use*, Gorongosa National Park, Mozambique, 13-17 September, p. 115.
16. ibid. p. 119.
17. Yntema, C.L. 1976. 'Effects of Incubation Temperatures on Sexual Differentiation in the Turtle, *Chelydra serpentina*', in *Journal of Morphology*, Vol. 150, No. 2 (Oct.), Part 1, pp. 453-61.
18. _____ 1979. 'Temperature Levels and Periods of Sex Determination During Incubation of Eggs of *Chelydra serpentina*', in *Journal of Morphology*, Vol. 159, No. 1, pp. 17-28.

19. Hughes, G. 1971. 'Preliminary Report on the Sea Turtles and Dugongs of Mozambique', in *Veterinary Mozambique*, Vol. 4 (2), p. 59.
20. _____ 1969. 'Dugong Status Survey in Moçambique', in *World Wildlife Yearbook*, Ed. Vollmar, F., World Wildlife Fund, Switzerland, p. 137.
21. ibid. p. 138.
22. ibid. p. 139.
23. Hughes, G.R. & Oxley-Oxland, R. 1971. 'A Survey of Dugong *(Dugong dugon)* In and Around Antonio Enes, Northern Moçambique', in *Biological Conservation*, Vol. 3, No. 4, July, pp. 299-301.
24. Marsh, H. & Anderson, P.K. 1983. 'Probable Susceptibility of Dugongs to Capture Stress', in *Biological Conservation*, Vol. 25, pp. 1-3.
25. Tello, J.L. 1986. op. cit. p. 15.
26. ibid.
27. Tinley, K.L. 1971. op. cit. p. 132.
28. Loxton, Venn & Co. 1975. op. cit. p. 13.
29. Tinley, K.L. 1971. op. cit. p. 133-4.
30. Seaver, G. 1957. *David Livingstone: His Life and Letters*, Harper and Brothers, New York, p. 322.
31. Livingstone, D. 1961. *Livingstone's Missionary Correspondence*, Ed. Schapera, I., Chatto and Windus, London, p. 309.
32. Baker, C. 1980. 'The Chinde Concession, 1891-1923', in *The Society of Malaŵi Journal*, Vol. 33, No. 1, January, pp. 6-18.
33. ibid.
34. ibid.
35. ibid.
36. ibid.
37. Fairfax-Francklin, J.W. 1968. op. cit. p. 206.
38. Loxton, Venn & Co. 1975. op. cit. p. 28.
39. Winson, F. 1987. Personal communication.

Index

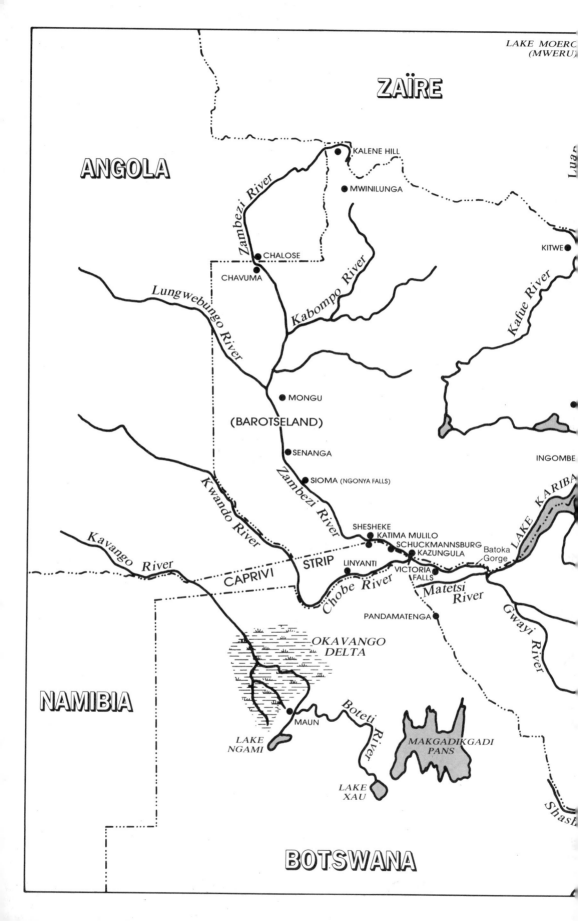